THE IDEA OF CONSCIENCE IN RENAISSANCE TRAGEDY

John S. Wilks

R
Routledge
London and New York

First published 1990
by Routledge
11 New Fetter Lane, London EC4P 4EE

Simultaneously published in the USA and Canada
by Routledge
a division of Routledge, Chapman and Hall, Inc.
29 West 35th Street, New York, NY 10001

Photoset in Helvetica Times by Input Typesetting Ltd, London
Printed in Great Britain by T J Press (Padstow) Ltd, Padstow, Cornwall

British Library Cataloguing in Publication Data

Wilks, John,
  The idea of conscience in Renaissance
  tragedy.
  1. Drama in English. Tragedies
  I. Title
  822′.0512

  ISBN 0 415 04454 5

Library of Congress Cataloging in Publication Data

Wilks, John S.,
  The idea of conscience in Renaissance tragedy / John S. Wilks.
    p. cm.
  Bibliography: p.
  Includes index.
  ISBN 0 415 04454 5
  1. English drama (Tragedy) – History and criticism. 2. English drama – Early
modern and Elizabethan, 1500–1600 – History and criticism. 3. English drama –
17th century – History and criticism.
  4. Conscience in literature. I. Title.
  PR658.17W5 1990
  822′.051209–dc20   89–10178

Contents

Contents

Acknowledgements

I wish to record my gratitude for the assistance and advice I received in the preparation of this study from the Director and Fellows of the Shakespeare Institute, University of Birmingham. My especial thanks are due to Dr Robert Smallwood, Fellow of the Institute, for whose patience, understanding and intellectual generosity I am deeply grateful; and to Dr Susan Brock, Librarian of the Institute, whose well-practised, wise directions saved me hours of fruitless toil. For whatever may be of merit in the following pages, they are in part the cause: whatever of demerit, I acknowledge mine.

Abbreviations

CHEL	Cambridge History of English Literature
DNB	Dictionary of National Biography
ESA	English Studies in Africa
JEGP	Journal of English and Germanic Philology
LTLS	(*London*) Times Literary Supplement
MLR	Modern Language Review
MP	Modern Philology
PBA	Proceedings of the British Academy
PMLA	Publications of the Modern Language Association of America
PQ	Philological Quarterly
QRL	Quarterly Review of Literature
REL	Review of English Literature
RES	Review of English Studies
SEL	Studies in English Literature
SP	Studies in Philology
SQ	Shakespeare Quarterly
TDR	Drama Review (*formerly* Tulane Drama Review)

Introduction

The idea of conscience as it occurs in Elizabethan and Jacobean drama reflects the maelstrom of controversy and debate concerning the moral nature of man raised by the conflicting issues of the Reformation, and sustained throughout the first part of the seventeenth century by the growing influence of Calvinist and Puritan ideas in English intellectual life. The momentous antinomies of grace and nature, faith and reason, which the schools managed to hold in harmonious counterpoise throughout the Age of Faith, had first been loosened by the advent of Ockhamite nominalism in the later Middle Ages, and then decisively sundered by the dark pessimism of Lutheran and Calvinist voluntarism in the sixteenth century. The Anglican church, seeking at one and the same time to adhere to its Henrician origins as a national church, and to define for itself a distinctive and systematic doctrine that would enable it to do so, attempted to resolve these profound dichotomies in a *via media* comprehending the widest possible spectrum of opinion; and in fact, the defenders of nature and reason contended with Puritans by recourse to a tradition rooted so firmly in patristic and scholastic authority as to threaten altogether the church's claim to be 'reformed'; whilst the exponents of grace and faith, resting their arguments on the extreme scripturalism of the Continental reformers, increasingly betrayed their impatience with a Church not sufficiently presbyterianized after the Genevan model, the austere disciplines of which the Marian exiles had had such recent experience.[1]

The distinctive intellectual achievement of the Middle Ages had been the fusing into one vast synthesis of the two great heritages to which it was heir, roughly analogous to the spheres of grace and nature: on the one hand the Scriptures, together with the commentaries upon them by the fathers and doctors of the Church; on the other, the extant fragments of the pagan philosophers. Perhaps the most heroic of these acts of absorption, and certainly that necessitating the most considerable readjustment in the mind of Christendom, was the induction and 'Christianizing' of

Aristotle during the twelfth and early thirteenth centuries; during which time the challenge represented by the newly discovered *Physics, Metaphysics, Psychology* and *Ethics* was successfully met and overcome, fused and in a sense defused by a self-confident Christendom in the schools of medieval Europe. The work of the mendicant orders, of Philip the Chancellor, Alexander of Hales (whose *Summa* was said to subsume the whole of Aristotle and his Arabian commentators), and principally of St Thomas Aquinas in the monumental *Summa Theologica* – the work of all these bore witness to the enormous energy with which the medieval mind laboured to bring about the successful reconciliation of faith and reason, thereby propitiating the twin poles of its own inheritance to the sensible detriment of neither.

At the heart of the *Summa Theologica* lies the premise that religion is intelligibly rational and reason fundamentally religious; although reason, being finite, must necessarily yield in the mysteries of revelation to faith, yet faith is not thereby contrary to reason, but completes it rather, just as grace perfects nature. The light of nature alone and the mere contemplation of His works attest the existence of God, and this alone is sufficient to excite man's reason to follow the precepts of that Law of Nature which best expresses both the execution of God's providence and man's proper realization of his own being as part of creation. The great principle of order, according to St Thomas, is a temporal force originating in a divine cause; all creatures exist, as Aristotle had taught, to realize their particular natures after their own kinds; but at the same time the pagan formulation was confirmed by what had been offered to man in the way of revealed truth: that not only does the whole of creation move around God at its centre, all things having been ordered towards their proper ends in the mind of God, but man alone is ordered to a perfection beyond himself – to a participation in the divine nature.[2]

In the shadow of these vast medieval postulates, annexing in like manner classical learning to scriptural authority, there grew up a series of minor treatises on the subject of conscience, the spiritual faculty by which man could perfect himself in this world and save himself in the next. Christ had described what is meant by conscience as 'the light within you' (Matt. 6:23), while St Paul had insisted on the power of conscience to anticipate the last judgement (Rom. 2:15, 9:1). In the Middle Ages, conscience came to be regarded as a volitional ability of the soul (*synderesis*), unimpaired after the fall, and related to the Natural Law, through which it was capable of inclining man to God.

This Thomist conception, a synergism of reason and revelation sustained within a comprehensive world-view, was to last over 300 years until fragmented by an equally comprehensive yet more forcefully enunciated systematic theology: that contained in the great Protestant summas, Luther's *The Freedom of a Christian*, and Calvin's *Institutes of the Christian*

Religion. If the alliance of faith and reason had been the harmonious diapason of scholasticism, their utter discord formed the primary doctrine of the reformers and challenged the entire Catholic system. Dismayed by the cheap grace offered by the Church's selling of indulgences, Luther propounded out of the Pauline epistles the notion that salvation, had already been won for man by Christ; it had merely to be voluntarily accepted in order to be achieved; man was justified by faith alone.[3] Calvin insisted further upon the utter depravity of postlapsarian mankind; that faith cannot be proved by reason, since not only is man's reason irretrievably vitiated by the corrupting effects of sin, but faith itself is founded upon an arbitrary mystery and the inscrutable fiat of God.[4] The scholastic impulse to order, the Natural Law, whose precepts were witnessed to in the rational soul of man as an act of conscience, only remained, according to Calvin, as a vestigial reminder of the perfect integrity of nature before the fall, in any case only dimly apprehensible to the conscience which was itself hopelessly perverted.

Whereas the schoolmen had defined the nature of conscience as intellective and rational, instinct with basic (or deontic) premises inclining it towards the good, the followers of Calvin determined it to be a connate faculty of the soul, arbitrating between God and man, but like reason in being debilitated to the extent that it could only resist the rioting passions and inveterate wickedness that are the consequences of the fall, through the regenerative effects of faith and obedience to God's work in the Scriptures. The good, in Calvinist thought, could only be apprehended by the clear conscience of the regenerate soul, redeemed by the blood of Christ, and informed in so far as may be by scriptural authority.[5] Even this affords only a partial sufficiency, for God's will, though to a limited extent discoverable by the light of revelation, yet remains forever partly hidden and mysterious, just as his justification, his election and his reprobation remain mysterious. In the voluntarist universe, God's will is the ultimate ethical imperative, divine fiat the awesome yet unknowable mandate to which man's will must conform; and because nature and reason are alike desecrated by man's original sin, God's will is often antithetical to both, an intervention in nature and an intermission in reason. The conscience is God's instrument, a forum between God and man, by which he excoriates the souls of the reprobate, and calls to repentance and godliness his chosen elect.[6]

All of these profound changes can be documented in post-Reformation England. Calvinist thought had early infiltrated the Church of England, and was yet more firmly implanted owing to the vigorous participation of the returned Marian exiles in the Elizabethan settlement, and the widespread acceptance of the Geneva Bible of 1560. Both Anglicans and Puritans stood essentially in the same field of the Reformation, and in the province of doctrine and soteriology the sensible differences were those of degree rather than of kind: both accepted the dogma of justification by faith, of the fatal effects of the fall, of election and reprobation. Yet within this broad framework there were variations: the rubric of identical statements of doctrine often overlaid furious controversy concerning matters of church polity, a controversy fuelled by yet more fundamental differences concerning the moral nature of man. For while both Anglican and Puritan alike accepted man's spiritual corruption after the fall, Anglicans insisted that of all man's faculties, reason had remained unimpaired; in the sphere of nature, man was capable of choosing the good, and this unaided by transfusions of redemptive grace.[7] In this way, moderate Anglicans looked back to the authority and traditions of the Catholic order of which they were no longer strictly a part; paradoxically they defended the English Reformation against Puritans with scholastic weapons. Not only is Richard Hooker's *The Laws of Ecclesiastical Polity* the first definitive statement of specifically Anglican doctrine, but, resulting as it did from a long and bitter feud with the Calvinist Thomas Cartwright, constituted for a time a bulwark in England against the increasing spread of Calvinism, and did much to shore up those venerable beliefs in a rationally apprehensible, causative and contingent universe, which had nourished Christendom over the previous four centuries. The *Laws* is rooted firmly in the classical and Christian traditions, and indeed owes much to Aquinas, especially in its elevation of reason and emphasis upon the divine sanction of Natural Law. For a time, there seemed a temporary recession in the pervasive ingress of Calvinistic doctrines, a brief respite coincident perhaps with the primacy of Archbishop Whitgift; but certainly after the accession of James I the growing self-confidence of Puritans and Calvinists meant that Genevan theology came increasingly to prevail in English intellectual life, at least until the growth of Arminianism and the advent of the Cambridge Neo-Platonists in the 1630s.

Circumstantial evidence, at least, of the growing spread of Calvinist ideas is testified to by the publication, from the latter part of Elizabeth's reign onwards, of increasing numbers of devotional works and volumes of sermons, overwhelmingly of Puritan inspiration, and designed to be read in the context of private and household worship by heads of families as an aid to Christian and godly living. Such works as William Cowper's *The Anatomie of a Christian Man* (London, 1613), Christopher Lever's *The Holy Pilgrime, Leading the way to Heaven* (London, 1618), or John Downame's *A Guide to Godlynesse, Or a Treatise of a Christian Life* (London, 1622) belonged to a type of literature that, as L. B. Wright has suggested, was first produced in Elizabeth's reign to compensate for a dearth of educated and competent clergy, and as a Puritan antidote against what they regarded as the stultification of God's word induced by the pulpit reading of the Homilies.[8] More germane to the present argument is the fact that a substantial corpus of this sort of literature consisted of treatises specifically on the subject of conscience, minutely anatomizing its nature, functions and offices, frequently, though not always, in the light of Calvinist teachings upon the moral nature of man, and documenting the proper exercise of the Christian conscience in the face of the manifold ethical decisions attendant upon living a godly life. Such works as those of the Puritan preacher Jeremiah Dyke, whose *Good Conscience: Or a Treatise shewing the Nature, Meanes, Marks, Benefit and Necessity Thereof* was published in 1624; or Ephraim Huit's *The Anatomy of Conscience*, published in 1626, represented a radical reformist style of casuistry. More famous, because prototypical of this particular sort of publication, was the work of William Perkins, the Cambridge preacher and theologian, who may with justice be regarded, along with his contemporary Richard Hooker, as one of the founders of the Anglican school of moral theology. Unlike Hooker, though, his writings were distinctly Calvinist in strain; and two of them are devoted entirely to the consideration of conscience: *A Discourse of Conscience*, published at Cambridge in 1597; and *The Whole Treatise of the Cases of Conscience*, published in London in 1611. Therein Perkins details the genus, offices and obligations of conscience, the consolations of a good conscience and the terrors of an evil one; the second work, in particular, amounts to a compendium of practical guidance in everyday decision-making, an attempt, as were all such works, in part at least, to assuage the possible tendency to spiritual desolation and despair that might be induced in the hearts of the faithful by the dark necessities of Genevan dogma.

Just as scholastic and Calvinist ideologies did not follow one from the other in a precise chronological sequence, so too did Anglican and Puritan conceptions of conscience interpenetrate, shot through on both sides with elements more properly belonging to scholastic or Calvinist theological systems. Perkins himself, for example, in spite of the decidedly Calvinist tincture of his writings, and his public stance as a moderate Puritan, yet saw himself as firmly within the Anglican fold, and in fact his work on conscience does show the influence of a number of Thomistic premises. The same might be said of other moderate Anglicans, John Woolton and John Hughes for example, who were scholastically inclined to a greater or lesser degree.[9] On the whole, though, the overwhelming tendency – perhaps most apparent during the early years of the seventeenth century – was for the published works of preachers and divines to disavow absolutely the conclusions of scholasticism regarding the conscience: first of all in almost uniformly deprecating the post-lapsarian viability of the Natural Law; secondly, in arguing the corollary that the Scriptures as the principal source of God's revealed will are thus the only means to an enlightened conscience; and thirdly, in insisting that the conscience is connative rather than intellective, an arbitrator divine in origin, superior to the other faculties of the soul which it uses in the process whereby it arrives at the truth.

Now it is my contention, and the object partly of this study to demonstrate, that this decisive shift in the fundamental axioms of moral theology which took place in England at the turn of the century diffused itself widely within other areas of English life and thought. Indeed, I take the point exhaustively made by Herndl that, allowing for a natural intercurrency and mutual permeation of ideas no doubt common to all such revolutions of thought, there was certainly 'more of scholastic rationalism and world-acceptance in Elizabethen years and of Calvinist voluntarism and world-rejection in the seventeenth century'.[10] The secular devolution of major doctrinal assumptions can be traced through the various scholasticisms informing the work of poets and scholars such as John Davies, Stephen Batman, and Thomas Wright, through to the occasional voluntarisms of such as Greville, Marston, Burton and the influential translations of Charron and the Huguenot poet Du Bartas. Some allowances must admittedly be made for inconsistencies and contradictions of belief; religious attitudes amongst the seventeenth-century laity had by no means set hard. Yet at the same time, the separation of grace and nature, faith and reason, explicit in Calvinist world-abhorrence, is paradoxically the implicit premise and point of departure for a number of tangential developments in the philosophies of Montaigne and Descartes; what they had in common was an empirical averroism that assigned matter and spirit to discrete orders of being, and which was ultimately, as Bacon foresaw, to leave the natural world for science to bustle in.[11]

Now if all this is true, and the hypothesis is accepted that this kind of evolution in man's profoundest assumptions about himself did in fact occur in the aftermath of the English Reformation, it is to be expected that some such change will similarly be reflected in contemporary dramatic literature; imaginative testimony, perhaps, of a shifting substratum of beliefs. In particular, it will be argued in the following pages that a gradual metamorphosis is discernible in the treatment of the idea of conscience from the substantially scholastic form that it takes in the works of Shakespeare, to a predominantly reformist conception in the works of his later contemporaries and Jacobean successors. Because the age which nurtured Shakespeare's own beliefs still inherited its doctrines and cosmology more or less unchanged from the Middle Ages, the idea of conscience manifests itself amongst a variety of religious concepts to which his characters refer – not, of course, necessarily in Christian terms – but, at any rate, as recognizably integral with an ontological framework scholastically orthodox in its assumptions about the moral nature of man. The Shakespearean universe is, moreover, intelligibly rational, and is everywhere suffused by Thomistic notions of the Natural Law: conscience is pre-eminently the litmus of any violation in man's teleological functioning in the great chain of being, and testifies internally and psychologically in the little world of man to what is manifest externally by violent and unnatural concatenations in the world of nature. Certainly by the time of the later Jacobean drama, any notion of the Natural Law by which evil confounds itself by causative repercussions in the body politic, has become extinct; the moral universe as portrayed in the plays of Webster, Massinger, and Ford has become, to use Calvin's words, nothing but a 'pollution of wickedness' and man's nature 'imbued with iniquity';[12] in the face of which his conscience, destitute, for the most part, of grace or enlightenment, remains powerless to resist a tragic bondage of the will to the slavery of sin.

The general intention, then, of the present study will be to trace the extent to which these moral and doctrinal postulates inform the notion of conscience as it appears in the plays of Tudor and Jacobean dramatists from approximately 1500 to 1640, and to analyse the literary–critical significance of the concept according to the hypothesis that some such seismic shift in scholastic and Calvinist world-views had subtle yet important repercussions in imaginative literature. A four-part scheme will be adopted for the book, whereby the religious and philosophical implications of the idea of conscience already glanced at will be made the subject of a more thoroughgoing contextual study by which to illustrate the literacy material to follow. Thereafter will ensue a discussion of the evolution of the dramatic character of Conscience in early Tudor interludes and morality plays of the sixteenth century, observing his changing role from that of rationalistic preceptor to tormentor, to agent of a largely scriptural enlightenment; a literary development which itself charts the cultural infiltration of voluntarist beliefs. Six such plays give a prominent role to the character of Conscience: *The World and the Child* (1500–22); *Impatient Poverty* (1547–58); R. B.'s *Appius and Virginia* (1559–67); Nathaniel Woodes's *The Conflict of Conscience* (1570–81); R[obert] W[ilson]'s *The Three Ladies of London* (c.1581); R[obert] W[ilson]'s *The Three Lords and Three Ladies of London* (1588–90).[13]

The last two sections of the enquiry will offer a comparison of Shakespeare with his contemporaries and successors, an arrangement that recommends itself firstly because Shakespeare is the most prominent heir to that scholastic and humanist tradition of which Aquinas and Hooker are the chief apologists; and secondly, because Shakespeare wrote more, and more richly, about conscience than any other dramatist of the period. As such, an interesting conspectus of the development of the concept within his work – through *Richard III* (1591–7), *Hamlet* (1591–c.1601), and *Macbeth* (1606–11) – would be less easily executed if strict chronology were made the presiding criterion of analysis, and every play included were treated *seriatim*. It has been thought advisable, moreover, to limit the selection of plays to those offering, implicitly at least, a Christian framework of values, for the sake both of clarity of exposition and pertinence to a common denominator of thought. On this principle, Brutus's scruples on the eve of the Ides of March have been omitted, even though Malefort's guilt-stricken passion for his daughter has been retained; for whereas Massinger's neo-Stoicism underpins a strident and explicitly Christian world view, Shakespeare considers in altogether more mutedly secular terms the moral predicament of his protagonist – a predicament which in any case is couched less in terms of a case of conscience (as is Malefort's) than of flawed judgment. Nor has this section the temerity to venture any further contributions to the vexed question of Shakespeare's religious affiliations; the problem is entirely outside the scope or relevance of this study, and only if it could with some certainty be demonstrated that Shakespeare was an extreme precisian – which on other grounds seems unlikely – would the conclusions reached here be seriously embarrassed.

Thereafter will follow a fourth section, more or less naturally providing a conceptual foil to the Shakespearean section, analysing once more the idea of conscience in various Tudor and Stuart plays, but employing, as a third term in the discussion, the Shakespearean conception of conscience: how it was antedated by, or in turn influenced, the literary heritage to which it contributed. Above all, an attempt will be made to discriminate between these plays according to whether they yield evidence of a received set of beliefs about conscience; not to commensurate complex dramatic meanings with an hypothetical Renaissance ideology, nor to make vain calculations about authorial intentions, but to disclose to modern sensibility the salience of opposed patterns of Renaissance ideas about an important moral concept. This section will include: Marlowe's *Doctor Faustus* (1588–92), Tourneur's *The Atheist's Tragedy* (1607), Webster's *The Duchess of Malfi* (1612–14), Massinger's *The Unnatural Combat* (1621–c.26), Massinger's *The Renegado* (1624), Ford's *'Tis Pity She's a Whore* (1629–33). Such a list makes no claim to comprehensivity. The intention of this study, and hence its principle of selection, is to explore those plays where the theme of moral choice is compounded with an internal recognition, by the protagonist, of the moral quality of motive and action.[14]

1

Discourses of conscience

Shakespeare and the scholastic tradition

Scholastic philosophy of the English Renaissance was, until the late six-teenth century, almost entirely derivative of the Middle Ages. Its concep-tual genesis is discoverable in Plato, Aristotle, the teachings of the Gospel, and Pauline theology, and it acquired its distinctive assimilative character as a rational, synoptic account of the created universe in the great thirteenth-century synthesizing work carried out by such as Abelard, Siger of Brabant, Bonaventure, and of course St Thomas Aquinas. As Curry states, its most widely accepted formulations were mediated to the Eliza-bethans via, on the one hand, a Franciscan tradition owing much to Augustinian precedent, and culminating in the somewhat unorthodox premises of John Duns Scotus; and, on the other, through the Dominican tradition associated with the Englishman's great contemporary, Thomas Aquinas.[1] Essentially, they were both the chief spokesman for the two great medieval orders to which the monumental task of assimilation had been deputed. These traditions held rival, but not necessarily dissimilar, conceptions of the human will: both held that it was fundamentally spon-taneous and free, but whereas the Franciscans believed it to be a neutral faculty, activated by representations of the good by the intellect, for the Thomists the voluntary act was intrinsically determined by the intellectual presentation of the complete good. In brief, the Franciscan school emphas-ized the independence of the will in both God and man: the ethical character of things was so because God willed it so; whereas to the Dominicans and to Aquinas, reason was the essence of God and man, the operant impulse of creation, and the sovereign faculty of the soul. But there is no question that, during the later Middle Ages, the latter concep-tion became overwhelmingly the received wisdom on the subject, the classic formulations of the *Summa Theologica* having long since rep-resented the mainstream of scholastic orthodoxy, to which Scotism entered an obscure caveat. And yet the caveat is important to record since, containing as it did the seeds of voluntarism, and acquiring in the fourteenth century the related impetus of Ockhamite nominalism, it was ultimately to burgeon forth at the Reformation as an important element in that violent recoil from reason and nature that characterized the presuppositions of Wittenburg and Geneva.[2]

But to all schoolmen, whether of Franciscan or Dominican persuasion, the faculties of intellect and will were understood properly to be components of the rational soul; they accepted, more or less unmodified, the Platonic doctrine of the trinity of the soul, expounded in the *Republic* (IV.435), and further elaborated by Aristotle in the *De Anima*. As the highest form of creation man possessed not only those aspects of soul subsisting in the vegetable and animal orders, but in addition a rational soul associated with ideation and will. Scholasticism 'absorbed' these classical postulates in the *Sententiae* of Peter Lombard (d.1160), a work which, because it contains an important reference to Jerome's *Commentary on Ezekiel*, was to become a source-book for medieval treatises on conscience. St Jerome, in discussing Ezekiel's vision of four men emerging from a fiery cloud, each possessed of four faces (that of a man, a lion, an ox, and an eagle) had correlated the first three faces with Plato's tripartite division of the soul, and the fourth with conscience.[3] Peter Lombard incorporated this conflation of the sacred and profane in what was, in effect, the first theological textbook,[4] and the *Sententiae* was to establish itself in the twelfth century as a work of enormous reputation in the universities, provoking over 200 commentaries upon it, and crystallizing for a Renaissance posterity the standardized teaching upon the structure of the soul. Stephen Batman states the Elizabethan consummation of the doctrine clearly:

> In diverse bodyes the soule is sayde to be three folde, that is to saye, Vegetabilis that giveth lyfe, and no feeling, and that is in plants and rootes, Sensibilis, that giveth lyfe and feeling, and not reason, that is in unskilful beasts, Racionalis that giveth lyfe, feeling, and reason, and this is in men.[5]

It is this concept to which Sir Toby in *Twelfth Night* refers when he asks:

> Shall we rouse the night-owl in a catch that will draw three souls out of one weaver?
>
> (II.iii.59–60)

Associated with the tripartite division of the soul were the three principal organs of the body, each serving its own faculty: the liver the vegetal, the heart the sensible, and the brain the rational aspect of the soul. At the same time, the rational soul which distinguished man from beasts was capable of functioning without the aid of bodily organs and was consequently immortal, able to contemplate spiritual truths. Phineas Fletcher describes this faculty as a Prince, a Vice-roy of the Divine Judge, situate in the little world of man, and constantly assaulted by the 'wavering mindes' of the inferior powers; capable, should he stand firm, of securing the soul to God, and for himself, eternal joy.[6]

Scholastic philosophy and psychology explained how the rational soul distinguished good and evil by positing the existence of two coefficients of the rational soul: a power of apprehension and a power of motion – the understanding and the will. The former – often exclusively designated the reason, or intellect – sifted by a process of enlightened cognition those impulses that came to it from the senses via the imagination. It also had the power to estimate and reflect upon the ethical status of these impulses in the light of certain instilled criteria by which the soul had implicit knowledge of both the Divine and the Natural Law.

Timothy Bright, in his *Treatise of Melancholie*, makes it clear that to conservatively inclined Elizabethans the act of conscience inhered in those operations of the soul governed by its relation to the Divine and Natural Law:

> From this [ingenerate knowledge] do springe three severall actions, whereby the whole course of reason is made perfect. First, that which the greekes call Sinteresis, the ground, whereupon the practise of reason consisteth, aunswering the proposition in a sillogisme: the conscience applying, the assumption: and of them both, the third, a certaine trueth concluded. . .[7]

Burton describes three innate species of the understanding:

> *Synteresis*, or the purer part of the conscience, is an innate habit, and doth signify *a conversation of the knowledge of the law of God and Nature, to know good or evil*. And (as our Divines hold) it is rather in the *understanding* than in the *will*. This makes the *major* proposition in a practick *syllogism*. The *dictamen rationis* is that which doth admonish us to do good or evil, and is the minor in the syllogism. The conscience is that which approves good or evil, justifying or condemning our actions, and is the conclusion of the syllogism. . .[8]

But whether situated primarily in the understanding or the will, conscience none the less continues to be seen as a separate and distinct attribute of the rational faculty, thus recollecting St Jerome's hypothesis concerning the fourth part of the soul as an inextinguishable 'spark', unassimilable with Plato's categories. Intrinsically it inclines towards good and hates evil, but as to what appears to be either good or evil, it depends ultimately for guidance upon the reason, or, because of the essential autonomy of the will, a rejection of some or all of the conclusions propounded to it by the reason.

The intellectual provenance of these ideas can be directly traced to St Thomas Aquinas, to whose formulations the Elizabethans merely gave plenary expression. Aquinas discusses conscience in three places: in his commentary on the *Sententiae* of Peter Lombard (1253–5); in the sixteenth and seventeenth of his *Debated Questions on Truth* (1257–8); and finally in the *Summa Theologica*, written about ten years later. In the second of these works, he begins by resolving once and for all the vexed question which had long exercised the medieval mind: the problem of the dual nature of conscience. Ever since the fourth century, when Jerome had displayed a gnomic inconsistency in his remarks on the longevity of conscience, apparently contradicting his imputation of a conscience even to Cain with a subsequent declaration that very wicked people cease to have a conscience,[9] medieval philosophers had tried to resolve the inconsistency by positing a distinction between *synderesis* and *conscientia*, the former being the 'spark' of conscience rather than conscience proper. They noted that even when an evil act is not attended by guilt, the evil-doer may still regret the consequences, if only because punishment ensues on that account. This residual regret they regarded as the 'spark' of conscience, which could plausibly be attributed even to Cain, since he evidently regrets his punishment (Genesis 4:13).[10] Thus there evolved a dual taxonomy concerned with *synderesis* on the one hand and *conscientia* on the other, implying the notion that while the one cannot be lost, the other can. St Thomas comprehends both categories, debating the distinctions in the usual scholastic form: arguing as to whether *synderesis* is a potentiality or a disposition of the soul; how it is related to reason; whether it can do wrong or be extinguished; whether *conscientia* is likewise binding, or can ever be mistaken.

St Thomas's answers to these questions are important in that they were substantially modified during the Reformation and in seventeenth-century Puritan works of casuistry. The first question, as to whether *synderesis* is a potentiality or a disposition, refers to Aristotle's classification of a potentiality as a native endowment by which the soul is able to acquire a skill to bring about actualization, whereas a disposition is a habit or tendency to one of two opposed courses of action.[11] St Thomas concludes that since God had not abandoned the soul, but assists it through instilling within it an appetite for the good, *synderesis* must be a disposition of the potentiality of reason, innate, by which basic deontic premises (i.e. those implying ethical obligation or permissibility) are known to man without reasoning.[12] The application of those premises to particular cases, on the other hand, is the province of *conscientia* – which is, in Aristotle's terminology, the actualization of *synderesis*.[13] Aquinas adds further that whereas *synderesis* can never be mistaken, *conscientia* can, since evil may arise in the syllogism by which the universal propositions of the former are misapplied to mistaken conclusions.[14] *Synderesis* can never be extinguished, properly speaking, since it is in virtue of its light that the soul is rational; but its operations can be impeded, and rationality vitiated therefore, where deontic propositions are wilfully and habitually misapplied.[15] For the will, though naturally inclined to submit to the practical conclusions of the *conscientia*, may be moved to error in its acts of free choice when reason's knowledge of the ultimate good is defective, or perverted by a 'vehement and inordinate apprehension of the imagination' which follows the passions of the sensitive appetite.[16]

At the same time the *conscientia*, however liable to error in this manner, is nevertheless binding on the actions of its possessor, even where it is actually mistaken. On this Aquinas says:

> it does not seem possible for someone to escape sin if his *conscientia*, however much mistaken, tells him that something is an injunction of God which is indifferent or bad *per se* and, such *conscientia* remaining, he arranges to do the contrary. For so far as in him lies, by this itself he has the wish that the law of God be not observed; hence he sins mortally.[17]

In general, then, a mistaken *conscientia* obliges even where the action in question is sinful. The only exception Aquinas allows is where the error arises from some factual mistake; but if the mistake is one of Law, then it is thereby rendered inexcusable, since a man who is ignorant of Law is culpably ignorant of something he ought to have known, and cannot therefore be mistaken in good faith.[18]

The assiduity with which St Thomas pursues this line of reasoning, though somewhat baffling to the logic of a later age, springs from the tendency among medieval writers to identify the objects of *synderesis* with the Natural Law. Belief in a natural law had a two-fold warrant in both reason and revelation. Aristotle's teleological ordering of means to ends in the created objects of the universe appeared to be confirmed by a widely influential passage in St Paul:

> For when the Gentiles which have not the law do by nature the things contained in the law, these, having not the law are a law unto themselves. Which shew the work of the law written in their hearts, their conscience also bearing witness and their thoughts the meanwhile accusing or else excusing one another. In the day when God shall judge the secrets of men, by Jesus Christ, according to my Gospel.
>
> (Rom. 2:14, 16)

St Thomas expounds the character of the Natural Law in a passage in the *Summa*, epitomizing the very spirit of scholasticism in its masterly concordance of the sacred and the profane, of St Paul with Aristotle. Divine wisdom, he says, having created all things in the character of a single idea, causes them to move to their 'due ends' in confirmity with the

Law inherent in that idea. This he calls the 'plan of government in the Chief Governor':

> it is evident that all things partake somewhat of the eternal law, in so far as, namely, from its being imprinted on them, they derive their respective inclinations to their proper acts and ends. Now among all others, the rational creature is subject to Divine providence in the most excellent way. . . . Wherefore it has a share of the Eternal Reason, whereby it has a natural inclination to its proper act and end: and this participation of the eternal law in the rational creature is called natural law.[19]

Consequently, man can discern good and evil according to a set of precepts implicit in the idea of the Natural Law, which in turn are deposited in that ineradicable habit or law of the mind already referred to as the *synderesis*: 'whence *synderesis* is said to incite to good, and to murmur at evil, inasmuch as through first principles [man] proceed[s] to discover, and judge of what [he has] discovered'.[20]

Now since the act of conscience more properly resides in the application of this universal knowledge to particular instances, St Thomas insists that man naturally partakes of the Eternal Law in a double sense, both 'by way of knowledge' and 'by way of an inward motive principle'. But, he adds, 'Both ways, however, are imperfect, and to a certain extent destroyed, in the wicked; because in them the natural inclination to virtue is corrupted by vicious habits, and, moreover, the natural knowledge of good is darkened by passions and habits of sin.'[21]

The great Elizabethan heir to St Thomas is, of course, Richard Hooker, upon whom the *Summa Theologica* exercised a profound influence. The argument of *The Laws of Ecclesiastical Polity* displays at every turn its intellectual debt to one or other of the ancient traditions, or to both as they are merged in medieval scholasticism. Defending church polity in the name of reason against a rival system which claimed to be founded exclusively upon Scripture, Hooker was less interested than Aquinas in anatomizing conscience, and more in demonstrating how God makes apprehensible his laws to the reason of man. Nevertheless, the demonstration is couched so recognizably in scholastic terms that the interchangeability of the concepts of reason and conscience may be all but taken for granted.

Firstly, Hooker addresses himself to the nature of the laws by which man lives. Originally there is the Law Eternal, by which God fashioned the universe: 'the being of God is a kind of Law to his working: for that perfection which God is, giveth perfection to that he doth.'[22] Contingent upon the Law that inheres in the first Cause, is the Law of Nature, the law which God has established for his creation to work by. 'His commanding those things to be which are, and to be in such sort as they are, to keep that tenure and course which they do, importeth the establishment of nature's law.'[23] The abrogation of the Law of Nature would bring about cosmic convulsions, a reduction to aboriginal chaos:

> Now if nature should intermit her course, and leave altogether though it were but for a while the observation of her own laws; if those principle and mother elements of the world, whereof all things in this lower world are made, should lose the qualities which now they have; if the frame of that heavenly arch erected over our heads should loosen and dissolve itself; if celestial spheres should forget their wonted motions, and by irregular volubility turn themselves anyway as it might happen . . . what would become of man himself, whom all these things now do all serve? See we not plainly that obedience of creatures unto the law of nature is the stay of the whole world?[24]

Natural agents keep the law of their natures unwittingly. The law by which man obeys God is the Law of Reason, which is merely the Law of Nature applied to intellectual beings who participate in it through reason; and though, as a 'voluntary agent', man's will is free, yet in his reason there exists an appetite towards the perfection that is God.[25]

The mandates of this Law are discoverable in man, moreover, by the unaided light of reason, in evidence whereof, Hooker continues, 'the minds even of mere natural men have attained to know, not only that there is a god, but also what power, force, wisdom, and other properties that God hath, and how all things depend on him'.[26] Similarly, the like natural inducement has 'brought men to know that it is their duty no less to love others than themselves'.[27] Man's reason, by nature alone, is sufficiently imbued with the laws of well-doing, therefore, to discover unaided those first two great commandments upon which, as the gospel declares, 'hang all the Law and the Prophets' (Matt. 22:40).

In his use of these concepts, and in his demonstration of the manner of their working, Hooker is clearly and orthodoxly Thomist; the 'Law of Nature' is Aquinas's Natural Law; Hooker's understanding of man's reason as appetitively inclined to the good is unequivocally a reformation of Aquinas's definition of conscience as a disposition; and both of them attest that basic deontic principles are instilled as axioms in the soul of man.

The dependence of all creation upon a Law of Nature assured the Renaissance, at any rate for a time, of the unity and ultimate correspondence of the whole of the phenomenal world in a providential design, a divine dispensation in which the interdependence of material with spiritual nature, of society with the individual soul, provided infinitely varied analogies for the same great mystery, whose ultimate solution was God. As an explanation, it embraces the realms of ethics, psychology, politics and religion,[28] the macrocosm and the microcosm. To Shakespeare the doctrine, implying as it did an infinitely recurring set of relationships connecting man with the universe, provided at any rate the basis for both a moral and an artistic vision: it infused the one and enriched the other. A frequent metaphor draws on the relation between the harmonious cooperation of man's faculties and the successful governance of a commonwealth. In *Coriolanus*, Menenius refers to his face as the map of his microcosm (II.i.62). Falstaff praises the effects of sherris-sack in terms of the body politic: it illumines the face 'which, as a beacon, gives warning to all the rest of this little kingdom', summoning the 'vital commoners, and inland petty spirits' to muster all to their captain, the heart (*2 Henry IV*, IV.iii.106–10).

The fundamental principle which at once maintained and described the unity of the cosmology was order: the order inherent in the Natural Law. The consummate Shakespearean expression of this principle occurs of course in *Troilus and Cressida*, where Ulysses depicts, in accents resonant of Hooker, the chaotic consequences that would inexorably follow should nature abandon 'the observation of her own laws'. What is significant in this speech is that Ulysses evokes the complex interfusion of the manifold variety of things in one great analogical scheme; whether in the realm of ethics, psychology, the heavens, the elements, or man's faculties, disorder in any one of these categories produces reflexive disorder in all the others.

Alfred Harbage argues that the medieval tenets of Hooker (whose *Laws* he calls 'the best of English expositions' of the traditional doctrines) were simply self-evident truths to a Renaissance itself steeped in the pieties of an earlier age, enunciated therefore, and fed into receptive minds by the

> very habits of speech of school-masters, local magistrates, and some of the preachers. A wealth of allusion in the later popular plays argues a general familiarity with the idea that man was the central figure in an orderly, beautiful and divinely planned universe. The salient fact was that it was a universe of law, not of chance or brute force.[29]

Hence what Ulysses could declaim from the stage was re-echoed resoundingly from the pulpit; indeed, the *Sermon of Obedience*, from whence derives the following, was as much a moral exordium as a political tract:

> In heaven (God) hath appointed distinct (or several) orders and states of archangels and angels. In earth he hath assigned and appointed kings and princes, with governors under them, all in good and necessary order. . . . And man himself also hath all his parts both within and without, as soul, heart, mind, memory, understanding, reason, speech, with all and singular corporeal members of his body, in a profitable, necessary, and pleasant order.

Take away obedience, 'and there must needs follow all mischief and utter destruction both of souls, bodies, goods, and commonwealths'.[30] This stern injunction is amply illustrated in the mind of Brutus, where the faculties of mind are in abject disarray; he reflects that between the acting of a dreadful thing and the first inclination towards it, the state of man, 'Like to a little kingdom, suffers then/The nature of an insurrection' (*Julius Caesar*, II.i.68–9). And the perturbations of his mind are correspondingly reflected in the disorder portents described by Casca.

The psychological processes involved in just such an insurrection in the state of man are described in detail by Thomas Wright in *The Passions of the Minde in Generall*. The sensible or irrational aspect of the soul is linked with a power of appetite common to man and beast; where the response of appetite to some desired object is in conformity with the Law of Nature it is deemed an 'affection'; where antagonistic, it is deemed a 'passion' or a 'perturbation'. Through the great correspondent impulse linking the chain of being, passions may actually produce physiological changes: they corrupt judgment, seduce the will and 'trouble wonderfully the soule'; whereupon animal spirits flock through 'certaine secret channels' from the brain to the heart, where they 'pitch at the dore' and make known whether the object is right or wrong. If the brain, seat of the rational soul, is apprehensive, it overwhelms the heart with spirits;[31] and if the apprehension is judged to be evil, it follows, according, this time, to La Primaudaye, 'that by reason of the great beating and panting of the heart, the tongue faltreth, and the voice is interrupted'.[32] Thus in *Measure for Measure*, Angelo, infatuated with Isabella, says:

> Why does my blood thus muster to my heart,
> Making both it unable for itself
> And dispossessing all my other parts
> Of necessary fitness?
>
> (II.iv.20–3)

Whereas in *Macbeth*, the mere contemplation of the crime produces unnatural effects in Macbeth's physical nature: the physiological moves in correspondent sympathy with the spiritual:

> If good, why do I yield to that suggestion
> Whose horrid image doth unfix my hair,
> And makes my seated heart knock at my ribs,
> Against the use of nature?
>
> (I.iii.134–7)

In fact so completely acquiescent was the Renaissance in the belief that the behaviour of the passions reproduced itself physiologically, that Elizabethans had little faith in the power of man to conceal the deepest motions of his soul.[33] Only those so dedicated to evil and so hardened in the usages thereof as to render themselves immune to the passions and to promptings of pity, conscience, and horror, could successfully conceal their motives. That one 'may smile and smile, and be a villain' was a phenomenon bafflingly unnatural to the Elizabethans, for it sundered the correspondence between soul and body. Only in cases of absolute degeneracy was there no art 'to find the mind's construction in the face'. Thus Richard can smile and murder while he smiles, whereas to Macbeth the process of learning to wear a mask succeeds in proportion as his soul becomes habituated to evil and therefore imperturbable. From being a book 'where men may read strange matters', Macbeth's soul becomes inured through 'hard use'; only when he has 'supp'd full with horrors' can he say.

> I have almost forget the taste of fears . . .
> Direness, familiar to my slaughterous thoughts,
> Cannot once start me.
>
> (V.v.9–15)

Such weary indifference and inertness of soul would be horrific testament of how far Macbeth had progressed down the primrose path to the everlasting bonfire. For conflict amongst the faculties of the soul was regarded as inherent in the very nature of man, partaking as he did in both the celestial and animal orders of creation. Medieval philosophers had held that the path of virtue could be taken only by that individual in whom the sensitive appetites remained conformable to the dictates of reason rather than the distractions of sensuality. Either course was open to the exercise of free will, counselled by an enlightened conscience.

The *loci classici* of this scholastic doctrine are to be found in St Anselm's *Liber de Conceptu Virginali et Originali Peccato* (3–4) and Philip the Chancellor's *Summa de Bono*, which variously distinguished between bodily appetites which are themselves good and the disordered bodily appetites not fully subject to the control of rational desire, wherein lies the impulse to sin.[34] The emphasis comes to assume an importance when contrasted with the reformist doctrines of man's total depravity: for Luther and Calvin, the impulse to sin is not just an affliction of concupiscence which affects reason indirectly; rather, it is total in the sense of affecting all the psychological powers equally.

Certain individuals, however, seemed to have been the unfortunate victims of an apparent contradiction in this scholastic theory, crushed, as it were, between the somewhat deterministic imperatives of the doctrine of correspondence and the supreme *bonum naturae* of mankind, free will. In formulating the principle that outer seeming reflected inner being, the Renaissance accepted the Platonic ideal as set forth in *The Timaeus*: 'For no man is voluntarily bad; but the bad by reason of an ill disposition of the body and bad education.'[35] The belief that deformities of the body may dispose one to evil receives the assurance of Bacon:

For the lineaments of the body to disclose the disposition and inclination of the mind in general; but the motions of the countenance and parts do not only so, but do further disclose the present humour and state of the mind and will.[36]

At the same time it was recognized that while in most cases physical deformity testified to spiritual degeneracy, nevertheless the freedom of the will was not essentially compromised: by a supreme effort, the will may amend the soul, and by the institution of right habits and custom, strengthen the conscience and bind it to God. 'For use almost can change the stamp of nature', says Hamlet (III.iv.168), and in this he is supported by Bishop Nemesius: 'our *habits* depend upon our *will*; and it is therefore the fault of our *will*, that we are evill, and not (*originally*) of our *nature*.'[37] And yet, having conceded the ultimate responsibility for action to man's free will, it remained true that even the most philosophically optimistic of Elizabethans would have regarded with extreme scepticism the possibility of changing the predisposing stamp of nature.

The whole metaphysical conundrum is quite remarkably documented in Shakespeare's conception of Richard III. As a misshapen stigmatic, a foul, indigested lump upon whom sin, death, and Hell have set their marks, he is clearly a vehicle for the doctrine that villainy in the soul was predicated by a correspondent deformity in the body. (It is also probably the classic formulation in Shakespeare; his later examinations of evil chart a developing awareness that evil's most problematic aspect is the difficulty of detecting it.) However, Richard's first soliloquy makes it clear that his dedication to evil is not wholly predestinate, but depends in the final analysis upon a degeneracy of mind wilfully determined. His ambitions for the crown, his plot to murder Clarence, may be said to be compensations for deformities which leave him no delight but to descant upon them and see his shadow in the sun – but mitigation may go no further than this. The mere fact that Richard offers his deformity as an excuse shows how far his choice of evil is rationally made, and we may be certain that, when he adds at the close of his soliloquy, the words 'Dive, thoughts, down to my soul', these represent the final perversion of an unresisting will, thus vitalizing the tenets of scholastic psychology. Will, denying the impulses of conscience, chooses a course to which the ill-assorted humours of a deformed body have previously inclined it. And yet, because the will inherently and by its nature loves the good, ultimately it is convicted by the conscience which testifies in Richard's dream how far will has violated its own disposition. Accordingly, even Richard's will could have imposed upon its inferior faculties; albeit we would do well to remind ourselves in addition, with Plato, that 'bad education' as much as physical deformity contributes to the rejection of the good and the atrophy of conscience. Shakespeare is careful to refer us to the circumstances of Richard's birth and the horrified reactions of his mother and the women who witnessed it; moreover, the Duchess's speech in Act IV recalls a frightful history of their relations:

> Thou cams't on earth to make the earth my hell.
> A grievous burden was thy birth to me;
> Tetchy and wayward was thy infancy;
> Thy school-days frightful, desp'rate, wild, and furious . . .
>
> (IV.iv.167–70)

Since, in addition to this, Richard feels himself deprived also of the many joys common to humanity, unworthy of love, and as well naturally disposed to evil by a crippled body, he determines to 'prove a villain' and substitute evil for good.

Hamlet's predicament is in complete contrast, for he is a man upon whom is imposed the hard necessity of action in a world so overwhelmingly flawed by the ambiguities of evil, that the principles of well-doing and any absolute certainty as to integrity of motive, are alike rendered obscure. In so far as he must act, there exist at the same time serious impediments to action of both an internal and external nature; but one powerful inhibition must be a conscientious doubt as to the ethical status of the action he is called upon to accomplish. For Hamlet's dilemma is that he reviles and despises his incestuous and murdering uncle, which excites in him the baser motive of a bloody but private revenge; at the same time this course is apparently sanctioned by heavenly mandate, together with obligations incurred by Hamlet's heir-apparent duty to execute public justice in the public interest. Apparently sanctioned – but for his conscience, as the scholastics had testified, that is pre-eminently the question. St Thomas had warned that sin committed through an error of conscience is almost invariably mortal, except in cases of factual mistake. And yet in the terms of Thomistic analysis, Hamlet's responsibilities seem exacerbated still further because they are governed by two contradictory deontic premises: that the heavens ought to be obeyed, and that man shall not kill. A lengthy discussion of this must, of course, be deferred to a later stage; suffice it to say that Hamlet's 'condition' is at least partly induced by an inner turbulence of conscience so profound that it causes him to doubt the authenticity of his father's ghost and the morality of its behests, because of the danger that his disordered passion for revenge might have provoked a visible conjuration of evil that would confound his soul.

In the case of Macbeth, free will seems, at least to begin with, entirely unconstrained; yet after he has committed what Speaight calls the 'hecatomb of crime',[38] we sense that his career in wickedness becomes more and more ineluctable, more fatefully preordained as sin plucks on sin and the good in him diminishes, leaving his soul a barren supulchre of evil. The stages in Macbeth's damnation proceed once again in accordance with the systematic conceptions of scholastic philosophy.[39] St Thomas had stated that sin may arise when reason's knowledge of the ultimate good is defective, or baffled by 'a vehement and inordinate apprehension of the imagination and judgement of the estimative power'. By these, will is distracted, and adheres not to those divinely instituted general principles instilled in the *synderesis*, but to a mutable good, the fickle, evanescent objective of the passions and the sensitive appetite.

As for Macbeth, it is safe to assume in him a pre-existent disordering of the imagination capable potentially of seducing the will. He is a mighty warrior, laden with royal honours, luxuriating in the golden opinions of all sorts of people. His service to Duncan in the wars has been glorious, and earns for him the epithets of honour 'valour's minion', 'Bellona's bridegroom'; and yet, significantly, Macbeth's prowess is depicted with that characteristic Shakespearean ambiguity reserved for all those in whom the service of *virtus* entails a partial surrender of *humanitas*. In Macbeth's wars, to 'unseam' a man 'from the nave to the chaps', and, with smoking sword to 'memorize another Golgotha' is to do what becomes a worthy gentleman: the same fateful equation made by Coriolanus in whom dedication to honour breeds a similar hubris. In Macbeth, that hubris is controlled, quiescent, satisfied with those dignities that for the moment may be worn in their newest gloss, and yet his first reaction on encountering the Weird Sisters shows that his imagination has before this commended to his self-love a putative image of the supreme mutable good – the golden round which Fate, metaphysical aid, and now his wife promise well to crown him withal. Still, Macbeth's conscience, reflecting the natural good in him to which his will continues to adhere, repeatedly warns him; Lady Macbeth, expressing it in a different way, calls this 'the milk of human kindness' – a revulsion of the soul against the mere contemplation of actions not in harmony with man's nature and the Natural Law.

Macbeth's temptations may therefore be seen as two-fold. His encounter with the Weird Sisters suggests to an already inordinate imagination the apprehension of a mutable good which excites the passions, distracts the will, and so clouds the judgment and reason that 'nothing is but what is not', and flawed logic suggests murder as the only means to the crown. None the less, conscience for the time asserts itself and Macbeth decides to 'proceed no further' in the business.

At this point, Macbeth's will becomes subject to a second, and this time, overwhelming onslaught. Lady Macbeth exerts her influence once again on the distracting effects of the sensitive appetites, and this time at their most vulnerable point. Her assault is upon her husband's conception of himself – the central idea of his warriorship which sustains him – undermining his hubris by imputations of weakness, of flaccid ambition and of cowardice. Her own remarkable capacity to banish all womanly qualities is a calculated affront to his own masculinity. And so his will, galvanized by the passions which in turn have been goaded to frenzied and inordinate apprehensions by the incitements of his wife, finally capitulates to a course against whose evil nature his repressed conscience never ceases to testify.

Descriptions of the nature and functions of conscience by contemporary theologians must be approached cautiously and with some regard for doctrinal differences of interpretation. Most, though, elaborate upon the Thomistic notion that the operations of conscience may be impeded by a wilful and habitual recourse to evil. Perkins, for example, is orthodoxly scholastic in saying that the conscience may be 'slumbering' or 'seared': the former 'commonly raignes in the hearts of drowsie Protestants' and accuses only for great sins; the latter 'doth not accuse for any sinne' and, inured to feeling or remorse, is characterized by the extinction even of the 'light of nature' in man, 'so that he judgeth evill good and good evill'.[40]

This seems aptly to describe Macbeth, in whom a 'slumbering' conscience degenerates to a 'seared' conscience, marked by an increasing insensitivity and an *exceeding greedinesse* to all manner of sinne'. Finally, at the nadir of wickedness, the conscience induces a sort of desperation 'whereby a man . . . comes to bee out of all hope of the pardon of his sinnes. This made Saul, Achitophell, and Judas to hang themselves.'[41]

Desperation, or despair, had not escaped the observations of psychologists such as Burton; it was regarded as a passion capable of perverting the instinct by which the soul should be made to desist from following after that which is impossible – not always to be 'discommended', says Burton, 'as in Wars it is a cause many times of extraordinary valour'.[42] A valour, indeed, which explains the hopeless desperation with which Richard 'enacts more wonders than a man' (V.iv.2) at Bosworth, and Macbeth, betrayed utterly by the juggling equivocations to which he had fastened his hopes, tries the last:

> Lay on Macduff,
> And damned be he that first cries 'Hold, enough!'
> (V.viii.334)

Repentance, of course, was the essential condition of forgiveness. Perkins, discussing the 'remedie' and the 'application' of it, writes: 'For nothing can stanch or slay the terrours of conscience, but the blood of the immaculate lambe of God . . . unfainedly to humble our selves before God for all our wants, breaches, and woundes in conscience.'[43] Thomas Playfere testifies similarly to the ultimately beneficent effects of a guilt-stricken conscience: of the contrite, he says, 'For this abhorring of himselfe is a recovering of himselfe: and the sooner hee repents in dust and ashes, the sooner he is freede from all his sinnes, and from all the punishments due to the same.'[44]

This is the remedy offered by Hamlet to his mother: 'Confess yourself to heaven' (III.iv.151), and, indeed, the object of the Duke's instruction to Juliet in *Measure for Measure*: 'how you shall arraign your conscience/And try your penitence' (II.iii.21–2). In fact, it may be averred that the theme of forgiveness, reiterated time and time again, is very close to the heart of Shakespeare's moral viewpoint.

In sum, then, the cosmology inherited by Hooker and Shakespeare is the rationally intelligible universe of scholastic patrimony; man's essential nature is his reason, indeed the Law of Nature is the law of his reason, and conscience, in its ability to formulate a priori deductions from that Law, the very predication of man's rationality. So long as his conscience observes the Natural Law, man puts himself into harmonious correspondence with the laws that subsist the universal frame, and of which his own creation was so manifest an execution. Nature in Shakespearean tragedy is always beneficent, and man's highest moral aspirations always accord with its law; even in the darkest of the plays, its most malign manifestations – the awe-inspiring fury of the elements in *Lear* and the unnatural shroud of perpetual night in *Macbeth* – are perversions of the cosmic order induced by man's dysfunction within it. Shakespeare's tragic heroes belong in the same moral category as Hooker's 'voluntary agents': their wills are free, counselled by the promptings of conscience to which they are either conformable or recalcitrant; and action derives from the freely determinate choices of the characters concerned. Evil rebounds upon evil-doers by an entirely natural reactive pattern of proximate causes in the macrocosm, and by an equally natural testament of guilty horror and condemnation in the conscience. The Shakespearean universe had inherently a legal foundation; it presumes that man is himself the author of his proper woe, and that there is a correspondent impulse linking man and society. As Hooker puts it, 'is it possible, that Man being not only the noblest creature in the world, but even a very world in himself, his transgressing the Law of his Nature should draw no manner of harm after it?'[45] That 'great bond' which Macbeth recognizes as the great ethical conflux of man in nature, and whose analeptic convulsions precipitate his personal tragedy and the restoration of the cosmic weal, represents, as in all Shakespearean tragedy, an artistic paradigm of a theological premise essentially scholastic in origin, and which in seventeenth-century drama began to deteriorate. In many of the Jacobeans, as Clifford Leech has said, 'there is a strong sense of determinism', an uneasy poise between the traditional belief in order and 'a conception of the universe as chaos'.[46] Moreover, the moral faculty in man, though capable of perceiving the good, seems subjected to a curious inanition: not only are the warnings of conscience subverted by a regressive degeneracy in the concupiscent appetites, but the natural order of society itself has disintegrated, made subject to the moral necrosis of a pervasive and insidious evil.

The slavery of sin: justification by faith and its consequences

The drastic revaluation of the nature of man and of the moral axiologies that in varying degrees sustained the universe of Jacobean tragedy, can be referred immediately to the post-Reformation diffusion in England of Lutheran and Calvinist doctrines which emphasized the transcendent glory of God by stressing the utter wretchedness and debasement of man. But the origins of that profound dislocation in the order of nature, so distinctively a characteristic of Reformist cosmology, must be sought paradoxically in the self-same medieval crucibles of thought as the conception which it so diametrically negated. The challenge to scholasticism which came first of all from St Thomas's English contemporary, John Duns Scotus, has already been remarked: whereas to Aquinas, reason was both the executive principle of God's providence and the faculty by which man ordered himself to its laws, Scotus insisted upon the supremacy of the will in God and man. Ethical distinctions were, for the Franciscan school, inaccessible to man's rational discrimination, and resided not in the essential nature of things, but in the arbitrary will of God; so, too, was the will of man an independent faculty of the soul, dispossessed, by an original permission at the fall, of that appetitive disposition imputed to it by St Thomas.

The concept of the arbitrary freedom of God's will was carried forward very largely by the nominalism of William of Ockham (c. 1290–1349).[47] The disputes between the nominalists and the realists from the twelfth to the thirteenth century had perhaps only an ephemeral impact on the consciousness of the Middle Ages; nevertheless the central epistomological problem they addressed – the problem of universals – was to have profound repercussions during the Reformation. Some degree of realism is implied in the majority of medieval thinkers; and the common assumption of scholastics such as William of Champeaux (1070–1121), Peter Abelard (d.1142), Albertus Magnus (d.1280), and of course his great pupil Aquinas, is the hylomorphic theory of matter and form which determined the status and relation of genera and species and the individuals belonging to them. Hylomorphism asserts the 'potentiality' of all matter, in that it cannot be said properly to exist until determined by form; form is what imparts to each thing its distinctive entity, and determines its essential singularity. The origin of the dispute centred on the Introductions by Boethius and Porphyry to Aristotle's *Categories*, which posed just such questions of genera and species: what was the nature of terms like 'animal' or 'man', and did they have a real and objectifiable existence outside the mind? The realists argued that they did; that individuals belonged to a species and defined their genera by means of a formal and essential identity, postulated in turn by the existence of a primal and irreducible basis of matter, potential of successive forms. If the reality of universals were denied, there was no means of theological discourse: as St Anselm said, 'How would he who does not understand that several men are specifically one man, understand that in the most mysterious of all natures, several persons, each of whom is a perfect God, is one God?'[48]

The nominalists, on the other hand, replied that universals were nothing but names, abstractions, and mental constructs that were the mind's response to an atomic and fragmented reality outside itself. Roscelin of Compiègne (1050–1125), and, in a later revival of nominalism, William of Ockham, held that only individuals were real, and the only valid knowledge was that which inhered empirically in intuitive experience, rather than abstractions. Universals were merely fictional labels by which to catalogue the apprehensions of the mind. The great importance of Ockhamism is that it dislocated, for a time at least, the very framework of scholasticism, since if there were indeed no universal essence common to a species, then not only could there by no Natural Law in the scholastic sense, but the manifold hierarchies of genera and kind that are the Elizabethan extensions of the principle must also collapse. The principle of order, according to the nominalists, was God's will, itself unconfined to rule or limit, since to argue, as Aquinas did, that God's purposes were reducible to law, seemed to impute a determining cause to the prime cause of the universe. And since God's actions are thus sublimely free of all coercion, a thing becomes right or wrong solely for the reason that He wills it so; good and evil are arbitrary categories imposed upon the universe, to man's reason incomprehensible, and to his nature essentially alien.

Although potentially subversive of the serene verities of scholasticism, nominalist ideas lay dormant for two centuries and exercised no further influence upon the mind of Christendom until they achieved a progenitive resurgence in the teachings of Luther and Calvin, who were both to profess themselves Ockhamists. In fact Luther's knowledge of Thomism was superficial, and he was far more familiar, outside St Augustine and the *Theologica Germanica*, with the nominalist commentaries on the *Sententiae* of Peter Lombard: those of Biel, d'Ailly, and in particular Ockham.[49] Luther was profoundly influenced by the nominalist conception of the divine will as absolute, ineffably beyond man's understanding, and unamenable to ethical categories. 'True, we must teach', says Luther, '. . . of God's incomprehensible and unsearchable will; but to aim at its perfect comprehension is dangerous work, wherein we stumble, fall, and break our necks.'[50] But it was from Ockham that Luther drew his pessimistic conclusions as to the utter depravity of man's nature: man's reason is corrupted by pride, and his will somehow curved in on itself (*'incurvatus in se'*), and both are bent ineluctably to sin. At the heart of Luther's doctrine of imputed righteousness lay the presupposition that man by his own efforts was helpless: neither by the light of natural morality, nor by the dedicated pursuit of good works, could man merit salvation; by faith alone could he be justified, and even then only as the passive recipient of a grace itself an imputative effect on the divine will. Similarly, Luther interpreted predestination in terms of divine fiat, once again uncon- ditioned by the formal necessities of nature and the laws governing crea- tures. As McDonough makes clear:

> If the Christian, the just man, intrinsically good in his nature and his acts and endowed with divine grace, merits Heaven, it is only due to the fact that God so ordains it *de potentia ordinata*; but He could or might, *de potentia absoluta*, refuse Heaven to the one possessing these qualities; or inversely, even impute justification and the right to Heaven to the sinful man.[51]

The agonized conclusions to which Luther was forced in wrestling with his own experience, were advanced still further with systematic rigour and implacable logic in Calvin's *Institutes* (published 1536–59). He too accepts the nominalist exaltation of the will: 'every event which happens in the world is governed by the incomprehensible counsel of God',[52] the authority for which he derives from Psalms 36:7. Although the will of God is partly accessible to man in the Scriptures, yet there are mysteries 'which far transcend the measure of our sense' since the 'admirable *method*' of governing the universe remains a function of God's will forever hidden.[53] Because of Adam's original sin, man's nature is twisted and perverted to evil: 'everything which is in man, from the intellect to the will, from the soul even to the flesh, is defiled and pervaded with . . . concupiscence . . . so that it is foolish and unmeaning to confine the corruption thence pro- ceeding to what are called sensual motions. . . . Here Peter Lombard has displayed gross ignorance.'[54] Calvin is still further from scholasticism in his wholesale deprecation of nature; Adam not only deteriorated his race by his fall, but 'perverted the whole order of nature in heaven and earth . . . through man's fault a curse has extended above and below, over all the regions of the world'.[55] In Luther and Calvin the divorce of nature and grace, reason and faith, is made absolute, and marks the decline of that philosophy which had ensured their hegemony over 500 years. 'Guilt', concludes Calvin, 'is from nature, whereas sanctification is from supernatural grace.'[56] In vain do we seek in our nature for anything good: 'When the will is enchained as the slave of sin, it cannot make a movement towards goodness, far less steadily pursue it.'[57]

To look ahead for the moment to the later Jacobean dramatists, it may now be possible to detect something of the form and pressure of reformist ideas in, say, Tourneur, Massinger, and Ford; an influence evinced most obviously in that pronounced pessimism and morbidity characteristic of seventeenth-century drama.[58] In particular, none of the plays of the drama- tists alluded to allows much scope for the idea of man's moral responsibility; and while everywhere is demonstrated the bottomless pit of stench and corruption to which man's degenerate and unbridled passions have reduced the world, there is nothing in the rendering of that evil which suggests that it is subject, as in Aquinas or Shakespeare, to a natural exorcism by a series of causative concatenations in the body politic. Moreover, characters surrender themselves helplessly to their passions in a manner which suggests that they are inevitably and by nature enslaved to them: a bondage of the will which enables the dramatist to secure for his characters on the part of an audience, either an extenuating and somewhat sentimental pity – as does Heywood for Anne Frankford – or a connivance at pragmatic opportunism – Bosola's – in the indubitably wicked world of Webster's Duchess. The alternative to this pervasive moral impotence is stark (for, as in Calvin's theology, there are no indeterminate ethical shades of grey in Jacobean drama – man is either justified, or he is not): just as Mistress Frankford, Bosola, and Giovanni are driven by the inordinacy of 'natural' forces beyond the control of their reasons, so too, do the priggish exemplars of an evidently Puritan-inspired pietism – the heroes of Tourneur and Massinger – radiantly transcend the sordid world, and, miraculously relieved of the drossy integument that had united them to it, stand forth against its temptations ineffably lapped in spiritual proof. The old Adam has been killed in them by a process dramatically unexplored, because inexplicable. Whereas in the scholastic paradigm to which Shakespeare adhered, man is born to the hard necessity of achieving his redemption, in Tourneur, Webster, and Massinger,[59] justification has the effect of being merely imputed to man, who is necessarily undeserving of it. What in fact these dramatists testify to is that inversion of the scholastic conception of moral responsibility, stated by Luther in *The Freedom of a Christian* as 'Good works do not make a good man, but a good man does good works; evil works do not make a wicked man, but a wicked man does evil works.'[60] When men are good or bad, not in act but in being, and where the consciously perceived effort of personal struggle is supererogated in the drama by a divine intermission – moreover, when the dramatic universe itself is no longer the rationally intelligible theatre of the autonomous and responsible will – at this juncture it is at least arguable that the conditions for the greatest tragedy no longer exist, and in fact the decline from Shakespeare to the Jacobeans is, to all intents, at one with the wholesale absorption in the latter of voluntarist doctrines.

We begin, of course, to find evidence of this philosophical change in secular works of all kinds which long antedate those of Shakespeare; indeed, as the present study will go on to suggest, the assimilation of reformist beliefs begins early on in the evolution of the English morality play, and is well established in, for example, Woodes's *The Conflict of Conscience* (published 1581). One could point as well to the pronounced fideist strain in Sir Philip Sidney's *Arcadia*, where the 'strange and secret workings' of a providential justice has as its corollary the metaphysical abasement of man's reason, the poet's Protestant scepticism coexisting somewhat uneasily with his Renaissance optimism. Faced with the serpentine and crooked line which brings the princes to be judged by their own kinsman Euarchus, Sidney intones the lines which, in a later generation, were to inspire the despair of Bosola: 'In such a shadow or rather pit of darkness the wormish mankind lives, that neither they know how to foresee nor what to fear, and are but like tennis balls, tossed by the racket of the higher powers.'[61] Sidney's friend Greville is likewise unimpressed by mankind's natural understanding, and endorses more thoroughly than does Sidney Calvin's estimate of a man as 'a worm five feet long':

> The last chiefe oracle of what man knowes
> Is UNDERSTANDING; which though it containe
> Some ruinous notions, which our nature showes,
> Of generall truths, yet have they such a staine
> From our corruption, as all light they lose;
>   Save to convince of ignorance and sinne,
>   Which where they raigne let no perfection in.[62]

But it is, as we have seen, in the dramatists of the early seventeenth century that we find the most thoroughgoing antithesis between the realms of nature and grace, reason and Natural Law. Thus Marston, in *The Scourge of Villainie*, anathemizes both free will and stoic destiny, and in doing so urges the Calvinist separation of grace from nature or philosophy:

> Wher's then (*I will*?) wher's that strong Deity,
> You doe ascribe to your Philosophy?
> Confounded Natures brats, can *will* and *Fate*,
> Have both their seate, & office in your pate?[63]

The same theme is merely recapitulated in his drama: the first part of *Antonio and Mellida* contains the lines

> Philosophy maintains that Nature's wise,
> And forms no useless or unperfect thing . . .
> Go to, go to; thou liest, Philosophy.
> Nature forms things imperfect, useless, vain.[64]
>   (III.i.28–36)

The axiom of knowledge, metaphysically suspect in Marlowe's *Faustus*, is further undermined in the antinomian tragedies of Tourneur and Webster, while the lugubrious moral insights of Ford's drama are heralded in his long religious poem *Christes Bloodie Sweat*, where

> men, that in a maze of deathfull errour
> [Do] treade the pathes of miseries and woe,[65]

These writers together express a view of nature anarchic, perverted –
that is, wholly contrary to the synchronous, morally kinetic universe of
law referred to, for example, by Hector in *Troilus and Cressida*: here, the
Natural Law accords with man's highest aspirations. Speaking of Helen's
return to the Greeks, and of the 'dues of marriage' which 'Nature craves',
he says:

> If this law
> Of nature be corrupted through affection,
> And that great minds, of partial indulgence
> To their benumbed wills, resist the same,
> There is a law in each well-order'd nation
> To curb those raging appetites that are
> Most disobedient and refactory.
>
> (II.ii.177–83)

Although it is true that Luther and Calvin speak of the law in this
Shakespearean sense, they differ from its scholastic implications by surbor-
dinating Natural Law to the absolute sovereignty of God; there can be no
law above or outside the undetermined will of God, which is the sole
source of order. Therefore God can only be obeyed by man's voluntary
response, an abasement in which man's perverted will is brought by the
secret processes of election to reflect the arbitrary will of God. Now the
primary source of man's knowledge of the Law is the divine will in so far
as it is revealed in the Decalogue and the Gospels, and it is by the
informing precepts of the Scriptures that man's conscience must struggle
to confirm itself, and even then the effort can only be made as an imputative effect of divine grace. Luther's moral pessimism was such that man's
enduring wickedness left no room for an upward movement of the soul
to God: justification was from God alone, and, devoid of redeeming grace,
man's reason was powerless to know, and his will helpless to perform, the
revealed will of God. None the less, both reformers were obliged to admit
that, despite his debased nature, man was still a rational creature endowed
with intellect and will; and even Adam's rebellion could not fully shake
the security of God's providential order. For Luther admits that St Paul's
reference to that order of knowledge which in pagans is 'written in their
hearts' (Rom. 2:15, 16) implies certain self-evident truths; namely, that
God is to be obeyed.[66] For Calvin, too, an external image of righteousness
still exists in man's reason and conscience by means of his perception of
a Natural Law;[67] and because man is a social animal, and cannot completely avoid the commands of God, he is driven by this to live up to a
minimal standard of civil harmony and justice.[68] Even though human
nature is 'so deluged, as it were, that no part remains exempt from
sin', nevertheless certain 'sparks' of reason remain: a limited power of
conscience to discriminate what is just and unjust, the 'seeds' of civil

order, along with practical gifts of reason in the fields of applied arts and liberal studies.[69]

The significance of this is that Luther and Calvin, despite their virulent attacks on the merits of human acts, admit of a certain unchanged onto-logical residuum in human nature. But that it is profoundly at variance with scholastic philosophy is demonstrable from the deep distrust mani-fested in the works of both for either reason or the Law. Of the 'sparks' of reason which differentiate man from the beasts, Luther admits that they may shed an obscure light on terrestrial affairs, especially those relating to self-interest; but the will is hopelessly defective and remains without grace, a slave to self and to evil.[70] Calvin is similarly dismissive: the 'light [of reason] is so smothered by clouds of darkness, that it cannot shine forth to any good effect'. In like manner, the will, because insepar-able from the nature of man, did not perish, but 'was so enslaved by depraved lusts as to be incapable of one righteous desire'.[71] Of the Natural Law, its precepts may sometimes be perceived, though always tortuously and frequently in vain; and it is in any case subjoined to God's arbitrary and inscrutable purposes. We must always return at last, insists Calvin, 'to the mere pleasure of the divine will, the cause of which is hidden in himself . . . the procedure of divine justice is too high to be scanned by human measure, or comprehended by the feebleness of human intellect'.[72]

These somewhat grudging gestures paid to the possible subsistence in man of an innate moral faculty, are written into the doctrines of voluntar-ism as a kind of rider to the overwhelming proofs of man's degeneracy; for in neither Luther nor Calvin's work is the primary purpose epistemo-logical, that is, to find out what the human mind, unaided by grace, can know with certainty. At the same time, the doctrine of predestination made the Reformers vulnerable to charges of antinomianism and the crimination of God; the former could only be met by admitting a residual rationality to man, while the dark shadow cast upon a divine justice that wilfully consigned a vast majority to perdition could only be countered by the supposition that they were in some obscure sense to blame. Above all, both Luther and Calvin had to account for St Paul's dictum that the Gentiles shall be judged according to their consciences instead of the Law of the Scriptures. They tried to cover all these objections by ascribing a purely negative signification to the Law and conscience: that is, that they provide enlightenment sufficient merely to ensure that the reprobate have no excuse. Says Calvin: 'The end of the natural law, therefore, is to render man inexcusable, and may be not improperly defined – the judgement of conscience distinguishing sufficiently between just and unjust, and by convicting men on their own testimony, depriving them of all pretext for ignorance.'[73] But, lest this hooded statement may seem to open the door to a scholastic sufficiency of reason, he reformulates his argument more precisely in a following paragraph:

For if the hearts of men are imbued with a sense of justice and injustice, in order that they may have no pretext to allege ignorance, it is by no means necessary for this purpose that they should discern the truth in particular cases. It is even more than sufficient if they understand so far as to be unable to practise evasion without being convicted by their own conscience, . . . Indeed, if we would test our reason by the Divine Law, which is a perfect standard of righteousness, we should find how blind it is in many respects.[74]

Calvin's teachings upon the nature and offices of conscience occur as a logical extension of these premises. For him, the conscience is the medium between God and man, necessarily vitiated, like all man's faculties, by the fall, and the centre, therefore, of unrelieved torment to him. Firstly, by revealing to him the extent of his disobedience, it brings him to conviction, dragging him forward as a culprit to the bar of God.[75] This down-pressing sense of sin makes the conscience a legal yoke, driving man against his will in the direction of the sovereign will of God, by causing him to despair in himself. At the same time, the Law contained in the Decalogue is consummate proof of what man, because of sin, is morally incapable of doing. Hence the conscience, originally free before man's fall, is constantly in terror under the dominion of the Law, and, moreover, tortured by a passion for harmony with God, which cannot possibly be satisfied since the whole nature of man is enfeebled by the flesh and enslaved to sin. So the conscience in 'natural' men feels 'anxious', craves 'confidence' in its cursed state, in the face of the 'terror' and disquietude induced in it by the haunting conviction of the Law.[76] Only in those who are conformed to the will of God in 'voluntary' obedience, obeying its precepts with 'alacrity' and promptitude, is the conscience at peace,[77] but since it is only in the elect that God initiates such a movement towards himself, the conscience remains tormented but impotent until fortified by divine grace. By this unaided, the conscience can simply compel and convict, but is very far from providing a basis for spiritual coherence in itself, as in scholastic thought; true, it has a myopic perception of a vestigial *ordo naturae*, but this merely directs the will in vain to something higher than itself as the true principle of order – namely, the causeless and arbitrary will of God. Only at the instant of regeneration, when the will of man is renovated and created anew as the 'handmaid' of prevenient grace, is the conscience made whole and entire,[78] and only in the elect, therefore, can the will be described as righteous, since everything proper to its own corrupt nature has been abolished.[79] In the reprobate, on the other hand, it remains under the necessity of sinning; since although such are not forced to be the servants of sin, they are nevertheless 'voluntary slaves'; though uncompelled to evil, their wills are nevertheless 'bound by the fetters of sin'.[80]

Clearly, Calvin's teachings on conscience are closely related to the doctrine of imputed righteousness, and both are at one with his overall conception of providence as manipulated and intrusively superintended by the inscrutable will of God. For the scholastics, providence is governed by a law inhering alike in God and the universe: the preservation of providence is the execution of that Law by which all things were created. Hooker, replying to Calvin, was to express it thus:

And as it cometh to pass in a kingdom rightly ordered, that after a law is once published, it presently takes effect far and wide, all states framing themselves thereunto . . . since the time that God did first proclaim the edicts of his law upon it, heaven and earth have hearkened unto his voice, and their labour hath been to do his will.[81]

Calvin's view is different:

It were cold and lifeless to represent God as a momentary Creator, who completed his work once for all, and then left it . . . faith must penetrate deeper. After learning that there is a Creator, it must forthwith infer that he is also a Governor and Preserver, and that, not by producing a kind of general motion in the machine of the globe as well as in each of its parts, but by a special Providence sustaining, cherishing, superintending . . . the sun does not daily rise and set by a blind instinct of nature, but is governed by Him in its course . . . every single year, month, and day, is regulated by a new and special Providence of God.

Those, moreover, who confine the providence of God within narrow limits, as if he allowed all things to be borne along freely according to a perpetual law of nature . . . defraud God of his glory.[82]

Now the Calvinist emphasis on God's immediate regulation of providence seems superficially to describe the moral universe of the Tudor chronicle plays, and especially that of Shakespeare's history plays. Characters cry out for divine vengeance to right the innocent, and hail as divine justice whatever nemesis is visited upon the unjust. Yet this providential retribution, if it is indeed such, is always in Shakespeare contiguous with a pattern in which a ramifying contagion of evil eventually engulfs the evil-doer, and precipitates a reactive series of convulsions in the natural order of things. In *Richard III* especially, as a later chapter will suggest, the hand of God is only ambiguously present in the affairs of those 'wrangling pirates' who so persistently invoke His intervention; and Richard himself is overtaken by contingent repercussions, concretely apprehended, which testify to his violations of both Law and conscience.

The most unequivocal dramatic portrayal of the absolutist conception of providence occurs in *The Atheist's Tragedy*. Here D'Amville is punished both for his atheism and the sins it allows him to commit, by the loss of his sons and the ultimate destruction of himself. But, as Herndl points out, the play is not a study of causes in human affairs;[83] the fate which overtakes D'Amville bears no rationally apprehended natural connection with the evil that precipitated it; retribution comes in the form of a divine intervention in nature, rather than a consummation of its impulse to order. On the contrary, the imposition of order is synonymous with divine fiat, and D'Amville's self-immolation at the end of the play is an assertion of the inscrutable and arbitrary justice of God. Of a piece with this is the overwhelmingly Calvinist conception of conscience at work in both D'Amville and the virtuous Charlemont. The latter, returning to find his father murdered by his uncle, is exhorted by his father's ghost to 'leave revenge unto the King of Kings' (II.vi.22): a commandment that accords fortuitously with his own inclinations, following as it does a sudden and unexplained conversion to grace. Thus happily insured – unlike Hamlet – against the contaminating effects of any further part in the divine economy of justice, Charlemont exhibits a Puritan serenity of conscience, passively complacent in the face of evil and death. On the other hand, D'Amville's conscience, unfortified by any such imputative effects of divine grace, convicts and excoriates him, albeit that this has little effect on his will, presumably for long enslaved to sin by the unholy practices of atheism. Finally, when himself about to carry out the execution of Charlemont, he dashes out his own brains by 'accident', a scenario deliberately chosen for its apparent impossibility, by which Tourneur suggests the intervention of God's justice. The whole play argues the falseness of D'Amville's position, based upon a blasphemous exaltation of nature and reason, and contrasts it with the patient Christianity of Charlemont, guided by divine grace, and beatifically resigned to the exercise of the divine will. Stumbling upon Charlemont and Castabella asleep in the graveyard, D'Amville acknowledges that theirs is a felicity to which his perverted reason had been incapable of attaining:

> Stay! Asleep? So soundly? And so sweetly
> Upon death's heads? And in a place so full
> Of fear and horror? Sure there is some other
> Happiness within the freedom of the
> Conscience than my knowledge e'er attained to.
>
> (IV.iii.283–7)

'Tis Pity She's a Whore similarly depicts a fallen world where Natural Law is pitted against Divine Law, and perverted reason seeks to justify a gross permission of the will in the name of what is 'natural'. The Friar attempts to warn Giovanni of the vanity of reason, inevitably misguided unless directed by the word of God. A dependency upon reason alone is apt to lead to that perverted and twisted rationalization of the sinful appetites that Calvin had insisted was characteristic of fallen man, and which Giovanni demonstrates with a tragic aptitude:

> . . . wits that presumed
> On wit too much, by striving how to prove
> There was no God, with foolish grounds of Art,
> Discovered first the nearest way to hell.
>
> (I.i.4–7)

The Friar concedes with Giovanni that incest might be justified according to the amoralism of the Natural Law; but God's will is above the order of nature, and the Friar is emphatic that incest is a sinful violation of the Divine Law, whose mysteries are inscrutable. Giovanni is, of course, half aware that what his 'natural' passions propose to his reason is sinful; aware also that yielding to them will lead ineluctably to his own destruction; and yet these shadowy insights are overwhelmed by a thraldom of the appetite and the degenerate will, and instead of continuing to struggle in accordance with the Friar's injunctions, he capitulates fatalistically, and indeed helplessly, to sinful corruption:

> All this I'll do, to free me from the rod
> Of vengeance; else I'll swear my fate's my god
>
> (I.i.83–4)

Indeed, the doctrinal implications of Ford's moral universe, and, it might be added, of the Jacobean dramatists as a group, seem to indicate a Calvinistic acceptance of the degeneracy of man; that lust, greed, and murderous ambition are endemic in the natural order of things, and are everywhere justified in the name of a twisted and perverted reason. But against this seamy backdrop, there stand out a chosen few, whose virtue is incorruptible, and who are frequently distinguishable by that calm assurance which is the chief comfort of a sound conscience.

The English casuistical tradition

The theology of conscience as expounded as a formal system in numerous treatises of the late sixteenth and early seventeenth centuries primarily manifests itself as a specifically Puritan branch of casuistical ethics, correlated with the great doctrinal and soteriological premises of *sola fide, sola scriptura*, and the total depravity of man. Though the hagiography of conscience has its Anglican exponents – John Woolton, John Hughes and Robert Bolton, for example, who accept a modified scholasticism in content and methodology – the vast majority, in this period at any rate, are firmly within a Calvinist tradition of devotional literature, which, as has already been made clear, fulfilled an overwhelming Puritan need for private study and prayer. In part this demand was a consequence of the great issue of religious allegiance, with its corollary of placing a heavier responsibility upon every individual for the conduct of his own religious life. But for the Puritan this responsibility was exacerbated by the yet more onerous duty of verifying the morality of his own actions in the light of biblical sanction, and by a corroborative search of his own conscience; as Horton Davies attests, the 'Protestant principle of the priesthood of all believers was taken in its fullest implications by the Puritan merchants of the middle classes'.[84] This emphasis on the supremacy of the conscience led, as Camille Wells Slights has ably demonstrated, to that largely seventeenth-century phenomenon known as case divinity, a branch of ethics pioneered by William Perkins and, a generation later, by William Ames, which attempted in compendious detail to resolve cases of conscience by the application of moral principles to the practical complexities of daily life.[85] Thus Perkins followed up *A Discourse of Conscience*, which is a purely theoretical study of the basis of casuistry, with the publication in 1606 of *The Whole Treatise of the Cases of Conscience*, whose purpose is essentially illustrative and multiplies, in a variety of permutations, particular moral instances and dilemmas. It is not, however, this empirical tradition of case morality, operating by distinctions and exceptions in the practical sphere, which is the principal concern of this synopsis,[86] but rather its theoretical basis in the soteriological dogmas that still dominated men's horizons in the sixteenth, and early part of the seventeenth, century. Indeed, with the exception of Perkins and Ames, whose *Conscience with the Power and Cases Thereof* did not appear in translation until 1639, most of the treatises that can be considered as having any bearing on the imaginative literature of the period were primarily of this academic sort: general instruments of moral theology, rather than collections of cases of conscience, limiting themselves to a consideration of the spiritual life together with the role of the conscience in its attainment, especially in relation to the definitive Reformation issues of grace, faith, the Law, and repentance. It is this formal and theoretical significance of conscience as a faculty of the soul – in Jeremiah Dyke's words, the 'Nature, Meanes, Marks, Benefit and Necessity Thereof' – which is most immediately relevant to the analysis of moral choice in the dramatic literature here to be surveyed, and the following pages will attempt to piece together, by reference to a number of such treatises, what, for reasons of space, can be no more than a composite profile of the reformist idea of conscience, and of the theological postulates which it subsumed.

The majority of the treatises under discussion begin by formulating a definition of conscience: its location in the soul, and its functions and offices. Nearly all such definitions owe something to the methods and the terminology of scholasticism, even those which most trenchantly refute its conclusions. Perkins, for example, follows the schoolmen in placing conscience not 'in the affections nor will, but in the understanding: because the actions thereof standes in the use of reason'.[87] His division, moreover, of the understanding into two parts called the '*Theoreticall*' and the '*practicall understanding*' is unmistakably a redaction of the scholastic terminology of *synderesis* and *conscientia*:

> The first [part of the understanding] is that which standes in the views and contemplation of *truth* and *falshood*: and goes no further. The second is that whiche standes in the viewe and consideration of every particular action, to search whether it be *goode* or *badde*. . . . And under this latter is conscience to be comprehended.[88]

In this conclusion, he is in complete agreement with others of more pronounced Anglican leanings, such as Robert Bolton and Richard Carpenter. The former, indeed, accepts without qualification the medieval theory:

> The whole and entire work of conscience, as you well know, out of the Schooles, consisteth in a practicall syllogisme: The proposition ariseth out of the [*Synteresis*], an habit of practicall principles, and generall fountaines of our actions. The assumption is properlie . . . *conscientia*, an actuall application of our knowledge to this, or that particular act or object.[89]

The Anglican Richard Carpenter, too, betrays a scholastic emphasis in dividing the faculties into 'Theorick' and 'Practicke', and designating them '*Synteresis* and '*Syneidesis*' after the 'Ancients'.[90]

However, these latter are quite exceptional; and most follow Perkins in the sudden recoil to a more orthodoxly Calvinist bias he makes in discussing the authority of conscience. First of all, he determines that it is a faculty of the soul, intermediate between God and man: conscience, he says, 'is of a divine nature, and is a thing placed of God in the middest betweene him and man as an arbitratour to give sentence and to pronounce either with man or against man unto God'.[91] Because of this absolute authority over conscience, God alone has power to bind the conscience directly: 'He which is the Lord of conscience, by his Word and lawes binds conscience . . . because he once created it, and he alone governs it.'[92] Jeremiah Dyke supports him in this conclusion, declaring likewise that conscience is a '*faculty*' of the '*soule*' and assenting to what crystallizes in later treatises to a primary dogma concerning its intermediate and authoritative status, quite distinct from all other faculties of the soul: it 'is not in the understanding alone, not in the memory, will affections alone, but it hath place in all the parts of the soule . . . . Conscience is placed in the soule as Gods spy, and man's superiour and overseer.'[93] This is corroborated by the Puritan Immanuel Bourne, writing in 1623; discounting Aquinas and the schoolmen, he prefers to agree with those 'later Divines [who] think [conscience] to be an office or function of the Soule, set as an *Arbitrator*, not onely to examine, but to give evidence and judge of particular actions between God and man'.[94]

In all these, as in others, is manifested a growing divergence between the Puritan definition of conscience as a connate 'faculty' subject to the absolutist sway of the divine will, and its elucidation in Thomistic thought as an act of the practical understanding instinct with the normative prescriptions of the Natural Law. Furthermore, the conscience, in common with all the spiritual faculties, is blighted by the degenerative effects of original sin. In emphasizing this, the Puritan Thomas Morton is rigorously Calvinist in tone:

As touching mans conscience in his corrupte estate, this must of necessitie be granted, that where the whole is corrupted, there everie severall part is corrupted . . . so that nowe the conscience is a false witnes, and doth judge of right and wrong, of life and death so as a blind man judgeth colours, saying that blacke is white . . . : and yet as the minde is not so wholly blinded, but that there remaine in it some reliques of knowledge, trueth and light: So the conscience hath his part as well of this light . . . and by vertue thereof, doth sometimes speak the trueth.[95]

This moral myopia of the conscience is stressed also by John Downame writing in 1622; although, at the creation, conscience was an 'upright Judge', yet after the fall, 'the understanding being darkened with ignorance, and the judgement corrupted, doe offer unto the conscience false rules and Principles, and so cause it to give wrong evidence and erroneous judgements'.[96] Downame accounts for this by invoking directly the Calvinist dogma of the utter extirpation of the light of nature resulting from the primal curse:

The which commeth to passe, because the light of nature is through the fall almost extinguished, and the booke of the Law written, according to which, conscience should judge and testifie, is not understood and knowne, or because it is blinded by lusts and passions . . . hath the mouth stopped with the bribes of worldly vanities.[97]

The Puritan tendency to emphasize the importance of consulting the Word of God in order to instruct the conscience, must be seen as a logical corollary of the fact of its ignorance in the face of the perversions inherent in the Law of Nature. Perkins insists sternly that

Whatsoever we enterprise or take in hand, we must first search whether God give us libertie in conscience, and warrant to doe it . . . .
    First, if a thing done without good direction of conscience be a sinne, then much more that which is done without direction of Gods word is a flat sinne; for without direction of Gods word, conscience can give no good direction. . . . And here by the Word, I meane no thing but the Scriptures of the olde and new testament which containe in themselves

sufficient direction of all actions. As for the law of nature, though it affoarde indeede some direction; yet it is corrupt, imperfect, uncerten.[98]

A Calvinist scripturalism is similarly evident in John Downame, who adverts to the 'Rule and Touchstone [of conscience], whereby all divine truth is to be tryed, namely, when it agreeth with the truth of God revealed in the Scriptures'.[99] Richard Carpenter, too, disavows his otherwise Anglican defence of reason to subscribe firmly to the truth of the Scriptures in cases of error: 'For the avoyding of all which errours . . . Search the Scriptures, Joh. 5. . . . for . . . they give best testimony both of Gods will concerning his own service, and of his good will in Christ to all his faithfull servants.'[100]

In spite of its dangerous liability to error (or possibly because of it), these Puritan divines show rather less leniency in cases of an erroneous conscience than did St Thomas, of whose strictures on the culpability of ignorance there is in the majority a very marked evidence. Perkins's teachings in fact contain the germ of all later seventeenth-century animadversions on this point, which is essentially reducible to the principle that a morally good action cannot exist unless it flows from a good conscience. For, as he states,

> this is the beginning of a good worke, that the conscience first of all gives her judgement truly, that the thing may be done, and is acceptable to God. . . . From this former rule arise three other: the first, Whatsoever is done with a doubting conscience is a sinne. . . . The second, Whatsoever thing is done in or with an erronious conscience, it is a sinne. . . . The third, What is done against conscience though it erre and be deceived, it is a sinne in the doer.[101]

William Ames, the great Puritan theologian and pupil of Perkins, was later to elaborate more fully on these principles. He, too, emphasizes the absolute obligations of an errant conscience, for 'conscience, though erroneous, bindes alwaies so, that hee that doth against it, sinneth. The reason is, because he that doth against conscience, doth against Gods will; though not materially, and truely; yet formally, and by interpretation.'[102] The error arises admittedly out of ignorance, 'because those things which God in the Scripture hath commanded us to beleeve, are not sufficiently understood', or, 'because the assent of Faith is not given to those things which ought to be beleeved'. But such ignorance can never be condoned: 'The cause . . . (besides God's secret judgements) is either the not considering of those things which ought to be considered, or some evill disposition'.[103] Like St Thomas, the Puritans could never accept that a man could commit evil in good faith; but unlike the scholastics, who argued that this was the case because the *synderesis* was inscribed with basic deontic principles, they by and large accepted the Calvinist position that ignorance itself is a spiritual blemish, in that it represents a lapse of faith in the word of God. For this they cited the authority of St Paul: 'And he that doubteth is damned if he eat because he eateth not of faith: for whatsoever is not of faith is sin' (Rom. 14:23). The implications of this fideistic absolutism are pressed to an inevitable paradox in the pages of John Woolton, who asserts that sin must always result if the 'least Scruple' remains in the conscience. 'For although the deede in it selfe be good in Gods sight, yet man doth it doubtingly, whether it be good or no: which doubt and staggaring of the mind is offensive and condemneth a man.'[104]

The early seventeenth-century divines in particular have much to say about the various offices of conscience, comparing its functions to those of a Book, Recorder, or Judge. Richard Carpenter envisages it as serving 'in the understanding as Judge, to prescribe, prohibit, absolve and condemne *de jure*; in the memory, as Recorder and witnesse testifying *de facto*; in the will and affections, as rewarder and punisher'.[105] A more gloomy eschatological view is taken by Jeremiah Dyke: conscience 'keepes a Diary, or a Journall of everything that passes in our whole course'. It bears witness, moreover, at the Last Judgment:

And this is the end of the former office of the Conscience. For therefore is it exact and punctuall in setting downe the particulars of a mans whole life, that it may bee a faithfull witnesse either for him, or against him. . . . This office it is ready to doe at all times . . . and most of all at the last day.[106]

Richard Bernard demonstrates an even more exhaustive range of metaphors: conscience is variously '*Mans Over-seer*', his '*Director*', a '*Register*', a 'Schoole-Master', a 'Witnesse', and last but not least, 'a just Judge of Oyer and Terminer'.[107]

A similar proliferation of categories is evident in the ever-more-refined analyses of different types of conscience. William Jones refers to such categories as the '*erring conscience*', the '*sleeping conscience*', the '*seared conscience*', and the '*accusing conscience*'.[108] Immanuel Bourne diagnoses the 'good' and peacable conscience, the '*erroneous*' and the 'evill' conscience. Of the latter there are two sorts: the '*conscientia mortua*, a dead and cauterized Conscience' and the '*Conscientia desperata* . . . too sensible both of the sting of sinne, and wrath of God against it'.[109] He also distinguishes a third type of evil conscience: the '*Conscientia spatiosa*, a large and spatious *conscience*, for it can hold a volume of impiety'.[110] By others this last affliction is termed a 'cheverill' or 'secure' or 'sleeping' conscience. But it is in the work of Jeremiah Dyke that the pathology of the ill conscience reaches an apotheosis. Of the secure conscience he asserts:

This conscience wants not an eye, but onely a good tongue in the head.

It sees its master to doe evill, and knowes it to be evill, but either cares not to speake, or els is easily put off from speaking. . . . being sleepy, heavy, and drowsie.[111]

A seared conscience, on the other hand is

That which *Paul* speaks of in 1 *Tim.* 4.2. *A cauterized Conscience.* . . . Thus it is with many mens Consciences, commit they whatsoever sins they will, yet their hearts are so hardened thorough long custome in sin, that they feele no gripings, pinches, or bitings at all, but are growne to that dead, and dedolent disposition.[112]

But it is in treating of the effects of sin or righteousness in the conscience, that the majority reserve their most vehement flights of eloquence. The possessor of an evil conscience, to the Puritans, endured the utmost conceivable agonies of the mind, and lived out in anticipation the torture of hell-pains. For Robert Harris, a bad conscience

puts one to intolerable paines, it racks the memory, and makes it run backward twenty yeeres, as *Josephs* brethren, and *Aristocrates* in *Plutarch*, yea, it twinges for sinnes of youth, as *Job* complaines, it racks the understanding, and carries it forward beyond the grave, and makes it feele the verie bitternesse of death and hell, before it sees them; it racks the phantasie, and makes it see ghosts in men, Lyons in children, as it is storied of some.[113]

Worse still, it causes the reprobate to fall into desperation and despair, themselves sinful states of being because a breach of faith in the free mercy of God's justification; therefore, says William Ames, it

is not only *Evill* in respect of *trouble* and *vexation* but of *sinne* . . . *A Desperate Conscience* (fully representing all sinnes, together with their exceeding great and unpardonable guilt, and Gods feareful wrath abiding upon Sinners . . .) is Gods most powerfull meanes to torment the Reprobate; like unto a worme, that most sharply biteth and gnaweth their hearts for ever . . .[114]

The only way to ward off the terrors of an evil conscience, and to avoid the pitfalls of despair, is by an act of repentance and an appeal through faith to the absolving grace of Christ's redemptive blood. But this turning away from sin to repentance is a process initiated in the soul of man by God; and Ames goes on to affirm the Calvinistic logic by which faith itself is an imputative effect of grace:

For to the end a Sinner may escape Gods *judgement*, he must *judge* himself. . . . Unto this judgement of Conscience, stirring up sutable affections; if God of his great mercy adde a *change* of *minde* with an *appealing* by Faith to the Judgement Seat of Gods mercy in Christ; then is that true . . . that the *Judgement of repentance maketh voide the judgement of punishment.*[115]

Christopher Lever, too, is adamant on the need for restorative grace:

for when God shall please to call his servants to a knowledge of himselfe, and to a detestation of sinne; the grace of his holy Spirit moveth in the heart of such a one, and first awaketh the conscience, . . . giving [it] sence to understand sin, and Spirit to reprove it; is the first degree of our reformation, and the preparation to our spirituall conversion: GOD himselfe beeing the prime and principall Author thereof.[116]

If an evil conscience symbolized for the Puritan the very nadir of earthly misery, the possession of a good conscience by contrast was thought to be a source of comfort and fortitude, for it assured him of God's election, and shadowed forth that vision of profound peace and unspeakable joy promised him in the hereafter. A good conscience, Robert Harris maintains,

is the sweetest friend in the world: if naturall cheerfulnesse be so good a house-keeper to a good man, that it feasts daily (as Solomon saieth) O then what be the bankets of conscience, sanctified and purified what joies those which will carry a man above ground, and make him forget the best of natures comforts? what comforts those which will make one sing under the whip, in the stocks, at the stake indespight of the fire? what the strength of conscience, that can sooner tire the Tyrant than the Martyr? and can carry weake strength . . . in triumph through a world of bonds, rods, swords, racks, wheeles, flames, strappadoes, and whatsoever else?[117]

Since its efficient cause dwells in the inscrutable will of God, and was inferred by Puritans to be a certain sign and forerunner of salvation, the regenerate conscience is clearly related to the doctrine of predestination. The mysteries of election and reprobation were not, of course, comprehensible to the human mind, but Puritan divines attempted a little to soften the harsh rigour of Calvinist determinism, rightly sensing the dangers of spiritual despair to which the faithful were made vulnerable. It is to these dangers that Thomas Morton addresses himself when he says, concerning the conscience and the certainty of salvation:

For what neede he who knoweth certainly that he shal be saved, take paines, and sustaine trouble and griefe in working his owne salvation by a Godly and holy life? To this we answer, confessing that the number of the reprobate or elect canot be knowen, & also that this knowledge is not gotten by any immediate revelation.

But he continues in the words of St Paul: 'they who are truelie regenerate are truely called, they who are truely called are justified, they who are justified are . . . glorified.'[118] Ultimately, a man may be reasonably certain of his salvation if he has a clear and regenerate conscience, for

> regeneration being a totall and a supernaturall change of the minde, will, affections, thoughtes, wordes and dedes of a man, cannot be hid or doubtfull for any long time, but will shewe it selfe both to the eyes of other men, and much more to the conscience of the beleever himself.[119]

In conclusion, then, the foregoing conspectus, epitomized still further, would seem to warrant the following inferences. There is deducible a gradual change to regarding conscience as a spiritual intermediary directly controlled by God, and superior to the other faculties of the soul, an evolution evidently coordinated to the Calvinist concept of God's immediate regulation of providence. Conscience, for Puritan theologians, is merely the spiritual instrument of the divine will, and the impotent agent of its inscrutable purposes. Increasingly, then, and by consequence, there is little reference, from Perkins onwards, to the scholastic notion of an intellective faculty, and still less that it is dispositionally oriented towards the good; on the contrary, it could not be located with any certainty in the understanding since it responds to an order entirely above reason. Even then, it is capable of discerning the good only when sustained by redemptive grace; otherwise it is egregiously subject to error, and never more fatally than when it relies on the light of nature alone. Even when the conscience is enlightened by a proper recourse to God's word, it seldom rises above its purely negative character as a register of man's chronic burden of guilt – as Calvin said, a 'yoke', always in some degree evil. Only in the chosen is it really capable of reforming the will and controlling the passions: that is, when it is regenerated by God, which blessed state is itself a forerunner of His otherwise secret election.

This, then, is the starkly voluntarist view taken of the nature and conscience of man in seventeenth-century moral theology. It will be shown that a correspondent impression is yielded by the moral universe of certain Jacobean playwrights – in particular by those characters who act out their destinies with a resigned and desperate fatalism, obscurely conscious of the right, but impotent of its actualization, irrationally yielding to desires speciously made rational in a world irredeemably corrupt. The tragic pattern of Shakespeare's plays, by which characters are redeemed to full humanity by a moral struggle, gives way to a voluntarist formula by which a few individuals are mysteriously translated to a serene transcendence: a metamorphosis apprehensible neither to reason nor to dramatic logic, but apparently induced by the sanctification that precedes the salvation of the elect. Thus does the Jacobean drama explore time after time the theatrical implications of a cosmological theory itself strangely theatrical, the solution to which, as to the drama, is the *deux ex machina* of the Calvinist God.

2

The character of conscience as depicted in Tudor interludes and morality plays

The moral history of theatre, of course, begins much earlier than with Jacobean tragedy. By way of preliminaries we must proceed by making the assumption that the concept of conscience will be evinced with greatest clarity in the interludes and moralities of the sixteenth century containing a character of that name, concerned as such plays are with the staging of abstractions clearly derived from the canons of metaphysical theology. Since all moralities were, in the first place, purely religious dramas, and only partially surrendered their homiletic character in the face of an increasingly secular and classical bias, it is perhaps natural to assume in them an accurate sensitivity to the great doctrinal controversies attendant upon the Reformation, and in particular to the changing philosophical premises which underprop the concept of conscience.

These changes are most evident, obviously, between the largely scholastic assumptions embodied in the only pre-Reformation play to deal with the subject directly, *The World and the Child*, and its five post-Reformation successors; but there is nevertheless a perceptible increase, in terms of the conspectus here surveyed, in the assimilation of reformist and voluntarist doctrines, which exert a subtle yet profound pressure on the dramatic portrayal of the character of Conscience. It is hardly to be expected that this process of assimilation will exhibit a pattern in any degree progressive or regular in outline, since allowances must clearly be made for competing and conflicting influences, some of them organic changes within the morality repertoire itself, but most dependent upon the increasingly idiosyncratic and inventive usage made by individual dramatists of the stock framework of the morality. Perhaps most notable in this connection is R. B.'s *Appius and Virginia*, where the growing secular trend of the interlude genre has partly released the author from the restrictive homiletic formulae of the *psychomachia* (and also to some extent, from the yoke of theology) to a new tragic conception of internalized moral struggle which looks forward to the great Elizabethans, Marlowe and Shakespeare. Robert Wilson, too, in *The Three Ladies of London* and its sequel, reshapes the traditional conventions of the morality idiom to support a superstructure of social satire and farce, promoting Lady Conscience in the process to the status of a fully developed character in her own right, rather than the episodic and functional abstraction of earlier plays. In general, however, the dramatic portraits of Conscience subscribe in greater or lesser degree, but in most significant respects, to the contemporary postulates of moral theology, for which the interlude form remained, until its demise in the later years of Elizabeth's reign, by definition a popular vehicle.

The World and the Child, printed by Wynkyn de Worde in 1522,[1] is an entirely allegorical treatment of the progress of man's life from birth to old age, representing symbolically the moral conflicts experienced by the hero in his passage through the stages of sin, repentance, regression, and ultimate redemption assisted by Conscience and Perseverance.

Renamed by Mundus in recognition of his youthful dedication to sin, Manhood is challenged in the middle of a thrasonical and vainglorious account of his grisly career-at-arms by Conscience, who warns him of his dangerous allegiance to the Seven Deadly Sins. Somewhat piqued by this unsolicited intervention, Manhood at first addresses Conscience in haughty, irreverent terms, but, persuaded of the value of the spiritual 'lyght' offered him by Conscience, gradually accedes to his counsels, eventually allowing that the qualities of 'measure' and 'discrecyon' are better guides to government on earth and salvation in heaven than his erstwhile subjection to the 'kynges of synne' (sigs.A4–B3ᵛ). Conscience warns him especially to avoid that composite embodiment of all sin, the Vice Folly, ever 'full of false flatterynge'; a denunciation which signals in turn Folly's prompt appearance on stage. Folly succeeds in persuading Manhood to renounce both Conscience and his precariously won conversion, and accompany him to London, there to undertake a bout of licentious indulgence centring on the stews and the Pope's Head tavern. As they depart, they leave Conscience and his 'borne broder' Perseverance to deliver a homiletic address to the audience, deploring human frailty in general, and Manhood's present fall from grace:

> Lo Syrs a grete ensample you may se
> The freylnes of mankynde
> How oft he falleth in folye
> Through temptacyon of the fende
> For whan the fende and the flesshe be at one assent
> Than conscyence clere is cleane out cast . . .
>
> (sig.C4)

It is this fall, coupled with the passage of incorrigibly misspent years, which brings Manhood to his final estate; now denominated Age, he enters clinging to life like a 'clodde in claye', and, bewailing the moral and material bankruptcy to which his sins have led, delivers himself up to despair:

> I stare and stacker as I stonde
> I grone glysly upon the grounde
> Alas dethe why lettest thou me lyve so longe . . .
> (sig.D1^v)

Even at the eleventh hour, however, Perseverance enters, advocating repentance and contrition, and applies spiritual balm and comfort by citing the example of the saints, thereby saving Age from despair and directing him further in the path of salvation by recourse to the twelve articles of faith and the sacraments of 'holy chyrche' (sig.D4).

This latter and other homiletic injunctions delivered by the two virtues, Conscience and Perseverance, identify the play as a pre-Reformation moralilty infused unequivocally with the doctrines of the Old Faith. A Catholic emphasis upon a proper obedience to the authority of the Church is indicated in the advice of Conscience to Manhood to 'Mayntayne holy chyrches ryght' and in his further admonishment to attend 'matyns' and 'masse'. In the province of soteriology, Perseverance, as has already been remarked, urges Manhood to merit his salvation by participating in the sacraments, and invokes the example of the saints and the intercession of the Virgin Mary (sigs.D2ᵛ, C4ᵛ). Furthermore, the justification proffered by Conscience to Manhood is a Catholic one involving works as well as faith: discussing the last of the seven deadly sins, Conscience counsels that 'covetous' is not always evil; covetousness in 'good doynge' is, on the contrary, 'good in all wyse' (sig.B2).

Given this traditional pre-Reformation framework of theoretical divinity, it is unsurprising that certain aspects of the presentation of Conscience are substantially in accordance with orthodox scholastic premises. Conscience intervenes at the height of Manhood's thraldom to the sin of Pride, announcing in typical morality fashion his general homiletic function: all mankind, 'yonge and olde both ryche and pore', must 'knowe' Conscience if they aspire to heaven's bliss (sig.A6). Accosting Manhood, up to this point evidently unacquainted with any moral scruples whatsoever, he introduces himself as a 'techer of the spiritualete' and 'all that be leders into lyght' (sig.A6ᵛ); and it is this scholastic emphasis upon ethical guidance rather than spiritual chastizement that actually determines the role of Conscience in the play. Thus his purpose, as he himself attests, is to counsel 'both hye and lowe', and although he subsequently alludes to bearing 'grete blame' and to experiencing 'shame' (sig.A6), these afflictions are hardly referred to again, and are certainly not worked out in terms of anything than can be construed as spiritual torment or psychological suffering. The punishment Manhood actually suffers after disregarding the precepts of Conscience, is a final degradation to poverty and physical misery that are the entirely natural consequences of his own attachment to worldly vanity and folly:

> At the pasage I wolde playe
> I thought to borowe and never paye
> Than was I sought and set in stockes
> In newgate I lay under lockes
> If I sayd ought I caught many knockes
> Alas where was manhode tho
> Alas my lewdenes hath me lost
> Where is my body so proude and prest
> I coughe and rought my body wyll brest
> Age dothe folowe me so . . .
>
> (sigs.D1–D1ᵛ)

Furthermore, the authority by which Conscience instructs Manhood is derived from no fideistic adherence to the Scriptures, but from a variety of Catholic doctrinal propositions: Conscience is clearly concerned more with an obedience to the canonical traditions of the Church, than to the biblically revealed word of God. Entirely compatible with scholastic assumptions also is Conscience's apparent appeal to reason in advocating the qualities of 'measure', 'good governaunce' and 'discrecyon' in daily conduct (sigs.B3–B3ᵛ); a rationally apprehensible sense of moral equilibrium and due proportion in human affairs, to be achieved, as Conscience advices, by the use of the 'wyttes' with which man has been furnished by God. A useful gloss on the idea of reason as the arbiter of moral balance and commensurability in man's affairs is provided by Aquinas, where he argues that the rule and measure of all acts is the reason: for

> it belongs to the reason to direct to the end, which is the first principle in all matters of action, according to the Philosopher . . . but the principles impressed on [the human reason] by nature, are general rules and measures of all things relating to human conduct, whereof the natural reason is the rule and measure.[2]

The ultimate source of Conscience's remarks, as Aquinas's citation of the Philosopher suggests, is indirectly traceable thus to the *Nichomachean Ethics*, where in Books II and III, Aristotle treats of moral excellence as a mean or temperate course avoiding extremities of conduct. Aristotle is here talking of *akolasia*, or intemperate desires, the satisfaction of which causes man to lose his sense of proportion: 'such gratifications should be moderate and rare. They should never clash with the rational element . . . which should govern the appetitive part of us.'[3]

Yet it remains true that the insights provided by Conscience in the play are only the first stage in the salvation of Manhood's soul: his chief role is to instill in the universalized hero a knowledge of the Law, which he does by a stern recital of the commandments. At the same time, Manhood is unable to conduct himself in accordance with that knowledge; indeed, his repentance is made with no very firm purpose of amendment, for, as he says:

> Thoughe the worlde and conscyence be at debate
> Yet the worlde wyll I not despyse . . .
> The worlde fyndeth me all thynge
> And dothe me grete servyse . . .
>
> (sig.B4)

Hence, in accordance with the progressive impulse of the play's homiletic logic, it is fitting that Conscience should give way in the second half of the play to his didactic successor, Perseverance, who, with the aid of the 'grace of god almyght', actually completes the hero's redemption.

Interestingly enough, that redemption describes precisely the scholastic pattern of salvation, by which man is first provided with a knowledge of the Law, and then favoured by grace as the means of obtaining it. Speaking of the extrinsic principles of acts, Aquinas says: 'But the extrinsic principle moving to good is God, Who both instructs us by means of His Law, and assists us by His Grace: wherefore in the first place we must speak of law; in the second place, of grace.' For, he continues, 'in the state of corrupted nature man cannot fulfil all the Divine commandments without healing grace'.[4] Thus it appears that the author of *The World and the Child* has indeed, as Bevington suggests, made a 'virtue of limitation';[5] the early suppression of Conscience in favour of Perseverance is doubtless justified as a means of dramatic economy in a play designed for only two actors, but the exigencies of production are also made very neatly to serve the homiletic design, which discloses its theological basis in demonstrating the dual stages in man's sanctification.

No such artistic integrity is discernible, however, in the interlude of *Impatient Poverty*: 'newlye Imprinted' in 1560 by John King, but written perhaps as many as ten years earlier,[6] its comparatively simple plot is clumsily executed and disorganized by a series of random and badly articulated digressions. It concerns primarily the fate of the titular hero, who to begin with is persuaded by Peace to forsake wrath and envy in favour of Christian patience and a charitable love of his neighbours; and, as an earnest of the material rewards contingent upon such a conversion, is renamed Prosperity. Later on, the Vice Envy plots with Misrule to separate Prosperity from his newly won thrift, delivering him over to the attentions of a French card-sharp named Colhazzard, by whom he is quickly reduced once again to the name and status of Poverty. Summoned before an ecclesiastical court and sentenced to do penance, Poverty is brought to a state of humility and becomes once more a disciple of Peace.

The role given to Conscience in fact constitutes the play's major digression, and involves a somewhat rambling and largely misdirected attempt to reform the habits of a similarly unrelated character, the usurer Habundance, who makes a further appearance at the trial scene towards the end, unemcumbered this time by his 'ghostly' instructor. The episode is only very tenuously linked to the main plot, with whose theme of the spiritual dangers of 'unmeasurable spendynge' it is arguably consistent (l.934); in all other respects it is difficult to see in it more than a parenthetic irrelevancy to the story of Impatient Poverty, whom Conscience never actually meets. It may be remarked in passing, however, that a perceptible development in the character and role of Conscience has occurred since his largely Catholic embodiment in *The World and the Child*. In this play, Conscience is seen as a spiritual tormentor, as well as a guide. In his efforts to persuade Habundance to call for grace and amend, Conscience advises him to risk material loss rather than 'spyll' his soul, presaging the awful consequences of finding the gates of mercy shut against him, and citing from Scripture a minatory example of God's wrathful vengeance upon usurers and oppressors.

The play's structural imperfections have prompted at least one of its editors to advance the theory that it is really a botched revision of an earlier play,[7] and indeed, the theory is substantiated by the fact that its anarchy of form is matched by a corresponding incoherence in its religious point of view. It is true that *Impatient Poverty* lacks the rich theological allusiveness of earlier plays, yet it is not primarily this attenuation of metaphysical scope that has made it difficult for literary historians to decide the vexed question of its religious affiliation. The fact is that the play seems in a curious sense creedless; or rather, it implies unsystematically and with a somewhat veiled ambiguity an indiscriminate dependence upon Catholic and reformist doctrines alike. Bevington presumably credits its author with a circumspectly uncontroversial approach, when he argues that the play's appeal is 'broadly national';[8] Peter Houle, however, asserts unreservedly that it is a pro-Catholic play of Mary's reign.[9] Neither position seems wholly satisfactory.

McKerrow's largely bibliographic hypothesis, that an early play has here been refurbished for presentation on the Elizabethan stage,[10] accords squarely with my own impression that the presentation of the character of Conscience is in significant respects doctrinally anomalous. He cites topical and textual evidence to arrive at the conclusion that the episodes involving Habundance, Conscience, and the court Sumner are late interpolations in a play predominantly of Philip and Mary's reign, amended to suit that of Elizabeth; some further support may be adduced for this view by the argument proposed here, that the principles underlying the concept of conscience are predominantly Protestant in an otherwise Catholic play.

Leaving aside for a moment the disputed scenes, there is certainly evidence (in addition to that advanced by McKerrow to establish its period of composition) that the main plot is decidedly pro-Catholic in its theological stance. It is reminiscent of much earlier moralities such as *Nature* and *Wisdom*, and indeed *The World and the Child*, in the use it makes of Renaissance Aristotelian ethics – not, of course, exclusively indicative of Catholic bias, but the exhortations of Peace, urging Poverty to be governed by 'reason' and 'discretion', and to 'forsake sensualyte' in order to become wealthy (ll.145–63) are significantly unqualified by any reformist deprecation of man's nescient inability to remain so governed. More convincing testament, perhaps, of the play's Catholic orientation is the indiscriminate distribution of oaths and profanities involving the saints, an incidence not confined, as in later Protestant polemical plays, to the Vice and his evil associates. Hence, though it is true that Envy and Misrule variously take in vain, so to speak, the names of 'Our Lady of Wolpit' (l.81), 'Sainct John' (l.612), 'our blessed ladye' (l.641), and swear by 'Goddes brede' (l.188), this is clearly undetermined by any intention to identify theological evil in the Vice characters as such, since Prosperity also uses expletives involving, amongst others, 'saynt Chadde' (l.754), and 'saynt Jame' (l.560), the Apostle of works so denigrated by Luther. But the play most tellingly evinces its Catholic inspiration in the circumstances of Poverty's penance in the 'courte spirituall' towards the conclusion (l.959). Here Poverty enters, according to the stage direction, with 'a candell in his hande doyng penaunce aboute the place', and, whilst the exact nature of the penitential exercise is unspecified, its accomplishment clearly requires the Somner to clear the court ('Rowme syrs avoydaunce') and to insist that Poverty's 'sin' be fully expiated:

> Pover[.]   Now have I my penaunce done
> Somner[.] Nay thou shalt aboute ones agayne

The performance of such expiatory exercises, or 'satisfaction', is one element in the Catholic sacrament of Penance, the two others being contrition and absolution. But the Reformers denied the necessity of satisfaction as a means of meriting divine forgiveness, which had already been earned for man by Christ. Luther is appropriately comminatory on the subject:

> [the Romanists] are so insistent on satisfaction, and construe it as necessary in such a way, that they leave no room for faith . . . [they have] brought the world into such disorder that men think they can propitiate God for their sins by means of their works, whereas He is propitiated only by faith in the contrite heart.[11]

The strength of the denunciation derives from Luther's evident identification of penitential satisfaction as the doctrinal germ from which sprang the Church's abuse of Indulgences; and in view of this, while it would certainly be somewhat inconsistent to find a reference to the practice in a Protestant play, it is not inconceivable that in a Catholic play revised for a Protestant audience such as this appears to be, the relatively obscure point should have been overlooked.

The Protestant accretions, such as they are, consist entirely in the presentation of the role of Conscience, in his lengthy interlocution with Habundance. The object of his harangue is exclusively to denounce the sin of usury to which Habundance owes his living, but it is not so much their homiletic import as the manner in which they are sanctioned by scriptural example that betrays the reformist bias of his remarks. Upon being challenged by Conscience, Habundance disingenuously pleads that the methods by which he has grown rich amount to nothing more than 'playne byenge and sellynge' (1.310); whereupon Conscience explains how false usury transgresses the laws of God, and that the obligations of charity require that loans made to the needy should be gratuitous. Unimpressed by Habundance's claim that his methods represent merely the customs of the country, and are commonly used by men of the highest reputation, Conscience advises that the sole remedy is for the usurer to make 'restytucyon' of the profits he had acquired thus wrongfully by oppression, quoting in support of this judgment the words of St Augustine:

> Quia non dimittitur peccatum
> Nisi restituatur ablatum
> ye muste restore to theym, ye have offended unto . . .
>
> (ll.353–5)

The source of the Church's opposition to usury is, of course, well known, originating as it did in the Aristotelian concept of the sterility of money, and the patristic commentaries on the Old Testament; for the scholastics, usury was properly a sin against commutative justice, as such carrying Augustine's obligation of restitution.[12] But this opposition cannot, of course, thereby be described as exclusively, or even mainly, a Catholic objection, nor need the remarks of Conscience on the subject be correlated unilaterally to this tradition. For the reformers – Luther, Melanchthon, and Zwingli – were equally adamant in their condemnations of usury, and indeed, the former's denunciation of those who imposed extortionate rates of interest, with its emphasis on the necessity of restitution, almost paraphrases the arraignment of Habundance by Conscience: 'Manifest usurers', says Luther, 'should be excommunicated'. If the usurer is penitent, he 'must become a Zacchaeus and return what he stole in excessive interest to those out of whom he sweated it'.[13]

Conscience's censure of usury is therefore only an equivocal index of his theological pedigree, being a matter indifferently inimical to all shades of religious opinion; but Conscience then goes on to augment his teachings by reference to scriptural authority, relating from the first Book of Kings a salutary instance of the divine wrath visited upon King Ahab. Such is the condign punishment meted out by God to all usurers and oppressors, warns Conscience, and should be the cause in Habundance of dread and repentance. As has already been remarked in the Introduction, the idea that the conscience should be instructed by the biblically revealed Word of God is exclusively a Protestant concept, deriving from the great catalytic principle of the Reformation, *sola scriptura*. The absolute predominance of the canonical Scriptures over apostolic tradition, first enunciated in the Bohemian Confession of 1535, was by 1553 written into the doctrines of the Church of England: the sixth of the Forty-Two Articles read: 'Holie Scripture conteineth all thinges necessarie to salvation.'[14] Bishop Hooper, Protestant victim of the Marian persecutions, bears witness in his *Confessions of Faith* (1550) to the intense suspicion with which the Scriptures were regarded by the Catholic Church, particularly in the vulgate:

> I believe that the reading of the same word . . . ought not, neither can it be prohibited and forbidden from any manner of person, of what estate, sort, or condition soever the same be of; but it ought to be common unto all the world, as well to men as women; yea, and that in a vulgar or common language.[15]

The Catholic antipathy towards the Scriptures is satirized in John Bale's *Three Laws* as early as 1538, anticipating by some years the Council of Trent's belated attempt to clarify the Church's position on the issue. Here, the Catholic Vices seek to beguile men by sophistry, philosophy, and logic, maintaining them in ignorance of the Scriptures by the use of Latin at services. Avarice admits of one exception:

> If they have Englysh, lete it be for advauntage,
> For pardons, for Dyrges, for offerynges, and pilgrymage.
> I recken to make them, a newe Crede in a whyle,
> And all in Englysh, their conscyence to begyle.[16]

But in *Impatient Poverty* it is patently not the intention of Conscience to 'begyle' by rendering a scriptural passage thus in the vulgate; and the impression by now apparent, that the informing principle of the character's creation appears predominantly Protestant, is confirmed still further by the fact that Conscience is evidently unable to restore Habundance to grace, and is in any case hopelessly and sinfully contaminated with the selfsame corruption for which he hypocritically blames the usurer. The latter, perhaps justifiably, feels no obligation whatsoever to heed the words of Conscience:

ye have ryches wythout measure
And of the flesshe ye have youre pleasure
ye can fynde no wayes to amend your self I you insure
Therefore rebuke not me for my synne ne good.

(ll.400–3)

With these words, Habundance places himself once and for all beyond the reformative influence of Conscience, who shortly afterwards suffers a further setback in being forced abjectly to flee the country: circumstances themselves atypical of the earlier pre-Reformation moralities, in which the hero is invariably redeemed by the influence of the Virtues. After Habundance's unrepentant departure, Conscience delivers himself of a dehortatory address to the audience, in tone implicitly reformist in its recognition of man's irredeemable depravity:

Odulle wyte plunged by ygnoraunce
Regardynge nothynge of ghostly instrucyon
Settynge more hys minde on worldly substaunce
Then on everlastynge lyfe that is to come
God wyl stryke when he lyst, ye know not how sone . . .

(ll.405–9)

Given the extreme religious sensitivity to all such issues in post-Reformation England, at least until the irenical measures introduced by Elizabeth, it seems on the evidence unlikely that the episode in *Impatient Poverty* depicting the moralizing of a biblically-inspired Conscience – a scene so precisely emblematic of Protestant individualism – could have been originally part of an otherwise Catholic play written in the reign of Mary Tudor.

Appius and Virginia, though printed in 1575, seems to have been written some years earlier, possibly by Richard Bowers, Master of the Chapel Children from 1545 to 1561.[17] It is predominantly classical in tone, and yet the Prologue commends its story as a moral example of zeal and love, to be noted well by the 'Lordings' and 'Ladies' and 'Virgins' evidently present in the audience (ll.20–4). Together with *Horestes* and *Cambises*, similarly hybrid specimens, *Appius and Virginia* represents a type of transitional interlude; an attempt, in the words of Tucker Brooke, 'to graft a plot of classic gravity upon the amorphous stock of the native interlude', which, though artistically a 'failure',[18] nevertheless symbolizes a perceptible shift in the direction of pre-Shakespearean tragedy. As Peter Happé points out, the play is manifestly tragic by authorial intention, announcing itself as a 'Tragicall Comedie' on the title-page, and as a 'Tragidie' in the Prologue;[19] and indeed, most critics concur in finding its most important feature to be its experimental, prototypical concern to invest the ethical dilemmas of the phychomachia with a new and potentially tragic significance.[20]

This significance is primarily a consequence of the changes R. B. makes to his principal source, Chaucer's *Physician's Tale*, specifically in the field of characterization. Virginia, originally in both source and play a chaste, beautiful, but otherwise unremarkable votaress of the cult of Diana, is endowed by R. B. with a certain tragic pathos in herself preferring death to dishonour, instead of, as in earlier versions, maintaining a dutiful acquiescence in the fate proposed for her by her father. At the climax of the play, it is Virginia who takes the initiative, begging her father to kill her rather than allow her to submit to the importunities of the corrupt Judge Appius: 'Graunt me the death, then keepe I my treasure' (1.931); and it is this index, however nominal, of a dynamic conception of character, that in the end gives to her death a sublimity uncovenanted by anything in her life as portrayed in the early part of the play. A similar tragic depth and stature is revealed in the character of the tyrannical Judge Appius; as Peter Happé has observed, Chaucer adverts to the onset of lust in Appius as a practically instantaneous change of 'herte' and 'mood',[21] whereas R. B. shows, with considerable psychological penetration, the processes of an interior struggle to subdue that lust, of whose evil consequences Appius is only too well aware. Perhaps the most signal indication of the play's transitional and evolutionary status is that, in contrast to the earlier moralities, the moral battle is fought out within, rather than over, the soul of the protagonist; while the traditional apparatus of Vice and abstract Virtues is retained, it is nevertheless subordinated to a new psychological realism, and only seriously resorted to by the author in order to provide a somewhat arbitrary solution to these larger issues which the dramatist otherwise lacked the technical means to resolve. Thus the justice which results in the imprisonment and eventual death of Appius, is providentially imposed by the abstractions Justice and Reward, while the ethical triumph symbolized by the unsullied death of Virginia is celebrated and underscored by the participation of Fame, Doctrina, and Memory at her funeral rites.

Consistent with the play's distinctively tragic treatment of a classical theme, the character of Conscience is here attenuated of almost all overt metaphysical and theological significance, and his role abbreviated to three somewhat inconsequential attempts to win the soul of Appius; both features are a measure of the extent to which the protagonist's moral struggle has been internalized. In comparison with *The World and the Child* and *Impatient Poverty*, where Conscience was an independent and external entity, unassimilated to the soul of the beleaguered hero, here it is very clearly Appius's own warning conscience which rebukes him, and whose first appearance in dumb show augurs his ultimate departure from the soul of the tyrant. The stage direction reads:

Here let him make as rhogh he went out and let Consince and Justice come out after him, and let Consience hold in his hande a Lamp burning, and let Justice have a sword, and hold it before Apius' breast.

(sig.C1)

Appius's accompanying soliloquy foreshadows the future partition of his soul:

> But out, I am wounded, how am I devided?
> Two states of my life, from me are now glided . . .
>
> (ll.501–2)

But it is not until that division is actually accomplished that Conscience acquires an independent voice; on his second appearance, Conscience, reverting once again to conventional precedent, delivers a traditional homiletic plaint upon Appius's determination to 'persever' in his guilty design, in which he alludes to the imminence of spiritual death, and in his despair, abandons Appius, intending to crave the help of the 'gods':

> O cleare unspotted giftes of Jove,
> How haps thou art refused?
> Oh Consience cleare, what cruell minde
> Thy truth hath thus misused?
>
> (ll.534–7)

Conscience's final exclusion from the soul of Appius is symbolized by a third and last exchange, in which the Virtue's by now disembodied voice, emanating this time merely from 'within', attempts feebly to prevail upon the remorseless temper of the tyrant's mind, by citing the bloody death and everlasting shame which rewarded Tarquin's enforcement of Lucrece (ll.646–50). But Appius, in whom the earlier departure of Conscience had occasioned terror and alarm, now remains impervious to its dire prophecies, dismissing them with a testy and scornful indifference. His mind wrought up to 'range at large my will for to expresse', he casually derides the moribund tones of Conscience as a 'pinching sounde', adding the peremptory injunction, 'declare be breefe'. Conscience laments that though 'at point nere hand to die', he is nevertheless compelled to cry out against wickedness with trembling soul; and thus fatally stricken by Appius's sinful obduracy, he expires, his last utterance seeming to imply the proximate death of the tyrant's soul:

> Ah Gods, what wittes doth raine, and yet to you unknowen?
> I die the death, and soule doth sinke, this filthy flesh hath
> sowen . . .
>
> (ll.671–2)

The religious connotations of conscience are here difficult to perceive;

it is, indeed, tempting to consider that in plays such as *Appius and Virginia*, the drama is on the threshold of its emancipation from theology, and that the dramatist is much more interested in his creation *qua* dramatic art than as a theologically accurate homiletic instrument. There is certainly insufficient evidence to discriminate a Protestant or Catholic bias; Conscience is made to appeal to the 'Gods' in accordance with the play's overall mythological superstructure. Nevertheless, the dramatist seems aware of a few general beliefs about conscience: there appears, for example, to be a vague Aristotelian basis to the articulation of the moral norm to which the family of Virginius subscribes. The chorus of the song they sing, celebrating the positive virtues of family life, insists upon 'measure' and 'reason in season' as the elements best guaranteeing stability and coherence in human relationships (ll.163–4). It is this order that Haphazard the Vice endangers with his anarchic advice to flout the moral basis of societal relationships by taking a chance, to hap or hazard all in the hope of a dubious gain. A very generalized scholastic schema of the structure of the tripartite soul seems to be the origin of Conscience's remark (l.538) that he has been spotted by 'wilfull will' and by 'lawles love and luste'; a somewhat obscure recognition by the dramatist that sin results from a disorder in the soul, by which conscience and reason are unnaturally overthrown by the will's surrender to the concupiscent appetites. Otherwise there is discoverable practically nothing of that direct equation of homiletic theme with the principles of theoretical divinity so evident in the plays previously discussed. There is only one explicitly Christian reference in Appius's conscience-prompted realization that 'fier eternall, my soule shall destroy' (l.508); and this marries with other hints – Appius's conjuration of 'hellish houndes' to haunt the parricidal Virginius (l.1051), and the pious tone of the Epilogue – that suggest a predominantly Christian eschatology. Appius destroys himself by his own hand, and in this, or course, R. B. is governed by his source material; but the manner in which he is brought to justice by the agents of the 'Gods', Justice and Reward, suggests the possibility of Protestant influence in the play's metaphysical design. It clearly accords with the classic setting and imagery that justice should be thus divinely imposed, but taken with the Christian tone of the Epilogue, in which the audience is adjured to earn 'his love that all in all hath made', it seems to hint at the settled reformist conviction of God's immediate regulation of the universe.

But the fact is that in *Appius and Virginia*, with its overtly secular blend of tragedy and romance, the drama has ceased merely to be the handmaiden of theology; just as the character of Appius himself is a literary conception of greater complexity and sophistication than the rudimentary Everyman character from which he drives, so too has the abstraction Conscience been supererogated in the play by R. B.'s attempt to represent ethical conflict as a psychological manifestation of Appius's tragic decline. In this sense, there are two parallel conceptions of conscience at work in the play: on the one hand, the somewhat redundant vestige of earlier and entirely symbolic representations already alluded to in *The World and the Child* and *Impatient Poverty;* on the other, an internal study of guilty horror and perturbation of the soul that anticipates the superlative Shakespearean studies of moral conflict in *Richard III* and *Macbeth*, and might be said to mark the beginning of a new phase in the theatrical treatment of conscience. The tragic decline of Appius has been ably and exhaustively dealth with by Peter Happé and Judith Anne Wall,[22] and it would be otiose to do other than to offer one or two observations on Appius's moral awareness in relation to that decline.

To begin with, R. B. quite deliberately locates the origin of evil within the soul of his protagonist rather than in the Vice; as Peter Happé remarks, this has the effect of implicating Appius deeply in the moral situation.[23] Like Macbeth, in whose soul the juggling equivocations of the Weird Sisters catalyse an already pre-existent evil, Appius is fully acquainted from the beginning with the improbity of his desires, a predisposition to sin that makes him in turn vulnerable to the evil instigations of the Vice; in both plays the agents of evil are seen as malevolent *succubi*, preying on the secret thoughts of their victims, with which they seem in an obscure sense familiar. His first lines testify to the extent to which Appius's sinful love of Virginia had disordered his soul, and overridden his better nature:

> Judge Apius I the princelest Judge, that raigneth under sonne,
> And have bene so esteemed long, but now my force is done:
> I rule no more, but ruled am, I do not Judge, but am Judged,
> By beuty of Virginia, my wisdome all is trudged . . .
>
> (ll.413–16)

Baffled and frustrated, he rails against the gods, knowing better than to crave them for the satisfaction of his lust, but none the less accusing them of being 'Unrighteous' and 'unequall' in allowing him thus to become a slave to desire, whose consummation is forbidden by the gods' own ordinance. His agony is exacerbated not only by the certainty of divine nemesis, by the 'yre' and 'Plague' with which the gods threaten all such offences, but by the more mundane realization that 'with Trump of carelesse fame', his name will be eternally forfeited to dishonour (ll.437–48). Yet these considerations, at first so rationally perceived, become subtly less distinct in the self-delusive logic by which Appius consents to listen to the glozing counsels of the Vice; ambiguously offered the means of easing his 'hart', Appius speciously invokes the thundering gods, disingenuously pleading that even they, so sternly censorious, would crave counsel in such a predicament. This moral blindness is the first in a series of steps by which the Vice, delivering him ever further into a web of illusion and unreality, ensures his ultimate downfall. When Conscience and Justice manifest themselves as substantial entities before Appius, Haphazard persuades him to disbelieve the evidence of his own eyes, dismissing them as mere 'thoughts', and, confounding the specious with the frankly implausible, goes on to convince the by now credulous Appius with a story that Conscience has been drowned, and Justice corrupted (ll.511–22). So far has Appius's rationality been impaired by the counterfeit presentiments of the Vice and his by now corrupted passions, that when Conscience encounters him for the last time – incidentally carefully distinguishing himself from the promptings of 'flesh' and 'filthy lust' – and warns the judge with 'trimbling soul' of his imminent demise, Appius perversely misconstrues this as a threat merely to his physical health, to be assuaged only by the possession of the fair Virginia:

> Why no disease dath me approche, no griefe doth make me
>   grudge,
> But want of faire Virginia, whose beauty is my Judge . . .
> (ll.666–7)

This degenerative moral awareness in Appius foreshadows a similar regressive impairment of the moral faculty in Macbeth, in whom the precarious insight that 'nothing is but what is not' does little to prevent the subsequent cumulative irrationality that precipitates him ever further towards damnation and the everlasting bonfire. In both tyrants, 'the insane root,/ That takes the reason prisoner' (*Macbeth*, I.iii.84–5) is an insidious familiarity with the idea of evil that debilitates the rational soul; a process which aptly describes the scholastic paradigm by which man's *conscientia* may gradually be vitiated by an inveterate indulgence of the passions and the sensitive appetites. In the wicked, says St Thomas, 'the natural inclination to virtue is corrupted by vicious habits, and, moreover, the natural knowledge of good is darkened by passions and habits of sin.'[24] In the case of Appius, his natural inclination to virtue, embodied externally in the character of Conscience, and psychologically in the tortures induced by the 'furies' of 'Lymbo Lake' (1.580), is finally extinguished in both dimensions with the death of Conscience, whose hopeless utterance *in articulo mortis*, 'Ah Gods, what wittes doth raine' (1.671), suggests just such a usurpation of the rational soul as Aquinas refers to, and anticipates the tyrant's self-destruction in prison, 'desperate for bluddy deede' (1.1151).

Thus perhaps the most promising aspect of this early attempt at tragedy is its concern to internalize the moral dilemmas of the *psychomachia;* a promise only partially realized, since the homiletic design of the play is precisely what prevents it from becoming truly tragic. The dramatic potentialities inherent in a maturing complexity of characterization, combined with a realignment of the moral order which centres responsibility firmly in man, are undercut by a solution imposed by the aetiolated framework of the morality. Harmony and justice are restored through the agency of abstract characters, which, as Judith Anne Wall has observed, makes the ending of the play seem 'undramatic, stiff and formal'.[25] Nevertheless, it argues considerable dramatic tact and accomplishment in the author, amounting to an evolutionary advance within the morality idiom, that in the case of Conscience, the rigid conventions of the earlier mode are to some extent abrogated by a vision at once more realistic and more humane.

Most commentators concur in assuming Nathanial Woodes's *Conflict of Conscience*, printed in 1581, to be a somewhat reactionary return to an earlier, more purely religious form of the morality play, an ecclesiastical departure from the increasingly classical and secular tenor of the popular convention, of which *Appius and Virginia* is a more typical, if progressive, illustration.[26] Written with an excess of reformist zeal by a clergyman of pronounced Calvinist leanings, it is clearly a late amateur attempt, in the words of David Bevington, 'to restore the morality to its prime concern with matters of the spirit';[27] as a consequence the idea of conscience is treated with a degree of particularized theological erudition unsurpassed in any of the plays so far considered.

The plot, which is derived from an historical instance of a notorious case of conscience, concerns the apostasy of one Philologus, who, according to the Prologue, 'through love of worldly welth' and fear of death at the hands of the Inquisition, falls from God's grace, loses his faith and suffers the pangs of conscience, ultimately falling into desperation and despair. The play exists in two issues of a single edition; in the first, the title-page and the Prologue both refer to 'Frauncis Spera',[28] and the actual career of the Italian lawyer whose celebrated recusancy forms the basis of the drama, is herein more accurately described when, in the last two lines, the Nuntius enters to announce the death of Philologus by suicide. In the second issue, however, the author, possessed evidently by the desire to universalize the homiletic appeal of his work by making it less historically specific, makes no mention of the name of his Italian prototype. The Prologue instead urges the audience to identify with the 'deserved fault' of the generic protagonist Philologus, one who 'loves to talke' but has no 'further care' for God's Word (ll.43–4); and, at the same time, a happy ending is substituted by which Philologus, won over by the godly counsels of his friends, is reconverted to Protestantism, repenting of his errors 'with manie bitter teares'.

The story of Francesco Spiera upon which the play is based was enormously popular throughout the sixteenth century; born in 1502, a citizen of Citadella, he recanted his lately acquired Protestant convictions upon being arrainged before the Papal Legate at Venice on a charge of heresy. This denial subsequently so tormented his conscience, and obsessed his mind with thoughts of his ultimate damnation, that, in spite of the united eloquence of certain scholars of the University of Padua who sought to assuage his despair, he succumbed so far to desperation as to attempt suicide. The eventual circumstances of his death in 1548 are not recorded; but within two years of this event there had appeared accounts of the lawyer's apostasy and despair written by four of the distinguished scholars of Padua who had so vainly disputed with him. All of these accounts were widely disseminated throughout Europe, and created for the tale an extraordinary currency. An English version of one of these accounts, that of Matteo Gribaldi, was published in 1550 with a preface by John Calvin, translated out of the Latin by E[dward] A[glionby]; and in the opinion of Celesta Wine, it is the second edition of Aglionby's translation, published in London in 1570, which forms the principal source of Woodes's play.[29]

Two elements in Spiera's horrifying experience would seem to have impressed themselves upon Woodes's imagination as he sought to transmute that experience into homiletic drama; like all Protestants, he seems to have construed the Italian's fate as a minatory example of what might be incurred by any Protestant who abjured his faith in God, and rejected the tenets of the Reformation, merely out of worldly consideration. The Prologue makes this quite explicit:

> The argument or ground wheron our Author chefely stayed,
> Is (sure) a Hystory straunge and true, to many men well knowne,
> Of one through love of worldly wealth, and feare of death
> dismaide,
> Because he would his lyfe and goods, have kept still as his owne,
> From state of grace wherein he stoode, was almost
> overthrowne . . .
>
> (Prologue, ll.29–33, Second Issue)

The second salutary element in his source material which seems to have borne heavily upon Woodes's intentions, was its depiction of the terrifying spiritual agony which afflicted those who were from 'state of grace' thus 'overthrowne': an agony of the conscience in particular, which made the Protestant sinner especially susceptible to the ultimate sin of despair in God's mercy and to self-slaughter. This aspect of the tale is treated exhaustively in the drama, in the course of an extended fifth-act interlocution between the protagonist and his friends Eusebius and Theologus, who both attempt to rescue Philologus from the desperate conviction of his own reprobation. These two elements, the abjuration of faith and its attendant vulnerability to despair, which Woodes derived from his principal source, make it clear that the play's presiding theme is not, as Bevington suggests, to show that 'God sends affliction to men in order to bring them to patience',[30] but a polemically inspired illustration of the central Protestant doctrine of justification by faith alone. Philologus's 'deserved fault' is specifically a theological crime: lack of faith is not only the moral flaw implied in the name of one who displayed insufficient 'care' for God's Word; the same lack of faith precipitates his apostasy and, in the first version, makes its impossible for him thereafter to repent of it. In the second version, the Prologue makes it clear that repentance, and with it relief from the excoriations of a guilty conscience, can only come as an imputative effect of divine grace: thus Philologus's faith is restored to him as an act of God, he himself having

> no power at all, in heart firme fayth to have,
> Tyll at the last, God chaunged his mynde his mercies for to crave . . .
>
> (Prologue, ll.34–5, Second Issue)

The long fifth act especially demonstrates how dangerously susceptible were believers in the Protestant soteriological doctrines to diabolically inspired despair; since the more a man believed that his justification depended on faith alone, the more easily could his faith be corroded by a conscience which persuaded him he could not deserve that justification. It is this paradox, elements of which are to invest the similar fates of Faustus and Giovanni, which ultimately ensnares Philologus after he has been visited by Horror; urged by Theologus to call on God for redeeming grace, and to put his faith in the mercy of Christ, Philologus answers stonily:

> I have no fayth, the wordes you speake my hart doth not beleeve,
> I must confesse that I for sinne, am justly throwne to hell.
>
> (ll.2087–8)

The conscience was, of course, God's means of correcting sin; but so easily could its excoriations thus turn faith to despair, and in this way be appropriated to the evil ends of Satan, that Calvin felt impelled to address a warning to the elect of the perils of immoderate remorse: there is, he said,

> nothing to which trembling consciences are more prone than to rush into despair. This, too, is one of Satan's artifices. Those whom he sees thus overwhelmed with fear he plunges deeper and deeper into the abyss of sorrow, that they may never again rise. . . . And yet we must always beware, according to the apostolic injunction, of giving way to extreme dread, as this tends to make us shun God while he is calling us to himself by repentance.[31]

The presentation of the character of Conscience is in terms once again reminiscent of the *pyschomachia:* Conscience and Sensual Suggestion fight for dominance over the beleaguered soul of Philologus. The nature and function of Conscience are clearly determined by the doctrinal premises of Calvinism: professing his ability to foresee the plagues and torments due to sin, Conscience quotes liberally from the Old Testament and the New in an effort to inform Philologus of the precepts of the Law Divine, but his efforts are rendered ineffective, and his insights obfuscated, by the glib readiness of Sensual Suggestion to quote Scripture for his own disingenuous purposes. There ensures, therefore, a somewhat recondite debate between the two abstractions, replete with prolix biblical allusions, and the fact that Philologus cannot distinguish between the promptings of either, nor espy the spiritual dangers that attend on such confusion, is attributed by Conscience, with full Reformist rigour, to that blindness which both Luther and Calvin imputed to man's reason:

> Such is the blindnesse of the flesh, that it may not descrie,
> Or see the perrils which the Soule, is ready to incurre:
> And much the lesse, our owne estates, we can ourselves espie:
> Because Suggestion in our hartes, such fancies often stirre . . .
>
> (ll.1748–51)

The debate centres upon the spiritual errors which Philologus seems 'ready to incurre': the forsaking of his faith in favour of worldly vanities and because of his fear of death; and the dangerous assumption, insinuated by Suggestion, that Philologus may avert his punishment by means of an eleventh-hour repentance.

On the first point, Suggestion castigates Conscience's utterances as 'glosinges untrue' (l.1764): that the accumulation of riches and worldly goods is not itself a bar to salvation is proven by those rich men – Abraham, Job and David – who 'dwell in Gods kingdome'. This Conscience counters by affirming that only certain kinds of acquisitiveness are sinful, citing Solomon's wealth in the first Book of Kings in support of the view that 'riches are the creatures of the Lorde:/Which of themselves, are good ech one' (ll.1772–3). Christ's parable of the camel and the needle's eye means, according to Conscience, not that heaven is categorically denied to the rich, but only to those who, like Philologus, have 'fastned' their 'love' upon 'worldly dust' to the exclusion of God (l.1779).

This brings Conscience to the second topic of debate: it is precisely because Philologus's faith is weak that he does not yearn, like Conscience, to join Christ in Heaven; indeed, so abject is his fear of death, that he would abandon his faith altogether rather than submit to it. In this he fails miserably to uphold the example of St Paul, who in the Epistle to the Philippians evinced such affection for Christ that he wished for death, in order that he might be 'to God disolved' (l.1806). Refuting Suggestion's submission that all living creatures are naturally endowed with a fear of death, and are justified, as were Paul, David and Christ himself, in taking steps to avoid it, Conscience points out that all of these fulfilled in their lives a higher purpose, yielding themselves to death and 'everlasting treasures' when that purpose was complete (l.1837). Philologus, on the other hand, would selfishly prolong his life, not to glorify God, but, by dedicating himself to mundane joys, to defame and dishonour him.

Finally, Conscience exposes the fallacy of relying upon the deathbed repentance recommended by suggestion, affirming that a trust in God such as Suggestion claims for Philologus is logically incompatible with a lifelong abandonment to 'wicked Mammon'; moreover, such a trust is in any case implicitly denied by Philologus's evident unwillingness presently to confide himself to the protection of God. Conscience further reminds Philologus that though God is merciful,

> Yet is he just sinnes to correct, and true in that he speake,
> Wherfore he sayeth, who so my name, before men shall not know,
> I shall not know him, when as Judge I shall sit in my seate.
>
> (ll.1874–6)

So it is that Philologus, his 'flesh' and 'Spirit' thus contending, and wretchedly doubting which best to trust, appears nevertheless partly conscious that Conscience 'speaketh truth'; but even more fearful of death, he resolves to ignore his Conscience, apprehensive at the same time of the torments and 'griping greefes' that await him in the shape of Horror (ll.1893–901). As he departs, Conscience delivers the homiletic address, and, pointing a characteristically reformist moral, laments the frailness of mankind, and the vanity with which he trusts to his own vitiated reason:

> Oh cursed creature, O fraile flesh, O meat for wormes, O dust
> O blather puffed full of winde, O vainer than these all,
> What cause hast thou in thine owne wit? to have so great a trust:
> Which of thy selfe canst not espie, the evils which on thee fall,
> The blindnesse of the outward man, Philologus shew shall . . .
>
> (ll.1909–13)

Philologus's fatalistic capitulation to the promptings of his fleshly reason proceeds according to a number of Calvinist postulates: the idea that conscience, albeit properly instructed by God's Word, is by itself impotent and helpless in the face of man's depravity; that his reason, upon which man has a deadly tendency to rely, is darkened and clouded by ignorance; and that the concupiscent appetites, here represented by Sensual Suggestion, are miserably enslaved to sin. Conscience's final judgment upon Philologus is, in fact, irresistibly reminiscent of John Calvin's perfervid censure of his prototype, Francesco Spiera, in his preface to Gribaldi's historical account; a resemblance perhaps less than surprising in view of Woodes's considerable reliance upon his source. For Calvin, Spiera's fate was a terrible example of the condign wrath of God, merited in part because he was 'a vaine fellowe puffed up with ambicious bragging, [who] would prophanely dispute and teache in the schole of Christ'. This he did in spite of the face that 'in the common life of men (if a man would viewe every estate and degree) there appereth nothyng but horrible blindnesse.'[32]

A further indication of Woodes's voluntarist conception of providential justice is the fact that Philologus's tragic decline is the result of no reactive impulse concretely apprehended within the nature of things. On the contrary, his apostasy brings in train all the worldly delights promised by Sensual Suggestion, and which, perceived in the latter's enchanted mirror, prompts Philologus's recantation. Installed at the top of fortune's wheel, he is not only appointed a judge and invested with sundry munificent offices of state; he has also preserved his immediate family from disgrace and poverty, a fact which his son Gisbertus gratefully acknowledges:

> Indeede, good father, we have cause, to praise your gravitie,
> Who did both save your selfe from woe, and us from begging
> state . . .

> (ll.1944–5)

Here, the 'natural' rewards of sin are wholly beneficent, nature and society demonstrating an amoral fickleness in favouring the wicked completely at variance with the ethical cogency inherent in the scholastic conception of the Natural Law. The retribution visited upon Philologus is an entirely supernatural one, brought about through the agency of Horror, who is assigned, as he says, by God to correct impenitents with 'torment of Conscience' (l.1976).

The arrival of Horror indeed marks the beginning of Philologus's precipitate descent into mortifying desperation and the deadly sin of despair, and completes that homiletic progression that is described in the triple stages of his spiritual struggle. This progression is traced, with precise theological accuracy, through the protagonists' previous encounter with the Holy Spirit, then with Conscience, and now finally with Horror. The Spirit, who appears to Philologus after his cross-examination by the Cardinal and his aides Hypocrisy, Avarice and Tyranny, offers to be the hero's guide, warning him not to captivate his conscience to mortal sin (ll.1701–2); yet Philologus ignores him, seduced by the fleshly delights he spies in the glass of Suggestion. This in turn brings on his 'crased' Conscience, who, as we have seen, foretells for him the 'plagues and torments' to which he will be sentenced by the 'just Judge' whom he so carelessly denies (ll.1742–3). Finally, his negligence of Conscience provokes the appearance of Horror, who transforms the glass of vanities offered by Suggestion into a reflection of his deadly sins; by which Philologus is thrown headlong into despair, convinced that he is beyond God's grace or mercy, his belief in his own election utterly confounded:

I am refused utterly, I quite from God am whorld:
My name within the Booke of life, had never residence,
Christ prayed not, Christ suffered not, my sinnes to recompence
But only for the Lordes elect, of which sort I am none . . .

(ll.2032–5)

Here, what Bevington calls the 'principle of ordered suppression' – by which Spirit gives way to Conscience and Conscience to Horror – is justified by a more than merely 'theatrical expediency'.[33] Their functions are superseded one by the other according to a theologically defined sequence, a retrogressive declension of Calvinist soteriology, by which Philologus, reduced from his presumptive status as one of God's elect, degenerates ever further into sin and despair. That he is, to begin with, ostensibly regenerate, is clear from his visitation by the Spirit, for, according to Calvin, it is by means of the Spirit that God prepares his elect for the hearing of his Word. Indeed, in the *Commentary upon Ezekiel*, the reformer makes it clear that it is only by opening the way into their minds by means of the Spirit, that God's Word can be made effective:

> God indeed works efficiently by His own Words, but we must hold that this efficacy is not contained in the Words themselves, but proceeds from the secret instinct of the Spirit. . . . But a distinction is made, that we may know that the external Word is of no avail by itself, unless animated by the power of the Spirit. . . . We hold therefore that, when God speaks, He adds the efficacy of the Spirit, since His Word without it would be fruitless.[34]

By turning a deaf ear to the Spirit of God, Philologus therefore 'captivates' his Conscience, binding himself under its condemnation; yet for all Conscience's erudite exposition of the biblically revealed Word, his preaching and exhorting remain ineffectual because of Philologus's previous dismissal of the Spirit. This process is made clear by Horror, who in announcing his intention to inflict 'torment of Conscience' upon Philologus, emphasizes his spiritual destitution:

> And where thou hast extinguished, the holy Spirit of God,
> And made him wery with thy sinnes, which dayly thou hast done,
> He will no longer in thy soule, and spirit make abode:
> But with the Graces, which he gave to thee, now is he gone,
> So that to Godwards, by Christes death, rejoycing thou hast
>   none . . .

(ll.1977–81)

The ordered principle that determines Woodes's homiletic method, therefore, is the imputative pattern of Calvinist election or reprobation, by which Philologus is either justified or damned (depending on the version) by the direct intervention of the Spirit of God, through whose power the conscience is in turn made effective.

After the appearance of Horror, by whom Philologus is convinced that he is become 'a child of condempnation', there follows an extended colloquy between the recusant and his friends Theologus and Eusebius on the possibilities of penitence and salvation. Examples of divine clemency are afforded to Philologus: the case of Peter, who, after denying Christ, bewailed his 'cryme'; and of the thief, who was at his death 'received into grace', though in wickedness he 'had spent his dayes'. Both these instances should persuade the sinner to plead for grace, urges Theologus:

> The hand of God is not abridged, but still he is of myght,
> To pardon them that call to him unfainedly for grace . . .
> (ll.2079–80)

Enjoined by Theologus to rehearse for them the chief points of his former faith, Philologus makes clear his belief that he is reprobated on account of his own wickedness: notwithstanding his erstwhile belief in the truth of the gospels, and in the doctrine of justification through faith in Christ, the root cause of his despair is that he charges himself with an antinomian lapse by which he made the sufficiency of faith an excuse to sin. His own faith, he is convinced, could never have been whole and entire, since he

> . . . tooke the faith of Christ, for lybertie to sinne,
> And did abuse his graces great, to further carnall lust,
> What wickednesse I did commit, I cared not a pinne:
> For that, Christ discharged had, my ransome, I dyd trust . . .
> (ll.2223–6)

Philologus evidently believes that, contrary to the Protestant belief by which good works were held to be the fruits of faith, his own life evidences the 'foule discorde' of an 'evill life' ensuing 'good words' (l.2243); his former presumption of perfect faith and God's election is in retrospect nullified by his failure to maintain the 'holy lyfe' which should be the outward and visible sign of regenerative grace. The vertiginous logic by which Philologus damns himself through despair (or risks that damnation in the reissued text) is elaborated for the audience by his friend Theologus: those who 'usurp' the gift of faith in the conduct of their own lives ignore the opinion of St Peter that the faithful make known their election by their works (ll.2276–82). It is this, as we have seen, that induces in Philologus that helical reasoning by which sinners consign themselves to Satan; the burden of his sins tempts him to distrust the certainty of his own election, which in turn corrupts the faith by which alone he may be justified. As Theologus points out, such reasoning is an evil perversion of the truth; referring to Philologus's forebodings of hell, he says:

> Your minde corrupted dooth present, to you, this false illusion,
> But turne awhile, unto the spirit of trueth, in your distresse,
> And it shall cast out from your eies, all horror and confusion:
> And of this your affliction, it will you soone redresse . . .
>
> (ll.2189–92)

The true purpose of the horror by which Philologus's conscience is chastized is reformative, a remedial punishment meted out, according to Theologus, by God

> Who doth correct you in this world, that in the lyfe to come,
> He might you save for of the like, the Scripture beares
>   recorde . . .
>
> (ll.2315–16)

That salvation is implied only in the second issue of the play, where, to the consternation of his critics, Woodes narrowly averts the tragic conclusion of the first by the substitution of one or two words. Philologus, who in the first instance is reported by the Nuntius to have 'hanged himselfe with coard' (l.2412, First Issue), is transmuted by a textual feat miraculous in its implications, into he 'that would have hangde himselfe with coarde,/Is nowe converted unto God, with manie bitter teares'. No doubt the author felt constrained thus to idealize his conclusion for the reasons deduced by Robert Potter, realigning his play with the conventional morality pattern of mercy and salvation to avoid an otherwise gratuitous violation of his audience's traditional expectations.[35] The reason he is able to do so with a seemingly sublime indifference to the assumptions of tragic decorum is that Woodes's theology is allowed entirely to dictate the form of his play, which the Prologue begins by deprecating as a 'recreance' produced for the edification of the godly when the author's mind was 'wearied' with graver works. Philologus's last-minute salvation is accommodated, not to the mundane necessities of plot and motivation, but to a Calvinist schema in which predestination to life is arbitrarily assigned to man as part of a secret process ineffably beyond his comprehension.

In contrast to the specifically theological crime of which Philologus is convicted, R[obert] W[ilson]'s *The Three Ladies of London*, published in 1584, deals rather more generally with commercial evils, of which society at large, and particularly London, is comprehensively indicted. Perhaps the most immediately noticeable feature from the point of view of this analysis, is that Conscience here emerges as a fully developed character in her own right, contrasting with the episodically curtailed presentation of the character in previous plays. Peter Houle describes the play as a 'social "estates" morality',[36] while for Tucker Brooke it has an evolutionary significance in showing the interlude form 'in the last phase of its drift towards city comedy';[37] both definitions accurately reflect the play's bourgeois setting in which the author deploys large numbers of representative social types, whose almost universal adhesion to venality and the unprincipled pursuit of worldly gain is presided over by the character of Lady Lucre. London is seen therefore as the capital of commercial sin, resorted to by 'foreign' Vices such as Dissimulation, Fraud, Simony, and Usury, and where the corruptive power of money is such that Lady Love is converted to lust, and Lady Conscience morally compromised.

Thus the main theme, summed up by the Judge at the end of the play as the 'unsatiate desire of vanishing earthly treasure' (sig.F3ᵛ), means that the idea of conscience is here defined by her somewhat specialized concern with the ethical uses of wealth; and, indeed, this theme is dramatized to a very considerable extent in the successive scenes where Conscience's advice is repeatedly flouted or ignored, until, along with Lady Love, she is abandoned by nearly everyone in favour of Lady Lucre. Hence the first half of the plot depicts the efforts of a merchant, a craftsman, a lawyer, and a priest to gain the patronage of Lady Lucre through the mediation of her clients, Dissimulation, Fraud, Simony, and Usury. The merchant, an Italian by the name of Mercadore, applies to Dissimulation, promising to export valuable commodities in exchange for such trifling vanities as will defraud English 'Gentlewomen' (sigs. B2–B2ᵛ). The craftsman, Artifex, reduced to penury by following the precepts of Conscience, promises Fraud henceforward to produce deceitful work, such as will 'please the eie' (sigs. B3–B3ᵛ). The lawyer, similarly brought to beggary by pleading for Love and Conscience, determines to render himself serviceable to Lady Lucre. Finally, a clergyman, Sincerity, unprovided with a benefice by Love and Conscience, applies also to Lady Lucre; but unable first of all to bribe Simony, he finds himself granted the living of St Nihil and the patronage of Sir Nicholas Nemo. Later on in the play, by contrast, an ignorant parson, Sir Peter Pleaseman, is helped to preferment by Simony on the promise of a yearly payment to the latter of one-half his annual income.

Thus beleaguered by society in its unscrupulous dedication to Lucre, the two virtuous Ladies are evicted from their house by Usury, their difficulties further exacerbated by the latter's murder of Hospitality. Conscience attempts to stave off utter destitution firstly by selling brooms, but ultimately succumbs to the pervasive corruption she condemns by becoming a bawd to Lucre, for complicity in whose crimes she is finally brought to trial and imprisoned.

As well as on the level of plot, where the play's homiletic theme is thus communicated through the progressive alienation of Conscience and love, other social vices are attacked or effectively satirized through the medium of dialogue. Hence Simony is said to enjoy 'great familiaritie' with the clergy (sig.F2^v); he and Dissimulation allude to the kind of tailor that out of a doublet and a pair of hose can steal his wife an apron (sig.E2^v); Sincerity complains of the irreligious who would rather play bowls than listen to God's Word (sig.B4^v); Lucre refers to the extortionate rents she charges 'straungers' (sigs.B3^v–B4). Turned out of her house, Conscience laments that any alternative accommodation would be likely to offend her; here her moral indignation amounts to a plenary indictment of ubiquitous corruption, and is made the scourge of all the 'Estates' for whom the play is offered on the title-page as a 'perfect patterne':

> If I goe lie in an Inne, I shall be sore greeved to see,
> The deceit of the Ostler, the powling of the Tapster, as in most
>   houses of lodging they be.
> If in a Brewers house, at the over plentie of water, and the
>   scarcenes of mault I should greeve,
> Whereby to enrich themselves, all other with unsavorie thinne
>   drinke they deceive.
> If in a Tanners house, with his great deceit in tanning,
> If in a Weavers house, with his great coosening in weaving.
> If in a Bakers house, with light bread, and very evill woorking
> If in a Chaundlers, with deceitfull waights, false measures, selling
>   for a halfepeny that is scant worth a farthing.
>
> (sig.D3)

In a manner reminiscent of her counterpart in *Impatient Poverty*, who is forced to flee the country, Lady Conscience is thus excluded by her own righteousness from any further participation in a society so dishonestly addicted to material gain. She resolves therefore to remove to some 'solitarie place', submitting to her 'crosse' with 'patience', and leaving Simplicity to point the moral:

> Simplicitie singes it, and sperience doth prove,
> No biding in London for Conscience and Love.
>
> (sig.D3^v)

Although the play's treatment of virtue and vice is largely secular in tone, there is still much to suggest that its moral stance derives from a substrata of religious ideas. Since, however, it marks, like *Appius and Virginia*, a further stage in the development of the Morality idiom, where religious polemic begins to merge into a genuinely dramatic interaction of ideas and characters, the doctrinal affiliation of those ideas is not in any real sense explicit. It seems, it is true, to align itself with the popular Protestant mood of the age in jibing at the Pope (sig.B2) and the various Romish tributes exacted from England before the Reformation. But concerning the author's treatment of Conscience we are on somewhat firmer ground, since her spiritual function is interpreted in a precisely Protestant way: not only are her precepts sanctioned by scriptural quotation and example, but in thus applying theological principle to issues of practical conduct and everyday moral contingency, she symbolizes dramatically that casuistical impulse by which all Protestants felt bound to search the Scriptures for individual guidance.

That guidance is here particularly concerned with the moral basis of worldly gain. Thus, when Lucre taunts Conscience with having turned her out of her house, and prophesies that before long she will come 'puling' to her for relief, Lady Conscience rebukes her persecutor's arrogance, and, retorting that pride will have a fall, quotes St Matthew on the vanity of acquisitiveness:

> What avauntageth it thee to win the world, and lose thy soule
> withall?
> Yet better it is to live with little, and keepe a conscience cleare,
> Which is to God a Sacrifice, and accounted of most deare.
>
> (sig.D2ᵛ)

Similarly, when Conscience enters selling brooms, she desires God to 'mollifie and lesten' Usury's heart in order to preserve the poor from penury. She laments the fact that though usury is tolerated amongst Christians, it nevertheless gives rise to unlawful extortion, resting her case upon the traditional teaching that according to God's Law, usury is wrong:

> But if we should follow Gods law we should not receave above
> that wee lend.
> For if we lend for reward, how can we say we are our neighbors
> friend?
>
> (sig.D4ᵛ)

The source of the Christian teaching at this point is referred once again to the Scriptures, this time, with a somewhat cavalier disregard for accuracy, to St Paul, who, according to Conscience, allegedly

> Calleth them theeves that doth not geve the needie of their store,
> And thrise accurst are they that take one penny from the
> poore . . .
>
> (sig.D4ᵛ)

Even Conscience's fall from grace enacts symbolically a passage from Scripture. Lucre promises her 5,000 crowns in order to 'decke up' her cottage, on condition that Conscience permits it to be used for immoral purposes by Lucre and her familiars. To this proposal Conscience finally acquiesces, resigned to following Lucre since it is evident that she now leads 'the worlde in a string'; and the contamination of the former is emphasized by an elaborately orchestrated piece of symbolism. Usury is bidden to fetch the 'boxe of all abhomination', from which Lucre daubs the face of her latest conquest, proceeding according to the stage direction: 'Here let Lucar open the boxe and dip her finger in it, and spotte Conscience face' (sig.El^v). The informing principle appears to be a recollection of Luke 16:15, where Christ warns the Pharisees against the impossibility of serving two masters, God and Mammon, together: 'And he said unto them, Ye are they which justify yourselves before men, but God knoweth your hearts: for that which is highly esteemed amongst men, is abomination in the sight of God.'

But it is not until the last scene of the play, with its eschatological overtones, that the concept of conscience draws to any considerable extent on ideas recognizably derived from moral theology. Conscience is brought to trial along with Lucre and deformed Love, in a court-room scene the apocalyptic imagery of which is clearly meant to evoke the Last Judgment. Lady Lucre, arraigned for adultery, robbery, and conspiracy to murder Hospitality, is condemned to the 'lowest hel' and the company of 'infernall sprites and damned ghostes' on the testimony of Conscience, whose own implication in the universal guilt is made clear:

> My good Lord I have no way to excuse my selfe,
> She hath corrupted me by flatterie, and her accursed pelfe:
> What need further triall, sith I Conscience am a thousand
>   witnesses?
> I cannot chuse but condemne us all in living amisse,
> Such terror doth affright me, that living, I wish to dye:
> I am afrayd there is no sparke left for me of Gods mercy.
> (sigs.F2^v-F3)

The idea here advanced, that of conscience as a witness, was originally propounded in the Pauline Epistles, and is made instantly recognizable to an audience by Wilson's quotation of the current proverb, 'Conscience is a thousand witnesses'; a usage which interestingly anticipates Shakespeare's adaptation of it in *Richard III:* 'My conscience hath a thousand several tongues' (V.iii.194). But it will be recalled from the Introduction that the wider notion that the conscience performs this function at the Last Judgment is a recurrent motif in the Protestant casuistical tradition, reiterated time and again by popular preachers and in books of sermons, and, as we shall see, explicated as a dramatic device in the dramatic literature of the succeeding age. One such example, from John Woolton, will suffice:

> This conscience so wonderfully fram'd and fashioned in man by almighty God, to be a witnesse and an informer of mankinde . . . Summoneth us as it were before the tribunall seate of God, sometime accusing, sometime excusing.[38]

Thus testifying against herself, therefore, and censured by the Judge for permitting 'cankered quoyn' to corrupt her heart, Lady Conscience is committed to prison until the day of the 'generall session', presumably hopeful of the eventual mercy and forgiveness of God. In this her fate contrasts with that of Lady Love, who, for marrying Dissimulation and thus selling her soul to Lucre, is condemned to suffer in hell 'like torment' with her erstwhile benefactress. The precise nature of the punishment Love will receive is elaborated for her by the Judge, and consists in an everlasting affliction of the worm of Conscience:

> Which torments comprehended are in the worme of Conscience,
> Who raging still, shall nere have end, a plague for thine offence.
> Care shall by thy comfort, and sorrow shall thy life sustaine,
> Thou shalt be dying, yet never dead, but pining still in endles
> paine.

> (sig.F3ᵛ)

The idea, which again recurs in *Richard III*, by which the remorse of conscience is metaphorically construed as a worm, everlastingly gnawing the souls of the damned and forming one of the chief torments of hell, is derived once more from a scriptural source, this time from Mark 9:43–8, where he talks of cutting off offending members 'rather than to go into hell, into the fire that never shall be quenched: Where their worm dieth not, and the fire is not quenched'.

Some of these ideas are taken up into the next play by the same author, *The Three Lords and Three Ladies* of London; printed six years later as a sequel to *The Three Ladies*, it is at once more allegorical in tone, and much less earnest in its social concern. The former play's lengthy exposure of social evils is to some extent limited and qualified in the sequel by Robert Wilson's more positive intention this time to show a London cleansed of its erstwhile corruption, into which the three Ladies are rehabilitated and from which the four Vices are finally exorcised. H. S. D. Mithall has suggested that Wilson wrote the sequel in order to provide his first play with a resolution more in accordance with the morality convention, which traditionally exhibited the triumph of good over evil, and from which *The Three Ladies* was clearly a deviation.[39] At all events, it continues the general Protestant tone of the first part: the central episode involves a timely evocation of the Spanish Armada, in which the 'Catholicos Castillianos' are symbolically vanquished by 'los Lutheranos Angleses' (sig.G3), the three Lords of the title undertaking the defence of a London once more graced by the newly redeemed Ladies, against the evil Lords of Spain, Pride, Ambition and Tyranny.

The regeneration of London and its Ladies is initiated by the three Lords, Policy, Pomp, and Pleasure, who, having determined to wed them, apply to Judge Nemo for their release. Addressing him in terms once again suggestive of his divine nature – 'thou spotlesse Magistrate' who 'never spill'd, whom he could save' (sig.C3ᵛ) – they plead with him to revoke his previous sentence, thus redeeming them from perpetual imprisonment. Nemo consents to clear them of their former crimes 'no blemish left to see', provided that he may dispose them in marriage to which of the Lords he thinks best (sigs.C4–C4ᵛ). Shortly the Ladies are brought forth by Sorrow, and, displaying a newly acquired repentance and shame which induces them to veil their faces, are made to sit upon three penitential stones, marked Remorse (Conscience), Charity (Love), and Care (Lucre) – a purgatorial experience designed, as Nemo later explains, to persuade them of their 'true condition' (sig.E1).

All the Ladies recount the pains they have suffered during their infernal imprisonment. Lady Conscience voices once again the idea of the especial punishment reserved in hell for those who die with a guilty conscience: the perpetual torment of remorse affecting the souls of the damned as the stinging of a worm, which never dies:

> O Sorrow when? when sorrow wilt thou cease
> To blow the sparke that burnes my troubled soule?
> To feede the worme that stings my fainting breast,
> And sharpe the steele that goares my dieng heart?
>   (sig.D1ᵛ)

A reformist motif emerges too, in Lady Love's recital of her punishment: she also has suffered the never-ending throes of spiritual death and the inextinguishable tortures of the immortal soul. But, significantly, she interprets her sinful folly, not as an offence against an *ordo naturae* of scholastic provenance, but as induced rather by a frailty implicit in nature itself, by which her corruption was made inevitable:

> Yet never dead, and yet Love doeth not live,
> Love that to losse in life her follie lent,
> Folly the food whereon her frailtie fed
> Frailtie the milke that Natures breast did give . . .
>   (sig.D1ᵛ)

Thus her fall seems determined by the voluntarist assumption that the natural order is irredeemably perverted, enunciated in Calvin's dictum that 'Guilt is from nature, whereas sanctification is from supernatural grace'.[40]

The theological antithesis between the guilt that is from nature, and a supernaturally contrived salvation seems further to inform the contrite resignation with which the Ladies accept the purgatorial inflictions arranged for them by Nemo. Although Conscience remains convinced that their distress will move 'smal ruth' (sig.D2ᵛ) in those who witness it, Love resists the temptation to despair that Conscience's words imply; and all three Ladies, consoling themselves with the idea that hope, in those that pray 'with faith', directs a 'readie way' to heaven, thus await a heaven-sent release from shame. Says Conscience:

> Then veile our selves, and silent let us stay,
> till heavens shall please to send some friends this way . . .
>
> (sig.D3)

The fortitude of the Ladies' reformation is immediately subjected to a moral assay with the ironic reappearance of the four 'friends' – Fraud, Simony, Dissimulation and Usury – whose falsehood and double-dealing had originally precipitated their mistresses' downfall (sig.D3). This time, however, the Ladies Love and Lucre, mindful of their recent dear-brought repentance, successfully resist the beguiling blandishments of the Vices, and adhere resolutely to the guidance of Lady Conscience.

Much of the remainder of the play continues to trace the growing effectiveness of Lady Conscience and her gradual reinstatement in the popular regard. Thus Nemo, faced with a predictable dilemma, in that all the Lords desire only to wed Lady Lucre, to the exclusion of Love and especially of Conscience, decides to overcome that failing in men by which they are 'forgetfull of their greater good' (sig.E4ᵛ), by means of a trick. By passing her off as Lucre, Nemo succeeds in matching Conscience with Pleasure, justifying his device in the light of his conviction that 'Conscience cleare indeed's the greatest gaine' (sig.E4ᵛ); a conviction that Pleasure himself comes to confess in his realization that Conscience is, after all, 'welcommer' to him than either Love or Lucre (sig.F1ᵛ). A further stage in the moral ascendancy of Conscience is reached when first Policy, and then all three Lords, together assure her that their collective defence of England against the Spaniards will be conducted chiefly in her service, notwithstanding the individual partiality of Policy for Love and Pomp for Lucre (sig.F2). The spiritual vindication of Lady Conscience in the life of London is finally confirmed when the Vices are forced to abandon the city, their credit disastrously undermined by a growing disposition to virtue generated in society by the prospect of the Spanish invasion. Says Fraud:

> the Spaniards are comming thou hearest with great power, here is no living for us in London, men are growen so full of conscience and religion, that Fraud, Dissimulation and Simony are disciphered, and being disciphered are also dispised.
>
> (sig.F4)

The resolution of the play is finally a comic one, and the multiple marriages at the end consolidate the theme of London's moral apotheosis. England's triumph over the various forces of evil, and the future security and prosperity of London, is celebrated and confirmed by the homiletic 'completion' of Policy by Love, Pomp by Lucre, and Pleasure by Conscience, to which latter Lord, Conscience had earlier commended herself as a wife to measure delights by 'reasons rule' (sig.F1). And to Pleasure, fittingly, is given the closing speech, in which he invokes a divine benediction upon London's inhabitants, praying God to 'poure downe' grace that they may live in fear and, 'dying well', earn by these means a place in Heaven.

H. S. D. Mithal in his combined edition of *The Three Ladies* and *The Three Lords and Three Ladies*, surmizes from an oblique reference in the epistle to Nashe's *Menaphon*, and a remark, possibly of autobiographical inspiration, put into the mouth of the priest Sincerity concerning the unprofitability of studying divinity at Cambridge, that Wilson, too, abandoned a similar preparation for orders in favour of a more lucrative career in the theatre.[41] The claim is yielded a certain circumstantial validity by his portrayal of Lady Conscience, and would explain the somewhat haphazard collocation of scriptural quotations and references, some apparently only half-remembered, with which Conscience is supplied in the first play. Perhaps the most that can be said of either play is that while, with their sprawling plots and absurd lack of focus, they are almost completely devoid of literary or theatrical merit, they are at the same time not without documentary significance, since Wilson's evidently serious concern to reflect current social issues is matched by an intelligent appreciation of the tenets of contemporary moral theology, to the popular dissemination of which Lady Conscience must be supposed some sort of index. More important is the extent to which it is here demonstrated that even very late moralities such as these, avowedly comic by intention, and broadly satiric and secular in tone, still communicate their themes within a religious framework of values, presuming in their audiences a level of awareness of such values sufficient in this case to comprehend the specifically doctrinal premises which inform the character of Lady Conscience.

Certain conclusions seem deducible from the foregoing analysis which provide valuable testimony of the altering postulates underlying the idea of conscience as it develops in Tudor interludes and morality plays. Firstly, the concept of the sufficiency of reason, upheld by Aristotle and the scholastic tradition, and apparent in *The World and the Child*, is uniformly denigrated by the reformist presuppositions manifest in *Impatient Poverty* and *The Conflict of Conscience;* correlatively, whereas in the pre-Reformation play, Conscience as a dispositional faculty of the reason retains its integrity and indirectly brings about the salvation of Age, in the two latter moralities, and also in *The Three Ladies of London*, there is a strong suggestion of its inveterate corruption, the judgments of the conscience being contaminated by its own complicity in evil. As a further corollary, all the post-Reformation plays here considered (with the possible exception of the second version of *The Conflict of Conscience*) demonstrate the hopeless ineffectuality of conscience upon the will of man, in turn Calvinistically enslaved to sin. The scholastic impulse to order, the Natural Law, by which the universalized hero of *The World and Child* is punished for infringing the precepts of conscience, gives way in *The Conflict of Conscience* and *The Three Lords and Three Ladies of London* to a retribution providentially imposed, and imposed most horrifically in the torments of conscience by which God castigates sinners. Moreover, all the post-Reformation moralities (excluding *Appius and Virginia*) teach that ethical guidance, and ultimately salvation itself, depends upon a conscience enlightened and informed by the biblically revealed Word of God.

Many of these theological postulates, of course, provide the shaping philosophical premises for those later dramatized studies of conscience and moral choice which this thesis has yet to address. In particular, Woodes's *Conflict of Conscience*, as a graphic analysis of theological despair, anticipates, in a variety of ways that have been explored by Lily B. Campbell, Marlowe's *Doctor Faustus*, and provides a model, however indirect, for numerous similar portraits from Webster's Aragonian brethren to Massinger's Grimaldi. By the same token, that deterioration and impairment of the moral faculty in Appius alerts us to a like prognosis in a long line of obdurate sinners, from Macbeth and D'Amville, to Malefort and Giovanni; while the commercial ethics of *The Three Ladies of London* which denigrate the 'insatiate desire of vanishing earthly treasure' communicate a homiletic strain common to much Jacobean satire, and re-emerge as a latent theme in Bosola's contempt for a world he is no more able to resist than is Wilson's Conscience figure.

That Shakespeare is dependent upon the Morality tradition in some of his greatest work is by now a commonplace of critical discussion. Indeed, the interaction of the Mankind figure with his conscience, though openly mocked at in the Launcelot Gobbo scenes of *The Merchant of Venice*, and in the colloquy between the murderers of Clarence in *Richard III*, contributes, on a more serious and doubtless more generalized level, much to the substantial meaning and structure of the Henry IV plays and to *Hamlet*. But the enormous advance upon this tradition that Shakespeare's plays represent, in terms both of moral vision and artistic richness, is accompanied paradoxically by a return to an earlier rationalistic metaphysic, salvaged from the post-Reformation ruins of man's total deformity by Hooker and revived intermittently in the following century by men such as Laud, Chillingworth, and Milton, which predicated an organic universe of intelligible moral causation in human affairs. The rehabilitation of reason and the emancipation of conscience that is evident in Shakespeare's work is the immediate subject of the next section of this book; subsequent chapters will explore the gradual erosion of the axiom of knowledge, overthrown in the ceaseless dialectic, the mortal and intestine jars, which occurred in sixteenth- and seventeenth-century England between the opposed theologies of reason and knowledge on the one hand, will and nescience on the other.

3

Richard III

In considering *Richard III* one is inescapably reminded of Hector's words on the nature of value:

> But value dwells not in particular will:
> It holds his estimate and dignity
> As well wherein 'tis precious of itself
> As in the prizer.
> (*Troilus and Cressida*, II.ii.54–7)

Value in Shakespeare's plays has an objectivity, a *quidditas* of this sort, but it is never obvious and seldom sustains a moral universe in which complacencies such as Hector's are allowed any absolute conviction. On the contrary, value frequently seems to dwell in a given point of view or disposition of events, but is then subsequently, or upon closer examination, found to be undermined or criticized by an altogether different collocation of value. Thus Hector's argument, when applied to the heady idealism of his Trojan companions, appears incisively to expose it for what it is: the baseless fabric of a dream of honour. But in the very next moment, the force of Hector's wisdom is ironically dissipated by his capitulation to the arguments of Troilus and Paris. All that is apparently objective and rationally absolute in the moral chiaroscuro implied in what Hector 'knows as truth', is thus in its turn qualified by juxtaposition with the rich subjective intimations of 'a promis'd glory' figured to him in the heroic vision of his brothers, whose appeal is actually to what is noblest in him. In this way is truth made apprehensible in the Shakespearean universe; 'persistive constancy', in men as in values, is discoverable only with difficulty in a mutable world, whose slippery turns in the interminable gyre of time threaten the general dissolution of all codes of value; and yet discoverable it is, providing we accept it as Shakespeare intends – as a chastened and attenuated thing, moulded and sculpted by a thousand equivocating ironies. A major corollary of this is that a Shakespeare play enacts such truths as a consequence partly, indeed, of the integers of characterization and poetry, but as a function, more broadly speaking, of its own construction, and that these factors subtend the kind of attention the play solicits for the values it embodies.

Any undue prolixity in these introductory remarks may perhaps be extenuated by their immediate application to *Richard III.* For here is a play not untypically Shakespearean in offering mutually qualifying systems of value expressed as inherent facets of the play's structure.[1] The crucial dilemma is whether that structure belongs more properly to the genre of history or tragedy: crucial because the dilemma is not alone an aesthetic problem. Such is the tectonic conformation of value in the Shakespearean universe, that the moral insights discovered in this place by the play as history coexist to all intents somewhat uneasily with those discovered by the same play considered as tragedy. Thus Shakespeare's 'authentic' moral viewpoint, at the best of times elusive, appears here functionally dislocated, permeating Janus-like two disjunct conceptions of the same play.

The point is an important one in so far as it affects the possibility of discussing Richard's conscience as an organic concept consistent with the development of his character within a play concerned at other points and in other ways to dramatize the concept.[2] Ever since the rehabilitation of Shakespeare's play in the theatre, critics have tended to justify those elements which Cibber had excised as undramatic – in particular, the 'croaking quartet of she-ravens', King Edward and Clarence, whose utterances do so much to refer the play morally to a framework of divine nemesis and dramatically to a culminating position in the tetralogy beginning with *Henry VI.* Hence R. G. Moulton's thesis, that the play is an elaborately wrought pattern of nemesis, of which Margaret is the oracle and Richard the instrument, has for long been a critical commonplace.[3] It is largely echoed by A. P. Rossiter when he argues that the play accepts the simple doctrine propounded by the Tudor historians that England rests under a chronic curse: 'the curse of faction, civil dissension and fundamental anarchy, resulting from the deposition of the Lord's Anointed (Richard II)'.[4] The bloody history of the Wars of the Roses are the catastrophic consequences of this moral rent in society, which Richard cauterizes, and to which Richmond applies the balm, both as agents of an outraged Deity. These somewhat naive suppositions concerning the doctrine of providence were undoubtedly ready to Shakespeare's hand in Hall and Holinshed, where in the latter, the apportionment of blame between the houses of York and Lancaster is secondary only to the imputation of absolute wickedness in Richard, in order to justify the Tudor settlement:

And as it thus well appeared, that the house of Yorke shewed it selfe more bloudie in seeking to obteine the kingdome, than that of Lancaster in usurping it; so it came to passe, that the Lords vengeance appeared more heavie towards the same than toward the other, not ceassing till the whole issue male of the said Richard duke of Yorke was extinguished. For such is Gods justice, to leave no unrepentant wickednesse unpunished, as especiallie in this caitife Richard the third.[5]

This is the sort of historiography that at one level at least, undoubtedly informs *Richard III*, and considered as a history play these are the somewhat limited truths that it dramatizes. Critics are right who point to the providential design of the play: divine retribution *is* clearly at work in the play and victims of the accumulated slaughter cry out for and upon God's wrath at the moments of their 'taking off'; there *are* associated supernatural manifestations, in the bleeding wounds of Henry VI, the punctilious fulfilment of curses, and the ghostly parade of victims; and Richard *does* appear to be the 'scourge of God', an evil instrument of divine justice, just as Richmond is a correspondingly righteous instrument. And yet to insist too far upon a reading of the play as history is necessarily to acquiesce in the values, however paradoxical, of the history upon which it is based: viz. that the security of the Tudor settlement depended on seeing Richard at once as an evil monstrosity, a demon incarnate. This is all very well as far as it goes: a belief in providence, especially of the rather ingenuous variety demonstrated in Shakespeare's source material, was regularly, almost instinctively, invoked in Renaissance England as a means of imputing a larger logic to the random vicissitudes of worldly circumstance, and existed in a variety of formulations, from neo-Stoic to Calvinistic. The trouble with the intrusive, meddling figment of the Chroniclers, simple-mindedly Old Testament rather than in any sense rigorously Augustinian, is that it subordinates human motivation to the kind of philosophical determinism that is actually consistent *only* with a view of the play as history. But a view of Shakespeare's art which construes all as puppets, caught up in the mechanical coils of a divine master-plan, does less than justice to its full significance; and the spiritual response of his characters to their predicament, even in this early work, promises more than is adduced by those ritualized litanies of revenge and counter-revenge whose morality the Deity is so dubiously called upon to sanction.

This is, as A. P. Rossiter remarks, the framework of 'moral history',[6] and it is not surprising that its somewhat medieval pattern should have suggested to Shakespeare the appropriateness of wedding to the idea of Richard as 'scourge of God', the equally traditional idea of Richard as Vice; and once again, vestigial elements of the Stage Vice *do* appear in his extraordinary mental resilience, his dangerous and deadly whimsicality, his dissimulation, and, more importantly, in his apparent capacity to deny the claims of conscience.

The point here is that *Richard III* seen as history play – that is, exclusively in the light of the naive theology of its sources – yields a range of values not only paradoxical, but difficult to recognize as Shakespearean. It compels us to admit that those most evil (the murderers, Margaret, Richard) can do no wrong; that the virtuous (Hastings, Anne) are foolishly contemptible, that mercy is excluded in favour of nemesis and that God's justice is essentially repugnant. Moreover, in this view the attribution of a conscience to Richard must necessarily be seen as artistically tactless, inconsistent with the hitherto external development of his character, and no more than a gesture paid to the morality pattern of the play, by the conventions of which Vice was made to undergo – in the words of M. M. Reese – 'an awkward five minutes before the end' as a belated recognition that wickedness does not pay.[7] Thus for Sen Gupta, the development of Richard's character is not dramatic in the true sense, 'for there is no inner connexion between the man who had mocked conscience and the man who is now mocked by it'.[8] Consequently, when Richard suddenly holds himself guilty of murder and perjury, 'the change is neither probable nor necessary'; a charge also supported by M. M. Reese. For him, no sense of tragedy attaches to the predestined doings of a monster in evil; 'we are watching the headlong career of a monster, not the withering of a human soul'.[9]

The downright apposition of a sense of 'tragedy' with 'predestined doings', of a 'monster' with a 'human soul', defines precisely the limitations of this view of the play, and I shall want to argue that what are here expressed as alternatives are actually compatible if we regard *Richard III* as Shakespeare's first attempt to make a tragedy out of an historical theme. It can be admitted that Shakespeare here acknowledges the same simplified Tudor patterns of retributive reaction as he adopted in the *Henry VI* trilogy, and there is certainly much evidence that we are meant to take them seriously; at the same time, the play's evolutionary tendency towards tragedy throws up a different order of value, an order presented with so much more imaginative vigour as to suggest irresistibly that it is in this tragic mode that the *imprimatur* of Shakespeare will be found. For him, an order of history that is written in the heavens and imposed upon mankind is uncongenial and perhaps even fundamentally at variance with the dramatist's art; much more satisfactory would be the order of tragedy that is worked out in the souls of men, and towards which he was groping in *Richard III*. Here the second order is offered simultaneously as a kind of palinode upon the first; for by showing the moral firmament to be less crudely immanent, less compromised in prospering the criminal designs of men, Shakespeare substitutes for the naive absolutes of Hall and Holinshed, a typically pervasive set of ironies and relativities.

In making distinctions such as these, it is useful to invoke Lily B. Campbell's definition of that which separates tragedy from history: the division of morals into the private and public spheres, a description she culls from Spenser and Raleigh. Accordingly, tragedy deals with the ethical world, history with politics; and what contributes to the impression that *Richard III* is a tragedy is precisely this ethical emphasis given to historical incident: the killing of the little princes, rather than the usurpation of the throne; Clarence's dream of divine retribution, rather than any sustained conviction of his family's right to rule.[10] Above all, the imaginative energies of the play are centred, not in the inchoate succession of incident and event that is history, but in the unifying and dominant character of Richard himself, who alone forges any kind of dramatic nexus with the audience. That relationship is composed of various elements: on the one hand, an insinuating and deadly confidence; on the other the shared enjoyment of murder as a grisly joke. But more important than these is the accessibility in Richard of elements more typically tragic: the nurture of ambition by envy and hatred, the onset of fear and passion, and the ensuing perturbations of conscience expressed as babbling dreams. This interior and psychological account of justice construed organically, by which the evil soul ultimately confounds itself, it the one most vitally conceived, and renders almost peripheral the externally imposed mechanism of providential justice. For an audience, indeed, the emotional satisfactions afforded by the sterile rhetoric through which the patterns of retributive justice are conveyed are about as limited as the intellectual inferences they enforce. 'History' in *Richard III* unfolds to a very large extent in the ritualized, repetitive tedium of the lamenting dowagers and the almost reflexive platitudes of numberless victims, which refer the play to a divine schema; tedium and platitude perhaps inevitably testifying to the indifference with which Shakespeare responded to the Old Testament morality of the Chroniclers, and the externality of a providence so conceived.

If *Richard III* is a tragical account of history, then we shall expect to find inscribed, as it were, on the anthropocentric vaults of the transcendental scheme, an emergent human system of justice, consistent with that developed by Shakespeare in his later tragedies, by which the diseased society purges itself and the causal nature of evil entails its final recoil upon the diseased soul. And in fact, there are numerous instances where just such an ironic tension is set up between the natural and the supernatural. On the one hand, the curses called down upon Buckingham and Richard by both Margaret and themselves are addressed to a God who appears punctiliously to answer them. And yet there is nothing unequivocally supernatural about either their invocation or their fulfilment: they are at best a dubious form of prayer, at worst as evil as what they attack.[10] Margaret's role as providential oracle is sanctioned at one level by her delivery of these curses in a ritual incantation; but this does not disguise their thoroughly evil nature, and their other, entirely natural character as the accumulated bile of a woman whose own past wickedness is constantly compared with that of Richard himself:

> The curse my noble father laid on thee
> When thou didst crown his warlike brows with paper,
> And with thy scorns drew'st rivers from his eyes,
> And then to dry them, gav'st the Duke a clout
> Steep'd in the faultless blood of pretty Rutland -
> His curses then, from bitterness of soul
> Denounc'd against thee, are all fall'n upon thee,
> And God, not we, hath plagu'd thy bloody deed.
>
> Q. ELIZ.: So just is God, to right the innocent.
>
> (I.iii.174–82)

Here, the reverberating ironies threaten the destruction of the whole panoply of a justice so conceived; the point being, of course, that no one is actually innocent, and no one can claim the exclusive alliance of God in plaguing bloody deeds, with the possible exception of Richmond. The theological position is more precisely defined by Clarence:

> If God will be avenged for the deed,
> O know you yet, He doth it publicly;
> Take not the quarrel from His powerful arm.
> He needs no indirect or lawless course
> To cut off those that have offended Him.
>
> (I.iv.204–8)

Here Clarence cites the orthodox belief that God's vengeance was enacted publicly by his magistrates in the administration of justice. In the case of Clarence's death, as with all of Richard's victims, it is only private revenge that masquerades as public vengeance, and is actually therefore a usurpation of divine justice.

For a right understanding of the organic impulse within the play-world to which all the personages of the drama ultimately propend, it is worth recalling the precepts of St Thomas Aquinas. Divine wisdom, he argues, having created all things in the character of a single idea, causes them to move to their 'due ends' in conformity with the law inherent in that idea. Divine providence, according to Aquinas, is not the external and manipulating figment of the Chroniclers, but

> that which the rational creature is subject to . . . in the most excellent way . . . Wherefore it has a share of the External Reason, whereby it has a natural inclination to its proper act and end: and this participation of the eternal law in the rational creature is called the natural law.[11]

The emergent moral design of this tragedy is actually very similar to that of Shakespeare's greatest tragedies, in that it is the participation of all things in the Natural Law that provides the philosophic correlative to the dramatic principle of causative design. Not, of course, that the doctrine of divine superintendence was incommensurable with such a design: on the contrary, Aquinas insists that God's providence cares for all individuals immediately, but that its execution is carried out by secondary causes, among which contingency and human free will must be counted. Evil exists not as a function of the divine decree, but inheres in the voluntary acts of human agents, whose partial imperfections are permitted in order to serve the perfectibility of the whole, since all things are ordered towards a final end in goodness.[12] Hence the existence of causes in human affairs is as important for Aquinas as for Shakespeare; for as the philosopher says, 'if there were no intermediary causes to execute divine providence, there would be no order of causes in the world, but of effects only'.[13] Presented in his source material with a series of historical effects merely, Shakespeare at once sets himself to explore their causes in the world of man, attempting, however imperfectly, to reconcile the perspectives of history with those of tragedy, providence with those of the human conscience. In Shakespeare's mature art, the great principle of order is perceived as a cosmic supra-personal justice whose medium is not the thunderbolts of an outraged Deity, but the infinitely complex, teleological bias of myriad acts of human free will. This principle, almost as it were Newtonian in its conception that to every action there must needs be an equal and opposite reaction, is incipiently at work in *Richard III* and is observable in two dimensions: societally, in the outer world of the commonwealth, where the atrocities of tyranny create the resistance which eventually overthrows it; and individually, in the inner world of conscience, where evil confounds its perpetrator.

In the first dimension, then, Shakespeare documents by a series of oblique touches what is to become his classic statement on the contagious nature of evil: that evil such as Richard's can only exist in a society already fatally flawed by it. The chief personages of Richard's world all share in the general guilt, either for what they were, or what they become. Margaret and the wailing dowagers have all contributed in greater or lesser degree to the conditions in which a 'bloody tyrant and a homicide' (V.iii.247) can subject them still further to the miseries they undoubtedly deserve; Anne and Hastings are no less corruptible in the face of evil for being apparently virtuous; and even the unexceptionable Scrivener and the honest Brackenbury compromise their integrity in a fearful compact with despotism. Hastings prophesies for England 'the fearfull'st time' (III.iv.104), and the citizens muffle their deepest misgivings, knowing full well that under Richard, 'such ill-dealing must be seen in thought', and that men may be 'sent for to the Justices' without knowing exactly why (III.vi.14; II.iii.46).

The familiar image of England as a garden, subject to the withering and destructive forces represented by Richard, is also much in evidence. 'When great leaves fall, then winter is at hand', remarks the Citizen (II.iii.33), a

meteorological quality that Richard recognizes in himself: 'They that stand
high have many blasts to shake them', he admonishes Queen Elizabeth.
Somewhat less appropriately, he refers to himself as a 'weeder-out' of his
enemies, and as having 'cropp'd the golden prime' of a young Prince
Edward; and elsewhere, a perennial image reliant upon the tempest-
disorder symbolism is applied to him:

> Q. ELIZ.:   And I in such a desp'rate bay of death,
> Like a poor bark of sails and tackling reft,
> Rush all to pieces on thy rocky bosom.
>   (IV.iv.233–5)

And yet, for all the undeniable complicity of these people in the evil
of which themselves are chief victims, there is none the less an unseen
groundswell of resistance, almost imperceptible at first, but accumulating
in strength as the accompanying vituperative clamour of the women rises
in ever more frenzied crescendo. This is at first felt in the darkly uttered
comments of the Scrivener who recognizes Hastings's death as a 'palpable
device' but confines himself to silence (III.vi.11). So too with the citizens
whose deadly pallor on being harangued by Buckingham does not start
them out of the 'wilful silence' which dumbly accuses Richard and his
confederates (III.vii.28). Out of this soundless opposition emerges a
mounting wave of reaction. At the meridian of power and ambition,
Richard's support begins to shift and totter. Buckingham, so long a stal-
wart accomplice in wickedness, now begins to grow 'circumspect' and to
look with 'considerate eyes' at the King who will give him no pause in
the unabated rush to slaughter yet more innocents (IV.ii.30–2). Catesby,
heretofore a reliable lackey of despotism, and likewise faced with yet
another political murder, this time of Anne, grows sufficiently amazed at
the pace and violence of Richard's behests as to be caught dreaming.
Tyrrel, one whom corrupting gold will 'tempt to anything', is overcome
by remorse, and describes the murder of the princes he has just commissioned as 'ruthless butchery', a 'piteous massacre' to which he was
suborned by a 'bloody King' (IV.iii.2–22). And in the wake of this, successive messengers bring with accelerating rapidity, the news first of Buckingham's rebellion, closely followed by that of Richmond and the wholesale defections of Morton, the Guilfords, and many more of their
'competitors' to the Tudor cause, until the sense of momentum which had
always attended Richard, has, by a convulsive reaction in the body politic,
transferred itself to Richmond. And the multiplicity of this reaction culminates in the appearance to Richard of his ghostly victims, who by sheer
weight of numbers, symbolize the revulsion of the moral order to the
cancer that consumes it. Correspondingly, the humane imperatives of
'kindness' begin to reassert themselves in Stanley's blessings upon
Richmond:

> Farewell; the leisure and the fearful time
> Cuts off the ceremonious vows of love
> And ample interchange of sweet discourse
> Which so long sunder'd friends should dwell upon.
>
> (V.iii.98–101)

But the 'fearful time' which thus curtails the vows of love, is nearly over; the creed of kindlessness epitomized in a tyrant who sunders friends is shortly to be disavowed, and the 'great bond', cancelled and torn to pieces by Richard as by Macbeth, begins to make itself whole. In fact, Stanley's speech denotes exactly the equivalent process of moral restitution prefigured in the Lord's words to Lennox on the purpose of Macduff's appeal to Northumberland and Siward:

> That, by the help of these (with Him above
> To ratify the work), we may again
> Give to our tables meat, sleep to our nights,
> Free from our feasts and banquets bloody knives,
> Do faithful homage, and receive free honours,
> All which we pine for now.
>
> (*Macbeth*, III.vi.32–7)

The cumulative effect of all this is to compel our awareness of an organic sense of purpose in the universe, as it were, an ethical field of force, which, in galvanizing multiple acts of individual conscience, results in a cathartic disgorgement of the evil which it harbours. Here it is expressed dramatically: Richard is an unnatural monster, an offence against the ethic of order which underpins the Shakespearean universe. Expressed as moral philosophy, the process arises out of an enactment of that Natural Law to which created nature defers, and the conscience inclines, out of an intrinsic and instilled knowledge of its precepts.

This might seem an over-secular account of things, but it is important to understand the extent to which the whole process involved a very precise relation between man and both Divine and Natural Law. In God's ordering of the created universe there were observable two stages, distinguishable as cause and effect: the reason of order, and the execution of order. By the first, all things were ordered towards their proper ends in the mind of God; they expressed that mind in the act of creation and by virtue of this partook in God's providence. But the execution of the providential design was the function of Government, through which God as universal Cause governs, but only indirectly, through a mediate chain of secondary causes inherent in the nature of things themselves. Any perversion of the execution of order in the individual was witnessed to by the act of conscience.[14]

The notion of conscience may thus be seen to have reference to the social and the universal order; just as it is not sufficient to describe Natural Law in terms simply of the phenomenal world, so it is not alone adequate to describe conscience in terms merely of the human psyche. The complex interfusion of what the author of the *Sermon of Obedience* terms 'souls, bodies, goods and commonwealths'[15] in the great analogical scheme of the universe meant that the sum of creation expressed, and was expressed by, its individual parts, and the spiritual world correlated with the physical; so that what responded to the Natural Law as a supra-personal embodiment of the collective will, responded in the individual reason as an act of conscience. And it is this internal aspect of conscience which *Richard III* also invites us to consider, coincident as the play is for Shakespeare with a developing awareness of character, and the origin of evil within it. For what is intimated in the Clarence scenes is an exploration of depth of the personal consequences of a commitment to evil.

The torments of conscience in Clarence and Richard resultant upon past occasions of sin, afflict them in the form of terrible dreams, an implicit recognition of the extent to which in both men the warnings and accusations that are the functions of a healthy conscience have hitherto been ruthlessly repressed. Clarence's dream is for the most part an orthodox representation of the effects of sin upon the conscience, resulting in the 'dismal terror' of a despairing soul: a condition reminiscent of Appius and Philologus, and one which looks forward to a whole range of desperate sinners from Faustus to Grimaldi of *The Renegado*. The incorporation into the episode of classical references, for example, to the 'sour ferryman' and the kingdom of 'perpetual night', does not quarrel with the essentially Christian experience to which Clarence testifies; according to Clemen, the episode follows the tradition (perhaps specifically Senecan in this case) of adopting as its model dreams from classical drama dealing with the conscience and judgement.[16] What is remarkable about the passage is its rich subjective, almost symbolic, colouring quite at odds with the rhetorical, objective utterances of other characters, and it is this development that generates the possibilities of a profounder conception of character than is observable anywhere else in the play. Moreover, the range of theme embodied in a new subtlety of poetry actually means that the complex meanings thus symbolically expressed are only partially assimilated with the rest of the play. The dream itself is a premonitory anticipation of Clarence's own death; his vision of an undersea world scattered with wrecks and skulls, a mordant vision of the grave. The juxtaposition of the earthly-precious in the shape of gems, and the rotten skulls is a grisly *memento mori*, recalling not only the transitoriness of life, but also the inevitability of death, the final arbiter of all value. Here men's skulls mock in death what in life men strive for; the idea certainly has a general relevance to the dreams of worldly power and ambition that motivate Clarence and Richard, and the ultimate meaninglessness of all such dreams; but it is not an insight the play otherwise concerns itself with, and indeed is not developed again as an idea in Shakespeare until Richard II embodies it in the notion of the 'antic' death, scoffing at state and grinning at pomp.

However, Clarence's dream is 'lengthen'd after life' (I.v.43), and on his descent into the kingdom of perpetual night he meets the spirits who pass judgement upon his soul. The accusing shades of his father Warwick and Prince Edward are actually the personified voices of his own conscience convicting him of perjury and murder, a fact which Clarence is able to recognize:

> Ah, Keeper, Keeper, I have done these things
> That now give evidence against my soul . . .
>   (I.iv.66–7)

The power of conscience to prefigure for the sufferer both the moment of his own death and the accusations of the Last Judgment was, as we have seen, well documented in the Pauline tradition of scholastic philosophy. Just as a scenario is exploited at the end of Robert Wilson's *Three Ladies*, and gives to the climacteric scenes of *Faustus* much of their power. In this case, the idea that the voice of conscience could be personified and its accusations embodied in the images of past sin is aptly illustrated in the following extract from Henry Smith, whose sermons were received enthusiastically by the London of Shakespeare's apprenticeship. On the sinner and his conscience he had this to say:

> Who can express that mans horror but himselfe?
> Nay, what horrors are they which he cannot
> expresse himselfe? Sorrowes are met in his soule
> as at a feast: feare, thought, and anguish, divide
> his soul betweene them. All the furies of hell
> leape upon his heart like a stage. Thought
> calleth to Feare: Fear whistleth to horror:
> horror beckeneth to despaire, and saith; come
> and helpe mee to torment this sinner. One
> saith, that shee commeth from this sinne: and
> another saith, that shee commeth from that sinne:
> so he goeth through a thousand deaths . . . [17]

Clarence's dream is an evocation to him of everlasting perdition, a result of his despairing soul which fears death because of what must seem inevitably to follow. His visionary hell comprises Furies, which at the bidding of Clarence's shadowy victims, will hurl him into torment, where a legion of foul fiends will environ him and howl in his ears. And yet of course, such terrors are merely hallucinations: however evil they may seem, the excoriations of conscience were held to be ultimately remedial, and its horrible visions merely analogies; analogies with a fairly wide currency at that. Perkins would have been ready with a very prompt diagnosis: 'heathen Poets', he says, '. . . have compared evill conscience to Furies pursuing men with firebrandes'.[18] Elsewhere he expounds the essentially positive function of such visions: 'though conscience bee thus tearmed evil, yet hath it some respects of generall goodnesse, in as much as it is an instrument of the execution of divine justice'.[19]

Thus for Clarence, the punitive element in his conscience certainly caused him to suffer the consequences of his wickedness in so far as he has offended against the execution of providence; nevertheless, the 'generall goodnesse' in such punishment appears not to have been entirely wasted. There is at least some hope in the 'deep prayers' with which he offers to appease God, that the contrition and repentance that charge his heavy soul will deliver him from the hell to which his own worst fears condemn him (I.iv.69).

Meanwhile, with the entry of the two murderers, the theme of conscience is again taken up, this time modulated in the half-menacing, half-playfully ironic argot that Shakespeare reserves for all his common conspirators. Conscience is comically objectified, somewhat in the manner of Launcelot Gobbo's musings upon the propriety of leaving his master's employ; but here the dialogue between man and the deepest stirrings of his soul is articulated in concrete images whose triviality does little to lessen the evident seriousness of the debate. Both are afflicted by the pangs of conscience; the second murderer, in whom the word 'Judgment' first breeds a disinclination towards the deed, appears the more tender-hearted (I.iv.105); yet neither is the first murderer altogether immune: 'Zounds, 'tis even now at my elbow, persuading me not to kill the Duke' (I.iv.140). Such monitory intimations of the inevitable results of sin are the only acknowledgement made in the play of a characteristic feature of conscience referred to in contemporary treatises and the sermons of Smith, Perkins, and others. Conscience had the power to anticipate the occasions of sin as well as to punish and accuse when its warnings were ignored. Thus, in *The Betraying of Christ*, Smith has this to say: 'There is a warning conscience, and a gnawing conscience. The warning conscience commeth before sinne: The gnawing conscience followeth after sinne. The warning conscience is often lulled a sleepe: but the gnawing conscience waketh her againe.'[20]

The second murderer actually demonstrates the meaning of this when he urges his companion not to betray his scruples to the Duke of Gloucester: 'Nay, I prithee stay a little: I hope this passionate humour of mine will change. It was wont to hold me but while one tells twenty' (I.iv.113–15). In convincing his companion that his warning conscience is lulled asleep, and that his passionate humour had indeed changed, the second murderer offers a lengthy diatribe on the material disadvantages of meddling with conscience:

> I'll not meddle with it; it makes a man a coward. A man cannot steal, but it accuseth him; a man cannot swear but it checks him; a man cannot lie with his neighbour's wife but it detects him . . . every man that means to live well endeavours to trust to himself, and live without it.
>
> (I.iv.128–38)

The equation of conscience with cowardice, and its corollary that worldly success entails trusting to oneself, are here offered as a proleptic counterpoint to the Machiavellian creed enunciated in Richard's 'Conscience is but a word that cowards use', and the solitary individualism to which that condemns him. The terrible consequences that the 'gnawing conscience' unerringly visits upon the upholders of such a creed are aptly illustrated in the remorse of the second murderer immediately following the death of Clarence, persuading us that those consequences will be no less terrible in the case of Richard. Like Brackenbury, who tries to shirk the burden of guilt by ignoring the meaning of his orders, the second murderer attempts in vain to renounce his part in the crime by relinquishing his blood-money:

> A bloody deed, and desperately dispatch'd.
> How fain, like Pilate, would I wash my hands
> Of this most grievous murder.
>
> (I.iv.261–3)

Clarence's own attempts to avoid becoming the victim of 'this most grievous murder' are advanced on different levels, their earlier confidence giving way to the piteous appeals of a frightened man. At first Clarence addresses his assassins in the clipped, authoritative tones of patrician hauteur: 'I charge you'; 'Erroneous vassals' (I.iv.178,184); and his arguments, pitched at an abstract and theoretical level, remind the murderers that his offence has not been tried by 'lawful quest', and that shedding his blood will imperil that final redemption bought for them by 'Christ's dear blood' (I.iv.173,179). That they come by command of the king is not sufficient: they will none the less be spurning at the edict enshrined in the 'table' of the King of Kings, who holds 'vengeance in His hand' for those that commit murder (I.iv.185,188). But the murderers counter this deftly by pointing out that if God made of Clarence a 'bloody minister' to strike dead Prince Edward, the more likely is their deed to represent God's vengeance upon Clarence for breaking His Law in 'such dear degree' (I.iv.209,199). Such claims to the administration of divine justice are, of course, equivocal. As Sanders rightly points out, though Clarence deserves to die, his murderers are not thereby justified in killing him;[21] at the same time, notwithstanding the wrongness of what they choose to do, the operations of providence will be fulfilled inasmuch as they act only by its permissive power. The point confirms that made in a previous context; God here merely suffers, rather than identifies himself with, the acts of private vengeance meted out one to the other by the 'wrangling pirates' of York and Lancaster in their discreditable feud. To do so would be needlessly to desecrate the ends served by such profane means; as Clarence points out, God

> needs no indirect or lawless course
> To cut off those that have offended Him.
> (I.iv.207–8)

The only unequivocal expression of God's displeasure is in the punishment Clarence's God-given conscience has already dealt him; just as the only unequivocal instance of his intervention is the direct aid he gives to his 'captain' Richmond in service against 'God's enemy', Richard (V.iii.253).

Having cited in vain the claims of justice both temporal and divine, Clarence now in desperation throws himself upon the mercy of his assassins, appealing to their consciences and invoking brotherly love, in exculpation first of his own misdeeds (done 'For Edward, for my brother, for his sake', I.iv.201), and then ironically as a guarantee of the reward for his life that Richard's 'kindness' will cause him to offer them. Little does Clarence realize that Richard's kindness has the blighting effect of 'snow in harvest', while his brotherly love is of the sort to deliver Clarence from this earth's thraldom to the joys of heaven – whither, without very much more ado, his murderers proceed to assist him.

Such is the relatively sophisticated inner exploration of the afflictions of conscience in Clarence, in which past sin is expiated as a consequence, not so much of divine retribution, as of an internal process whereby the soul recognizes its own alienation from the Natural Law. The questions thus explored here will probably be found to be broached rather more tentatively in the case of Richard, since, for reasons we shall return to later, his development is to some extent held hostage to the ascendant fortunes of a later age. Nevertheless, the implications of the Clarence scenes ought perhaps to prompt a closer scrutiny of the presentation of Richard's character, since it is frequently urged that the belated revelation of conscientious scruples in the soul of one hitherto apparently altogether soulless is dramatically superfluous.

It is certainly true that Holinshed's conception of Richard, derived almost intact from More's scheming Machiavellian monster, seems to have imposed itself upon Shakespeare's mind during the first three acts of the play, almost to the exclusion of the prototypical, psychologically more realistic Richard of Gloucester in *Henry VI, Part III*. There the dramatist had been more concerned to render an account of the origins of evil with some particularity, managing to suggest the psycho-social conditions in which envy, bitterness and thwarted pride can generate a monstrous perversion in human nature. In *Richard III*, however, More's Machiavellian supervenes; and moreover, to this Shakespeare had added a comic dimension taken from the moralities: the stage convention of the Vice. As Wilbur Sanders puts it, Richard, like Vice, depends for his very existence 'on a kind of conspiratorial collaboration with the audience' – a relationship established in the early soliloquies where his 'tongue-in-cheek self-exposition' and 'the patronizing airs of a master-of-ceremonies' combine to make him less humanly vulnerable than any mere man could be.[22] Critics who attend too exclusively to Richard's incarnations as Vice and Machiavel (Sanders is not one of these) come dangerously close to supposing Shakespeare to have been merely the prisoner of his sources; that he simply accepted the externally conceived account of the character up to its termination in More, at which point the morality pattern of the play takes over, entailing a slight tendency to internalize the meaning of events, so that Richard can be made to undergo the formal capitulation to the claims of conscience that the convention required. Once again, we find that the historical account coordinates rather clumsily with the morality pattern, though undoubtedly both bore heavily upon Shakespeare's mind as he wrote *Richard III*. And yet, at the same time, there is surely traceable a parallel Shakespearean conception of character, honoured in the Clarence scenes and at least partially endorsed in the post-coronation scenes of the play; a conception, indeed, originally vouchsafed in *Henry VI, Part III*, where Richard first makes an impact.

In the trilogy, there is clearly a marked contrast between the defective conscience displayed by Richard, and the wholly conscienceless, unhesitatingly self-interested conduct displayed by Henry's ruthless nobles. An almost psychopathic state of mind is evidenced by the speeches of Cardinal Beaufort and, interestingly enough, in the soliloquies of Richard's own father, York. In the latter, a primitive single-minded ambition is enunciated uncomplicatedly as part of a psychological process whose genesis Shakespeare is unconcerned to explore; but Richard's own lust for the crown, though asserted with the same claims to ruthlessness and treachery, is clearly a more complex phenomenon, betraying a remarkable vulnerability entirely consistent with a later manifestation of the same weakness on the eve of Bosworth. Here Richard's musings have an almost dream-like quality:

> And yet I know not how to get the crown,
> For many lives stand between me and home:
> And I, – like one lost in a thorny wood,
> That rents the thorns and is rent with the thorns,
> Seeking a way and straying from the way;
> Not knowing how to find the open air,

But toiling desperately to find it out –
Torment myself to catch the English crown . . .
                    (*3HVI*, III.ii.172–9)

Even more remarkable is the passage which that follows, in which eloquent testimony is given of the extent to which Richard's lust for the crown is but a perverted expression of a human need for love frustrated by his terrible deformities, a compensation for the love that forswore him at birth, and a revenge upon corrupted nature:

I'll make my heaven in a lady's lap,
And deck my body in gay ornaments,
And 'witch sweet ladies with my words and looks.
O miserable thought! and more unlikely,
Than to accomplish twenty golden crowns.
Why, Love forswore me in my mother's womb:
And, for I should not deal in her soft laws,
She did corrupt frail Nature with some bribe,
To shrink mine arm up like a wither'd shrub;
To make an envious mountain on my back,
Where sits Deformity to mock my body;
To shape my legs of an unequal size;
To disproportion me in every part,
Like to a chaos, or an unlick'd bear-whelp
That carries no impression like the dam.
Am I then a man to be belov'd?
O monstrous fault to harbour such a thought!
                    (*3HVI*, III.ii.148–64)

The anguish and bitterness displayed here is of course Shakespeare's answer to the Renaissance belief in the notion that outer seeming predicated inner being; he does not so much contradict it as qualify it by demonstrating the intense malignity with which the emotionally deprived are likely to expend their pent-up resentments upon a nature which has so cruelly cheated them. Richard's conception of himself as monstrous has been confirmed in him ever since his birth, in the fear and loathing of the women who attended his mother, and her own sense of outrage at his very existence:

The midwife wonder'd, and the women cried
'O Jesu bless us, he is born with teeth!'
And so I was, which plainly signified
That I should snarl, and bite, and play the dog.
                    (*3HVI*, V.vi.74–7)

His mother's detestation of him since then appears to have been unremitting.

From *Richard III* we learn that his childhood has been almost classically delinquent:

> Thou cams't on earth to make the earth my hell.
> A grievous burden was thy birth to me;
> Tetchy and wayward was thy infancy;
> Thy schooldays frightful, desp'rate, wild and furious . . .
>
> (IV.iv.167–70)

Such is their mutual antipathy that Richard does not hesitate to calumniate his mother's chastity in starting a rumour to the effect that Edward's sons' claim to the throne is void through a species of double illegitimacy.

So it is that the notion of the conventional villain, conveyed to the Renaissance imagination by the correlation between wickedness and physical deformity, is subtly undermined in Richard by Shakespeare's concern to suggest how the 'tetchy and wayward' infancy, and the 'wild and furious' boyhood, has resulted in the consummate Machiavellian that is Richard III. For the consequence of these insights is that Shakespeare succeeds in retaining some shred of sympathy for his protagonist, allowing an audience, on one level, the queasy gratification of being made accessory to evil, but at the same time permitting them the suspicion that much of the vaunting hysteria of Richard is no more than a cry to be recognized, an appeal for a just hearing:

> And therefore, since I cannot prove a lover
> To entertain these fair well-spoken days,
> I am determined to prove a villain . . .
>
> (I.i.28–30)

Reference has been made elsewhere to the fact that these lines show how Richard, though naturally disposed towards evil by a crippled body, actually subordinates his will to the pursuit of evil as an act of free choice. Yet if his natural disadvantages do not extenuate his moral degradation, nevertheless Richard repeatedly offers them as such; for his 'villainy' is offered the excuse of not being able to 'prove a lover'.[23] Even if we cannot accept the justness of the balance, the fact of the appeal itself has a great deal to do with our feelings for his common humanity. More than this, a soliloquy which affects to prove that Richard 'ought' to be bad, whether to compensate for fate's injustices, or because the arts of peace are beyond his capacity, suggests a mind not wholly at ease with its own inclinations – in short, a conscience.[24] Even in the first part of *Richard III*, then, when striving most to be a man without a conscience, Richard succeeds only in appearing to be so, since the very stridency with which he claims immunity from conscience betrays his lack of success. What ought to make us less likely to overlook this and, on the contrary, to expect the collapse at the end, is that he is contrasted with every hired murderer, with Edward and with Buckingham, all of whom are conscience-stricken while he remains apparently unmoved. But the hysterical self-assertion, the contempt for his victims, the arrogant sense of isolation, above all the intoxicated zest for histrionics, all are features of a defensive carapace which begins to disintegrate shortly after Richard's coronation.

At this point Shakespeare, undoubtedly released to some extent from the imaginative restraints of his sources, begins to document an almost dialectical pattern of moral disintegration in Richard, perceived as an occasional glimpse into inner turmoil, followed by a hard sudden reversion to egocentric nerveless invulnerability. Hence the plot to murder the Princes is urged upon Buckingham somewhat apprehensively, with Richard betraying a fastidious disinclination even to name the deed he would execute, begging the approval that his own conscience will not supply. The extent to which that conscience is still active has earlier been made clear by the Lady Anne:

> For never yet one hour in his bed
> Did I enjoy the golden dew of sleep,
> But with his timorous dreams was still awak'd.
> (IV.i.82–4)

But immediately, the momentary hesitation revealed in dialogue with Buckingham is hastily obliterated; no more shall the duke be 'neighbour' to his counsels, and Richard's doubts are submerged in ever more frenzied plotting.[25] But within a short time he is brought up short again; the deeds commended by policy do not commend themselves so readily to conscience. Moreover, Richard begins to perceive the ineluctible reactive pattern by which 'bloody instructions' recoil upon the perpetrator in accordance with the Natural Law:

> Uncertain way of gain! But I am in
> So far in blood that sin will pluck on sin;
> Tear-falling pity dwells not in this eye.
> (IV.ii.63–5)

Once again, the momentary hesitation, the temporary access to remorse, is stopped up by the somewhat unconvincing stridency of the last line, a stridency made even less convincing by the subsequent interview with Tyrrel, and Richard's characterization of the Princes as 'Foes to my rest, and my sweet sleep's disturbers' (IV.ii.72).

The growing dissolution of Richard's confident persona, his flagging morale, is implied in a series of oblique touches by which Shakespeare demonstrates the King's growing ineffectuality. The triumphant finesse with which the wooing of Anne had been conducted, is paralleled by the somewhat less adroit wooing-by-proxy of the Princess Elizabeth. Whereas before, obstacles in his path had seemed to provide a stimulating challenge to his ingenuity, now the accumulating reports of rebellion jostle a pre-occupied Richard into an irritated incompetence. Catesby is a 'Dull unmindful villain' for omitting to carry out instructions he has not been given (IV.iv.445); Ratcliffe's orders are changed arbitrarily for the reason, merely, that 'My mind is chang'd' (IV.iv.456); while the third Messenger is struck for bringing what turns out to be good news. These are the actions of a man the inner turmoil of whose mind has up to this moment only been glimpsed; the inescapable dramatic logic of both the inferences urged upon us by the action, and by what has been covenanted in the Clarence scenes, is now towards the development of Richard's character on a profounder level, and a treatment of conscience not just more thorough, but capable of being assimilated with different levels of the play's meaning.

In contrast with Clarence's dream, Richard's is highly formalized and schematic, the ghosts conveying their messages in a rhetorically symmetric pattern significantly reminiscent of the choric utterances of the women. There are, it is true, similarities with the earlier dream sequence: Richard's past sins also seem to have taken on visual shape, in order to torment the conscience of a man considerably more guilty than Clarence. One is drawn irresistibly to the conclusion that Shakespeare is here attempting simultaneously to redeem obligations incurred by the ambivalent nature of the play's structure. The logic of history seems to require that the ghosts function as part of the same order of divine providence as the lamenting dowagers, and as such their choric refrain is pitched at the same tonal frequency. In this scene the possibility that they have some objective validity as agents of the transcendental scheme remains conjectural; Shakespeare clearly felt the necessity of showing here at the end of his play, that Richard's damnation coincided with England's salvation at the hands of Henry Tudor, and hence makes the same ghosts appear to both. At the same time, the concurrent logic of the play as tragedy induces Shakespeare to permit a coexistent possibility: that an apparition existing outside of a conscience-stricken mind could, without losing its reality, be simultaneously symbolic of conflict within the mind of the sinner. Accordingly, while other victims (Hastings, Buckingham) offer valedictory confirmation that their deaths fulfil the inexorable exactions of nemesis, Richard's ghosts never mention revenge, nor does Richard ever refer to his own death as just such a fulfilment of the curses of Margaret or Anne.

The soliloquy following the dream can probably only be acted satisfactorily as a distraction, with Richard only half-awake and still subject to the afterglow of nightmare horror, which he attempts desperately to shake off. Though still in the rhetorical mode of the dream, it forms in both content and style the strongest possible contrast to Richard's earlier soliloquies. There, Richard had established a qualified relationship with the audience, disclosing those aspects of himself that suited his purpose as scheming politician and comically gloating Vice; now the old confident bravura is only fitfully reclaimed, and Richard has clearly lost the dramatic advantage. In short, the soliloquy of direct address has given way to the soliloquy of introspection. For the first time, Richard is really alone; he strives in vain to repossess his old confidence, but vaunting egotistical assertion is constantly undermined by self-contradiction and confusion: 'Richard loves Richard, that is I and I' (V.iii.184). Whereas before we inferred a conscience to Richard, and felt the disintegrating of the defensive persona, now the process is actually demonstrated by which 'I' and 'myself' divide and fall into confusion and evasiveness. No matter that Richard fights desperately to repress it, his defences crumble before the compulsions of conscience: 'Fool, of thyself speak well! Fool, do not flatter' (V.iii.193). Conscience, reviled as a coward at the commencement of the soliloquy, now recoils upon him, delivering its accusations in an overwhelming babel of voices, multiplying the villainies of Richard's nature in 'a thousand several tongues'. As W. H. Clemen remarks, the inventory of Richard's sins 'mounts to a climax in a dramatic image reminiscent of the allegorical style of the late Middle Ages':[26]

> Perjury, perjury in the highest degree;
> Murder, stern murder in the direct degree;
> All several sins, all us'd in each degree,
> Throng to the bar, crying all, 'Guilty! Guilty!'
> (V.iii.197–200)

Exactly the same doctrinal assumptions lie behind this image as were noticed in the similar instance of Clarence's dream; the image takes its strength from the fact that Richard is living out in advance the circumstances of his own damnation, and that conscience had the capacity not only to anticipate for the sinner the Last Judgment, but once having arrived, there to accuse him of his sins. Thus Perkins:

> when a man dies, conscience dieth not: when the body is rotten in the grave, conscience liveth and is safe and sound: and when we shall rise againe, conscience shall come with us to the barre of Goddes judgement, either to accuse or excuse us before God.[27]

In his oncoming despair, Richard approaches the nearest he can be permitted to full moral self-realization. Certain ethical truisms have indeed come full circle. Conscience, for so long jauntily repressed as a 'word that cowards use', now induces terrors which Richard can only flee by plunging desperately into battle. The terrible pathos of the boast 'I am myself alone' is answered in the despairing cry wrung from him in final recognition of his tragic isolation:

> There is no creature loves me,
> And if I die, no soul will pity me –

> And wherefore should they, since that I myself
> Find in myself no pity to myself?
>
> (V.iii.201-4)

And yet, as a tragedy, *Richard III* is attenuated, docked of full significance because the didactic necessities of history in the end make it impossible that Richard should undergo any regenerative or expiatory process.
Upon his unredeemed degeneracy, after all, rested in large measure the
claims of the Tudor settlement. Consequently, Shakespeare has effected
a compromise; and the limited significance allowed in the soliloquy to a
tragic exploration of guilt and conscience, we can see in retrospect to have
been qualified still further by the rhetorical style of the soliloquy, the
fragmentary rhythms of internal debate in Richard's soul being the direct
correlative of the ritualized thematic utterances of the ghosts. What is
averred by the content of the soliloquy – the warring selves suggesting the
nature of a psychological insight – is actually retracted by its style, where
the antinomies of truth and falsehood, conscience and the evil soul, are
couched in the neat and formal register by which Shakespeare elsewhere
intimates the providential order at work.

As a consequence, the implications of the tragic stature momentarily
conferred upon Richard by the soliloquy, are hastily disavowed. He is
made contemptible, taking refuge in eavesdropping. The lesson that 'sin
will pluck on sin' has been well learnt: the meaning of a crown got by
plotting the downfall of others is that others for the same goal will similarly
plot his: 'bloody instructions' indeed, returning infallibly to 'plague th'
inventor'. Even his final courage is a perseverance in evil from which his
conscience cannot deter him, and for which he must therefore be finally
damned, and moreover seen to be so beyond any doubt, in order that the
regeneration of England may be confided to the divinely sanctioned Henry
Tudor.

Consequently, it is the transcendental order which supervenes at the
end of the play, in bowing to which necessity Shakespeare discharges his
obligations to the didactic purposes of his sources, and finishes the task
he began with in *Henry VI*. And yet, like Prince Hal, he almost manages
to pay several debts he never promised: those incurred by the emergent
tragic order shadowed forth in a profounder exploration of man's relation
to evil. This conception released him to a consideration of justice organically conceived, by which man is punished by his sins, rather than for his
sins, and by which the Old Testament theology of the Chroniclers is
augmented by a scholastic conception of the Natural Law, and an examination of causes located primarily in the affairs of men. It is this system of
moral order, only imperfectly actualized here, which comes eventually to
sustain the universe of Shakespeare's mature tragedies; an order where

infringement is witnessed to in the commonwealth as an act of purgative reaction, and in the individual as an act of conscience.

4

Hamlet

In *Richard III* the exploration of conscience is tentative and inconclusive, vitiated to some extent by an ambivalent conception of moral justice working itself out in a dramatic form itself lacking any clarity of definition. Richard himself is very largely an unhesitating sinner, and only becomes conscious that he is so after a very lively career in crime; there is little evidence of that warning conscience so eloquently described by Henry Smith, and identified by Burton as the '*dictamen rationis*', and this in turn is so because the entire problem of moral choice anterior to the occasions of sin, so profoundly analysed in *Hamlet* and *Macbeth*, there remains untouched. The similarities between all three plays are, of course, numerous. In each, the justice that works, though divinely sanctioned, is first and foremost an expression of the Natural Law, immanent within all created things which causes them to react expulsively to evil. In the public external order, this reaction manifests itself as a multiple concatenation of events and circumstances which forces evil to recoil upon its perpetrator; while in the little world of man, the reaction expresses itself psychologically, either in rioting passions which usurp the sovereign reason, or in the supervenient lacerations of conscience. Thus in all three tragedies, treason and murder reduce a kingdom to chaos, but out of that chaos are forged the instruments of order and restitution, a dialectic which ensures that the usurper, whoever he may be, is killed by the forces that his own evil rouses against him. By a contingent process, that usurper suffers the horrible tortures of the mind that are the inward consequences of such evil. The great difference between them is, of course, the emphasis with which these inward manifestations are explored in the mind of the *protagonist*. It will be recalled that, in the case of Richard, our impression of an organic conscience, reflecting any sort of moral catalysis in the individual, had necessarily to be underwritten imaginatively by our sense of an emergent moral pattern described in the public and external world of the body politic. In *Hamlet*, that pattern is still present to the imagination, though subordinated to a profound and deeply penetrating exploration of the conscience in the practical act of moral discrimination; yet it is precisely a curious, one might almost say, anomalous, absence of any real remorse in the prince that differentiates the play as a study in moral conflict, and it is in this sense untypical of the series with which we have to deal. Only in *Macbeth* is the full process enacted, from choice to consequence, from *synderesis* to *syneidesis*; only here shall we find the protagonist evincing a clear-sighted and conscious awareness of the implications of the evil he chooses, and being tormented thereafter by the worm of conscience.

That in *Hamlet* we are witnessing a conflict of conscience immeasurably more complex than, but not essentially unlike, those experienced by the universalized heroes of the Morality tradition, is a critical assumption by now largely unexceptionable.[1] According to this school of thought, and by extension a major premise of this argument, Hamlet's predicament evokes that of man, in that not only is he confronted by a fallen world in which ancient evil bafflingly presents an aspect of goodness, but, in being called upon to oppose that evil, is in the end mortally disabled by its mysterious intimacy with his own soul, the 'dram of eale' which insidiously corrupts man's virtues and undermines the integrity of his motives. In addition, the realities upon which Hamlet is obligated to act are purveyed to him in riddling terms disquietingly in tune with the play's pervasive metaphysical uncertainties and, moreover, powerfully evocative of that other supernatural soliciting in *Macbeth*:[2] the Ghost's command indeed commences in a truth – that concerning the circumstances of the King's murder – but ends with an unholy exhortation to revenge, the implementation of which would seem inescapably to 'couple hell' (I.v.93). Part of Hamlet's 'problem' is that, in so far as he can be said to be aware of a moral scruple which inhibits action, he consciously perceives it in terms merely of the first of the Ghost's intimations, and not of the second; that is, he sees only the Ghost's revelation of evil as problematic, rather than the means by which that evil is to be countered. Consequently, he embarks upon an elaborate attempt to identify the Ghost and the truth of its witness, by means of *The Mousetrap*; yet this by itself does not unravel the ethical ambiguity implicit in its enunciation of a barbarous moral principle, the *lex talionis*; and it is this latter ambiguity which Hamlet, though his determination to act in the face of it is evidently confounded throughout by some uncomprehended scruple, nevertheless utterly fails to address, or at any point consciously to analyse in terms of an inner conflict.

Thus it has seemed necessary for the large number of critics venturing, in the wake of Rosencrantz and Guildenstern, to pluck out the heart of Hamlet's mystery, to attribute his delay – a prevarication that continues to puzzle his will until well after the *experimentum crucis* of *The Mousetrap*

– to a 'conscience' which never fully objectifies in the Prince's soul the damnable consequences of a course so dubiously congruent with his own base passions. In other words, Hamlet's mystery is in greater or lesser degree impenetrable, coexistent with a moral void at the centre of his consciousness. He is either the victim of gross self-deception, through which, in John Lawlor's words, he 'never penetrates his inability to be the avenger';[3] or he is permitted the obscure and half-realized awareness that by his actions, for example, he has 'forfeited the role of God's minister . . . and . . . become instead a scourge',[4] an insight which likewise presumably never hardens to the status of an explicit judgement. One or other of these propositions is, broadly speaking, admitted by those critics who share in the assumption that Hamlet's conscience in some way inhibits his 'native resolution'; Catherine Belsey, for example, appears to subscribe to the latter consensus when she argues that Hamlet's ethics are more subtle than those of the play's other revengers, and that, in some sense, he 'sees' the ambiguity of his position,[5] while never consciously debating it; McAlindon, on the other hand, places himself squarely in the former camp in pointing out the Prince's moral, logical and rhetorical confusion, and in demonstrating how 'unconscious equivocation' contributes to his undoing.[6] The phrase aptly describes the utterances of some critics: a momentary confusion on Eleanor Prosser's part, for example, whether conscious or not, allows her to have the best of both worlds, at one point assuring us that Hamlet 'knew' that his own personal motives were evil in origin,[7] and at another that he is 'blind' to the shifting contradictions in the reasoning by which he takes Fortinbras to be a moral exemplar.[8]

Allowing, of course, for differences in emphasis, all these critical statements attempt to account for a curious dislocation in Hamlet's psyche, by which he appears in some degree obliquely to recognize his passionate, crudely self-castigating soliloquies for what they are, yet invariably responds to them as good; and further than this, to describe a conscience which on the one hand apparently induces the Prince to blame himself for 'shirking a plain duty',[9] and on the other, afflicts him with an unassimilated scruple antithetical to it, the full implications of which he never consciously articulates. If, for the most part, these explanations fall short of complete illumination, couched, as they all too often are, in vague and anachronistic modern psychological jargon, it is largely to the extent that they have overlooked the fact that Elizabethan moral philosophy would almost certainly have construed Hamlet's confusion as a classic instance of a 'doubting' or 'erroneous' conscience, the aetiology of which condition originated, as we have seen, in medieval scholasticism, and was subsequently documented in, or indirectly influenced, a large number of sixteenth- and seventeenth-century treatises and devotional works already referred to. The contention of this chapter is that to analyse Hamlet's dilemma in the light of scholastic philosophy is not only to gain a clearer understanding into why what G. R. Elliott calls the 'unconfessed conflict of passion and morality'[10] in the Prince remains unconfessed, but also to reconcile that tragic variance by which ruthless savagery comes to be committed in the cause of right by one whose 'virtues else' are 'pure as grace' (I.iv.33); and perhaps above all to explain how it is that Hamlet's crimes – the butchering of Polonius, the sudden and unshriven deaths of Rosencrantz and Guildenstern – are attended by no sense of guilt, on the contrary, being seen paradoxically by the Prince as justifying his own 'rashness' and 'indiscretion' (V.ii.7,8).

An account of *Hamlet* which endeavours to analyse his predicament in terms of a moral struggle, the terms of which, because only partially discovered to his reason, throw his conscience into doubt and error, must naturally begin with the malign source of that confusion, the Ghost. The spirit which Hamlet sees upon the battlements of Elsinore in the dead waste of the night 'May be a devil, and the devil hath power/T'assume a pleasing shape' (II.ii.595–6) is a presentiment hauntingly present to his imagination until it is ostensibly abrogated by the *Murder of Gonzago*; and it goes without saying that a contemporary audience would have had no difficulty in understanding Hamlet's doubts of the Ghost as arising from quite ordinary and conventional beliefs in the possibility of fiendish juggling. Indeed, Shakespeare seems to have intended imaginatively to engage the beliefs of his audience at this level in the huddled, nervous colloquy between the sentinels in the first scene, as, harrowed with 'fear and wonder' (I.i.47), they speculate upon the nature of the apparition. To Horatio, it is from the very first inauspicious: not only does it bode 'some strange eruption to our state', but, charged by him significantly in the name of 'heaven' to stay and speak, it is manifestly offended, and stalks away (I.i.52,53). The uneasy inference he draws for his awestruck companions is that the Ghost is a portent of cataclysmic and cosmic disorder, an example of those unnatural harbingers which, like the stars appearing with 'trains of fire and dews of blood' before Caesar fell, always act as 'prologue to the omen coming on' and fatefully precede the passage of feared events (I.i.120,126). Hence Horatio pursues a second psychomantic encounter against his own better judgment, determining this time to 'cross' the illusion even in face of the possibility that it may 'blast' him, the further to divine its secret:

> If thou are privy to thy country's fate,
> Which, happily, foreknowing may avoid,
> O speak . . .

> (I.i.136–8)

The Ghost's reaction appears to confirm all the worst suspicions of its bewildered witnesses; upon the cockcrow, it starts, according to Horatio 'like a guilty thing/Upon a fearful summons/ (I.i.153–4); the implications of which observation are re-echoed in Marcellus's avowal that when the cock crows at the season of 'our Saviour's birth', the 'nights are whole-some', thereby, it seems, not congenial to such unhallowed and ungracious spirits as this appears to be (I.i.164,167).

The tentative conclusions reached by Horatio and the Watch in their distracted and extemporized attempts to discriminate the nature of the 'thing' they have seen, would accord substantially with the scholarly axioms propounded in contemporary pneumatological treatises, by which the Ghost would also be understood as wholly evil, an infernal illusion seeking to procure the damnation of the unwary. The evidence predicated by these treatises has been comprehensively documented by such scholars as Dover Wilson, B. L. Joseph, and Eleanor Prosser,[11] and, though mar-shalled to marginally different conclusions by each, is sufficiently well known not to require yet another rehearsal of its substance here. Suffice it to say that the occasion of the Ghost's appearance to Hamlet is emphati-cally not of the sort likely to be permitted by God; and biblical and other injunctions taught Elizabethans to identify as irredeemably cursed any person or thing which attempted to procure so gross a violation of the teachings of the Church. The Ghost's command, which finds so apt and tragic a response in Hamlet, runs absolutely counter to those teachings, founded as they were in the Old and New Testament ordinance, 'Ven-geance is mine, saith the Lord, I will repay.'[12]

It is against this carefully insinuated backdrop, replete with all the cautionary implications of the Ghost's first unpropitious visitation, that Hamlet's own interview with the spectre must be considered. Nothing concerning the identity of the Ghost is at this stage certain, of course; an audience, however possessed, like Horatio, of the atmosphere of premoni-tory foreboding that invests the first scenes, is likely to be disarmed, like Hamlet, of its more clamorous suspicions by the spectre's meretricious appeal to the Prince's tenderness, and confounded utterly by the spurious morality of its precept to 'Taint not thy mind' (I.v.85). Doubtless these illusory provisos, an attempt to sugar o'er with a saving grace the diabolic command to revenge, contribute to Hamlet's own confusion; but we should also notice how his initial passionate rush to identify the Ghost as that of his father – 'I'll call thee Hamlet,/King, father, royal Dane' (I.iv.44–5) – actually pre-empts in the Prince a rational process of appraisal, and is, moreover, subtly indicative of an emotional disequilib-rium infinitely vulnerable to the kind of temptations to which he is so dangerously exposed. Heedless, therefore, of the proverbial wisdom which warned that the Devil could quote Scripture for his own purposes; heed-less, too, of the commonplace so fatally ignored by Macbeth, that the instruments of darkness tell us truths only to betray us in deepest conse-quence, Hamlet, like Macbeth, accords to the Ghost not only a credence wherein lies its principal power to destroy him, but also a distorted belief in its claims upon him which insidiously endorses the latent desires of his own disordered passions. That Hamlet, overwhelmed by pity and love, should react at first towards the apparition as if it were his father's spirit, is understandable. Rather less so is his determination to speak to it in spite of his manifest awareness that it comes in questionable shape, and might as easily be a 'goblin damn'd' as a 'spirit of health' (I.iv.40). Yet still more ominously, he defies Horatio's warning that to follow it might be to cloud his brain with 'toys of desperation' (I.iv.75), placing in jeopardy his very sovereignty of reason. But the possibility that Hamlet's reason might already be to some extent jeopardized, and his mind tainted, by 'unmanly grief' and 'obstinate condolement' (I.ii.94,93) is one to which an audience has previously been alerted by Claudius. It is true that the unctuous platitudes are to a degree debased in the mouth of one who has shown himself all too ready to violate the laws both of heaven and nature in serving his own corrupt passions; yet the words none the less legitimately convict Hamlet of a will most incorrect to heaven, nature and reason in its impassioned opposition to the inevitability with which 'all that lives' must pass 'through nature to eternity' (I.ii.72–3).

But the sinister obverse of his embittered and melancholic refusal to accept as 'common' the death of his father, is his almost physical disgust and loathing for the 'satyr' who has replaced that father with such unseemly dexterity in the affections of his mother; a loathing at once enkindled and confirmed by the Ghost's revelation of absolute evil in his uncle, and further distilled to a black and leprous intent within Hamlet's soul by the damnable exhortation to revenge. 'Taint not thy mind' sounds a note of Christian forbearance harshly ironic in the circumstances; but it is the principal source of that confusion about the Ghost by which Shakespeare appears deliberately to contrive a pneumatological mystery for the sake of dramatic impact.[13] To act may be to enlist the 'host of heaven'; but the fugitive intuition that it might alternatively be to 'couple hell' (I.v.92,93), though it remains troublingly with an audience (and intermittently with Hamlet), is now obliterated by the Prince's hysterical resolve, leaving an abeyance of doubt into which is assumed, with a passionate conviction, the Ghost's commandment:

> And thy commandment all alone shall live
> Within the book and volume of my brain,
> Unmix'd with baser matter.
>
> (I.v.102–4)

But even if Hamlet is fully blinded at this point to the evil implications of his revenge motive, surely, it is argued, the Ghost's disclosure of 'something rotten' in Denmark imposes some sort of obligation upon Hamlet to act, both as the son of a 'dear father murdered', and as the princely executor of justice in a state whose King is become the fountainhead of injustice? To discuss what Hamlet ought to do in the circumstances, revenge being damnable, is to an extent otiose, since the answer resides in what he actually does in the final scene, when once he has rid himself of that passionate importunity raging in his blood, which ever urges him to 'sweep' to his revenge against his better nature. For some critics, it seems, any resolution of the tragedy in which Hamlet finally takes arms against Claudius is morally unsatisfactory, and they seek presumably to improve upon both the Prince's motives and the course of events, by canvassing for him other, more edifying, spiritual postures, such as 'creative mercy'[14] or 'Christian patience',[15] as the proper response to evil. The latter alternative, the course of stoic passivity which would leave Claudius, like Gertrude, to heaven, is in fact raised fleetingly by Hamlet, as in soliloquy he considers whether ''tis nobler' to suffer unresistingly an outrageous evil, and is rejected emotionally by him as by an audience, almost at the moment of recognition. Yet as an alternative it interestingly illustrates the terrifying consequences to the sinner in being thus left to heaven; for the justice that works retributively in the little world of man is executed in its most agonizing form, not through any human agency, but in those thorns that prick and sting the conscience; there, as Claudius discovers, there is no 'shuffling', and sin lies in its 'true nature' to condemn the soul.

Yet the meaning of events in *Hamlet* is wider in scope than this interior and spiritual account of justice will permit: Claudius may be punished by his conscience, but he is not thereby induced to repent so far as to yield up the 'effects' for which he did the murder. Moreover, he is a king, whose rank offence is the source of that corruption through which Denmark has become an 'unweeded garden', and our awareness that the restitution of order and justice has this public aspect, more than is bound by the 'single and peculiar life' (III.iii.11), is one with Hamlet's eventual recognition that Claudius is a 'canker' in 'nature' (V.ii.69), to be prevented from further evil. But in the cyclic and mysterious processes by which nature, operating according to its divinely instituted Law, itself will excise the canker represented by Claudius, there exists, as in all things, a 'readiness'. The ramifying contagion of evil initiated by Claudius's original crime, ineluctably corrupts and destroys each 'small annexment' and 'petty consequence' until, in working itself out, the whole commonweal is threatened by a 'boist'-rous ruin' (III.iii.21,22). Yet this mortal process of disease actually provokes a purgative reaction in the body politic, analogous to that organic principle by which evil confounds itself in the individual conscience, until Claudius is destroyed by a reflexive concatenation of events and circumstances which ultimately commends to the King's lips the 'poison temp'red by himself' (V.ii.333).

In this way, the operations of providence proceed through an entirely natural sequence of events, apparently the collateral and random effects of fortune coadjutant with man's free will, but at the same time, instinct with the great ethical bias by which the whole of creation conforms to the enactments of the Natural Law; so that the economy by which evil is employed to its own destruction, and by which 'foul practices' turn against themselves, though infinitely mysterious, expresses simultaneously a moral design publicly expressive of the glory of its Creator. Says Bishop Hall: 'Nothing more honours God, than the turning of wicked men's forces against themselves. There are none of his enemies, but carry with them their own destruction.'[16] And in the execution of divine justice, there inheres, for Bishop Hall as eventually for Hamlet, a readiness or ripeness, consistent with the maturation of wickedness to the point where it destroys itself:

> It is the wisdom of God, to take his best advantage: to suffer us to go on, till we should come to enjoy the fruit of our sin: till we seem past the danger either of conscience or punishment . . . but where he means utter vengeance, he lets men harden themselves to a reprobate sense-lessness, and make up their own measure without contradiction, as purposing to reckon with them but once forever.[17]

That this process is both publicly apprehensible and pre-eminently legal in character, is reflected elsewhere in Shakespeare: as Clarence recognizes in an earlier play, 'If God will be avenged. . . . /O know you, yet, He doth it publicly';[18] and Hamlet's initial fault is to circumvent the machinery of providential justice in rashly committing himself to an indirect and lawless course. In so far as Hamlet eventually resigns himself to the providential scheme, and divests himself of the passionate motive of revenge so guilefully enjoined upon him by a secretive Ghost, he becomes a willing minister of grace, his conscience 'perfect' (V.ii.67) and fully reconciled both to what he must do and the principles of Natural Law by which it must be done. An Elizabethan audience would look back, at the end of the play, upon the thread of apparent coincidence and chance occurrence, and acknowledge in the pattern by which Claudius is ensnared by his own machinations, a numinous and down-pressing sense of divine justice working through a series of natural agencies, of which Hamlet, duly tempered to the task, becomes one.

The foregoing digression will have justified itself if it offers, from a similar retrospective position, an insight into the 'cause in nature'[19] that delivers Hamlet's conscience over to confusion and error. For if it takes time for Hamlet to win through to a recognition of his role in the divinely instituted order of nature, it is partly that in placing upon him the tragic burden, the Ghost confuses his reason by appealing equivocally to nature and the violation of its laws:[20] 'If thou hast nature in thee, bar it not' (I.v.81). Ostensibly, Hamlet is being summoned to act in accordance with the laws which hold together the universal frame, to acknowledge the natural obligations of consanguinity, in requiting the 'foul and most unnatural murder' of a king and father, whose 'questionable' apparition is itself a manifestation, to use Hooker's words, of a 'singular disgrace of Nature'.[21] More confusing still is that the imperative thus to set right a time gone 'out of joint' (I.v.197,196) is plausibly addressed to Hamlet in the name of filial piety – 'If thou didst ever thy dear father love' (I.v.23) – sanctioned implicitly by the Decalogue. As Catherine Belsey points out, it is undoubtedly the specious conjunction of love, nature, and the commandments that generates Hamlet's conviction of heaven's interest in revenge.[22] Yet at the same time, the Ghost's command, uttered obliquely in the name of nature, entails a fateful paradox: a murder which was 'most foul, strange and unnatural' (I.v.28) will be revenged by acts themselves 'carnal, bloody, and unnatural' (V.ii.386).[23]

In this sense, the connotative ambiguities insinuated by the Ghost extend to that theological disparity between man's ideal nature and his fallen nature, and seem designed to enlist that original depravity in man which, intrinsically rebellious to the law of his reason, can make of him, in the words of Hooker, 'little better than a wild beast',[24] and indeed, has already made of Claudius a 'lord of beasts' (V.ii.87). Revenge – brutal, retaliatory murder – belongs to this unregenerate order; but the Ghost knows, as does Hamlet in a moment of truth, that the attraction of evil and the potency of its appeal lies in its being addressed precisely to that ancient frailty in man by which 'virtue cannot so innoculate our old stock but we shall relish of it' (III.i.117–18). That Hamlet responds to the Ghost's evil injunction as good is primarily, therefore, a mistake in his reason, for the mere fact that in the world evil is ever seeming-virtuous is no cause for not discerning it as such; for though, as Hooker says, 'if that be desired which is evil, the cause is the goodness which is or seemeth to be joined with it',[25] none the less 'There is not that good which concerneth us, but it hath evidence enough for itself, if Reason were diligent to search it out.'[26] And it is this original failure rationally to discriminate the moral implications of his commitment that contributes to Hamlet's chronic vacillation between half-admitted doubt and relative error in the conscience, and which in turn prompts the illogical synthesis of both heaven and hell in the task he will accomplish paradoxically as a scourge and minister.

Now the categories of the 'doubting' and 'erring' conscience were widely known to seventeenth-century divines and moral philosophers, and, indeed, have already been discussed at some length in the introduction to this study. William Perkins,[27] John Woolton,[28] Immanuel Bourne,[29] and William Ames[30] among others[31] express themselves largely on both topics, the substance of their remarks mainly conducing to illustrate the principle that a morally good action cannot exist unless it flows from a good conscience. Briefly, it may be recalled that Perkins declares flatly that whatsoever is done in or with a doubting or erroneous conscience is a sin,[32] while the rather more scholastically inclined John Woolton also adverts to the dangers of doubt and ignorance in the conscience: 'For if the least Scruple remaine in the minde, whether a man doe according to the motion of his Conscience, or agaynst it, he sinneth grievously.'[33] Puritan animadversions such as these were vigorously enunciated in contemporary casuistical literature because of what was felt to be the dangerous liability of the conscience to error; but the origins of the idea that the conscience might in any way be rendered defective in its apprehension of good and evil must be sought primarily in the formulations of school philosophy, which made a distinction between *synderesis* and *conscientia*, respectively the theoretical and practical aspects of conscience. A closer look at these formulations may be appropriate at this point.

This scholastic terminology was quite familiar to the Renaissance, and an act of conscience was widely understood to inhere in the syllogism by which the innate knowledge of the *synderesis*, imbued with universal propositions discernible in the natural order, was applied through the *conscientia* to particular cases. It will, perhaps, be remembered that for Timothy Bright, 'Sinteresis' is 'the ground, whereupon the practise of reason consisteth', the conscience itself restricted merely to 'applying, the assumption' in a syllogism;[34] a distinction adduced similarly by Burton, where he describes *synderesis* as 'the purer part of conscience', and con-science as that which is the 'conclusion of the *syllogism*'.[35] Some Puritan divines, such as Perkins, appear to prefer to disguise an overt philosophical debt to scholasticism by anglicizing its terminology; but his division of the reason into the '*Theoreticall*' and '*practicall understanding*', under the latter of which 'is conscience to be comprehended',[36] correlates quite plainly with the Anglican Robert Bolton's less qualified acceptance of the medieval theory, which he sets forth succinctly as follows:

> The whole and entire work of conscience, as you well know, out of the Schooles, consisteth in a practicall syllogisme: The proposition ariseth out of [*synteresis*], an habit of practicall principles, and general foun-taiens of our actions. The assumption is properlie [*syneidesis*], *conscientia*, an actual application of our knowledge to this or that particular object.[37]

It was precisely in order to explain how the conscience, albeit dispos-itionally inclined towards the ethical imperatives of the Natural Law, can nevertheless pervert and misapply its own precepts, that scholasticism originally posited the *synderesis/conscientia* distinction. Philosophically to pose the question whether or not a man's conscience was right or wrong could attract no simple answer; since if it were possible for it to be mistaken about basic general principles, then, as Aquinas suggests, there could be no stability or certainty about anything; accordingly, therefore, the moral basis of an action must be construed in terms of a dual sense of 'conscience' by which *synderesis* is never mistaken, but *conscientia* is susceptible to error. Philip the Chancellor gives an example of how a correctly apprehended universal principle may be irrationally misapplied to a particular instance, provoking a mistaken belief, in the individuals so affected, that they are conscientiously obliged to a particular course of action: 'Suppose', he says in the *Summa de Bono*,

> that it is written in *synderesis* that everyone who makes himself out to be the son of God, and is not, should die the death; but that this man (pointing to Christ) makes himself out to be the son of God, yet is not; it is then supposed: therefore he should die the death. What was contributed by *synderesis* was unchangeable and dictated only good, but this conjoined with what was contributed by reason dictated sin. So, therefore, *synderesis* plus the reason for a free choice makes *conscientia* right or mistaken.[38]

Here a false contingent premise contributed by the reason is subjoined to a basic deontic proposition, the object of the *synderesis*, which is then actualized in the *conscientia* to a mistaken conclusion. Philip is careful to explain, furthermore, the non-deliberative character of *synderesis*, distinguishing it from the act of practical reasoning by which conscience itself is properly to be understood: 'there is no deliberative judgement in *synderesis*, only executive. For it determines the good . . . without deliberation.'[39]

In these particulars, Philip's treatise is very largely confirmed by St Thomas Aquinas, who, in discoursing upon the relation of the *synderesis* to the reason, similarly conceives of it as a passive potentiality, exercised in apprehension merely, without active enquiry;[40] this latter activity is more accurately the province of *conscientia*, whose morphology suggests that it applies knowledge deliberatively: 'for', as he says, 'the noun "*conscientia*" signifies the application of knowledge to something, so that to be conscious of something (*conscire*) is, as it were, to know simultaneously (*simul scire*)'.[41] St Thomas, too, expounds upon the ways in which a false conclusion may be derived from a general deontic proposition, either by an erroneous inference, or by assimilating it with a false contingent premise, illustrating the latter by an example reminiscent of that afforded by Philip the Chancellor:

> When a false conclusion is drawn in some piece of reasoning from two propositions, of which one is true and the other false, the error in the conclusion is not attributable to the true one, but to the false one. Hence in that judgement by which the killers of the apostles thought that they did God a service, the sin did not come from the general judgement of *synderesis* that God's will is to be complied with, but from the false judgement of higher reason, which thought killing the apostles

to be pleasing to God. Therefore it does not have to be allowed that they were disposed to sin by the actualisation of *synderesis*.[42]

It therefore follows that the 'dispositional light' of *synderesis*, whose purpose he elsewhere confirms is to 'murmur back' in reply to evil,[43] can never be extinguished in respect of a general judgment. But the actualization of *synderesis* in the conscience, where it concerns a particular judgment, may be obstructed when 'the power of appetite or of something else to which one is subject so swallows up reason that, in choosing, *synderesis* does not apply the general judgement to the particular actualisation'.[44] Nevertheless, 'this does not extinguish *synderesis* without qualification, only relatively', since, as he says, its light 'belongs to the very nature of the soul, since it is in virtue of [this] that it is rational'.[45]

For both philosophers, then, error in the conscience resides in the process by which the innate, theoretical and non-deliberative apprehensions of the *synderesis*, being compounded with a false judgment of the reason, are distorted to mistaken conclusions in the conscience; and this distortion occurs typically when, as Aquinas says, reason's knowledge of the ultimate good is defective, or perverted by 'a vehement and inordinate apprehension of the imagination',[46] induced by the passions of the sensitive appetite.

Now this scholastic analysis appears almost exactly to define the origin and nature of Hamlet's moral 'dilemma' – a dilemma only imperfectly apprehended and never fully realized in his own conscience, owing to his signal failure ever to specify and test the hypothesis that private revenge is justifiable. Here, too, reason's knowledge of the ultimate good has been occluded by the opaque intimations of a diabolic illusion, by which those inordinate and murderous instincts towards his uncle, hitherto latent in Hamlet's soul, are at once sanctioned and inflamed by what appears to be a sacred duty. His reaction to the Ghost is immediate and passional, conducing to a false judgment of the reason by which Hamlet comes mistakenly to believe, after a momentary qualm, that he is conscientiously obliged by the 'hosts of heaven' to a course of bloody revenge. Or, employing scholastic terminology, we might say that the intuitive knowledge of his *synderesis*, which had before this been competent to recognize the deontic premise that the canon of the Everlasting is fixed against self-slaughter, and even at the moment of temptation couples the unadmitted suspicion of hell's intrigue, fails to actualize in his conscience a related canon against the slaughter of others, owing to a false contingent premise supplied by the reason which collocates heaven, nature and love in the demoniac logic of revenge. That this logic is never finally acted upon is attributable to a residual moral scruple remaining within Hamlet's soul, and intimated therein as a 'passive potentiality' and in 'apprehension merely' as a non-deliberative judgment of the *synderesis*; but this intuition is irrationally and habitually misapplied in the conscience, resulting in that erroneous conviction by which Hamlet feels ennabled by 'cause, and will, and strength, and means' to do what so inexplicably remains undone (IV.iv.45).

Consequently, Hamlet constantly goads himself towards the deed in soliloquies of passionate and guilty self-excoriation, and it is at such moments as these, when he feels himself to be spurred to revenge by duty, example, and opportunity, that his conscience is in a state of absolute error. At the same time, the 'dispositional light'[47] of *synderesis*, only relatively impaired by the wholesale forfeiture of conscience to error, exercises within him a latent and uncomprehended restraint, an involuntary antipathy to the dictates of his own fallacious reason, and which the latter, so long as it remains clouded by disordered passions, prevents Hamlet from fully objectifying to himself: 'I do not know', he confesses, 'Why yet I live to say this thing's to do' (IV.iv.43–4); while his inability to explain this prevarication either in terms of too much or too little thinking is further evidence of a lack of insight into his own motives.

On the other hand, on those occasions when the ambiguous nature of his commitment is admitted to a conscious process of dubitation in the practical intellect, and awakes in his conscience both the possibility of damnable abuse by the Devil, and the question 'Whether 'tis nobler . . . to suffer. . . . /Or to take arms against a sea of troubles' (III.i.57–9); on such occasions, and such scruples are subjected to intellectual scrutiny, they throw Hamlet's conscience into a condition of 'doubt' – a doubt which he attempts to appease by *The Murder of Gonzago*, and will later thrust aside altogether in the renewed impulse to revenge.

Thus Hamlet remains paralysed in the grip of a dilemma, the implications of which he only partially perceives, vacillating between the state of doubt and error in the conscience according to the ebb and flow of his passions, all of which derives from that original failure in reason to discern what Aquinas calls the ultimate good.[48] This hypothesis allows us to appreciate above all, not only the origin of that curious reversal of values which occasions in Hamlet a series of shocking brutalities towards Ophelia, Polonius, and Rosencrantz and Guildenstern, but also the paradox by which a prince, supremely sensitive to the principles of reason and religion, and whose intention palpably is to destroy evil, none the less comes so preposterously to further it.

The immediate aftermath of Hamlet's impetuous vow to 'remember' the Ghost, and to commit himself unreservedly to its commandment, ushers in the first of those recurrent lapses of time and passion in him, which so aptly demonstrate the psychological truth enunciated by the Player King: purposes of violent birth are but the *'slave to memory'*, and *'Most necessary'* it is indeed that *'we forget'* them (III.ii.183,187). Coincident with this waning of passionate intensity in Hamlet, is a gradual incipience of doubt in his conscience, a doubt overtly acknowledged in his 'To be or not to be' soliloquy and before that suggestsed in the recoil to a more temperate circumspection indicated in his determination to have 'grounds/More relative' as the basis for his actions (II.ii.599–600). But his initial intemperance, in relation to which his assumed madness is at once the symptom and the mask, has already begun to erode in the Prince the 'pales and forts of reason' (I.iv.28); and his histrionic repudiation of Ophelia in her closet, and subsequent denigration of Polonius as a 'tedious old fool', are merely the first perceptible stages in that tragic falling off in Hamlet that is signalled in his determination to alienate from his soul 'all forms, all pressures past' (I.v.100) – in short, all humane obligations incommensurable with that monadic and inhumane compulsion laid upon him by the Ghost. At the same time, the audience is alerted to the inauspicious consequences of such a course by being offered what Catherine Belsey has called a 'counter-image' of revenge:[49] the Prince's evocation of the *'hellish Pyrrhus'*, *'horridly trick'd/With blood'* (II.ii.459,453–4), infers to him a black purpose which ironically lends a *'tyrannous and a damned light'* to Hamlet's own (II.ii.456), and represents a correlative by which the values of revenge may be perceived and rejected. That this signification is lost to Hamlet – the 'poison of deep grief', as it were, urging him to identify with the victims of tyranny (Priam and Hecuba) rather than its perpetrator – seems plain in the long tirade of self-vilification that follows the departure of the players, where the accents of revenge – 'fatted all the region kites', 'slave's offal', 'Bloody, bawdy villain' (II.ii.575–6) – recapitulate in an ironic refrain the dubious imagery of his Pyrrhus speech. Yet once before we have been given evidence of a fleeting intuition, the confused and unacknowledged apprehension of his *synderesis*, that his chosen course has been commissioned as much by hell as by heaven; and the possibility now recurs, uttered once again as a cryptic and subliminal insight (II.ii.580), but this time actuating in him the cognitive awareness that 'The spirit that I have seen/May be a devil', and finally contributing a tangible doubt to Hamlet's conscience, where, in the fourth soliloquy, it is subjected therein to a conscious process of introspection.

But both the staging of *The Mousetrap* and the 'To be' soliloquy, considered as attempts by Hamlet to sift his own motives and allay his doubts, are undermined at the outset, respectively by that original misconception in his reason, and by the prior emotional commitment to revenge by which it is so chronically prejudiced. Hence Hamlet fails to detect the unsoundness of the argument by which he presumes to confirm the propriety of revenge by the tenting of guilt in his uncle:

> If his occulted guilt
> Do not itself unkennel in one speech,

> It is a damned ghost that we have seen,
> And my imaginations are as foul
> As Vulcan's stithy.
>
> (III.ii.80–4)

'If a do blench,/I know my course' (II.ii.593–4) is an assumption that Hamlet trusts to restore him to his previous certainties regarding the integrity of the Ghost and its revelation; and yet it is founded on the same illusory premise that spirits who tell the truth are necessarily honest, and that evil spirits are capable only of lies. In recognizing the power of evil to dissemble and 't'assume a pleasing shape', Hamlet is utterly unmindful either of its corresponding capacity to equivocate some truths as prologue to his own damnation, or, indeed, that the unkennelling of guilt in Claudius might not lessen the possibility that it is indeed a 'damned ghost' who solicits the Prince to the hideous implications of 'my course'. Hamlet thus excogitates the basis of his dilemma in terms merely of verifying injustice in Claudius, rather than examining the grounds upon which he himself proposes to execute justice.

Similar fallacies in reason are detectable in the tortuous and affective logic by which Hamlet attempts to ponder, in his new mood of self-restraint, the objective doubt that has secreted itself into his conscience. We are not to suppose that the doubt canvassed in this soliloquy is one provoked yet again by Claudius's as yet unsubstantiated guilt, since it would be dramatically superfluous to show Hamlet articulating an anxiety he has only just arranged to test; his scruple here is rooted more essentially, if elusively, in the question of taking arms at all. Nor do the dialectical alternatives of 'To be' or 'not to be' ostensibly include the possibility of suicide at the outset of Hamlet's discourse; none the less, the ethical implications of such a course intrude themselves halfway through the soliloquy, where they are evidently seen by the Prince as having an obscure bearing on his predicament. In this connection, we remember that Hamlet has, on a previous occasion, acknowledged the canon of the Everlasting against self-slaughter; and some unmediated recollection of this deontic proposition is evidently the moral absolute towards which his ratiocination, through a series of disjunctions and non-sequiturs, inevitably moves. What follows from the antinomies of 'to be' and 'not to be' are two divergent possibilities: 'to suffer', or to 'take arms' against, the diffuse vicissitudes suggested by 'Fortune' and 'a sea of troubles' (III.i.57,59). The latter proposition invites in Hamlet the speculation, converted to actuality by the passage of events, that opposition to his troubles might also entail his own destruction, diverting his thoughts thereby to the even more shadowy assumptions of 'not to be'. If to die is merely to sleep, oblivious of everything, then that is indeed a 'consummation/Devoutly to be wish'd' (III.i.63–4); but if there are dreams hereafter, then to suffer these carries a still more awful significance of 'to be', which gives Hamlet pause . . . and yet the dilemma is left in suspension, and the sort of opposition which might deserve the affliction of bad dreams remains unspecified. Instead, Hamlet shifts to a parallel: a fear of the life to come similarly deters those wretches who seek to escape in suicide the miseries of this one. Here he is on firmer ground; having himself rejected suicide in recognition of the Divine Law which condemns it, he is more clearly aware also of the relatedness of this injunction to that 'dread of something after death', the awesome consideration that 'makes calamity of so long life' (III.i.78,69).

By a subtle transposition of the argument, Hamlet appears to be struggling to define his own vaguely apprehended doubts, by comparing the taking of arms against others with what he knows more clearly to be the consequences of taking arms against oneself. In some unspecified sense, his conscience opposes the former just as it opposes the latter; but whereas on that previous occasion, the divine ordinance against suicide was clearly actualized as a judgement of the conscience, in this instance the cognate ordinance against revenge remains an obscure apprehension, sufficient merely to confuse the conscience and puzzle the will, but otherwise lacking intelligible definition. Even this partial and unconstituted doubt is potentially undermined by a predisposition of the emotions, all but swept away in the indiscriminate reversal by which the taking of arms in either dubious cause becomes an enterprise of 'great pitch and moment' (III.i.86); and Hamlet is suborned, once again by the inordinacy of his own desires, into making that disastrous equation of conscience with cowardice, which is ever the prelude, in Shakespeare's villains, to dispensing with it altogether, and the almost inevitable adjunct to further wickedness from the Morality tradition onwards.[50]

It is at this unpropitious moment, when the cautionary doubt in Hamlet's conscience is all but disorientated and overwhelmed in the counter-swell of bitter emotion, that Ophelia intervenes; and her appearance immediately provokes the flash and outbreak of that pent-up resentment and sex-nausea which his mother's remarriage has occasioned in him, and which now extends by association to all women. Unrestrained now by the 'pale cast of thought', and surrendering himself wholly to the poisoned impulses of his own 'foul imaginations', he vents upon the unsuspecting Ophelia the brunt of his anguished cynicism and disgust, making her the misplaced symbol for that pervasive spread of seeming-virtue and hypocrisy in Denmark against which Hamlet feels himself incoherently obliged to act. It is precisely to expose the iniquitous source of that hypocrisy and corruption, the smiling serpent Claudius, that Hamlet had arranged, in a more moderate moment, to show guilt, as it were, its own feature by means of *The Mousetrap*. And it is the necessity of attending to this that mitigates in him the whirlwind of his passion, begetting in its stead the temperance he commends to the players, and above all, awakening in his soul the oblique awareness, confided to Horatio, that the effort of coming to terms with evil will entail not the abject enslavement to passion implied by the nunnery scene, but a more harmonious commeddling of blood and judgement:

> Give me that man
> That is not passion's slave, and I will wear him
> In my heart's core, ay, in my heart of heart,
> As I do thee.
>
> (III.ii.71–4)

That a man representative of such an ideal, whose equanimity in the face of fortune's buffets and rewards argues the just conformity of passion to reason, should thus be affiliated to Hamlet's purpose, is itself a favourable augury, betokening a renunciation in the Prince of the self-imposed secrecy of his compact with the Ghost, and pre-figuring that final dispensation of events, the justice of which is witnessed by all; *both* their judgements now will join in censure of the tesimony of *The Mousetrap*. And yet, the evidence to be yielded by this means is itself inadequate, for, as we have seen, the device is predicated upon the inferred hypothesis that the authentication of guilt in Claudius will legitimize a murderous revenge in retaliation. Even as the performance proceeds, Hamlet's salacious banter with Ophelia, and the gloating and hysterical glee with which he descants upon the ironies of the play's 'argument', reveal how far his judgement is swayed by blood-inspired appetite and hopelessly compromised by the obsession which sits in brood upon his soul, like the raven, impatient for revenge.

Once Claudius has fallen into his trap, Hamlet will 'take the ghost's word for a thousand pound' (III.ii.280–1); he is restored, by the King's evident perturbation upon the talk of poisoning, once again to that objective certainty in the propriety of his mission, according to which he had believed that heaven, nature and filial piety cohered to endorse in his conscience a sacred duty of revenge. The spectacle of Claudius, 'frighted with false fire' (III.ii.260), is sufficient to erase his last conscious scruples on that score, and the false reasoning by which it does so infers to his conscience a palpable and gross error, so that the effect of its explicit moral judgments is paradoxically to sanction and confirm his rash and bloody deeds, and to engender, moreover, that guiltless and pathological conviction by which he believes that his worst brutalities are commissioned, not by his own violent passion, but by a divine and summoning justice. This conscience-inspired belief in his role of heaven's minister explains the hieratic tone of his interview with Gertrude, where he fulminates in the name of 'Heaven's face' and in defence of 'sweet religion' to procure in his mother a confession of her 'black and grained spots' (III.iv.48,47,90).

The deluded self-righteousness of his diatribe, and the moral myopia which provokes it, is ironically emphasized by the fact that it is conducted over the corpse of Polonius, the 'unseen good old man', whose officiousness in the wrong cause made him the victim of the Prince's impetuous sword-thrust through the arras. Hamlet's hideous blunder lies in its true nature for all except Hamlet to see; an audience instinctively applauds Gertrude's exclamation: 'Oh, what a rash and bloody deed is this!' (III.iv.27); but for her son, Polonius's death is just, the proper consequence of being too busy, and the inevitable fate due to a 'wretched, rash, intruding fool' (III.iv.31). As a result, Hamlet rails at Gertrude to repent and confess herself to heaven for an act which, at the worst, no more than merely 'blurs the grace and blush of modesty', in the meantime dismissing his own sin with a perfunctory gesture of regret – 'For this same lord/I do repent' – and laying to his soul the flattering unction that 'heaven hath pleasd it so' and that he must be 'cruel only to be kind' (III.iv.41,174–80).

In fact, Hamlet's offence is rank; like Claudius's crime, it, too, 'smells to heaven'; but unlike Claudius, Hamlet remains unassailed by any compunctious visitings of remorse, since the objective conclusions of his conscience are yoked to an original misapprehension in his reason as to what constitutes the ultimate good. A kindred distortion exists in that insidious inversion of moral values by which Hamlet plots with a cold malice to blow his two school-fellows at the moon, and later attributes to heaven's ordinance the adventitious set of circumstances which enables him to do so, sending them, without a shadow of regret, to a sudden and largely unmerited death, 'not shriving-time allow'd' (V.ii.47). But the consignment of souls to unshriven death is unequivocally the devil's business;[51] and the process by which Hamlet's erroneous conscience actually permits him to endow the perpetration of wickedness with a specious sublimity of motive, reminds us of those earlier words of Polonius, which gave so smart a lash to the unregenerate conscience of Claudius:

> We are oft to blame in this,
> 'Tis too much prov'd, that with devotion's visage
> And pious action we do sugar o'er
> The devil himself.

(III.i.46–9)

But for all that, the conscience of Hamlet is only imperfectly synchronized to the machinations of Hell; and the reappearance of the Ghost to whet the Prince's 'almost blunted purpose' is prompted by what Hamlet himself is able to acknowledge: that the shriving of his mother is merely a substitute for the 'important acting' of its 'dread command' (III.iv.109), a perfect opportunity to implement which he had unaccountably let slip on the way to Gertrude's closet. This continued negligence is partly conditioned by the anodyne of time upon passion; partly by the compulsive and misdirected exercise of that passion, by which Hamlet again unpacks his heart, this time with cruel dagger-words directed at his mother. But leaving the tragic and interjacent consequences of his attempts to do so, Hamlet's inability to act purposively upon the Ghost's command itself, nor, indeed, ever consciously to penetrate that inability, must be sought at a deeper level of his moral psyche; for we have also to explain how it is that, following the success of *The Mousetrap*, and wrought up by both passion and conscience to a renewed aptness for the deed, he nevertheless recognizes its obscure affinity with evil. For though the deliberative judgments of his conscience are, as we have seen, erroneously misapplied, and delusively coordinated moreover to a chthonian logic, still there remains that dispositional light by which the purer part of conscience, the *synderesis*, apprehends intuitively, *qua* passive potentiality as it were, the knowledge of Divine and Natural Law. Thus, immediately after the play-scene, the evidence of which has lent to the Ghost's words a specious reality, Hamlet rededicates himself to his terrible purpose in words whose very utterance implies the hellish source of that resolve, and unconsciously subverts his self-assumed role of divine justiciar:

> 'Tis now the very witching time of night,
> When churchyards yawn and hell itself breathes out
> Contagion to this world. Now could I drink hot blood,
> And do such bitter business as the day
> Would quake to look on.
>
> (III.ii.379–83)

Similar antithetical impulses explain, furthermore, the curious reasoning by which Hamlet chooses not to avail himself of the 'pat' opportunity provided by the King at prayer, to execute the 'bitter business (III.ii.382) for which he has just claimed so bloodthirsty a relish. Once again, the words themselves, as Dover Wilson has remarked, testify to the genuineness of Hamlet's hatred;[52] but from the outset, his intention is phrased conditionally[53] – 'Now might I do it' (III.iii.73) – which leads us in turn to expect the rationalization by which he summarily abandons it; rather less comprehensible, especially to an audience which has just witnessed Claudius's climactic struggle for his soul, is the frightful blasphemy inherent in that rationalization, by which Hamlet intends to ensure beyond doubt his victim's damnation. In reality, the impasse is a moral one, a manifestation of a conscience that has moved into error, and that seeks moreover to satisfy itself in the debased justice of revenge, rather than the 'hire and salary' of immediate execution; at the same time the intuitive knowledge of the *synderesis*, unactualized in the conscience, nevertheless latently and by implication deters him from what, in its true nature, is indubitably 'horrid'.

Other intermittent and unassimilated insights of his *synderesis* give rise to an odd series of paradoxes: in spite, for example, of the vaunted 'virtue' by which he catechizes Gertrude's 'vice' (III.iv.154), and in pursuance of which he intends to outmanoeuvre his school-fellows, none the less there is present in that intention the tacit recognition that in the encompassing of craft in Rosencrantz and Guildenstern, he will himself be marshalled to further 'knavery' (III.iv.207). In the same way, it contributes the con- fused and unadmitted possibility that in his precipitate butchering of Polonius, Hamlet may have been acting as heaven's 'scourge' rather than its 'minister' (III.iv.177). In every instance, that which satisfies his uncon- trolled passions and his mistaken sense of obligation, is articulated by his *synderesis* in vocabulary which latently and by implication condemns the horrid nature of what he contemplates. That Hamlet does not accede to this knowledge at a conscious level is at once a measure of how far passion has blinded his judgement, and a recognition by Shakespeare that the mode of this particular moral insight is passive and nondeliberative in character.

These discrepant and unrelated impulses in Hamlet's moral awareness are concentrated and taken up into his final soliloquy of self-exhortation, in which Fortinbras, leading the powers of Norway to gain a patch of ground having 'no profit but the name' (IV.iv.19), is consciously adopted as a moral criterion, a spur to right action, but with an admiration that converts implicitly to censure even in the course of expression. The spe- cious deductions and mistaken conclusions in the Prince's reasoning sug- gest that his conscience continues to be bound erroneously to the impos- tures of evil; and, indeed, the whole argument, in so far as it rests upon a syllogistic distortion, is remarkably amenable to the scholastic analysis of moral choice, where the knowledge of the good is perverted and con- founded in the syllogism by which the theoretical propositions of the *synderesis* are misapplied to particular cases in the conscience.

Hamlet admits unconditionally therefore, as to a universal axiom, the immorality that resides in the casual consignment of 2,000 souls to per- dition, merely to debate the question of a straw; and the same generalized denunciation governs his related perception of the expedition as a symp- tom of societal degeneracy, the 'impostume of much wealth and peace' (IV.iv.27). That this is indeed a reliable judgment is evident moreover in its congruence with Horatio's earlier deprecation of the 'lawless resolutes' of Fortinbras, 'Shark'd up' to any enterprise of 'stomach', and, like the universal wolf of Ulysses, productive only of discord and mere chaos (I.i.101–3). But this proposition, abstractly conceived, is fallaciously mis- applied to the practical instance of Hamlet's own 'dull revenge', by being combined with the false contingent premise that the uses of 'godlike reason' are somehow synonymous with the 'Excitements' of blood (IV.iv.33,38,58). Thus, by a diametric transposition of value, the 'imminent death of twenty thousand men' for a 'fantasy and trick of fame', led thereto by a 'delicate and tender prince', comes now to be perceived as an example 'gross as earth', an exhortation to all that 'fortune, death, and danger dare' (IV.iv.60–1,46,52). Moreover, such action is seen as the very purpose of man's existence, an attribute of reason sanctioned implicitly by him 'that made us', and the apotheosis of those whose spirit is by 'divine ambition puff'd' (IV.iv.36,49).

Thus, Hamlet's conscience arrives through the by now familiar misalignment of reason and heaven with the object of his 'bloody' thoughts, at an explicit approbation of what by 'cause and will and strength and means' he seems required to do. At the same time, the generalized premise with which the discourse was prefaced – in scholastic terminology, the innate apprehension of the *synderesis* – communicates nevertheless an unconscious coloration to the meditative arguments in which the ostensible conclusions of the conscience are urged; for to weigh the integrity of one's cause by analogy with the indiscriminate posturings of a Fortinbras, is perforce to reduce it to a mere 'eggshell' vanity, a 'fantasy and trick of fame', and the arbitrament, moreover, not so much of honour, as of 'Bestial oblivion' (IV.iv.61,40). These nescient ambiguities are epitomized, as is often pointed out, in the lines in which Hamlet attempts the elucidation of true greatness: if the meaning of greatness is, indeed, *never* to stir without great argument, it is in this sense incompatible with that greatness which resides in finding 'quarrel in a straw/When honour's at the stake' (IV.iv.55–6) – and wholly antithetical to the overt signification of the rest of the soliloquy. Yet the line as it stands, with its equivocal omission of the double negative, resonates ironically with Hamlet's evanescent deontic recognition of the vanity of debating thus all such questions of straws, and by implication queries whether the honour that insists that we do so, is not rather the 'impostume . . . That inward breaks', showing no cause 'Why the man dies' (IV.iv.27–9).

This question is never actualized as a palpable doubt in his conscience, of course; by that, Hamlet is 'shamed' out of his apathy, incited by the spectacle of futile courage into a like acceptance of the obligations of honour and of nature; yet, as Traversi remarks, the 'note of stagnation' evident in Hamlet's reasoning,[54] attributable in this study to the unreconciled and subliminal promptings of his *synderesis* (by which he 'does not know' why what he ought to do is so glaringly left undone), allows us to anticipate that the contrarieties in Hamlet's moral awareness will lead, after his sojourn in England, not to a recrudescence of his revenge motive, but to its continued atrophy.

If the prospect of Fortinbras's reflexive and compulsive violence commends itself subjectively to Hamlet as an excitement of 'reason' and 'blood', an audience is likely to respond to the same prospect with a more considered objectivity; remembering the sanguinary Pyrrhus, they will perhaps conclude further that an enterprise which requires the imminent destruction of thousands over a worthless plot not large enough to entomb the slain, represents, on the contrary, an utter divorce of blood and that same judgement without which we are in very truth, 'pictures, or mere beasts' (IV.v.86). That objective conclusion is only confirmed by the reintroduction, in symbolic counterpoint, of the play's other precipitate revenger, the young Laertes, whose rebellious haste at the head of a rabble subversive of the fabric of both antiquity and custom suggests his invidious moral affinity with Fortinbras and his 'lawless resolutes'. But by Laertes's case, we may see more clearly the portraiture of Hamlet's. Laertes is also pricked on by nature and by honour to revenge. Like Hamlet, he divests himself of all former vows and allegiances in dedicating himself exclusively to its accomplishment; but unlike the Prince, he will do so fully conscious of its damnable implications, electing in sensible despite of both the worlds to consign 'Conscience and grace, to the profoundest pit' (IV.v.132). Inasmuch as Laertes comprehends the evil nature of what he intends, the origin and commencement of his resolution has an unsanctified cogency of purpose that Hamlet's has ever lacked; but just because its satisfaction must in this manner knowingly shove by justice, conscience, and grace, Laertes's passion is even more vulnerable than Hamlet's to the 'wick and snuff' that will in time abate it. This Claudius recognizes, as he seeks to infuse Laertes's undirected energy with something of his own calculating and malignant intensity:

> That we would do,
> We should do when we would: for this 'would' changes
> And hath abatements and delays as many
> As there are tongues, are hands, are accidents,
> And then this 'should' is like a spendthrift sigh
> That hurts by easing.
>
> (IV.vii.117–22)

Just as Hamlet's conscience is inverted, ensnared to what it 'would' by his baffling encounter with hell and the devil, so, by a parallel process, evil is insidiously converted to moral principle in Laertes by the seeming virtue of Claudius, the potency of whose hypocrisy has delivered the whole of Denmark to the predicament, in the words of B. L. Joseph, of 'acting falsely in trying to be true'.[55] 'Now must your conscience my acquittance seal' (IV.vii.1) glozes Claudius in Laertes's ear; and in this manner, both hero and anti-hero are imposed upon by the counterfeit pretensions of evil to innocency, deluded alike by a satanic forgery of shapes and tricks, the dubious effect of which is to set a varnish on the impious course of retaliatory murder, and to sanctify a boundless revenge.

And yet Hamlet never at any stage consigns conscience and grace to hell; and in the aftermath of his sea voyage there is born in him a new sense of poised equanimity, partly coincident, no doubt, with that attrition of time upon the sharper edges of grief and passion, a predictable blunting of the shards of memory and thus of purpose, which it had been the object of the Ghost's visit to exacerbate. But in the meantime, as Eleanor Prosser has pointed out, the gravedigger's discussion places in the perspective of eternity man's ultimate responsibility to the Law divine, and reminds us that judgment hereafter will rest upon legal distinctions encoded in that law. Moreover, not only does Hamlet come now to accept as 'common' the universal fact, so greenly resisted heretofore, that 'all that lives must die'; he also arrives at a supervenient awareness in the light of this fact, of the vanity and ephemerality of all mundane striving. 'I am very proud, revengeful, ambitious,' Hamlet had confided to Ophelia, in a moment of savagely ironical self-deprecation (III.i.124–5); yet the graveyard comes now to infer to him that 'fine revolution' by which the ambitions of the politician, 'one that would circumvent God', are over-reached ultimately by the 'ass' who digs his grave, and even crimes like that of Cain, 'that hath the primal eldest curse upon't', will be revenged in the fulness of time by the fell sergeant, Death (V.i.76–91). The subsidence in Hamlet of virulent revengefulness and hatred is marked by his admission that he 'lov'd Ophelia', and the justice of his claim to be 'not splenitive and rash' is substantiated in fact by the chastened self-control with which he attempts to hold off the murderous attack of her grief-maddened brother.

Yet in spite of his accession to a renewed temperance, Hamlet's regeneration can be seen only as partial and conditional, characterized by no tragic *anagnorisis* or retrospective recognition of either the origin or nature of his inner conflict. Having abjured the excesses of spleen and rashness in himself, and mocked them ironically in Laertes, his subsequent relation to Horatio of the trickery by which he turns the tables on the unfortunate Rosencrantz and Guildenstern and compasses their unprepared-for deaths, attributes everything to the unlikely liaison of heaven's ordinance with the same hideous rashness, which, far from serving Hamlet well as he now supposes, has in fact precipitated that dark cataclysm of events which is eventually to engulf him. For Hamlet remains mortally culpable, inasmuch as his conscience was ignorant of what it ought to have known, for the unnecessary deaths of five innocent victims;[56] and even now his awareness of heaven's commission is only anamorphously related to any recognizable concept of theological jutice, since he sees in his recent deliverance a providential authority for his own impassioned rough-hewing.

None the less, the inference he now draws from the pattern of chance and coincidence that has delivered him to a final reckonng with his 'mighty opposite', is of a 'divinity that shapes our ends,/Rough-hew them how we will' (V.ii.10–11); and this, together with the demonstrable evidence that deliverance affords him of Claudius's compounded guilt, has in him the effect of resolving his inner discord, and harmonizing his previously flawed and dissociated moral sensibility to a new confidence in his task. He is still, as he says, 'constant' to his purposes (V.ii.197); but the clandestine and occulted purpose of revenge which had before blinded his reason and undermined his conscience, is now subordinated to the open and affirmative purposes of public justice, the execution of which is now become a rational necessity to which he is morally obliged in order to prevent further evil. Heaven being ordinant, it is now 'perfect conscience' to purge Denmark of the manifest source of its corruption, and 'damnable' to let 'this canker of our nature' infect further the life of the state; and Hamlet's wider awareness that the image of his personal cause is now reflected in a communal sense of outrage in the public domain elicits Horatio's choric inculpation of Claudius, 'Why, what a king is this' (V.ii.62), and prompts in the Prince the further determination to court Laertes's favours, federating both to a joint arraignment of tyranny.

Hamlet has foresaken the 'deep plots', rough-hewed in the importunacy of blood and passion, by which he had sought to implement the Ghost's evil injunction, and from this moment submits his will to the machinery of providential justice, tempered both to exact its punishment upon Claudius at such time as heaven's shaping ordinance and the 'king's fitness' shall speak, and readied even to an acceptance of his own death, should that also be decreed. 'There is special providence in the fall of a sparrow . . . The readines is all' (V.ii.215–18); and in thus coming to terms with the enactments of the universal order of nature, he comes to terms also with his own conscience, since it now witnesses wholly and perfectly to the innate apprehension of that order which is its proper object. Whereas before, the indiscriminate taking of arms had excited in his conscience the 'dread of something after death', now the prospect of 'not to be' can be viewed, not only with the optimistic fatalism suggested by 'If it be now, 'tis not to come'; but as well with the fortitude born of an acceptance of man's limited capacity, in his fallen state, to know 'aught' of what he leaves, or to penetrate finally the mystery of his own destiny.

Yet the audience is permitted an insight into the devious and ultimately incalculable workings of providence more profound than that attentuated awareness attained to by Hamlet, ever the victim of a fatal incoherency of motive; since Shakespeare traces throughout the play the cyclic and convoluted impulses by which nature itself forecloses upon the unnatural progenitors of disorder, according to the operations of its own divinely instituted Law. Thus the causative pattern of events, discoverable at first in the obscure mechanism by which 'Foul deeds will rise,/Though all the earth o'erwhelm them, to men's eyes' (I.ii.257–8), describes by a series of progressive and incremental steps the dynamic and entirely natural process through which providence works, and by which it ensures that evil finally recoils upon itself. What Horatio, in recounting to the as yet 'unknowing world' the manifold causes of the 'bloody question', will impute to the random operations of chance

> of accidental judgments, casual slaughters,
> Of deaths put on by cunning and forc'd cause,
> And, in this upshot, purposes mistook
> Fall'n on th'inventors' heads . . .
>
> (V.ii.387–90)

may alert the minds of an audience to the stragely just and propitious conclusion effectuated thus by chance, the chain of coincidence which results in the final defeat of evil growing, in retrospect, to something of great constancy. The havoc and chaos of the general slaughter is not without ethical signficance, since it marks the final analeptic convulsion by which the moral order reconstitutes itself, and by which the disease represented by Claudius, 'desperate grown' in the body politic of Denmark, is by 'desperate appliance' finally relieved. In fine, the apparently haphazard sequence of chance and coincidence that preserves Hamlet for a last and fatal duty – the discovery of the king's treachery, the timely arrival of the pirate ship which permits an escape from his captors, and finally the fortuity which yields to his hand the poisoned rapier – all this would have demonstrated to an Elizabethan audience, as it does distortedly to Hamlet, a moral design in the economy of natural causes through which a Divinity works, indirectly shaping events, and, through an immanent and proximate pressure upon the matrices of fortune and human free will, conforming them ultimately to its own inscrutable purposes. Inasmuch as Hamlet succeeds in the end in framing his actions according to this moral design, he not only becomes the willing minister of that supernal justice which vindicates itself to the court of Denmark in turning against evil its own treacherous instruments, but wins through to a redemption in which 'flights of angels' will sing him to his rest, and to the honour of a soldier's funeral and the 'rite of war' (V.ii.365,404).

5

Macbeth

This organic conception, by which tyranny, in so far as it violates the Natural Law, is overthrown by a congeries of unnatural acts which return to plague the inventor, is even more insistently present to the imagination in *Macbeth* than in *Richard III* or *Hamlet*. It is present, for example, in Act II, where the portents described by the Old Man to Ross refer Macbeth's crime to a universal frame of reference, where it reverberates the very frame and stasis of the ordered relationship between man and the rest of nature. It is present, too, in the tensity and resilience with which this relationship is bodied forth in that which prevails between Duncan and his thanes, an harmonious creative dependency of subject upon king replete with suggestions of natural growth (I.iv.32–3), a relationship thematically sustained in the images of natural procreation, by the naked babe imagery, and ironically by the 'procreant cradle' of the temple-haunting martlet.[1] Fundamentally this relationship is secured by the uderlying integrity of all nature inclining to the Natural Law which prescribes to each thing its purpose and fulfilment, and it is the correspondency of this impulse within their own souls which the Macbeths attempt to evade. Lady Macbeth, indeed, succeeds in curdling the very springs of natural affection, wrenching her femininity, as it were, from the fixed place, and blighting the very sources of creative life:

> Come, you Spirits
> That tend on mortal thoughts, unsex me here,
> And fill me, from the crown to the toe, top-full
> Of direst cruelty! make thick my blood,
> Stop up th' access and passage to remorse;
> That no compunctious visitings of Nature
> Shake my fell purpose, nor keep peace between
> Th' effect and it! Come to my woman's breasts,
> And take my milk for gall, you murth'ring ministers,

> Wherever in your sightless substances
> You wait on Nature's mischief!
> (I.v.40–50)

What she invokes of the spirits, Macbeth obtains of 'seeling Night' which with a bloody hand must 'Cancel, and tear to pieces, that great bond' by which his moral function is knit up with the great ethical impulse informing the providential scheme (III.ii.46–9). Yet cancellation of the bond, and the annihilation in themselves of all humanity and tenderness of feeling, cannot prevent, and indeed rather provokes, the dynamic reaction of the moral order which has been thus outraged. Macbeth himself shows an awareness of this cyclic process of providence when he acknowledges the way in which 'bloody instructions', even on this 'bank and shoal of time', ineluctably return to 'plague the inventor'; that an evil act can never be the 'be all and end all', and invariably has consequences that cannot be 'trammel[led] up' (I.vii.1–10). And it is precisely in keeping with this causal reaction in the public and universal sphere that it should be Macbeth's most horrendous act of tyranny in seizing upon Fife which should make of Macduff his most fatal 'consequence' of all, and forge in the Thane the providential instrument of Macbeth's final downfall.

In *Richard III* it was necessary to analyse the cyclic operations of the moral pattern in the social and public realm at some length in order to adumbrate its existence in the private world of Richard's conscience. But in *Macbeth*, as in *Hamlet*, a like compulsion to proof is almost entirely absent, for here that providence is more profoundly correlated with the inner development of character, and the logic which asserts Macbeth's personal disintegration is actually superincumbent upon the external logic by which the chain of being perfects itself. What is being commended to us chiefly in *Macbeth* is the spectacle of the punitive exactions of such logic upon the individual soul, and it is this spectacle that imaginatively pre-empts the manifestations of exterior disharmony in the universe, subordinating the macrocosmic convulsions almost to the status of a complex series of metaphors for what is happening in the microcosm.

Now it is worth recalling that in either dimension the process was pre-eminently a secular one; that is not to say that the supernatural never intervened on the earthly plane, but that, according to the scholastic tradition, the execution of the providential design resided in a mediate chain of secondary causes inherent in the nature of things. The secondary cause in the case of man was government, which both expressed and executed the Natural Law, and which was instituted by God to effect the plan pre-existent in his mind as Universal Cause. Though man's reason inclined to government out of an intrinsic and instilled knowledge of the precepts of the Natural Law towards which it was counselled by conscience, government was none the less necessary in recognition of the fact that the will of man was ultimately free. Indeed, the idea of conscience in scholastic philosophy actually presupposed the moral condition of man as free to make choices the ethical status of which it functioned as witness; a unilaterality of the will which was seen as a necessary component of that hierarchy of values whose perfection was God, and without which good and evil, perfection and imperfection would lose all distinction.

On these assumptions, then, that the existence of a conscience acting upon the free will of man was, for the scholastics, irreconcilable with the idea of an intrusive Deity or a destiny heavy with the sense of impending inevitability, the following inferences can be drawn. The numinous and extramundane, where it exists in Shakespeare's plays, and certainly in the three presently under discussion, bears an oblique and highly equivocal relation to reality. In *Richard III*, prayers offered to right the innocent appear to be fulfilled by a crudely intervening deity until it is remembered that such prayers are really venomous curses in the mouths of the irredeemably wicked; and as John Wilders observes, the God to whom such appeals are addressed turns out, on closer inspection, merely to be a variable and subjective conception in the minds of the characters, with only slightly more reality than the gods in *King Lear*.[2] In *Macbeth* the redemptive scheme, though pre-eminently dependent upon collateral ramifications arising out of the natural order, is likewise seemingly ratified by 'the grace of Grace' (V.ix.38); in particular, a supernal lustre plays about the idea of the benevolent Duncan, whose murder is announced as sacrilege, and also the mystical Edward, through whose sanctified hands heaven does 'miraculous work' (IV.iii.147). But in general, these are merely suggestive touches, sublime and celestial threads in the predominantly naturalistic warp of the play's metaphysical substance, a muffled antiphonal descant to Macbeth's unhallowed descent into evil.

Far more problematic is the question of the reality of the Weird Sisters, for inasmuch as they 'look not like th' inhabitants o' th' earth,/And yet are on't', they are neither clearly subjective nor objective (I.iii.41–2). They have sufficient reality and substance to claim for themselves a stage presence and the appearance of women; yet their uncanny presence forbids Banquo, at any rate, to interpret that they are so, and the 'truths' they tell are for him the gilded equivocations of all such instruments of darkness. On the other hand, the Weird Sisters seem to bear an obscure subjective relation to Macbeth's inner thoughts, the truths they tell for him being wakeful emanations of an imperial theme that has for long enkindled his imagination. Significantly, it is Banquo, who has 'a wisdom that doth guide his valour/To act in safety' (III.i.52–3) who finds the Sisters impossible to classify and for whom after their disappearance they were incorporeal as bubbles of the earth. It is Macbeth, as Sanders[3] points out, who is already committed to creating a reality for the witches and, indeed, whose unconscious adaptation of the witches' incantation in I.i.11

suggests a mysterious pre-existent communion in the miasmic evil suffusing the fog and filthy air of the gloomy heath – it is he who converts to reality their hitherto hypothetical status by a direct equation of prophecy with fact: 'Your children shall be kings' (I.iii.86). The inference is irresistibly borne in upon an audience that, properly speaking, the Sisters are neither wholly subjective nor objective; they inhere in a paranormal dimension, parasitic upon reality to the extent that, while unable to palter with Banquo, they can nevertheless batten on to a compliant host like Macbeth, who in turn confers reality upon them. This mysterious ambivalence extends also to the prophecies: that their partial truths are consecutively revealed as fact confirms Banquo's intuition that the Sisters are instruments of a supramundane maleficent Power, and this indeed is one with our suspicion that Macbeth is foredoomed from the start. On the other hand, Macbeth apparently proceeds, upon moral choices freely made, and in defiance of a conscience fully active, to embark quite deliberately and unnecessarily upon an evil course – to draw, in fact, all the unnecessary inferences from the prophecies: that chance will not crown him without his stir; to endow the augury 'Beware Macduff' with a fateful certainty by the needless slaughter of the innocents at Fife; and, moreover, to yield himself into the power of Macduff by the impolitic abandonment of his castle, merely because the siege he had said it would 'laugh to scorn' has appeared disguised as a moving grove of Burnam Wood. In all these instances, Macbeth apparently confers upon the prophecies their only power to destroy him; and yet even this proposition acquires a new and sinister complexity when exposed to the demoniac logic of Macbeth's fall. For if, as is true, the only future that is knowable is one that cannot therefore be altered, the predictions must inevitably presuppose Macbeth's unnecessary reactions to them. In this sense, Macbeth does indeed appear to struggle in vain in the deterministic jaws of some infernal trap. It is as if Shakespeare is paraphrasing one of the leaden truths purveyed to mankind east of Eden: that certain fruits of the Tree of Knowledge are fatal, and a knowledge of the future most deadly of all, because it merely induces in the prescient either an abject and torpid resignation to what he knows cannot be changed, or a ferocious and destructive desperation to alter the unalterable. These chilling ambiguities, some of which are explored by Marlowe and later by Ford, are wrought up in Macbeth's own response to them; in his desire to 'feel now/The future in the instant' (I.v.57–8), Macbeth trades a present freedom for the knowledge of a future that in the nature of things must enslave him; yet he never ceases to believe in his own freedom to act, either to circumvent the future by obliterating Banquo's issue, or by binding himself still further to its necessities in order to secure for himself a 'doubtful joy'.

These ambiguities can only partly be resolved, for the origins of evil in Macbeth are never fully disclosed; it is true that the supernatural solicits him in the aftermath of battle, and yet he starts and seems to fear, as if those fair predictions of noble having and of royal hope were merely a strange intelligence of what had for long since been foully lodged in his secret soul. It will be recalled from the introduction that the nature of this encounter shows the extent to which Macbeth's imagination and hubris have before this nourished a putative image of the supreme mutable good – that golden round which fate now proffers him. As Sanders puts it:

> What Shakespeare makes us feel . . . is the extremely tenuous division between the 'free' act and the 'determined' one, and the imaginative possibility of a world in which the balance has been imperceptibly tipped towards evil, so that man writhes and sprawls vainly on a greased slope that ends in perdition.[4]

We may argue that Macbeth, like Milton's rebellious angels, is free until he enthralls himself; that he himself revokes that freedom by his own revolt, until the fruits of knowledge and of evil yield him up, like Satan, to a greater power, and turn to bitter ashes in his mouth. But to reconcile in this manner Macbeth's increasing helplessness with an original responsibility for his fate, we must address the crucial question: upon exactly which bank and shoal of time does the greased slope actually begin?

Perhaps the nearest approach to an answer resides in Banquo's perspicacious extended metaphor:

> If you can look into the seeds of time,
> And say which grain will grow, and which will not . . .
>
> (I.iii.58–9)

Here Banquo seems to imply a vision of the future as a progressive actualization of events which exist merely as potentialities within the teeming womb of time, and that the germinal or generative impulse arises out of an anterior matrix of human choices which alone bring to fruition a given sequential chain of future events. Appropriate Duncan's words and apply them to the predicament of Macbeth, and the process by which he actually wills the maturation of the seeds of his own destruction becomes clear:

> Welcome hither:
> I have begun to plant thee, and will labour
> To make thee full of growing.
>
> (I.iv.27–9)

Macbeth therefore has an original freedom, but one that is gradually circumscribed as the embryonic evil in his mind is catalysed by the external promptings of the predictions which, it may be noted, augur forth an entirely circumstantial account of the future, never once suggesting evil as the means of effecting it. This last is Macbeth's own contribution, the germ of ambition which is at first fantastical, that lies wrought up in the secret recesses of his soul, smothered in surmise but, nursed into being by external temptation, infects and impairs his reason, debilitates his will, and so sunders his single state of man that 'nothing is but what is not'.

Set against the ambition which impels him towards the 'swelling act/Of the imperial theme' is, of course, his conscience,[5] which fills him with horror at the means to the crown his ambition has proposed:

> This supernatural soliciting
> Cannot be ill; cannot be good: –
> If ill, why hath it given me earnest of success,
> Commencing in a truth? I am Thane of Cawdor:
> If good, why do I yield to that suggestion
> Whose horrid image doth unfix my hair,
> And make my seated heart knock at my ribs,
> Against the use of nature? Present fears
> Are less than horrible imaginings.
>
> (I.iii.130–8)

Here the intensity of Macbeth's visual imagination suggests the divided soul in the moment of agonized indecision. The horrid image of the murdered Duncan as the condition of 'success' is an evil chimera that comes to Macbeth's mind unbidden by anything the witches have said; and though it chimes with his own ambition, it is nevertheless indubitably 'horrid', dressed by conscience in the habiliments of nightmare actuality, such that moral horror causes Macbeth's hair to unfix itself, and his heart to knock at his ribs 'against the use of nature'. On this occasion, however, conscience as the counsellor of the will prevails upon Macbeth to put aside the temptation: 'If chance will have me king, why, chance may crown me,/Without my stir' (I.iii.144–5). and yet the vocabulary of the soliloquy above shows how insidiously his conscience is undermined by a will that has to a dangerous extent already 'yielded' to the horrid image, and is moreover beleaguered by an anarchy of the soul beyond the possibility of conscious control.

Similar semantic ambiguities permeate Macbeth's next soliloquy, where the declaration of Malcolm as Scotland's heir-apparent seems to bring him to the point of decision; yet at the same time his conscience arraigns his guilty resolve and paradoxically invests it with a hideous reality that the stars, the light, and the eye dare not behold:

> Stars, hide your fires!
> Let not light see my black and deep desires;
> The eye wink at the hand; yet let that be,
> Which the eye fears, when it is done, to see.
>
> (I.iv.50–3)

Yet this time a perceptible equanimity has stolen over his soul; the horrid image does not now unfix his hair as it did before, and its darkening shadow is beginning to eclipse Macbeth's free will. There is a nightmare sense of helplessness in the imagery of these lines, an unwilling abdication of the moral faculty in order that the element of choice may be surrendered, and the conscience occluded, in the dark press of forces Macbeth would rather not control.

The exact composition of Macbeth's conscience is precisely analysed for us by Lady Macbeth as she muses upon those qualities in her husband that might yet impede him from the greatness that is promised him. He is 'too full o' th' milk of human kindness', ambitious, but without the illness, unholiness, and playing false that should necessarily attend such ambition (I.v.17–22). She fears his nature, not only because it expresses that humane sense of kindred that binds man to man, but because it is instinct with a proper sense of the sacredness of life. In short, Macbeth's most dangerous attribute is an enlightened conscience – everything, indeed, that had previously caused the image of murder to unfix his hair; and it is these promptings towards humanity and tenderness that Lady Macbeth hastens to chastize by pouring her spirits in at his ear. And yet before she can do this, she herself must make thick her blood, herself deny the compunctious visitings of nature, fusing them in the white heat of diabolic purpose; in conjuring the ministers of evil to take her milk for gall, she desecrates the most sacred bond of kinship and tender care, defiling the very sources of creative life. At the same time, the tone of Macbeth's letter, and of Lady Macbeth's reception of it, only strengthen the overall impression of him as one in whom conscientious scruples are reinforced by a sense of profound humanity: the note of tender consideration, enhanced by the parenthetical endearment, is unmistakable:

> This I have thought good to deliver thee (my
> dearest partner of greatness) that thou might'st
> not lose the dues of rejoicing, by being
> ignorant of what greatness is promis'd thee.
>
> (I.v.10–13)

Neither is this tone of solicitous sharing dispelled by Lady Macbeth's rapturous welcome of her husband upon his return; the bond of tenderness between them is paradoxically emphasized rather than negated by the managing, yet affectionate, condescension with which she insinuates to her husband's mind her diabolic and ruthless machinations. The tragic irony of Macbeth is that the gentleness and humanity associated with his good conscience are withered in him by a course of action which actually provokes his wife's conscience, now so effectively repressed, eventually to drive her to suicide.

Yet with Duncan within his battlements, and time and place thus favourably adhering with opportunity, still Macbeth's vivid imagination and agonized conscience make the decision to do evil very nearly impossible. In scene seven, Macbeth once again wrestles with his own divided consciousness; a consciousness on the one hand that insistently presents the deed to his mind, and on the other reproaches him in the accents of Christ betrayed by Judas (I.vii.1–2). What to his ambition seems so desirable that he will risk eternity and 'jump the life to come', is rendered palpably less so by the prudential wisdom that forces him to acknowledge the process by which 'bloody instructions' return 'to plague the inventor' (I.vii.7–10). His conscience then propounds to him more altruistic precepts, both private and public: the duties and obligations required of a loyal kinsman and a subject, which sustain the bonds of family and the fabric of society. Lastly, his conscience directs him to the cosmic implications of his crime, forcing him to contemplate Duncan's virtues pleading like angels, and the cataclysmic grief that will ensue when the deed is blown in every eye. With apocalyptic visionary anguish, Macbeth's conscience prefigures for him a glimpse of the Last Judgment, crowding his imagination with angels and cherubs as a defence against the chthonian potency by which his wife seems now possessed. An overwhelming sense of the foulness of what he intends grips his soul, and he confesses lamely and even regretfully the inadequacy of mere ambition as the motive for so horrendous a deed:

> I have no spur
> To prick the sides of my intent . . .
> (I.vii.25–6)

But this is a cue chillingly taken up by Lady Macbeth, to whom it now falls to effect what she intended in scene five: to pour her diabolic spirits in at his ear. On her appearance he accordingly conveys to her scornful understanding the irresolute conclusions to which conscience has driven him; yet, sensing her new-found moral imperviousness, Macbeth speaks evasively of honour and public esteem, rather than of the profound vision by which his soul has just been affrighted:

> He hath honour'd me of late; and I have bought
> Golden opinions from all sorts of people,
> Which would be worn now in their newest gloss,
> Not cast aside so soon.
> (I.vii.32–5)

Naturally fortified by the poverty of such reasoning, Lady Macbeth responds contemptuously to the opportunity thereby yielded her, to deride his flaccid will and empty ambition, goading his passions to frenzied perturbation by her taunts of cowardice and lack of love:

> Art thou afeard
> To be the same in thine own act and valour,
> As thou art in desire? Would'st thou have that
> Which thou esteem'st the ornament of life,
> And live a coward in thine own esteem . . .
>
> (I.vii.39–43)

And yet still his conscience jolts him to a painful awareness of what is rationally and properly entailed in being human, and he retorts angrily:

> I dare do all that may become a man;
> Who dares do more, is none.
>
> (I.vii.46–7)

With an almost satanic fury, Lady Macbeth rounds upon what she rightly perceives is the authentic basis of his scruples; it is not, after all, merely a cat's timorousness that has sapped his valour, but his conscience articulating the ethical precepts that nourish his deepest instincts as a human being, the almost religious odour of which infuriates his wife. With resourceful guile, she insinuates the authorship of their deadly enterprise upon her husband, taunting him with breaking a promise he never actually made:

> What beast was't then,
> That made you break this enterprise to me?
> When you durst do it, then you were a man;
> And, to be more than what you were, you would
> Be so much more the man.
>
> (I.vii.47–51)

In the face of her awful and yet heroic malignity, Macbeth's conscience wilts, and in the ensuing chaos to which conflicting passions reduce his moral being, he actually succumbs to the cowardice that she accuses him of, entering to her impressive determination the greenest and palest of all objections: 'If we should fail?' (I.vii.59). Yet eventually his moral capitulation is complete, and Lady Macbeth, elaborating to his quavering spirit a plan that will not fail, infuses him with something of her own infernal energies, so that she gains a complete victory over his will. But still his conscience has been, and continues to be, a terrifyingly active witness to the diminution of his moral being: had not natural ambition coincided fatefully with a number of external forces themselves pregnant with a dark immanence – the glorious victory, the installation of heir-apparent Malcolm – above all, had not these forces cohered with the pat opportunity and Lady Macbeth's precipitate urgings, then conscience might have prevailed upon his will, and his will imposed itself upon the evil inclinations of his passions, which are instead only too ready to endorse the terrible feat to which they are now bound up.

> I am settled, and bend up
> Each corporal agent to this terrible feat.
> Away, and mock the time with fairest show;
> False face must hide what the false heart doth know.
> (I.vii.80–3)

Even at the penultimate moment, waiting for the bell-signal from his wife, Macbeth's overwrought conscience projects a final desperate image upon his heat-oppressed brain, a fatal vision so vivid in its stark impress that he knows not whether it is sensible to feeling or purely imaginary. Entranced, he moves under its ominous compulsion to where it marshalls him – towards the chamber of the sleeping king; but, startlingly, there appear on the dagger's blade and dudgeon gouts of blood – the ghoulish premonitions of a guilt-stricken conscience. Earlier, Macbeth had exclaimed:

> Stars, hide your fires!
> Let not light see my black and deep desires;
> The eye wink at the hand; yet let that be,
> Which the eye fears, when it is done, to see.
> (I.iv.50–3)

Now, by an appropriate psychic irony, the very opposite ensues, and Macbeth is forced by his conscience to contemplate yet again the presumptive implications of the 'bloody business', which thus informs to his eye the everlasting affinity with murder and evil he will ratify for himself should he undertake such a monstrous act. But this time the sanctions of conscience are weaker in their effect; and Macbeth, who had successfully averted its adjurations in the name of pity and altruism, now sweeps aside this last and intimidatory vision with a contemptuous snarl: 'There's no such thing' (II.i.47).

The deed having been accomplished, Macbeth's conscience changes, by that spiritual metamorphosis to which Smith has before referred us, to a vengeful accuser, condemning him with occult voices and with the terrible lacerations of guilt and remorse. Returning from the chamber he announces his 'success' in two laconic phrases, heavy with significance in their oblique juxtaposition:

> I have done the deed – Didst thou not hear a noise?
> (II.ii.14)

Here a leaden hopelessness is displaced by a growing atmosphere of stifling anxiety. In the sense that the action has brought about the reverse of what the protagonists had intended, these lines sum up, as Toppen points out, what is at the same time both *peripeteia* and *anagnorisis*.[6] Now the damnable reality of what he has done assails Macbeth, gripped as he is by horrific memories of the deed he has just committed: 'Amen' sticks in his throat as if endorsing his earlier prevision of his soul's peril; a voice cries with hysteric insistency that Macbeth has murdered sleep; all of which 'brainsickly' musings Lady Macbeth listens to with increasing alarm. With grim foreboding, she intuits the dangers, not merely to the health of their enterprise, but to sanity itself, which can result from the livid figments of an imperfectly repressed conscience:

> These deeds must not be thought
> After these ways: so, it will make us mad.
> (II.ii.32–3)

And yet she too, now that her barbarous mood is beginning to dissipate, is increasingly vulnerable to such compunctious visitings:

> Had he not resembled
> My father as he slept, I had done't.
> (II.ii.12–13)

But faced with her husband's evident infirmity of purpose, she reassumes her self-command, and, affirming grimly that the 'sleeping, and the dead,/ Are but as pictures', proceeds with implacable courage to complete the task from which Macbeth demurs (II.ii.52–3). Nevertheless, the scene she then witnesses, in going to smear the faces of the grooms, so etches itself on her soul that it reappears eventually to haunt her dreams, hounding her to madness and suicidal despair. But for the moment she is alert and resourceful; the knocking which appals her husband, by now poorly lost in his thoughts, precipitates her to action, and she applies both the necessary rational astringencies to his baleful fancies, and the strategies that will safeguard them from discovery. But Macbeth, unresponsive to these necessities, gazes unblinkingly into the moral abyss that has opened within his soul:

> To know my deed, 'twere best not know myself.
> (II.ii.72)

The message of the air-drawn dagger reaches here a dreadful consummation, for Macbeth and his deed are inextricably bound up with each other, and he is indeed spiritually affined with murderers and the powers of darkness. To regain his integrity, to know himself once again, will necessitate the creation of a new psyche, centred upon the daunting recognition of his appalling crime; and it is the struggle to become, by just such a recognition, once more 'perfect', 'whole as marble', as 'broad and general' as the air, that causes Macbeth to violate still further the natural good within him.

Accordingly, there follows after the coronation a dismal hiatus, during which time Macbeth is assailed by excruciating agonies of the mind which testify to what extent he has infringed the principles of the Natural Law instilled within his soul; his conscience castigates him by afflicting him with terrible dreams that shake him nightly, putting rancours in the vessel of his peace, and provoking him to a despairing envy of the dead who sleep well after life's 'fitful fever'. But as his moral nature shrinks and deteriorates, so the light of reason in him thickens, slowly strangled in the murderous grip of racking passions and livid imaginings; all of which induce him to construe Banquo's knowledge and possible suspicion of his crime as the principal cause of his spiritual malady, which in his death 'were perfect'. Certainly his conscience still has the power to indicate to him with searing clarity the elemental causes of his distemper, yet such moments of truth are to become increasingly intermittent, constantly frustrated and misapplied by a will seeking to habituate itself to evil. He knows, for example, that in perpetrating the murder of Duncan he has 'fil'd his mind', and given away his eternal jewel; yet it never once occurs to him that, like his namesake Cawdor, he might confess his treasons, and set forth a deep repentance; on the contrary, he misinterprets the remedial prick of conscience, and fatalistically judges himself as unforgivable. He knows, moreover, in an oblique sense, that the restless ecstasies to which he is subject are really the reactions of conscience to the outrage done upon the instilled precepts of the Natural Law, that 'great bond' which keeps him pale; and yet he deludes himself that the anodyne to conscience lies in the utter extirpation, the complete cancellation of all such precepts in his own nature. The point is that such moral insights supplied by *synderesis* still fitfully enlighten the murky recesses of his soul, but they are fatally perverted, fallaciously misapplied by a treacherous paralogic of the will to the immediate circumstances with which it must deal. This, the doomed logic of reprobation, with its corollaries of murderous desperation, moral confusion, and a bleak imperviousnes of spirit, is well documented by Perkins. Of the notorious malefactor, he has this to say:

> How the heart of [such a] man beeing exceedingly obstinate and perverse, carrieth him to commit sinnes even against the light of nature and common sense: by practise of such sinnes the light of nature is extinguished: and then commeth the *reprobate minde*, which judgeth evill good, and good evill: after this follows the *seared conscience*, in which there is no feeling or remorse. . .[7]

Thus it is in the case of Banquo, in whom Macbeth instinctively recognizes a symbol of strength in virtue now become anathema to his own desecrated soul; that goodness, in short, by which the genius of evil must always feel itself rebuked. 'In the great hand of God I stand', Banquo had said (II.iii.130); and it is this moral integrity, a spiritual wisdom that guides him to act in safety while still permitting him to rest assured in the prophecies, that Macbeth envies. If Banquo's posterity may benefit by the predictions without his 'stir', then it is solely for his issue that Macbeth has 'fil'd his mind', succeeded moreover to a barren sceptre and a fruitless crown, and his

> eternal jewel
> Given to the common Enemy of man,
> To make them kings, the seed of Banquo kings!
>   (III.i.67–9)

Yet in his increasing unreason and moral myopia he confuses the sense of envy and despair thus provoked in him by Banquo, with a sense of outward insecurity, in an obscure way a rationalization of his own spiritual insecurity. He speaks misgivingly of his 'fears' that in Banquo 'stick deep', fears attributable to his 'royalty of nature', so real and present to Macbeth's imagination that they add an authenticity to the 'weighty' reasons with which he 'makes love' to the assistance of the murderers; Banquo is his enemy

> in such bloody distance,
> That every minute of his being thrusts
> Against my near'st of life . . .
>   (III.i.115–17)

And yet Macbeth is no coward, and it is difficult to concede that he actually dwells in abject fear of a man whom he admits to be virtuous; it is only the crepuscular light of his diseased reason that seeks desperately some analgesic for the torments of conscience that deludes him into thinking that the remedy for a mind 'full of scorpions' lies in the murder of Banquo and Fleance. That in his blindness Macbeth imagines that the balm of sleep which he had banished by his original crime may be restored to him, and harrowing care once again knit up in him, by the commission of a second murder, only goes to show how far his psychological insight into the elemental causes of his misery has been dimmed; an obtuseness that prompts him now to avert any further incubus of guilt upon his soul by instigating in the minds of two assassins his own deadly resolve.

The extent to which his essential humanity is also being obscured and diminished is evidenced by a growing abstraction and increasing isolation; he now keeps alone, even from the companionship of his dearest partner in evil, brooding instead on 'sorriest fancies' (III.ii.9). And indeed, he seems to gather a kind of strength from this: he who had earlier fought an unequal struggle with the 'compunctious visitings of nature' now seems proof against them, locked into a microcosm of despair that makes him as well both indifferent to his wife's solicitude and independent of her reassurance. Indeed, she seems more in need now of spiritual reinforcement than he does; bereft as she is of those demoniac energies that before had made of her a tower of strength to her husband, she is now become a prey to the corrosive insight that it is better to be destroyed, than by destruction 'dwell in doubtful joy', and can rise to no more than the languid and listless despondency of her advice to Macbeth:

> Things without all remedy
> Should be without regard: what's done is done.
> (III.ii.11–12)

But to Macbeth's fevered brain the remedy is plain; and partly to keep his wife from all such 'regard', but also becauses their guilt and spiritual isolation have caused a gulf to open up between them, Lady Macbeth is kept in ignorance of the plot on Banquo, told to 'present him eminence' who will never again appear alive if the murderer's commission is executed. To her question, 'What's to be done?', Macbeth replies with grim solicitude: 'Be innocent of the knowledge, dearest chuck/Till thou applaud the deed' (III.ii.44–6); but in view of their mutual solitude and his growing sequestration from humankind, this sounds less like a reaffirmation of his old tenderness than the successful implementation of his own hypocritical injunction to make his face 'a vizard to his heart', disguising even from his wife the evil it really harbours. In contrast to her, he cannot give up what is to become with him a *fata morgana* of the soul: the entirely chimerical idea that by destruction he can and will succeed to a kind of joy, that to become 'whole as marble', 'founded as the rock', rid forever of the racking tortures of conscience, needs but 'twenty trenched gashes' on the head of Banquo and the like for Fleance:

> There's comfort yet; they are assailable:
> Then be thou jocund.
> (III.ii.39–40)

These lines express not only the grim tensity of a man seeking peace and security through slaughterous thoughts, at any cost, 'even till destruction sicken'; as Toppen points out, they also form an ironical echo of the words of the bloody sergeant as, in his account of the battle, he described the onslaught of an earlier, and equally unforeseen attack upon Macbeth:[8]

> So from that spring whence comfort seem'd to come,
> Discomfort swells.
> (I.ii.27–8)

Now in retrospect they seem to form a preterite commentary, not only on the self-deluding way in which Macbeth diagnoses his spiritual disease, but one also drearily prophetic of the only future that can spring from such a diagnosis.

Ironically, the future that most immediately confirms the swelling discomforts that attend upon destruction, is that prescribed by the Weird Sisters, in accordance with which Banquo shall 'get kings' though he be none: Fleance escapes from the knives of the assassins, thus confirming in fact the fruitlessness of the crown for which Macbeth pawned his soul, and binding him still further to 'saucy doubts and fears'. Moreover, he is still 'but young in deed'; destruction has not yet dimmed to extinction his visualizing conscience. At the banquet, no sooner does he pay the vauntingly ironic compliment

> Here had we now our country's honour roof'd,
> Were the grac'd person of our Banquo present:
> (III.iv.39–40)

than the ghost of Banquo enters, with twenty mortal murders on his crown, provoking again, and exacerbating still further, that 'fit' of conscience from which Macbeth had sought an everlasting immunity by this very murder. He is unnerved, completely unmanned, his guilt by guilt exposed and left naked before his guests. Twice the spectral vision appears to appal Macbeth's sight, on each occasion called into visibility by the desperate bluster of a man whose vain attempts to repress a guilty conscience coexist partly with an apparently genuine belief that he has, on this occasion, nothing to feel guilty about:

> Thou can't not say, I did it: never shake
> Thy gory locks at me.
> (III.iv.49–50)

The nature of Banquo's ghost has something of the ambivalence of those of Richard's victims that appeared to him on the eve of Bosworth: Shakespeare is careful to preserve a certain enriching vagueness to all such emanations of the spirit, never permitting them characteristics accessible to the kind of proof which might confirm their status as either fully subjective or objective. Equally indeterminable as a specifically psychological or spiritual phenomenon is Banquo's ghost; indeed the cumulative evidence seems to indicate that the Elizabethan mind was not quite so obsessed with the ontological status of experience as is the rational scientific twentieth century. For Shakespeare's audience, Macbeth's experience would on the one hand invite Lady Macbeth's interpretation of it as 'the very painting of your fear' – like the air-drawn dagger a visible representation of conscience; on the other hand, they would acquiesce equally in the proposition that since conscience has origins beyond the mind, it had the power, already cited, to embody past sins pleading at the bar of God's judgment; and in this connection they would understand the ghost as confirming Macbeth's eschatological vision of the angels pleading 'trumpet-tongued' against Duncan's murder.

In the aftermath of the banquet, the lords having been hastily despatched, the Macbeths stand alone in the frigid half-light of dawn; she listless and numb, the infernal fires in her now exhausted and extinct; he alternately lost in gloomy thoughts, but a prey yet to the fretful agues and cramps of conscience that paradoxically keep his restless mind meditating and scheming, generating the reckless fears that lead him ever nearer his downfall. His partial recognition of the true status of his being – that the tendency to crime has habituated itself in him – only confirms in him the delusion that his present course, however wearisome, must end in some sort of relief:

> I am in blood
> Stepp'd in so far, that, should I wade no more,
> Returning were as tedious as go o'er.
> (III.iv. 135–7)

The determination to root out conscience has become the good for which 'all causes' must give way; indeed, the image of a decision resulting in a possible return is itself delusory. Not only is the element of quandary which had attended Macbeth's previous decisions entirely absent – this time the decision anticipates the image of division, and merely supports what has become a fixed prejudice of the mind – but the fact is that there is no wading through to the other side: he must inevitably be engulfed in the blood that 'will have blood'. And yet the notion of a possible return, albeit irreconcilable with dramatic logic at this point, and evidently unpalatable to the diseased rationality of Macbeth's degraded mind, is nevertheless a poignant reminder of the only true path to redemption and the easement of his soul – the forswearing of the crown for which he originally pawned it.

Instead, Macbeth returns to the Weird Sisters, determined to know, by the worst means, the worst, convinced that the horrific sights conjured in his mind by conscience are due merely to 'the initiate fear, that wants hard use' (III.iv.142). Only a bloody, bold, and resolute course can re-create that harmonious accord with providence that he has lost; for by these means can the chaos of his own soul be projected upon the exterior world,[9] even until 'the treasure of nature's germens tumble' and 'destruction sicken' – the ensuing dust and ashes of which will confer upon Macbeth a kind of negative peace. Now the 'very firstlings of [his] heart' become the 'firstlings of [his] hand', and the swiftness and violence of his deeds outrun the pauser, reason, in a truly infernal reflexive automation of the soul, by which act is synchronized with purpose, and ideation becomes the remorseless engine of the will. The equivocating prophecies of the apparitions seem to ensure him a charmed life, and grant him a delusive security that apparently innoculates him against further 'sights' and makes him immune to fear and remorse; yet the show of kings and the exhortation to 'Beware Macduff' induce in him the frantic resolve to hesitate no more, to seize on Fife, and give to the 'edge o' th' sword' the wife, children and dependents of Macduff, in an irrational bid to guarantee his own 'lease of Nature' (IV.i.151,99). Now a reign of terror is instituted; tyrannous atrocities are committed upon Scotland:

> Each new morn
> New widows howl, new orphans cry; new sorrows
> Strike heaven on the face, that it resounds
> As if it felt with Scotland, and yell'd out
> Like syllable of dolour.
>
> (IV.iii.4–8)

The divine order here moves in sympathy with the temporal, the whole of created nature recoiling in outraged anguish at the monstrous deeds perpetrated upon it in defiance of the Natural Law. The precepts of this Law, properly and originally implicit in the nexus of secondary causes, government, are now discarded; the graces of kingship, such as justice, verity, temperance, mercy, devotion, and patience, are malignantly perverted in Macbeth, negated by his original usurpation and the absence of natural good in him, to avarice, luxury, falsehood, deceit, suddenness.

But the peace that he wins through to by such means, though it secures him from the racking torments and spectral visions by which he had formerly been assailed, is not the sort which he expects or desires: conscience still obliges him to recognize the negative quality of evil, delivering him over to the spiritual doldrums of nihilistic calm and inducing in him a passive and listless indifference. He who had once won 'golden opinions' from all sorts of people, had been proud to wear them in their 'newest gloss', now discovers the comfortless aridities of a future laid waste by his own evil:

> And that which should accompany old age,
> As honour, love, obedience, troops of friends,
> I must not look to have; but in their stead,
> Curses, not loud, but deep, mouth-honour, breath,
> Which the poor heart would fain deny, and dare not.
>
> (V.iii.24–8)

Again, he too, who had once shared a dream of ambition with his dearest partner of greatness, to whom, indeed, he owed the most in trying to attain it, cannot now, in its nightmare aftermath, find in himself one spark of grief or regret at the news of her death:

> She should have died hereafter:
> There would have been a time for such a word.
>
> (V.v.17–18)

His words testify to a kind of *rigor mortis* of the soul; the peace to which he succeeds is that which has effected in his seared conscience a callousness to pain, and here induces an utter negativity, a spiritual paralysis that cannot respond either to his human need to sorrow, or to his own horror at his incapacity to do so. This, their final separation, the ultimate stage in the doomed logic which had long since ensured to each a lonely despair, provokes him to a grim peroration, an obituary not so much for Lady Macbeth, for she seems dreadfully absent to his thoughts, as for his own galling disappointment; not so much of grief as of bitter cynicism for the hopeless unmeaning of the life she has left him to. On the bank and shoal of time upon which Macbeth now stands, life seems to him capable of holding nothing of positive value; the past amounts to no more than a dreary series of yesterdays, lighting fools the way to dusty death; the future a meaningless tedium of endless tomorrows stretching to the grey horizon where time merges with eternity. This is the ultimate tragedy of Macbeth, as, in staring stonily across the void of his own spiritual annihilation, he utters what in these lines seems a negation of universal significance, a solemn affirmation of the worthlessness of life in general. Yet the inflation is unwarranted, however poetically rendered, merely the private chagrin of one whose soul has reached the stage described by Henry Smith, the phrasing of whose sermons bears an uncanny resemblance to Macbeth's soliloquy. Speaking of the wicked, he says:

> All his lights are put out at once: he hath no soul fit to be comforted. . . .
> Our fathers, marvelling to see how suddenly men are and are not,
> compared life . . . to a player which speaketh his part upon the stage,
> and straight he giveth his place to another. . . . If any of you go away
> no better than you came, you are not like hearers, but like ciphers,
> which supply a place, but signify nothing.[10]

The one who struts and frets, and whose life has been full of sound and fury, is Macbeth; his words evaluate not the worth of the external world, but the life of one who, to paraphrase Smith, went away not merely no better than he came, but in subtracting worth from himself, was thereby reduced to a cipher.

His confusion here is a consequence of that rational deterioration which has increasingly blinded him to the moral implications of his own situation, a deterioration that, as it atrophies his volitions, permits his acts of free will to become bound within the evil circumscriptions of the witches' prophecies. A kind of dual determinism, operating externally and internally, seems tragically to overwhelm Macbeth towards the end: ensnared, to all intents inescapably, in the ravelled coils of a self-elected fate, his struggles, partly because frenzied and unreasoning, only bind him tighter in its mesh. On the other hand, the precepts of the Natural Law inhering in his conscience have been repeatedly violated, so that, as Curry points out, irrational acts have established habits leading to further irrationality, resulting in the dire impairment of his liberty of free choice.[11] So it is that, in a mysterious sense, the baleful malignity of that dark Power to which Macbeth is bound by the prescriptive nature of the prophecies acquires in the end a moral penumbra, begins to move in the same ambit as that disposition implicit in all creation, by which providence knits together all things according to the ordered assignation of their due ends and acts. The shadowy conclusions to which we are impelled, and which in the final act begin to take on an obscure luminescence, are those that centre upon a deep equivocation in the moral universe itself; in an enigmatic sense, the Weird Sisters that take their being in the overmantling pall of evil, attendant upon the genesis of sin in the soul and insinuating their prophetic obfuscations to frail and peccant man – these are not the final reality in *Macbeth*, as he himself half-realizes. For the opaque intimations that the Sisters breathe forth are only the partial revelations of a future dispensation that is itself moral, that is shaped in accordance with the divine purpose immanent within the universe, and to which future even their predictions must give hostages such as Fleance, spared to the exigencies of a providence which evil cannot oppose. And it is this providence, working as much through the instrumentality of the witches as by the disabled volitions of Macbeth's own nature, that ensures the cathartic disgorgement of the evil he comes to represent; *sub specie aeternitatis*, the Weird Sisters in a curious sense serve the ethical impulse which, gestated through time and the hour, forecloses upon the victim of their prophecies, bringing to fruition in the seeds of time a glorious good out of tragic waste and decay.[12] This enormous metaphysical prevarication at the nexus of the coordinates of time and eternity, the 'future' and the 'instant', free will and determination, is one of which Macbeth is only intermittently aware: aware that this supernatural soliciting 'cannot be ill, cannot be good'; aware, too, that 'juggling fiends' may 'palter' with him in 'double sense'; yet it is an intuition that Macbeth fails to apply to his own conduct at the outset, and is thereafter only imperfectly accessible to his reason, as the light of his conscience thickens, darkens, and becomes finally extinct.

6

Doctor Faustus

Similar metaphysical ambiguities lie close to the heart of Marlowe's Play also, which, like *Macbeth* and the Satanic philosophers of *Paradise Lost*, debates the eternal questions of 'Providence, Foreknowledge, Will, and Fate', and does so within a rationalist universe, where moral choice and the act of conscience occur not as a result of absolute decree, but under the 'high permission of an all-ruling Heaven' (*PL* ii.559; i.212). But there are other ambiguities equally central to *Doctor Faustus*, concerning the extent of Marlowe's commitment to such a universe, which must be pondered in addition to the elevated arguments of its grand design. We may admit cautiously the proposition advanced by Roy Battenhouse, that *Doctor Faustus* represents the 'protest of traditional ethics against Renaissance individualism',[1] provided the counter-terms are used advisedly, and enlist our awareness of what precisely that protest is intended to mean. For although it is widely conceded that the drama is not *merely* a reactionary homiletic abrogation of all that is implied in the Renaissance humanistic impulse, there is far less agreement over the extent to which Marlowe's art accords a conscious validity to the humanist term: whether, on the one hand, as Marlowe the rebel he commits intellectual 'apostasy' in the face of a barbarous and 'fundamental creed';[2] or whether on the other, as Marlowe the quondam theologian he endorses the explicit values of the Prologue and Epilogue, and – however betrayed in this by the subliminal attractions of the Renaissance dream of limitless possibility – actually intended to write a quasi-morality on the sinfulness of earthly learning, and the vanity of earthly satisfactions.[3] Moreover, the assertion that such values are enforced in the name of 'traditional ethics' is partially disabled by an imprecision which allows to the phrase an almost protean versatility of meaning. For some commentators, the play dramatizes the reform doctrines of Wittenburg,[4] or again of Geneva;[5] for others, the informing dogmas are those of Augustine and St Paul;[6] for still others, the play offers a vague but triumphant vindication of Marlowe's 'unimpeachable' orthodoxy.[7] But Faustus's hubristic rejection of divinity and his addiction to 'devilish exercise' is in the play construed as a wilful, specifically *unfaith-ful* perversion of the plot of 'scholarism graced'; and Marlowe's protest may be seen at one level, and without any important anachronism, as embodying that of late scholasticism against what, from a Reniassance perspective, must always have seemed endemically the seeds of its own decay. Ever since an earlier Carolingian renaissance had brought them into being, the schools of medieval Europe had countered an incipient humanist appeal to the profane disciplines of the ancients – an appeal barely resisted by such as Roscelin and Aberlard – by first of all maintaining a clear distinction between the *artes liberales* and theology, and later by synthesizing them; but they insisted always on the ascendancy of grace over nature, *auctoritas* over *ratio*, subordinating the profane sciences to the status of *ancillae theologie*. Marlowe's orthodoxy is the orthodoxy of Hooker and of Shakespeare; and in the drama, it is clearly – one might say, necessarily – inimical to what Marlowe identifies as some of the more pernicious and disordered aspects of humanism's Renaissance apotheosis – an apotheosis that itself did much to undermine the old scholastic assumptions. Faustus's cry of 'sic probo', his desire to test by experience the unverified suppositions of medieval cosmology, his ironic refusal to accept, even from Mephostophilis, the received hypotheses concerning hell – all of this is emblematic of that fifteenth- and sixteenth-century assertion of empirical fact against metaphysical status of being; while the subordination of theology to philosophy, of faith to reason, which Faustus symbolically undertakes in the first scene, is a literary metaphor for the humanist ferment undermining the traditional hierarchies of virtue. The play is indeed 'the spiritual autobiography of an age';[8] an age which in *Doctor Faustus* is set historically at one remove from Marlowe's own, but one whose intellectual overthrows precipitated not just the related, but ultimately reactive, impulse of the Reformation – which sought to restore the hegemony of grace and faith by deprecating the spheres of nature and reason, but continued to reverberate well into the seventeenth century, expending themselves eventually in the new scientific philosophy, which for Donne, would throw 'all in doubt'.[9]

Hence the formal disciplines of scholasticism that Faustus rejects in favour of a distorted humanism, are their Elizabethan extension in moderate Anglicanism, imbued partially therefore with the dogmas of the continental reformers, and reflecting the ascendancy of Pauline and Augustinian fideism. Official Anglican orthodoxy had made justification by faith the eleventh of the Thirty-nine Articles, which if anything made it more suspicious of 'unsatiable speculation' than medieval scholasticism had been of '*curiositas*', yet in neither case were knowledge and reason anathemized as such, but were rather divorced from a proper contemplation of the supreme beatitudes of mankind, the way of salvation and the content of faith. This traditional suspicion of the disintegrating pursuit of natural philosophy at the expense of its divine counterpart – disintegrating because it threatened the whole metaphysical structure of thought, with its witness to other than empirical realities – goes some way to explain Marlowe's evident conviction that the traditional wisdom, embodied in the homiletic framework of the play, can still offer something cogent to the more disordered, albeit vigorous, energies of Renaissance humanism. Thus in portraying Faustus's ambition to 'live and die in Aristotle's works' (I.i.5) as merely the preamble to dispensing altogether with the divinity they are supposed to serve, Marlowe is dramatizing the centuries-old rebuke of scholasticism, this time to a species of brash new humanism which would indulge itself exclusively in profane philosophy, preferring the divinity of knowledge (Adam's sin) to a knowledge of the divine. La Primaudaye shares a similar Augustinian misgiving in *The French Academie*, where he makes it clear that those wise fools who cultivate philosophy *per se*, court a far more dangerous ignorance:

> Therefore, *S. Augustine*, reproving those to whom the bookes of *Plato*, and *Aristotle* were more delightfull than the holy Scriptures, calleth them fooles, as beeing people that learned a science like unto their studies, *videlicet*, leaves and no fruit, that is to say, faire words, and not solid and true virtues . . . [they are] sencelesse, because they under-stand not anything as they ought to doe, touching that which is requisite for them to knowe, thereby to obtaine eternall life.[10]

Marlowe, to be sure, gives imaginative sanction to the humanist aspiration and Faustus's rapturous lines celebrate all the idealized promise of that world of 'profit and delight,/Of power, of honour, of omnipotence', (I.i.52–3); a world indeed which, properly reconciled to faith, could accommodate an Erasmus or a Thomas More with ease. But Faustus's perverted ambition consists not only in an unnatural striving to make his dominion exceed its legitimate natural sphere, to 'raise the wind, or rend the clouds' (I.i.58); but in promoting the mind of man by means of necromancy to a god-like potentially, it also epitomizes the blasphemous exaltation of reason over faith, and re-enacts the presumption inherent in the fall of the angels and of man. It is not so much the humanist endeavour to which the play takes exception, for Marlowe underwrites its desperate enterprise for Indian gold, for 'strange philosophy' and all the 'princely delicates' of the new-found world with unqualified enthusiasm; not the generalized aspiration, but the manner of its peculiarly tainted realization in Faustus to which Marlowe's caveat is addressed; for Faustus elevates a Renaissance openness to experience above the traditional disciplines, and the *artes* above divinity, and in pursuing the humanist ideal, makes it antithetical both to nature and to God.

Faustus's exordial proposal to 'settle' his studies and to 'sound' their depth, is essentially nominal and schematic, intended not so much as an intellectually profound critique of the scholastic curriculum, as a psychic profile of the Doctor's attitude towards it, born as that is of spiritual pride and 'self-conceit'. It is pride, the fount and origin of all sin, which prompts him, from the very moment of his commencement, to be a divine merely 'in show', and to level instead at the end of the secular disciplines. Implicit in this primal dissatisfaction is the suggestion that Faustus's evaluation of divinity derives from a prideful and meretricious delight in 'excelling all' in theological debate, a delight jaded inasmuch as the depth of his concern is merely the limited and nugatory satisfactions of sterile dialectic, in which he has too easily 'gravelled the pastors of the German church' (I.i.112). His rejection of philosophy, physic, and law arises from similar motives: again the impression is of a monstrous arrogance, 'glutted' and cloyed with the learning it inevitably trivializes in the process of humouring its own vainglory. In levelling at the end of every art, both divine and secular, Faustus's purview is not only egocentric, but reductively anthropo-centric; for it is precisely in this finite and subjectively defined aspect that all modes of knowledge can be made to seem incompatible with the mounting reach of his own god-like ambitions, allowing their all-too-facile dismissal. If, therefore, it is true that 'logic's chiefest end' is merely to 'dispute well' (I.i.8), then Faustus has attained it already, and wishes for a 'greater miracle' (I.i.9). If, likewise, it be true that the end of physic is simply the 'body's health' (I.i.17), then in that too Faustus's achievement is such as to have made his 'common talk sound aphorisms' (I.i.19); but his vaulting pride, unsatisfied with this, wishes to be 'eternized for some wondrous cure' (I.i.15), affecting even the divine prerogative of raising the dead to life. If the 'universal body of the law' can be reduced to a 'petty case of paltry legacies' (I.i.33,30), then its servility and illiberality may conveniently be assumed. In every case, rejection is the consequence of a wilfully perverse logic, which in considering each category of know-ledge *in abstracto* and *in saecularis*, unassimilated, that is, to its status in the metaphysical hierarchies of the great university curriculum, is able to repudiate as the limited object of 'petty wits' what is manifestly incapable thereby of accommodating Faustus's blasphemous designs upon the div-inity of knowledge. Through a preexistent and sinful disordering of the imagination, Faustus arbitrarily reduces all intellectual categories to the service of his own spiritual pride, and then spurns them as insufficient to an even greater presumption. It is, indeed, a kind of intellectual idolatry finally: man's adoration of himself in revolt against God, which St Augus-tine and St Bernard saw as the origin of evil in man, and the cause of his intellectual ruin.[11]

Some intellectual impairment, together with a conscience inimical to the order of grace and the promptings of faith, must be held accountable for Faustus's obdurate blindness to those ultimate truths concerning the redemption of man and his eternal completion on a supernatural level, revealed in the Scriptures and professed by the very divinity in which he has so recently commenced. Taking up Jerome's Bible, Faustus collocates two of the most comfortless statements of the Law concerning the ultimate destiny of man: '*Stipendium peccati mors est*', and '*Si pecasse negamus, fallimur, et nulla est in nobis veritas*' – a syllogism apparently insistent, as Helen Gardner has said, on man's mortality and fallibility,[12] but the determinism of whose elided logic is entirely Faustus's own. Faustus's mutilation of the sequel to each truncated text cannot be because, as a Doctor of Divinity, he is somehow ignorant of the Gospel promise of divine mercy; rather, the selectivity is induced by a blind arrogance which seeks to depreciate all values, both human and divine, to the point where they can be shuffled off as merely insulting to the debased immortality of his own longings. And it is because this distorted perception of the Scriptures seemingly collaborates with, and even justifies, the animus of his disordered ambitions, that it comes to him with the full weight of a necessary and leaden conviction:

> If we say that we have no sin, we deceive ourselves, and there
> is no truth in us. Why then, belike, we must sin, and so
> consequently die.
> Ay, we must die an everlasting death.
> What doctrine call you this? Che sarà, sarà:
> What will be, shall be. Divinity adieu!
>
> (I.i.42–7)

There is no question that Faustus does not actually believe what he is saying here; indeed, sixteenth-century treaties, expounding the relevant Augustine doctrines, take pains to point out that, in the absence of grace – in this case, excluded from the soul of Faustus by his swollen pride – the accusing conscience remains bound to the conviction of man's culpability before the Law, immune both to the consolations of the Gospel and the prospects of divine mercy, out of a profound sense of guilt and original sin. Perkin's 'Of the nature and practise of repentance', first published in 1593, makes it clear that the conscience, proceeding through just such a practical syllogism as does Faustus, and arraigning the guilty soul before a knowledge of the Law and the Justice of God's wrath, remains petrified in this posture of condemnation, unless and until it is redeemed therefrom by a faith in divine mercy as revealed in the Gospel. A sinner having convicted himself in the knowledge of the Law, says Perkins,

> in the second place must follow the *Application* of the former knowledge
> to a mans own person, by the worke of the conscience . . . and this
> application is made in a forme of reasoning, called a practicall syllo-
> gisme, in this manner:

> *The breaker of the law is guiltie of eternal death*, saith the mind.
> *But I am a breaker of the Law of God*, saith the conscience, as a witnesse and as an accuser:
> *Therefore I am guiltie of eternall death*, saith the same conscience, as a judge.[13]

From this mortifying conclusion, says Perkins, arises such conscientious 'feare' and trepidation in respect of 'Gods judgement against sinne' that unless it be 'delayed by a knowledge of the Gospel, it brings man to 'desperation' and eternal damnation.[14] The man that looks forward to life everlasting must go further, applying to himself through conscience the revealed mercy of God in the following manner:

> *He that is guiltie of eternall death, if he denie himselfe, and put his affiance on the death of Christ, shall have righteousnesse, and life eternall*, saith the mind enlightened by the knowledge of the Gospell:
> *But I being guiltie of eternall death, denie my selfe, and put all mine affiance in the death of Christ*, saith the conscience . . .
> *Therefore I shall have righteousness and life everlasting by Christ.*[15]

Perkins is, however, explicit concerning the necessity for grace in this second and regenerative action of the conscience: elsewhere, he says that the soul of man, having been smitten by a 'Legall feare' in respect of its sinfulness, the 'action of Grace' may thereafter 'stirre up the minde to a serious consideration, of the promise of salvation propounded . . . in the Gospel'.[16] Faustus's conscience may therefore be understood to be in just such a state of desperate resignation, contumaciously resistant to the grace by which he might be redeemed, preferring with a fatal perversity an intellectual bondage to the Law which condemns him, and moreover, solely for the reason that the latter insists on precisely that sense of human confinement which he would perforce 'mount above'. In this way, Faustus's despair is born out of his presumption – is, indeed, a complex rationalization of it; and his offence against the first of the sins against the Holy Ghost necessarily brings in train the second. For the terrible price of his aspiration is to freeze his conscience in an abject condition of 'legal feare', a state of mortal danger in which he inevitably risks 'desperation' and the threat of 'eternal damnation'.

If Faustus's distortion of the Scriptures points thus to a case of conscience bereft of grace, to this condition also must be ascribed his subsequent inability to repent. And yet in neither instance is it true to say that grace is not offered to him, or, as several commentators on the play have asserted, that Faustus is 'a victim to Augustinian and Calvinist predestination'[17] and that the controlling deity is the 'Calvinist tyrant of mass reprobation'.[18] The complex relationship of divine grace to human free will was one of the central issues of the Reformation, and one to which Marlowe, as a Cambridge divinity student, could hardly have remained obtuse; certainly it is an issue crucial to our understanding of Faustus's repeated crises of conscience, convinced as he is by the Bad Angel's prophecy that he 'never shall repent' (II.ii.17) and that his heart is in some arbitrary sense 'hardened' (II.ii.18) by some inscrutable act of cosmic malevolence. And yet he is at the same time made intellectually aware, at least, of the ever-present possibility of forgiveness and repentance, both through the offices of the Good Angel and indeed of the Old Man, whose vision of the objective availability of 'precious grace' is an offer Faustus is none the less unable to appropriate through lack of faith.

In this lies the fundamental distinction between his case and the plight of Philologus in Nathaniel Woodes's *Conflict of Conscience*, with which Marlowe's play has often been profitably compared;[19] for although both protagonists become enmeshed in the coils of theological despair through a want of faith, implicit in Woodes's Calvinism is the premise that faith is the fruit of grace, from which Philologus believes himself 'secluded'[20] and reprobated thereby through the secret justice of the eternal decree. Marlowe, on the other hand, makes Faustus's damnable lack of faith and incapacity to repent the ineluctable and tragic consequences of his own obdurate will, 'sin by custom' growing so far into 'nature' (V.i.41) that he can scarce bring himself to name 'salvation, faith or heaven'; an impression entirely confirmed by the Old Man's valedictory censure of the Doctor as a 'miserable man' who from his own soul, actively 'exclud'st the grace of heaven' (V.i.117). What Sanders calls the 'predestinarian crux',[21] the doctrine whereby a few are effectually called and have faith and grace imputed to them, the rest being 'hardened' and reprobated according to a hidden higher justice, is entirely alien to the moral organization of Marlowe's tragedy. The Old Man's precepts concerning the continued amiability of Faustus's soul and the accessibility of grace reflect a scholastic and moderate Anglican emphasis upon the idea that the wicked render themselves incapable of salvation.

Hence, although predestination was written into the Thirty-nine Articles,[22] moderate Anglicans tended only to imply the negative consequence of the doctrine, namely reprobation, preferring, as had the medieval church, to dilute its Augustinian harshness with the milder concept of God's indiscriminate charity, and to characterize it as a relative, rather than an absolute, decree of the divine will. Accordingly, while for Perkins, wearing his Calvinist hat, it is 'not true, that all men are called to salvation' or that 'grace . . . is offered to all',[23] for Hooker, on the other hand, the 'natural will of God desireth to impart unto all creatures all goodness', all men thus being 'capable of inward grace', the decree of reprobation being only as it were 'a consequent will, forasmuch as it presupposeth in man a just and deserved cause leading him who is most holy hereunto'.[24] Since Faustus's conscience is mortified and in a manner rendered desperate by his original excision of the Gospel texts concerning the promise of salvation, he makes himself subject to this 'consequent will' of God; for although throughout his twenty-four years, hell has continuously to strive with grace for 'conquest' in his breast, he consistently shuns the latter out of a despairing conviction that he is not worthy of it. Thus he becomes, in the words of Hooker, one of those

> to whose charge it may truly be laid . . . that the grace which is offered they thrust from them; and do thereby, if not in word, yet in effect, pronounce themselves unworthy of everlasting life . . . And for this cause, that will of God which sin occasioneth to decree the just condemnation of many, is by the same necessity enforced to leave many unto themselves, whose greatness of sin hath constrained him to set down the sentence of death.[25]

And while Faustus's obsessive and morbid fatalism engenders in him the inference that God has 'hardened' his heart preparatory to condemning him, like Pharoah and Judas, Hooker makes it abundantly clear that Faustus's damnation is likewise a consequence of what divine prescience foresaw in Pharoah's heart, namely 'an obstinate will'.[26] As for the related delusion, constantly insinuated to Faustus's thoughts by the Bad Angel, that he is 'but a man condemned to die' (IV.v.21), Hooker would insist, on the contrary, that 'condemnation is not the end wherefore God did create any man', but rather 'it be an event or consequence which man's unrighteousness causeth God to decree'.[27] We may judge with Robert Bolton, that Faustus's hardness of heart has come about through a lasting addiction to the unrighteousness for which he will finally be condemned, a condition of reckless foolhardiness sometimes to be observed in the seared consciences of 'notorious malefactors': of such as these Bolton says, 'A long rebellious, and remorseless continuance, and custome in sinne . . . Satan's hot iron searing their consciences . . . so . . . that they are desperately hardned'.[28]

Thus Faustus's *hamartia* may be seen initially, like Hamlet's, as a mistake in reason; but here, more particularly, as a tragic disposition to elevate his fallible reason, glutted with its own conceits, above the transcendent realities of faith, which it so fallaciously repudiates. In this he sunders that organic nexus in which the scholastic tradition had held faith to be the precondition of all natural understanding; a supremacy which the Reformation was merely to render absolute by insisting on an original vitiation of man's rational powers. St Anselm's humble deprecation of reason in the introduction to his treatise *Proslogion* – 'I do not seek to understand so that I may believe, but I believe so that I may understand'[29] – reappears distortedly in Calvin's savage denunciation of man's cognitive insufficiency before the mysteries of faith: human intelligence, he says in the *Institutes*, is utterly destitute 'in reference to the knowledge of God'.[30]

Particularly ironic, therefore, is that Faustus's fateful rejection of divinity, which the Good Angel is to insist would have saved him had he so 'affected it' (V.ii.106), arises out of a specious syllogism, itself the diseased logic of a mind inured to faith, and to which divinity perforce seems 'Unpleasant, harsh, contemptible, and vile' (V.i.108). Necessarily, therefore, Faustus's appetite for knowledge resolves itself indistinguishably into an explicit and familiar form of Epicurean self-indulgence;[31] for Faustus's impulse is not to comprehend God, but to 'gain a deity' (I.i.62); not to strengthen faith by a speculative immersion in analogies of the divine in creation, but to degrade it to a blasphemous 'trust in Belzebub' (II.i.5), affecting thereby the necromantic 'cunning' of an Agrippa, and a specifically unnatural power over nature's elements. It is not just that Faustus's false humanism leads him to aspire to a knowledge-without-faith ironically debased at the outset by the grosser images of appetite in which it is couched; it follows inevitably from this that the satisfactions gained by such knowledge, endorsed as they are by the terms of his Satanic deed of gift, should prove humanly disappointing, and his deluded faith in Mephostophilis the cause in the end of his bitterest suffering.

Seen in this way, Faustus acquires an impressively tragic stature; Marlowe manages to suggest that the fate to which his protagonist yields and by which he is finally destroyed, is in large measure a subjective and psychic malfunction, the intellectual initiative involved in repudiating grace precipitating his conscience ever deeper into a spiritual vortex from which it cannot be saved except by faith. Nor is his tragic attempt at self-signification other than merely influenced by the extramundane order to which it appeals; for to the extent that this order permeates and interconnects with the real state of sublunary nature, its existence may be seen to be in some measure symbolic, the spirit entities merely the shadowy extensions of Faustus's own consciousness, externalizing impulses, either for good or evil, which it already contained.[32] In this eminently Elizabethan sense can be understood the Good Angel's vainly repeated attempts to interpret to him what evidently he already knows, namely the way of 'Contrition, prayer' and 'repentance' (II.i.16); while strictly speaking, the only 'power' either the Bad Angel or the devils have over him is to insinuate those entirely subjective doubts concerning his worthiness to be saved through which, paradoxically, he damns himself. In a manner reminiscent of *Appius and Virginia*, and as James Smith has pointed out, all the supra-human entities are both significant as symbols, and significant as themselves;[33] but, in spite of what Faustus himself may suspect, in neither order of potentiality do they have any more than a relative influence upon his actions, and certainly no absolute capacity to enforce him to a destiny he has not himself willed. Even Mephostophilis's apparent readiness to accept responsibility for that destiny, and his gloating confession that

'Twas I that, when thou wert i' the way to heaven,
Damned up thy passage; when thou took'st the book,
To view the Scriptures, then I turned the leaves
And led thine eye.

(V.ii.91–4)

does not represent a maleficent encroachment upon the unilaterality of man's free will, but adverts rather to evil's immanent attendance upon its exercise, awaiting, as it does, the opportunity of engrossing man's venial and petty impulses to a diabolic logic of hideous and unsuspected consequence. Faustus's sinfulness was, after all, not merely the result of Mephostophilis's turning the page, but the cause of it,[34] his incipient determination, having commenced, to 'be a divine in show', indicating much the same sort of moral frailty and corruptibility exhibited by those other victims of demonic exploitation – Philologus, Hamlet, and Macbeth – with which previous chapters have been concerned.

That having been said, some ontological and dramatic distinctions may be made between the relatively abstract device of the Good and Bad Angels, and the pantheon of stage devils – in particular, of course, the tormented and stricken figure of Mephostophilis, whose dramatic substantiality is such that his dominance over Faustus verges at times on a domination of the play itself. Both categories of spirit visitants, angelic and diabolic, derive of course from the homiletic framework of the moralities, where as primitive and literal embodiments of moral impulses they tended to fight over, rather than within, the soul of man. In *Doctor Faustus* a similar psychomachia takes place, but Marlowe's art has evidently etherialized the symbolic and psychological significance of the Angels to the point where they are very nearly abstractions, and at the same time emphasized the dramatic particularity and palpability of Mephostophilis and the hierarchy of hell to the point where they are fully developed characters in their own right. But the process is not carried so far as to reduce to a clear-cut intrinsicality or extrinsicality the significance of either source of influence upon Faustus's soul; for, as Sanders has argued, the apparent objectivity of Mephostophilis is qualified by his appearance '*per accidens*', the occult manifestation of Faustus's own thoughts emanating from an unlocalized hell; and likewise, though the formalized and symmetrical utterances of the Good and Bad Angels are sufficiently ritualized to make them most obviously the functions of Faustus's conscience, they none the less refer to a numinous order quite independent of human cognition.[35] And in this their more obvious aspect as symbols of internal conflict, the Angels in fact share many characteristics in common with the stock abstractions of the morality tradition.[36] In particular, the role and function of the Good Angel may be compared directly to those dialectical encounters of Conscience with his respective homiletic counterpart already discussed in a previous chapter; in the first scene, for example, the exhortation to 'Read, read the Scriptures' (I.i.72) is, as we have already seen, a typical corrective to sinful error, counselled repeatedly by the character of Conscience in post-Reformation plays, and nowhere more urgently than in the *Conflict of Conscience*, where Philologus's moral dereliction, like Faustus's, results *ab initio* from an insufficiency of 'care' for God's Word.[37] Similar traditional and generic resonances are awakened by the Good Angel's admonitions concerning the condign wrath of God and urging of the means of avoiding it through repentance. The advocacy of both visitants seems to imply an absolute moral antithesis between the world of grace and nature which appears to align *Doctor Faustus* yet again with Woodes's play and also with *Three Ladies of London*, in both of which the world is strictly the devil's province, and where mankind's characteristic frailty is anathemized as a 'love of worldly wealth' or the 'unsatiate desire of vanishing earthly treasure'. In a not dissimilar vein, the bad Angel accords an unholy sanction to Faustus's ambitions by inciting him to a mastery of 'nature's treasury' (I.i.74), which in turn proves to be the cause for which he is finally abandoned by the Good Angel ('thou didst love the world', V.ii.99). Yet there is no appeal to the Calvinism of either Woodes or Wilson; for it is not precisely that Faustus's dreams of power and wealth are intrinsically opposed to 'God's heavy wrath', as much as that they would unnaturally accomplish by blasphemous means ('that famous art') an equally blasphemous end (to be 'Lord and commander of these elements', I.i.73,76). None of these thematic parallels need imply, of course, that Marlowe was acquainted with any of the above-mentioned plays, although it seems on the whole likely that he was familiar at least with one or other version of the Spiera literature;[38] what is beyond doubt is that Marlowe stood in a field of the Reformation at any rate adjacent to that of his predecessors, and was able to draw on a variety of theological formulations, as well as upon an established dramatic tradition, concerning the determination of moral choice. Indeed, the overwhelmingly psychic and noetic function of the Good and Bad Angels, related as they are in a dramaturgical sense almost entirely to the processes of Faustus's own ideation and conscience, rather than to any character, seems to suggest a theological rather than a specifically dramatic provenance,[39] in concept closely related to the good and evil thoughts with which the conscience was said to be afflicted. In *The Burthen of a loaden conscience* (1608), Richard Kilby writes of the origin of good and evil in the soul:

An evill thought is sent from the devill, and if you entertaine it, it bringeth the devill. A good thought is sent from the holy Ghost, as a messenger unto your soule; if you receive it, and make much of it in

your heart, the holy Ghost will enter, and putting out the Devill, will
fill you full of heavenly grace.[40]

However this may be, Faustus, in the arrogance of his pride and presumption, and moreover, with a conscience recalcitrant either to grace or
its 'messenger', is prepared to entertain only thoughts of evil, ruminating
solely on that necromantic skill through which his dreams of wealth and
power are to be realized. Valdes and Cornelius assure him that their
books of magic will verse him in a 'cunning' that will be acclaimed by all
nations, making serviceable the spirits of every element in fantasies as
diverse as the dragging of argosies from Venice, or the impersonation of
'unwedded maids' (I.i.126). Yet, ironically, it is the knowledge of the
'concealed arts' rather than philosophy and divinity, which is to prove, in
all its odious obscurity, ultimately superfluous and unnecessary; since for
all its grounding in principles and pseudo-learning, the incantational ritual
of conjuring is only the accidental cause of Mephostophilis's appearance.
The real cause, as the fiend himself points out, is Faustus's previous
abjuration of the Scriptures and of Christ, the whole blasphemous para-
phernalia of lines, circles and the tetragrammaton having no more power
in themselves than to suggest to the powers of darkness his patent willingness to be damned. Therefore do they 'fly in hope to get his glorious soul'
(I.iii.49); and the ironies inherent in Faustus's exulting cry, 'I see there's
virtue in my heavenly words', are suggestive of the compound delusion
with which he flatters both his pride and his conscience. With virtue in
either sense Faustus's words have very little to do; Mephostophilis turns
out to be subject to 'great Lucifer' rather than to Faustus's commands; and
the invocation, far from being 'heavenly', is no more than the equivalent of
praying 'devoutly to the prince of hell' (I.iii.54). And yet the first delusion
is made to sustain the second; the dream of power, after all, depends
upon a profoundly ironic transposition of values by which Faustus will
constantly invest the service of the devil with the imagery of religious
worship, offering up to Belzebub the 'blood of new-born babes' (II.i.14),
in practice of that black art for which he and his companions hope to be
canonized (I.i.119).[41]

Deprived of heaven by divinity, or so he rationalizes, and therein condemned for an inherited human insufficiency, he will devote himself wholly
to the study of that knowledge by which his human limitations may be
transcended, finding out a new heaven, and indeed a new earth, in the
monarchy of hell. The soaring aspirations of false humanism, forbidden
by a Christian heaven, can be accommodated at a price, by an equally
orthodox hell; and by a wilful and self-induced myopia, therefore, which
now holds as a 'principle' (I.iii.55) the moral suzerainty of Belzebub,
Faustus deliberately confounds 'hell in Elysium' (I.iii.59), assuaging the
terrors of damnation in the serener visions of a pagan after-life. There,

his ghost will be 'with the old philosophers' (I.iii.60); and so long as Faustus is able to maintain this humanistic vision of a transmogrified hell, subjecting the moral premise it represents to his personal convenience; so long, in short, as he can construe it merely as 'sleeping, eating, walking and disputing' (II.i.139), Faustus will 'willingly be damned' (II.i.138), for in this aspect, hell promises nothing more painful than a metaphysical extension of those intellectual pleasures whose exercise had first enkindled his pride. Therefore Faustus remains illogically and resolutely obtuse to the reality of hell, the chief testament to whose objective existence is the anguished fiend who stands before him, and scornfully contemptuous of anything that Mephostophilis's own experience can tell him about the agonizing pains of being deprived of everlasting bliss;

> What, is great Mephostophilis so passionate
> For being deprived of the joys of heaven?
> Learn thou of Faustus manly fortitude,
> And scorn the joys thou never shalt possess.
> (I.iii.83–6)

In the same way, Faustus remains impervious not only to Mephostophilis's involuntary pang of suffering which provides his directest warning: 'O Faustus, leave these frivolous demands,/Which strike a terror to my fainting soul' (I.iii.81–2); but also to those implicit parallels between the Doctor's own hubris, and the original cause – in aspiring pride and insolence – for which Lucifer and the Angels were thrown from heaven. At the same time, the element of bravado and hollow self-assurance in Faustus's scepticism is implied in his preoccupied questioning of Mephostophilis concerning the possibility of a more orthodox hell – a hell of real pain and suffering – which not only intrudes upon his comforting notions of Elysian immortality, but is ultimately destructive of the human significance which they symbolize, and for which he would pawn his soul. Mephostophilis's repetition of the received Augustinian doctrines concerning the two-fold ethos of hell, which explained it not only as an undefined state of spiritual anguish commensurate with the mind of the sufferer, but as a substantive, fully objective locality of corporeal torture,[42] is just what Faustus cannot permit himself to believe; and what cannot easily be confounded in Elysium must necessarily be discounted as a 'fable', or as 'trifles' and as 'old wives' tales'(II.i.127, 135).

But the dual Augustinian nature of eternal punishment that Mephostophilis describes answers precisely and inevitably to the dual nature of Faustus's sin: the logical relationship is set forth in Robert Bolton's *Instructions*. Inasmuch as sin consists firstly in 'Aversion from an infinite, soveraigne, unchangeable good', and secondly in 'Conversion to a finite, mutable, momentary good', there is ordained an appropriate hell:

To aversion from the chiefest Good, which is objectively infinite, there answereth *Paine of losse*, as they call it, Privation of Gods glorious presence . . . which is an infinite losse. To the inordinate conversion to transitory things, there answereth *Paine of sense* which is intensively finite, as is the pleasure of sinne.[43]

The pain of sense, the vast perpetual torture-house of finite apprehension, is not physically disclosed to Faustus until the expiration of his twenty-four years; but the pain of loss, which is the spiritual corollary of his abandonment of God and 'inordinate conversion' to the transitory goods of power, wealth and 'all voluptuousness', afflicts him from the beginning as a stinging of the conscience. Alone in his study, and oppressed for the first time with a morbid sense of isolation ('Now Faustus must thou needs be damned', II.i.1), his resolution wavers in face of the summons of prevenient grace sounding in his ears ('Abjure this magic, turn to God again', II.i.8)[44] and the admonishments of the Good Angel ('think of heaven, and heavenly things', II.i.20). But these positive impulses are countermined by a conscience fatally susceptible to despair, and by an inordinacy of will which contrives to dismiss all such retrogressive doubts and fancies as essentially subversive of its own fixed predilection for 'honour' and 'wealth' (I.i.21):

> Ay, and Faustus will turn to God again.
> To God? He loves thee not:
> The God thou servest is thine own appetite
> Wherein is fixed the love of Belzebub . . .
> (II.i.9–12)

Thus Faustus's conscience, on this occasion, is easily overruled by the blandishments of the Bad Angel and the incontinence of his own desires, whose voracity will be sanctioned by Mephostophilis himself:

> Why, the signory of Emden shall be mine:
> When Mephostophilis shall stand by me
> What god can hurt me? Faustus thou art safe.
> (II.i.23–5)

By the chilling irony of inversion[45] in which Faustus's moral perceptions are increasingly rooted, he seeks a security from the 'hurt' of God in that very hell to which the justice of God must for that reason consign him.

But it is none the less a security of whose counterfeit character Faustus is increasingly made aware, first of all by the ominous presentiments of the conscience he would suppress, issuing in omens and hallucinations, and secondly, by its continued proneness to fits of harrowing despair. For the only security represented by the heinous deed of gift is that which Lucifer 'craves' (II.i.36); for Faustus, on the contrary, its endorsement validates nothing more propitious than his own extinction. Something of the enormity of the sin he commits in signing away his soul communicates itself to him in the congealing of his blood and in the appearance of the words '*Homo fuge*'; as in *Macbeth*[46] these are fatal visions, proceeding from the heat-oppressed brain, by whose flickering incandescence Faustus is brought momentarily to the brink of a terrifying awareness of his own spiritual bondage:

> *Homo fuge*! Whither should I fly?
> If unto God, he'll throw me down to hell.
> My senses are deceived, here's nothing writ:
> O yes, I see it plain, even here is writ
> *Homo fuge*! Yet shall not Faustus fly.
> (II.i.77–81)

To aid him in this recovery to an uncertain equilibrium, Mephostophilis, in what is to become a recurrent device in strengthening Faustus's 'resolution', stops up the access to debilitating remorse by providing 'somewhat to delight his mind' (II.i.82) in the form of a 'show' of dancing devils. Throughout the play such apparent delights will be proffered to Faustus as infernal palliatives to deaden the torments of conscience;[47] and in so far as he yields to them, he likewise yields himself further and further into the power of hell. In this respect, his perilous complacency identifies him as one of those 'bruit beastes' who, in the words of Richard Kilby,

> give credit to deceitful shewes and flattering enticements, and so are wilfully snared of the Devil, who with his alluring baites draweth them on to destruction; and the further he draweth them, the surer he is of them.[48]

But the pain of loss, that never-dying worm of conscience which is to Faustus a precursor of that personal hell attested to by Mephostophilis, can never be alleviated for very long; and Faustus's observation of the heavens affords him a glimpse of 'those joys' from which he deems himself everlastingly alienated, and for whose loss he blames the wickedness of his ministering fiend. Mephostophilis's reply is all gall and wormwood: 'Twas thine own seeking Faustus, thank thyself' (II.ii.4); and the subsequent inadvertency of the devil's denigration of heaven as less fair than the creature for whom it was made – though intended, as M. M. Mahood says, as a sop to Faustus's humanist pride[49] – ironically evokes in him a vision of legitimate human dignity which that same pride had caused him originally to repudiate:

> If heaven were made for man, 'twas made for me:
> I will renounce this magic and repent.
> (II.ii.10–11)

His wavering and uncertain thoughts are once again objectified by the entry of the two Angels, whose diametrical utterances concern once again the possibility of repentance; the Bad Angel, seeking as always to consolidate his victim's despair, and invoking plausibly the counterfeit authority of the deed of gift, suggests that as the 'spirit' Faustus has contracted to become, God 'cannot pity' him. But the compulsion of the bond's terms is implicitly negated by the otherwise superfluous appearances of the Good Angel; the reality, as Jump has pointed out, is that the deed is 'validated from minute to minute' by the inordinacy of Faustus's presumption and the inveteracy of his despair.[50] A fleeting perception of the ever-present feasibility of repentance and forgiveness is, however, mediated to his conscience by the Good Angel, and for a moment Faustus seems to escape the insidious logic of his own contumacy: 'Who buzzeth in mine ears I am a spirit? . . . /Yea, God will pity me if I repent' (II.ii.14, 16). Yet this transient insight, suggestive of the inchoate stirrings of the faith by which he might be saved, is obliterated once more by the dark prognosis of the bad Angel, and Faustus's incipient movement towards forgiveness is stillborn, dammed up by a fatal despondency: 'My heart's so hardened I cannot repent' (II.ii.18). Richard Greenham's *Two Treatises of the comforting of an afflicted conscience* indicates graphically how vulnerable the wounded conscience was thought to be to the mendacious 'buzzing' of sin and Satan, who pervert and misrepresent the doctrines of repentance in order to terrorize the sinner into a conviction of his own reprobation: 'there is', he writes,

> no time to late to repent in . . . howsoever sinne and Sathan . . . would especially perswade him. For as the humming Bee having lost her sting in another, doth still notwithstanding make a fearefull and grievous noyse by her often buzzing about us, but is nothing able to hurt us; so sin and death, having lost their stings in Christ Jesus, do not cease at all, even in the height of the parching heat of our consciences, to make a murmuring: and with the furious stormes of temptations to terrifie us and our consciences, albeit they can never sting us.[51]

Faustus's soliloquy reveals how frequently have such storms of temptations afflicted his conscience, echoing with a thunderous insistency the certainty of damnation; moreover, his own vertiginous inclinations have been aided and abetted by devils, who put into his possession various instruments of self-destruction: 'swords and knives/Poison, guns, halters and envenomed steel' (II.ii.21–2). Faustus is thus sucked down in such moments into a maelstrom of suicidal desperation well-known to sixteenth-century theologians: caught between the Scylla of his own hardened conscience, and the Charybdis of diabolic intrigue, he is reduced to that state of spiritual agony whereunto, in the word's of John Woolton, often times a man is drawn and tormented as it were of an hangman, by his own unquiet Conscience, or by the malicious and guileful temptations, of his mortal and capitall enemy the Devill.[52]

Faustus's withdrawal from the dizzying abysses of self-annihilation is accomplished through another of those evasions of responsibility only too readily available to him in the moral oblivion of 'sweet pleasure', ever the infernal anodyne to 'deep despair' (II.ii.25). It is true that here the theme of sweet pleasure seems to transcend all that is merely drossy and sordid in Faustus's Epicurean lusts, modulating in its poignant imagery all the objective validity of an uncorrupted humanism that in him was from the outset blighted:

> Have not I made blind Homer sing to me
> Of Alexander's love, and Oenon's death?
> And hath not he, that built the walls of Thebes
> With ravishing sound of his melodious harp,
> Made music with my Mephostophilis?
> Why should I die then, or basely despair?
>   (II.ii.26–31)

But Faustus himself seems partly to recognize that the plangent harmonies of Homer and Amphion are nothing more than the consolatory music of Mephostophilis, the siren accompaniment to his own damnation; and his tone of forced and querulous insistence, resulting in the salvage once again of his resolution, merely counterpoints the deeper misgivings of conscience.

Nor are these misgivings deferred other than provisionally by Faustus's escapist proposal to dispute and reason of 'divine astrology' with Mephostophilis; for he soon discovers that, in the province of learning as with his earlier request for a wife, the fruit of his compact with Lucifer is disillusionment. The devil's inability to tell him anything deemed to be 'against our kingdom' (II.ii.72), comes rather short of the sweeping unconditionality implied in the deed of gift, which was to render Faustus 'more than thou hast wit to ask' (II.i.47); on the contrary, Faustus's wit finds itself restricted and hidebound in its quest for knowledge, to 'freshmen's suppositions', and the 'slender questions Wagner can decide' (II.ii.55,49). More galling still is that the catechizing of Mephostophilis only confirms him in the knowledge of the old Aristotelian axiologies, and leads him by a process of reasoning which, as James Smith has indicated, 'resembles . . . the scholastic argument *a contingentia*',[53] ineluctably through the theory of intelligences to a consideration of the Supreme Intelligence, the Unmoved Mover at the centre of scholastic cosmology; the ultimate question for Faustus is, 'Now tell me who made the world' (II.ii.67).

Receiving no reply, Faustus for the first time perceives the loathsome-ness of his sin, dismissing to 'ugly hell' the 'accursed spirit' who would therein damn 'distressed Faustus' soul' (II.ii.76,77); and this provokes in him yet again a movement to repentance, the frenzied irresolution of his thoughts symbolized by the contrapuntal utterances of the Angels. On this occasion, the movement only just falls short of that full state of atonement implied in the offices of 'contrition, prayer, repentance'; but his precipitate impulse to call upon 'Christ, my saviour' for help in saving his soul is almost immediately deflected by the materialization, in a moment of dramatic and awesome peripeteia,[54] of the trinity of Hell, who reconfirm him in their sombre doctrines. But the arch-fiend Lucifer's assertion that

> Christ cannot save thy soul, for he is just;
> There's none but I have interest in the same
>
> (II.ii.85–6)

has no more substance than the bond by which that interest is claimed; equally without foundation is the suggestion that the gravity of Faustus's sin has put him beyond the pale of Christ's justice. Corrosive imputations such as these were widely recognized as a favourite device of the devil to undermine the faith of those labouring under a strong conviction of sin; and Faustus's facile credulity in this respect identifies him as one of those sinners who are, in the words of Robert Linaker, ever more ready

> to take the knowledge of [their] sinnes from
> Sathan . . . [who] will make them greater than they
> be, to throw [the sinner] headlong into dispaire.[55]

The incident marks a profound shift in the basis of Faustus's relationship with the infernal powers; for he who aspired to be 'as great as Lucifer' (II.i.52) is now his abject and servile slave; and though still prepared to gratify the god of Faustus's appetite, Lucifer will ensure the obedience of his servant hereafter as much by coercive threat as by the opiate of sweet pleasure. In short, hell is disclosed to Faustus in all its terrifying reality in order this time to frighten him into submission; yet another of the better-known subtleties of Satan, who, according to Robert Bolton, will only appear to his own in his 'true' and terrible likeness at such time as 'Hee have them at some dead list, and desperate advantage . . . And then hee playes the Divell indeed, and shewes Himselfe in His colours'. In the meantime, continues Bolton,

> Hee labours might and maine to keepe [his victims] in as merry a moode
> as may bee. He laies about Him, by all wayes and meanes, He can
> devise, to plot and provide for them, and that with great variety and
> curiosity, fresh successions and supplies continually, of pleasures,

contentments, the countenance and favours of the times, sensuall satisfactions, all earthly prosperities.

. . . For Hee knowes full well, that if they endured much hardship
in His service, they might perhaps thinke of seeking after a New Master;
that want of comfort in the world, might draw their hearts to delight in
the *Word* . . . lest thereupon, they breake out of His fooles-Paradise,
into the *Garden* of Grace.[56]

For just such a purpose does Belzebub extenuate the harsher threats of
Lucifer with the emollient and diverting attractions of a court masque; a
'pastime' in which the Seven Deadly Sins will appear in their 'proper
shapes and likenesses', and which Faustus welcomes with an ironic and
ill-omened propriety, as a sight 'pleasing' as was 'Paradise . . . to/Adam
the first day of his creation' (II.ii.105–6). More aware now of the realities
of hell, he is similarly more aware of the gardens of grace as a real, if
painfully inaccessible alternative, once by himself denied, but now by sin
denied to him. For one of the major ironies of *Doctor Faustus* is that in
attempting to exceed through devilish exercise the knowledge of what
heavenly power permits, he very quickly exhausts what is permitted him
to know by those whose power and dominion stretch no further than the
bounds of hell, and by whom the mind of man, therefore, must inevitably
be dissatisfied. It is thus entirely appropriate that after his cosmological
dispute with Mephostophilis, the pleasures offered him by the devil are
no longer of that heroic order of speculative discovery and learning which
led Faustus inadmissibly to the evidence of the Cause and End of all
knowledge, but consist almost wholly, from this point onwards, of the
inglorious pursuit of the innocuous and the trivial – what is not, in short,
offensive to 'our kingdom'.[57] In the episodes concerning Faustus's dashing
of the Pope's solemnity, his necromantic exploits at the courts of Charles
and of Vanholt, and his gulling of Benvolio and the horse-courser, the
high-aspiring dream of 'knowledge infinite' takes on the rather more
shrunken dimensions of a conventional and earth-bound Epicureanism.
Faustus seems here to be content with – perforce, indeed, must remain
so – 'all things that delight the heart of man' (III.i.60); and for what is
left to him of his four and twenty years, so he assures Mephostophilis

> I'll spend in pleasure and in dalliance,
> That Faustus' name, whilst this bright frame doth stand,
> May be admired through the furthest land.
>
> (III.i.62–4)

Faustus's degeneration is thus symbolized by the substitution in him of
the divinity of knowledge – itself blasphemous – for the equally damnable,
but more mundane vanities of mere fleshly pleasure: in Bolton's words,
those 'favours of the times, sensuall satisfactions and all earthly prosperit-

ies' that are the permitted consolations of the devil. And for the remainder of Faustus's unexpired time, these reduced and frivolous contentments seem wholly sufficient to his diminished vision; only on one occasion do the enfeebled stirrings of conscience intrude upon his self-forgetful surrender to a life of unmeaning inconsequence. In the midst of cozening a horse-courser, who believes that in buying a delusory horse, he is a 'made man forever', Faustus awakens briefly to an awareness of his own delusory bargain: 'What art thou, Faustus, but a man condemned to die?' (IV.v.21). But the despair that once again drives distrust into his thoughts is, in the hardened state of Faustus's conscience, only too easily confounded with a 'quiet sleep', its sharper passions absorbed and dissolved in the equally deadly sin of presuming upon the divine mercy:

> Tush, Christ did call the thief upon the cross;
> Then rest thee, Faustus, quiet in conceit.
>
> (IV.v.25)

In this manner, Faustus assuages his conscience yet again through the forgeries of his own self-deceit; this time yielding to the specious comforts of that spiritual state known to theologians as carnal security, the 'quiet' of which 'conceit' is treacherously short-lived. Richard Greenham's *Two Treatises*, for example, would convict Faustus of a mortal complacency in being one of those who

> going quietly awaie, and sleeping in carnall security . . . and neglecting to make conscience of their sinnes done long agoe; sodainely have falne into such horrour of minde, that (the violent remembrance of all their sinnes surcharging them) they have beene overwhelmed.[58]

It is the Old Man's intervention which both reawakens Faustus from this protracted and complacent torpor, and safeguards him from a sequent 'horrour of minde' in which he is tempted to use on himself the devil's dagger. Once again, his crisis of conscience assumes a nightmare quality of suspense, the opposed impulses towards repentance and despair resulting either in a fixed inanition of the will ('I do repent, and yet I do despair', V.i.68), or its sickening tergervization between the spiritual 'comfort' extended by the Old Man, and the physical torment threatened by Mephostophilis. The encounter not only externalizes the striving of hell with grace in Faustus's soul, but recapitulates in a moral and dramatic coda the entire syndrome of perversity and evasion by which his conscience has been hardened against that grace. The abiding factors in his inability to repent – the compounding of his initial pride and despair with a numbing complacency, his fatal susceptibility to either tactic of diabolic manipulation, whether it be the bait of sensual pleasure, or the rod of physical violence – all these contribute to and coalesce in Faustus's final act of repudiation, itself a logical consummation of the first. The Old Man's divinity restores those prospects of salvation censured in Faustus's original misprision; what to his unregenerate conscience appeared 'harsh, unpleasant, contemptible and vile', in the Old Man's discourse only '*Seems* harsh, and all unpleasant' (V.i.46).[59] To the eye of faith the rigours of the Law are merely apparent: Faustus, to be sure, is subject to the Law as a 'man'; but only if he perseveres in sin 'like a devil' will he be rendered liable to its execution; its precepts are thus expounded with a balance and proportion wholly absent in the Doctor's earlier rejection of theology, and delivered in the spirit of grace as a 'kind rebuke' in pity of Faustus's 'future misery'. For it is still not too late for him to repent; if 'sin by custom grow not into nature' (V.i.41), searing his conscience through an habitual and insensate wickedness, then Faustus's doom is by no means irrevocable, nor his soul irreclaimable. Even at this stage, his will remains free; but the Old Man shares Hamlet's insight concerning its critical susceptibility to the influence of 'monster custom', whose use 'almost can change the stamp of nature/And either [lodge] the devil or throw him out' (*Hamlet*, III.iv.170–1).

But neither does the Old Man allow an undue sufficiency to the will; that, as Brockbank has noted, would be to 'court the Pelagian heresy' which affirmed that the human will could attain salvation unaided by grace.[60] On the contrary, the Old Man's vision of the angelic vial implies not only the need for, but, as we have seen, the objective possibility of 'precious grace'; but it is a possibility subjectively attainable only through faith and the avoidance of despair. For a last moment, Faustus appears to waver; but his 'desperate steps' have in the past shown a precipitant incapacity to shun the 'snares of death' laid for him by the devil. And so it proves now; Faustus's unnecessary belief in the legitimate claims of hell's 'right' (V.i.54), prompts in turn not only his doomed acquiescence in the legitimacy of his 'arrest' by Mephostophilis for disobedience, but, moreover, his equally unnecessary subjection to the threat of diabolic torture. On the other hand, the Old Man's triumph, like the trials of David and Job, demonstrates both the ascendancy of faith over the powers of 'vile hell', and also the limited subordinacy of evil to the providential purposes of which it is but a part

> Satan begins to sift me with his pride,
> As in this furnace God shall try my faith:
>> (V.i.119–20)

For Satan, it seems, like the witches in *Macbeth*, is merely licensed to co-operate in the purification of virtue, sifting the faithful according to his own evil desires, but as part of a vaster process over which God himself presides.[61] This is strictly as far as Hell's 'right' goes; but Faustus, devoid of faith and subject to an overwhelming conviction of sin, cedes to it an exclusive interest in the possession of his soul coextensive with the illusory terms of his bond, and thereby surrenders to hell its only power to destroy him. By the continuing irony of inversion, Faustus repents not to God but to Mephostophilis, his act of contrition itself an infernal parody of the Christian means to repentance.[62] And this, his last renunciation of grace, is rewarded appropriately enough, by the 'pride of Nature's works'; in a final resurgence of humanist yearning, Faustus craves of Mephostophilis the ultimate distraction: to have for his paramour Helen of Troy, whose 'sweet embracings' will both glut the longings of appetite, and banish 'those thoughts' subversive of his newly affirmed vow.

Yet the 'heaven' which is in Helen's lips, and the 'immortality' conferred by her kiss, are merely the ironic precedents of an eternity of suffering in hell, to which his soul is in reality being sucked forth. The exalted imagery, all fire and air in the rapture with which it celebrates Helen's beauty as a symbol of Renaissance idealism, gives ambiguous life also to those baser elements in Faustus's consciousness, which compel him implicitly to recognize, and hence to sublimate, the destructive reality behind the celestial beauty of form. For the lyric intensity of vision which evokes the pagan comparisons with Semele and Arethusa is offset by the Christian context, which permits neither Faustus's muse nor his soul the untrammelled ecstasies of flight: both are betrayed by the more sinister connotations of fiery annihilation and extinction, which are written as an infernal palimpsest to the classical images of erotic consummation.

When we next meet Faustus, his 'changed' looks announce that mood of melancholy solitude and weary indifference which arouses the concern of his fellow-scholars, and is to convey itself in the apathetic tones of his farewell to them. Now that his last hours have come, what had seemed to him the apotheosis of his boundless and inexhaustible ambitions, the possession of the 'heavenly' Helen, triumphant symbol of all that had appeared unconfined to time or limit, is utterly forgotten: her phantasmic impermanence transmutes thus to a metaphor for all those transient and present pleasures indulged in by Faustus during life, which must now, in death, be sauced with everlasting pain. And it is to view his oncoming ordeal that the gloating triumvirate of hell ascend; during the course of the 'gloomy night' we witness, in a theatre of cruelty now entirely of the devil's making, those exquisite tortures of conscience, of apprehensive horror, pain and deprivation, which constitute the remainder of Faustus's earthly existence. The man who aspired to godhead, who sought to make himself a heaven on earth, finds now that hell must be his 'mansion, there to dwell' (V.ii.87): that is the final reality which cannot be overreached, and Marlowe spares us no details of the 'desperate lunacy' to which sinners like Faustus were held to succumb at the approach of death, and for which theologians reserved their most lurid prose. Of the eleventh-hour agonies of those to whom repentance comes too late, Robert Bolton has this to say:

> Give me a great man who . . . tumbles himselfe in the glory and pleasures of the present: Throw Him from the transitory top of His heaven upon earth, upon His last bed: present unto His eye at once the terrible pangs of approaching death; the ragefull malice of the powers of Hell; the crying wounds of His bleding conscience; the griefely fourmes of His innumerable sinnes; His finall farewell with all worldly delights; the pit of fire and brimstone, into which He is ready to fall; And I tell you true, I would not endure an houres horrour of His wofull heart, for His present Paradise to the worlds end.[63]

Faustus, too, has but 'one bare hour to live' (V.ii.132). So also are the impulses of his bleeding conscience externalized for the last time, the prophetic judgments of the Angels anticipating the eschatological justice of God's 'heavy wrath' shortly to be visited upon him. In like manner does the Good Angel deliver a poignant reminder of those worldly joys – 'riches, pleasures, pomps' (V.ii.101) – for which he has forever lost hope of 'celestial happiness' (V.ii.104), recalling irresistibly the Gospel words: 'For what shall it profit a man, if he shall gain the whole world, and lose his own soul?' (Mark 8:36). And finally, an actual 'pit of fire and brimstone', its jaws open ready to receive him, is physically disclosed to Faustus's terror-stricken gaze by the Bad Angel:

> Now Faustus, let thine eyes with horror stare
> Into that vast perpetual torture-house.
> (V.ii.114–15)

Deserted by the scholars, bereft of the lugubrious comfort even of the Good and Bad Angels, Faustus is reduced to a tragic isolation. Now the confining and earth-bound dimensions of time and place combine at once to affirm and thus to foreclose upon the humanity he had repudiated.[64] For he would have gained a deity, in vain to transcend all that moved between the quiet poles, finds himself bound by his creature status to the same silent and inexorable rhythms of the 'spheres of heaven' (V.ii.134) by whose ever-moving processes, all in nature passes to eternity. The stars continue to move, the clock will strike, and the logical impossibility of Faustus's pleas for 'a year, a month, a week, a natural day' in which to repent, serves only to make less credible the idea that he who had so signally failed to do so in twenty-four years, could ever do so now. His evanescent vision of Christ's redemptive blood streaming in the firmament merely confirms by its infinite remoteness the moral prostration of his soul; his upward yearnings – 'O I'll leap up to my God' (V.ii.143) – are fatally countermined by a profoundly oppressive knowledge of sin, Satan, and his own death, which pulls him down, rending his heart with a paralying sense of guilt:

> One drop would save my soul, half a drop. Ah my Christ –
> Rend not my heart for naming of my Christ;
> Yet will I call on him: O spare me Lucifer!
> Where is it now? 'Tis gone, and see where God
> Stretcheth out his arm, and bends his ireful brows:
> Mountains and hills, come, come, and fall on me,
> And hide me from the heavy wrath of God.
>
> (V.ii.145–51)

The momentary image of mercy is here replaced by that of avenging justice, the empyreal vision of Christ's blood banished by his mortified conscience just as it had earlier killed his own heart-blood (V.ii.12). For in the equation of man's ultimate destiny, Faustus's conscience is still bound to the irrationality of perceiving only a single term: the premise of sin, judgment and death upon which his whole career was predicated, and by whose doomed and circular logic his fate is sealed.[65] It is the inexorability of that judgment which now fills his mind's eye: and his appalled conscience reflects therein a terrifying apocalyptic vision of the God of Revelation, in order to escape whose heavy wrath Faustus longs for extinction: an extinction either of body – in the 'entrails of yon labouring cloud' (V.ii.158) – or of body and soul together, through metempsychosis into some brutish beast, which after death is 'dissolved in elements' (V.ii.176). All of these compulsions were held by writers on conscience to afflict sinners suffering from the final depths of extreme horror: the shrinking self-abhorrence, the rending of the heart with almost physical agonies of sorrow and guilt, the desperate craving for extinction – such descriptions were bound together with familiar scriptural intimations of the Last Judgment (via Hosea, Luke, and Revelation)[66] to convey something of the harrowing death-bed torments awaiting the impenitent. So Robert Bolton says of the conscience, in its penultimate moments, that it

> rents the heart in pieces with such desperate rage . . . it makes a man so extreamely miserable, that Hee would make Himselfe away; wishes with unspeakable griefe that Hee had never been; that Hee might returne into the abhorred state of annihilation; that hee were any other Creature; that Hee might lye hid world without End under some ever-lasting Rocke, from the face of God.[67]

This, as Roma Gill has said, 'is the final hope of the pride of Wittenburg';[68] and everything for which that pride had stood is abjured in Faustus's terminal utterance, an expiring and ineffectual attempt to appease God by apostasizing the doctrines of the devil: 'I'll burn my books' (V.ii.188).

But if Faustus attains here to an uncertain *anagnorisis*, the phrase harks back rather too equivocally both to the necromantic works of wise Bacon and Abanus (I.i.153), and to his later wish never to have seen Wittenburg, 'never read book' (V.ii.45), implicitly suggesting thereby that he imputes his downfall to the sinfulness of all learning as much as to its misdirected abuse. We may allow that the play itself shares something of Faustus's uncertainty, placing his Renaissance rebellion within a simplistic medieval framework which, in affirming the dangers of practising more than heavenly power permits, makes no absolute distinction between learning's golden gifts and its devilish exercise. Some of this ambiguity is traceable to the play's genesis in an age which saw a diffuse and undifferentiated threat to revealed 'truth' in any manifestation of the immorality of knowledge, whether it be the magic of a Cornelius Agrippa or a Doctor Dee, or the equally blasphemous innovations of a Copernicus or a Galileo. But in treating of the nature of Faustus's sin, and of the crises of conscience which it precipitates, Marlowe is on surer ground: in so far as Faustus sins, it is not what Perkins would define as an 'outwarde' sin – that is, in act and realization – but an inward corruption of the 'minde, will and affection', of which he cites two characteristic expressions: 'That there is no God' and 'That the paines of hel may be eschewed'.[69] Faustus's appetite for knowledge is therefore shown, in terms that a contemporary audience would not fail to understand, as debased from it inception by his abandonment of divinity and presumptuous denial of hell. Marlowe's own humanism, according to the allegations of the Baines note, was evidently permeated with just such a Faustian 'corruption' of the mind, will and affection; almost certainly he epitomized, in himself as much as his creation, that questing spirit of the Renaissance, which in one modern view, 'regarded human nature and human history as a realm of unmeasured possibilities and felt that medieval religion failed to do justice to human freedom and human destiny'.[70] But just as the spirit of humanism had eventually to reach an accommodation with the scholastic synthesis from which it sprang, so is the suggestion implicit in the Epilogue, that its uninhibited and wholesome growth in Faustus – obliquely, and perhaps significantly referred to as '*Apollo's* laurel bough' – might have been accomplished within the bounds of the traditional sanctions. The 'deepness' that entices 'forward wits' is that secular and purely atheistic impulse of the Renaissance which would indulge the speculative reason exclusively in the realms of nature and the world, and to which the Reformation restitution of faith came as a reaction. The history of the sixteenth century is the history of the tension between the two; and the unassimilated focus of the age, precariously divided in its loyalties between religion and knowledge, is unerringly reflected in what we know of Marlowe's own consciousness.[71] But his play, though in some respects similarly dissociated in its moral impulses, is, in the end, surer of them; for while Faustus's 'wondrous knowledge' is admired no less by his creator than by the

'German schools' he once ornamented, its abortive pursuit is condemned, explicitly and at every point, by heaven, hell and his own conscience, and is seen to merit the justice of that end which, notwithstanding, 'every Christian heart laments to think on'(V.iii.14).

7

The Atheist's Tragedy

Superficially, at least, *The Atheist's Tragedy* invites comparison with *Doctor Faustus* as a moral treatise directed, once again, at the presumption of those 'forward wits' who would exalt a puny rationalism over the mysteries of grace and faith, and whose addiction to a blasphemous and imponderable 'deepness' epitomized for the Renaissance a dangerous tendency to unsatiable speculation in nature and the world. Like Marlowe's, Tourneur's play is a tragedy of knowledge, a similarly graphic depiction, as Ornstein puts it, of yet another atheist's 'harrowing journey towards the spiritual and moral knowledge which is gained by less arrogant minds through a simple act of faith'.[1] There, however, the resemblance ends. Not only is D'Amville's creator less equivocally disposed than is Faustus's towards the heady prospects of knowledge infinite – the limitless exercise of man's aspiring mind resulting, for Tourneur, in nothing more heroic than the conventional villainies of a conventionally politic brain – but his perception of positive value in the Christian myth carries a more absolute certainty of conviction, and the sufferings of the impious who incur its exemplary sanctions are, in *The Atheist's Tragedy*, affirmatively counterpointed by the felicities of the pious who so beatifically transcend and vindicate them. Moreover, whereas Faustus's *hubris* affects a god-like potentiality over mundane phenomena, avid to discern, by supernatural and forbidden means, those mysteries above nature by which her elements may be controlled, D'Amville affects only such limited and material goals – pleasure, profit, power – as are consistent with his purely naturalistic and sceptical beliefs.[2] His atheism does not admit the hypothesis of a God-centred universe, and denies altogether the premise that the observable order of nature is completed by a numinous order of divine grace beyond man's rational comprehension. On the contrary, and like Shakespeare's Edmund, he makes a goodness out of nature, and binds his reason to the service of her mechanistic and amoral laws. But perhaps the most fundamental distinctions to be made between the two plays are those concerning their doctrinal and metaphysical allegiances, in which a profound transition is apparent. While Faustus's revolt represents a vigorous, if perverted, release of the energies of Renaissance humanism in the face of a confining scholastic synthesis which it threatens to fracture, it is wholly evident that in the decadent world which D'Amville inherits, that synthesis is already utterly dislocated, and his revolt against faith is a logical, if equally disordered, extension of a typically seventeenth-century emancipation of nature and reason. Tourneur's atheist is one post-Reformation consequence, just as Bacon was another, of that aggressive Renaissance secularism whose Elizabethan awakenings had been so powerfully symbolized in Faustus; for in labouring to indemnify faith by deprecating nature, Calvin hammered so relentlessly on the theme of their separation, as incidentally to prosper not only the cause of those empiricists and Pyrrhonists to whom the supernatural was unknowable, but of those sceptics and mechanists to whom it was neither knowable nor necessary.

The Atheist's Tragedy is, in short, the first of a series of Jacobean dramas which together present a changed picture of the idea of conscience. In them is bodied forth that stark voluntarist world of the early seventeenth century in which the old medieval assumptions, the common property of Marlowe and Shakespeare, are nowhere in evidence. D'Amville and Borachio, who identify wholly with the new spirit of scientific rationalism, and whose godless creed denies validity to all that lies beyond 'Nature and her large philosophy' (1.i.4), act out their vain and wretched pretensions in a theatre of cosmic justice directed now by a Calvinist god of unqualified will, whose secret counsels and undetermined decrees impose awful constraints upon man's rational powers. For Calvin, of course, as for Christian orthodoxy in general, atheism was the ultimate blasphemy. But doubly outrageous to him was the unspeakable presumption inherent in erecting its unholy propositions upon the enfeebled inferences of man's vitiated reason, inferences culled, moreover, from the irredeemably perverted order of nature, which atheists would exalt as the aboriginal cause of all being. To deny God, moreover, was to render man indistinguishable from the brute beasts; and those who, with D'Amville, observe the 'self-same course/Of revolution both in man and beast' (1.i.5–6), attributing solely to nature's power the cause of man's 'better composition', are condemned in the *Institutes* as much for their perfidious exaltation of nature as for their blasphemous disavowal of its First Cause. Of such naturalists and atheists, Calvin says, '[They] will not say that chance has made [them] differ from the brutes that perish; but, substituting nature as the architect of the universe, [they] suppress the name of God.'[3]

Tourneur's play is, of course, primarily conceived as a refutation of this heresy, its overwhelmingly contrived dramaturgy a demonstration of the two quintessential truths of man's condition, whose admission by the atheist serves as prologue to his own damnation: man's wisdom is, uncontrovertibly, 'a fool' (V.ii.248), and there is manifestly a 'power above [nature] that controls her force' (V.i.103–4). Far from removing God 'out of sight', or burying him in nature, Tourneur's most urgent concern is to make visible at every turn God's immediate regulation of the affairs of men; to dramatize the superintendent workings of a providence that, in Calvin's words, governs all natures by a process 'vigilant, efficacious, energetic, and ever active',[4] and by means which, characteristically, are above the ordinary course of nature. Neither in *The Atheist's Tragedy*, nor in Jacobean drama generally, do we find any trace of that Thomistic order of phenomena ruled and concatenated by laws, nor of that Shakespearean conception of providential justice which is executed through a series of rationally determinate secondary causes. Whereas for Aquinas, the perfection of divine providence required intermediary causes for its fulfilment, for Calvin and Tourneur the universe exhibits predominantly an order not of causes, but of arbitrary effects merely, not of reason, but of groundless will. Thus goodness, morality, and divine justice itself are beyond the scope either of man's reason to know, or his capacity to enact. The power that executes retributive justice upon D'Amville, contrives the arbitrary overthrow of his projects 'in their pride' (V.ii.272), and manifests itself ominously in extraordinary and elemental portents, is profoundly at variance with that entirely natural and reactive pattern of events which forecloses upon Richard III or Macbeth. Nor is the sudden and unexpected succour proffered to Charlemont and Castabella, which occasions in them a passive and resigned fortitude, in any way to be confused with that providence which Hamlet sees in the fall of a sparrow, and to whose eternal purposes, matured to ripeness in the nature of things, he eventually coordinates his perfected, but still voluntary, intents. Although *The Atheist's Tragedy* is the first play in which the revenge ethic is explicitly countermanded by the Christian *Vindicta Mihi*, nevertheless in the cases both of Charlemont and Hamlet, vengeance is in fact ultimately secured by the King of Kings;[5] but in each instance, the theatre of God's judgment is shaped and determined by mutually opposed theories concerning the precise mode of its dispensation. For the super-ordinant providence of Hooker and Shakespeare is pre-eminently that *universal* providence conceived of by Aquinas, which is reflected in the order of creation; they are indeed synonymous, for the most part, since both affirm the Law Divine which is the reason of order in nature. But while Calvin grudgingly concedes the existence of a corrupted order of nature instinct with a universal providence which sustains it, he submits both doctrines to that of a superintending, watchful, *special* providence, according to which nothing happens without God's counsel, and wherein all contingency dependent merely on fortune or human free will is necessarily and absolutely negated. For Tourneur, as for Calvin, the mighty are put down from their seats, and the righteous exalted, not by a teleological ordering of means to ends in nature, but by God's active and undetermined intervention in its ordinary processes; not by virtue of divine power, but as a consequence of divine decree. Thus it is that, in the metaphysically bisected world of *The Atheist's Tragedy*, where there is an absolute moral disparity between those that profess 'a divine contempt o' th' world' (I.iv.98) and those who are sinfully enslaved to its pleasures, we are evidently urged to the contemplation of that order of transcendental justice, the evidence of which Calvin describes in the *Institutes* thus:

> For in conducting the affairs of men, he so arranges the course of his providence, as daily to declare, by the clearest manifestations, that though all are in innumerable ways the partakers of his bounty, the righteous are the special objects of his favour, the wicked and profane the special objects of his severity. . . . His power is strikingly displayed when the rage of the wicked, to all appearance irresistible, is crushed in a single moment; their arrogance subdued, their strongest bulwarks overthrown, their armour dashed to pieces, their strength broken, their schemes defeated without an effort, and audacity which set itself above the heavens is precipitated to the lowest depths of the earth. On the other hand . . . the oppressed and afflicted are rescued in extremity, the despairing animated with hope, the unarmed defeat the armed, the few and many, the weak and strong.[6]

It is this voluntarist and determinist thesis of providence to which is conformed, in Bradbrook's phrase, the play's 'rigid pattern of incredible events';[7] and the apparently causeless web of coincidence and improbability through which the tragedy is resolved has for Tourneur this specifically hermeneutic significance.

Now, given this Calvinist metaphysic of intractable command, in which virtue is synonymous with divine fiat, and morality wholly unassimilated to nature, the conscience becomes merely instrumental in character, the operative and supra-rational medium of man's soul, through which the decrees of providence are transmitted and carried immutably into effect. Only to the elect is granted a partial knowledge of God's will, and the means of framing themselves in accordance with it; the rest are clouded in ignorance, their wills bound by the fetters of sin. In the case of Charlemont, the mysteries of providence are partially illuminated in his soul by the ghost's scriptural command, and thereafter he exhibits that passive patience and rapt serenity of conscience which are the inward blessings of those elected to the divine favour. As Herndl has remarked, helplessness and resigned fortitude are in general the marks of the Jacobean hero, indeed, the very measure of his virtue.[8] In this sense, the conscience of Charlemont is quite unlike that of Hamlet; for whereas in Shakespeare, the problem of evil demands action as an essential part of its solution, in

Tourneur the answer is quite specifically to take no action at all. Hamlet's conscience, moreover, is almost synonymous with that recurrent and objective process of ratiocination by which he repeatedly addresses the central epistemological questions of his own flawed universe. His ultimate perception of the good is a reasoned outcome of inferences drawn from a cumulative chain of causes in his own and others' affairs, which convince him of heaven's ordinance. Charlemont's conscience, on the other hand, is at once inimical to nature and transcendant over reason; for his moral struggle, in so far as it takes place at all, is typically not between the excitements of blood and the promptings of *reason*, but between 'the passionof/My blood and the *religion* of my soul' (III.iii.35–6).

In the evil characters, conscience is similarly opposed to nature, indeed, to that universal guilt in nature by which the unregenerate voluntarily, but necessarily, capitulate to every kind of corrupt depravation. Levidulcia is in some obscure sense aware of sin, but fatalistically regards her concupiscence as a 'natural sympathy', seemingly the 'free effect' of her own 'voluntary love', but an effect she can neither restrain, nor give reason for (IV.v.16–21). D'Amville, though similarly enslaved to sin, seeks to circumvent conscience altogether by rationalizing his perverted and unnatural lust for his niece, by an argument 'merely out/Of Nature' (IV.iii.135–6), whose logic he will enforce as a blasphemous and provocative challenge to her 'great supposed protector' (IV.iii.160). Conscience is in the wicked merely a 'yoke', silenced for so long, but sensitive in its moral judgments just so far as is necessary to drive them unwillingly and at last to a self-confessed conviction of sin, by which testimony they are, in Calvin's words, deprived 'of all pretext for ignorance'.[9] Thus it is that, although Levidulcia's suicide is committed in 'detestation of my deed' (IV.v.82), and D'Amville's self-destruction infers to him the 'judgement I deserved' (V.ii.266), neither character is capable of true repentance, merely of that remorse by which the inevitable fact of divine justice is automatically acknowledged.

The Atheist's Tragedy, then, is a dramatic dissertation which explores the theoretical implications of two mutually exclusive accounts of man's moral nature and metaphysical destiny.[10] On the one hand are the atheists, whose radical creed, illegitimately filiated to the new spirit of scientific enquiry, substitutes for the empiricist study of second causes, a wholly discrete and amoral belief in nature as an autonomous mechanism, governed by purely physical laws of cause and effect. Set against them are the Christians, Charlemont, and Castabella, whose invincible faith in a transcendental Being above nature, to which infinite power its processes are inscrutably subject, is so spectacularly vindicated in the climactic overthrow of their oppressors. D'Amville would have had an immediate and mythic authenticity for a contemporary audience; as an archetypal atheist, he represents a synthesis culled from popular opinion and various Renaissance confutations of atheism.[11] The antecedent elements of this synthesis have been thoroughly explored by Ornstein and others,[12] whose valuable researches have served to illuminate, through contemporary perspectives, the atheist's characteristically scientific outlook, his elevation of an inadequate natural philosophy, his view of man as animal, and his attachment to such typically Epicurean goals as pleasure, power and profit.

In a somewhat undramatic exposition, therefore, D'Amville and Borachio systematically rehearse the cardinal tenets of their 'large philosophy': nature's laws determine the 'self-same course/Of revolution both in man and beast' (I.i.5–6), who are in consequence only to be distinguished by 'man's . . . better composition' (I.i.9); his 'being's excellency', on the contrary, need to be ascribed to nothing above his 'Nature' (I.i.14,15). Since it is true, moreover, that all life must yield to 'Nature's weakness', and death casts up 'Our total sum of joy' (I.i.16,17), the rational man owes it to himself to accumulate and augment the earthbound felicities of which 'Wealth is Lord' (I.i.30), by the industrious increase of his own power and substance. Himself a part of nature's mechanism, he is nevertheless able through his intellectual capacity to understand and adapt to his own ends her autonomic processes, by these means ensuring the continuance of that posterity wherein lies man's only claim to eternity. By the energetic propagation of himself, both in his own progeny and the resources 'Whereby they live and flourish' (I.i.58), the rationalist may in some measure escape the central fact of human mortality to which his materialist creed condemns him. Thus D'Amville can say of Rousard and Sebastian:

> Here are my sons . . .
> There's my eternity. My life in them
> And their succession shall for ever live,
> And in my reason dwells the providence
> To add to life as much of happiness.
>   (I.i.123–7)

In this resides the chief difference between what Murray calls the rational atheists, D'Amville and Borachio, and their sensualist counterparts, Levidulcia and Sebastian, for whom reason is entirely submerged in the instinctive and indiscriminate indulgence of physical lust.[13] For them, a compulsive carnality is justified in the name of 'Wise Nature' (I.iv.78): Levidulcia upbraids Castabella for an unnatural chastity in refusing to wed the ailing Rousard, in a long harangue which repudiates the dictates of 'reason' and the 'barren mind' (I.iv.69) as essentially subversive of that 'work/Of generation' (I.iv.75) by which nature revives her age. Distinctly animal-like in her predatory licentiousness, Levidulcia exemplifies not so much reason's inadequacy as what Calvin describes as its total deformity and ruin.[14] D'Amville, by contrast, denigrates with Borachio the foolish improvidence of spending either one's substance or oneself on 'a minute's pleasure' (I.i.27), and his subsequent attempt to gratify his physical appetites by ravishing his daughter-in-law is subordinated to the eminently rational task of securing descendants. *The Atheist's Tragedy*, indeed, examines several varieties of godlessness,[15] and Soquette, Fresco and the false precisian Languebeau Snuffe collectively symbolize that irredeemably sin-laden and degenerate world which is so markedly a feature of the Calvinist *mythos*. But it is D'Amville primarily who exemplifies what, for his creator, is the monstrous iniquity, not only of accommodating nature's perverted amoralism to the depraved misuses of reason, but of blasphemously opposing the providence of a merely human reason to a divine providence whose very existence it would deny. In the voluntarist and dislocated universe in which he operates, the atheist is crushed finally by those vast metaphysical dichotomies whose sanctions he so casually pretermits, and the vanity of his ambitions is adumbrated in the series of ironic reversals by which they are successively and summarily negated. All his schemes and plots come to nothing: the murdered Montferrers reappears to haunt him, his disinherited nephew returns to claim his lawful patrimony, the enforced marriage of Rousard and Castabella proves sterile, and the judgment intended for Charlemont falls quite literally upon his own head. But more than this, their overthrow awakens him to a conscience-stricken perception of his own guilt and the generalized inadequacy of human reason that testifies irresistibly to the reality of an avenging and outraged Deity.

In thus objectifying D'Amville's *anagnorisis*, Tourneur clearly takes his cue from the ideas propounded in prose confutations of atheism;[16] for it was widely recognized that no matter how vaingloriously such scoffers made 'pregnant wit' the architect of their own 'commodious providence' (I.i.110,112), they were nevertheless unable to escape the fearsome agonies of conscience. William Vaughan's treatise reaffirms Calvin's dictum that the vulnerability of atheists in this respect amounted to 'an example of the fact that some idea of God exists in every human mind',[17] notwithstanding that such knowledge may be temporarily effaced or obscured by repeated wickedness. In *The Golden-grove* (pub. 1600) Vaughan declares:

> Thus we see, that there is engraven in the hearts of men a certaine feeling of Gods nature, which can never be rooted out. And although swinish Atheists doe laugh at that, which I have written touching the Godhead, *yet that is but a laughter from the teeth outward, because inwardly the worme of conscience gnaweth them much more sharply then all hote searing irons*.[18]

So it is that D'Amville, to whom the murder of Montferrers is but a matter for 'violent laughter' (II.iv.89) and who seems able to 'disburden' his conscience by the 'satisfaction' of further crimes (IV.iii.96), comes to realize before he dies that a creed built upon the freedom of the reason can only deliver him at last to a 'loathsome horror' of sin (IV.iii.225) and an abject terror of death.

Given this connate and finally inextinguishable insight available even to the unregenerate conscience, it is easy to appreciate the widespread Renaissance supposition that those who attempted to root out its 'engraven' knowledge of God's nature were nothing but fools. D'Amville and Borachio congratulate themselves on their 'amplitude of wit' (I.i.119), and the 'judicious' design of their Machiavellian plot (II.iv.101), but the final cataclysm which overwhelms him demonstrates to D'Amville the precariously limited strength of natural understanding. In spite of the vaunted wisdom by which he attempts to outreach other men's wit, D'Amville's self-inflicted death-stroke duly humbles him to the Psalmist's truth ('The Fool hath said in his heart, There is no God': Psalms 14:1), and justifies the scathing obloquies enunciated in such treatises as Fotherby's *Atheomastix:*

> But what is the *Atheist* then, if he be not a man? I finde it affirmed, in the writings of the learned, both of *Divines*, and *Philosophers*, both of *Christians* and *Pagans;* yea, and that by full consent; that all impious *Atheists*, and deniers of God. . . . are in very deed, not better than mere *Fooles*. Who, being destitute of reason (the true specificall difference of a man) cannot truly be called men, but in an abusive and unproper acception.[19]

But although before his death and judgment, D'Amville experiences the 'fearful torments' of conscience, and confesses to the foolishness of unbelief, there is for him neither hope of conversion nor escape from the unalterable decrees of a providence which strikes down the wicked even as it safeguards the innocent. For atheists were authoritatively considered to be numbered among the reprobate, eternally predestined to damnation; and of those 'beastes' who make 'open profession of contempt against [God] and all religion', John Dove has this to say:

> But as for these, they mocke God in despight of him, they sinne upon malice, and therefore their blasphemye is against the Holy Ghost, which is love and charitye. There is no hope of their conversion, because our Saviour hath already pronounced sentence of damnation against them, saying: Their sinne shall never be forgiven, neither in this life, nor in the life to come.[20]

If the course of D'Amville's damnable career ironically describes, in its purely secular orientation, that 'self-same course of revolution' as more fundamental forms of life – its genesis, state and decay yielding in a limited and finite sense to 'Nature's weakness'[21] – that of Charlemont suggests the regenerate progress of a soul elected to the divine favour and therein confidently assured of its salvation. Symbolically drowned in the wars and 'buried' by his uncle, he is metaphorically reborn, in the aftermath of the ghost's visitation, to a blissful and self-reliant piety, schooled to attend with patience that 'success of things' by which he ultimately inherits all the blessings he formerly 'Stood ready to be dispossessed of' (V.ii.280). He embodies, with Castabella, the Calvinist virtues of patient fortitude, chastity, and a passive submission to the divine will. After his imprisonment, he is translated to that serene state of grace and peace of conscience which distinguish the adopted souls of the elect, and bears himself thereafter, in the manner of his father, with such a native goodness as if 'regeneration had been given/Him in his mother's womb' (II.iv.66–7). The wholesale transformation that comes over Charlemont,[22] from a wayward 'inclination' and 'affection to the war' (I.ii.2,14) that would place the obligations of family honour above its mutual and 'contracted life' (I.ii.93), to a humbled and obedient acquiescence in the will of providence as revealed by the ghost, seems in this light not so much an inconsistency in Tourneur's characterization, as a deliberate attempt to suggest that moment of regeneration which Calvinists believed manifested itself as much in the outward demeanour of the believer as in the inner assurance of his own conscience. 'True regeneration', says Thomas Morton, in his *Treatise of the threefolde State of man*,

> is not so small a matter, neither maketh so light a chaunge in a man, but that it may be plainly discerned where it is present . . . For regeneration being a totall and a supernaturall change of the minde, will, affections, thoughtes, wordes and dedes of a man, cannot be hid or doubtfull for any long time, but will shewe it selfe both to the eyes of other men, and much more to the conscience of the beleever himselfe.[23]

It is partly because the change of 'minde' and 'conscience' is 'totall' and moreover 'supernaturall' in origin, that its psychological implications remain unexplored in Charlemont. On the contrary, change is merely imputed to him without inner turmoil or obvious moral struggle, somewhat in the manner of 'that fire' which, in the words of his counterfeit funeral oration, 'revive[s] the ashes of/This phoenix' (III.i.35,36), so that divinity comes to seem, in very truth, the description, rather than the instruction, of his life (III.i.40–1). Nevertheless, its outward effects are clearly evinced in the graveyard: for what to D'Amville is a place 'full/Of fear and horror' (IV.iii.285), its disinterred death's-heads mortifyingly vexatious to his conscience, to Charlemont and Castabella, on the contrary, is as 'fit a place for contemplation' (IV.iii.3) as for sleep. Moreover, the sight of their innocent composure convinces the atheist that there is indeed

some other
Happiness within the freedom of the

Conscience than my knowledge e'er attained to.
(IV.iii.285–7)

But the play also develops, in its opening scenes, two other patterns of contrast sub-joined to the central metaphysical debate between the values of godliness and godlessness: the contrast between honour earned and honour bought, and between love and lust. The dramatic purpose of these minor themes is at an obvious level further to distinguish the Christians and the atheists, but they serve also to underline that universal deformity of both reason and nature to which the whole of creation is heir. Charlemont, in his desire to fight in the wars, is identified with family honour rather than with his uncle's dynastic acquisitiveness; but from the very outset, he too demonstrates the inadequacy of his reason. Encouraged by his uncle's offer of gold to supply his expenses, he advances the claims of honour in a moving interview with Monteferrers, the ironic effect of which is to remind us how far the unreasoning naiveté of the soldier has been manipulated by the scheming politician.[24] For Charlemont's sincere desire to *earn* honour has been seconded, and thus subtly undermined, by his uncle, who would 'disinherit' his 'posterity' to secure its '*purchase*' (I.i.88–9). Moreover, it is D'Amville who originally applies the epithets of honour to a project rooted merely in Charlemont's unthinking 'disposition' and 'affection' for the wars, and does so in order to coordinate his nephew's somewhat nebulous and irrational motives to the unscrupulous machinations of his own Machiavellian intellect. The reasons of honour are properly neither Charlemont's own, nor, from his point of view, fully rational; for they are allowed to predominate over both his obligations to Castabella and his duty to his father. Indeed, as its only surviving scion, the increase of honour to his 'house' actually threatens its survival. Nevertheless, we are meant to admire the sincerity, if not the soundness, of his motives, their nobility, if not their logic; for it is the 'soldier's heart' in which love and courage are so 'near allied' (I.iv.48) that is deliberately opposed to the perverted rationality of the atheist, simultaneously indifferent to all egos except his own, and all motives other than power and wealth.

Just as Charlemont's quest for honour demonstrates the frailty of his understanding, so Castabella's fidelity in love is never permitted to question the play's general thesis concerning the wholesale depravity of purely 'natural' instincts. For Castabella, love is opposed to lust just as in the broader dispensations of the play-world, morality is abstracted from nature, a term which, for Christians and atheists alike, carries the same meaning.[25] She therefore never directly denies the arguments of nature, whether addressed, by Levidulcia, to her 'blood', or by D'Amville, to her reason; but rather sublimates her love as a 'chaste affection of the soul', above the adulterate promptings of the flesh, a virtue she describes as the very 'minion of Heaven's heart' (II.iii.1–4). Forced to marry Rousard against her will, she refuses to submit divine ordinances to the judgement of reason, and yields her 'duty' if not her 'heart' to heaven's 'pleasure' (II.iii.13–14). These antitheses are more fully debated in the charnel-house, where D'Amville rationalizes his incestuous designs upon Castabella by arguments drawn from that 'general liberty/Of generation' which nature allows to all creatures other than man:

> Incest? Tush!
> These distances affinity observes
> Are articles of bondage cast upon
> Our freedoms by our own subjections.
> (IV.iii.124–7)

Castabella's protests are not addressed to the logic of D'Amville's philosophy, only to its insufficiency; for, as she points out, to argue 'merely out/of Nature', prescribing authority and law from its example, not only ignores the omnipotent goodness of God, but is unworthy the 'Prerogative of Nature's masterpiece' (IV.iii.135–6,138). Confessing that the 'horror' of the argument confounds the capacity of her 'understanding', she commends herself to the protection of 'patient Heav'n', and prayerfully invokes the thunderbolts of its wrath (IV.iii.163–4).

Whereas for the atheists, the moral law represents an artificial restraint upon man's natural freedoms, for the Christians it supererogates the laws both of nature and reason. Their translation to the realms of grace is apotheosized above all in the graveyard, where their chaste slumbers – in a place, moreover, where on every hand, lust and murder commit sin together – symbolize a blessed indifference either to sense or sensuality, and a supreme confidence in the directing hand of heaven. This sublime contempt of a world conceived of as a charnel-house of moral decay and corruption – a world from which only the elect can remain aloof – is surely the dramatist's attempt to give meaning to the central Calvinist theorem of a fragmented and divided universe, wherein all 'Guilt is from nature, whereas sanctification is from supernatural grace'.[26] To D'Amville, the sight of Charlemont and Castabella asleep among death's-heads, suggests a peace of conscience beyond the scope of knowledge; and indeed, divines such as Thomas Morton would have confirmed that the excusing consciences of the faithful in regard both of their own and imputed righteousness could deliver them to just such a state of serene transcendence over sin, death and suffering: 'This excuser' [sic] he says,

> is he who only can abide the trials of God's justice, who maketh the faithful rejoyce in all miseries; yea secure in regard of danger. It maketh them triumph over sinne, Sathan, hell, death and damnation, and

replenisheth their hearte with such a perfect peace, whereby they feele the joyes of heaven, even whilst they live upon earth.[27]

But, as Morton goes on to point out, this kind of excusing conscience 'commeth of a true faith';[28] a faith which, inaccessible to merely rational knowledge, is awakened in Charlemont by the summoning mandate of heaven, revealed in turn by his father's spirit, whose essence is, by definition,

> Above the nature and the order of
> Those elements whereof our senses are
> Created.
>
> (III.i.85–7)

Charlemont's moral development in the play, therefore, to some extent counterpoints D'Amville's own, and involves his progress from an earthly code based upon the rationale of honour, to a heavenly code of patience; from a somewhat passionate impulsiveness, to the ineffable peace of conscience; in short, from the folly of corrupted reason, to the supra-rational wisdom of faith. Thus his initial pursuit of honour not only leads him unerringly to that species of 'ill success' previsioned in the forebodings of Montferrers and the presageful tears of Castabella; but its brittle logic is unilaterally abrogated by a divine imperative which insists that the onus of revenge, to which Charlemont is by honour and convention ostensibly bound, is the absolute prerogative of the King of Kings. But even then, Charlemont's 'doubtful heart' (II.vi.67) is slow to credit the full implications of what has been revealed to him: he attempts first to rationalize the ghost's appearance as an 'idle apprehension' or a 'vain dream' (II.vi.61), and even a second visitation fails to rid him of the painful conviction that his wrongs are both heavier than 'patience can endure to bear' (III.i.145), and that their cause is the business still of his 'understanding to deliberate' (III.i.136). Only after his fight with Sebastian, during which the ghost, reappearing for the third time, interposes between Charlemont and the prosecution of his revenge, is he finally content to resign the dubious propositions of both honour and passion to the ultimate dispositions of 'Him . . . /to whom the justice of revenge belongs' (III.ii.33–4).

Partly as a result of his religious forbearance in not striking down Sebastian whilst he had the chance, Charlemont is arrested and thrown into prison, an experience which so humbles the 'pride' of his 'mortality', and so arms him against the weight of his afflictions (III.iv.27–9), that he becomes heir to what Calvin called 'the exulting confidence of the saints'.[29] As with Job, the value of suffering for Charlemont lies in simply accepting its incomprehensibility, and he learns the absolute futility of all efforts to commensurate divine with human justice, of all attempts to measure 'our conditions' by our deserts. (Cf. Job 6:2, 'Oh that my grief were thoroughly weighed, and my calamity laid in the balances together'.) For to submit providential punishment to the judgment of unaided reason is merely to increase its power to hurt; in this sense, 'profane conceit' and 'our own constructions' are, as Charlemont comes to acknowledge, the 'authors of/Our misery' (III.iii.13–16). To accept such affliction, on the other hand, is to acquire not just a 'heart' above the reach of maliciousness, and a 'fortitude' in scorn of all contempt, but a sovereign ascendancy over the passions:

> But now I am emp'ror of a world,
> This little world of man. My passions are
> My subjects, and I can command them laugh,
> Whilst thou dost tickle 'em to death with misery.
> (III.iii.44–7)

Charlemont's stoical fortitude epitomizes the Christian mystery of redemptive suffering expressed in Matthew 24:13, that 'he that shall endure to the end, the same shall be saved'; a truth vindicated in retrospect, when, standing possessed of all the symbols of heaven's favour and the world's regard, Charlemont's triumph is declared by the Judge to illustrate 'the power of that eternal providence', which, he affirms

> Hath made your griefs the instruments to raise
> Your blessings to a greater height than ever.
> (V.ii.271–4)

Above all, it is Charlemont's submission of his conscience to this directing power that not only enables him miraculously to elude the mortal dangers to which he is everywhere exposed, but delivers him up to that euphoric acceptance of mortality in which the churchyard's 'humble earth' comes to seem the 'world's condition' (IV.iii.21–2) at its best, and death, a victory, whose 'honour' lies beyond the exigent of a merely mundane existence. In short, his conscience is imbued with those 'inestimable felicities' which, according to Calvin, sustain the 'pious afflicted' once the light of providence has entered their souls:

> But once the light of Divine Providence has illumined the believer's soul, he is relieved and set free, not only from the extreme fear and anxiety which formerly oppressed him, but from all care. . . . This, I say, is his comfort, that his heavenly Father so embraces all things under his power – so governs them at will by his nod – so regulates them by his wisdom, that nothing takes place save according to his appointment; that received into his favour, and intrusted to the care of his angels, neither fire, nor water, nor sword, can do him harm, except in so far as God their master is pleased to permit. . . . Hence the exulting

confidence of the saints. . . . 'The Lord taketh my part with them that help me' (Ps.cxviii.6) 'Though an host should encamp against me my heart shall not fear' (Ps.xxvii.3) 'Yea, though I walk through the valley of the shadow of death, I will fear no evil' (Ps.xxiii.4).[30]

But the intimately regulated order of effects predicated by the Calvinist conception of providence, though it frequently supercedes, does not ultimately pre-empt the existence of what the reformer calls 'inferior causes' in the dispensation of divine justice; indeed, it is often through such causes that the divine will is visibly manifested, affording categorical proof that *all* events, whether in or above the realm of nature, proceed from the secret counsel of God. To this end, Calvin affirms in the *Institutes:*

> the Christian will not overlook inferior causes . . . If he is not left destitute of human aid, which he can employ for his safety, he will set it down as a divine blessing; but he will not, therefore, be remiss in taking measures, or slow in employing the help of those whom he sees possessed of the means of assisting him. Regarding all the aids which the creatures can lend him, as hands offered him by the Lord, he will avail himself of them as the legitimate instruments of Divine Providence.[31]

The fixed contemplation of a superintending providence therefore enables Charlemont to entertain each and every opportunity of escape as evidence of its beneficent favours. Thus he accepts the offer of money to redeem him from prison as the induction to 'some end/Of better fortune' (III.iii.59–60), acknowledging the courtesy of Sebastian in being its instrument. Later on, having killed Borachio in self-defence, he again makes his escape, forswearing his own inclinations to submit to the law, on the supposition that 'It may/Be Heaven reserves me to some better end' (IV.iii.35–6). Finally, it becomes clear that the better end for which he has been preserved is to become just such a 'legitimate instrument' of providence, as those inferior causes of 'aids' and 'means' by which he has hitherto been assisted. Entering in time to interrupt *ante flagrantem* the graveyard assignation of Soquette and Snuffe, he appropriates the latter's disguise of sheet, hair and beard, wisely forbearing to 'expostulate' the purpose of such a 'friendly accident' (IV.iii.71–4); a purpose which in fact triumphantly declares itself when he is made the means of Castabella's deliverance from 'the arm of lust', frightening D'Amville away by his opportune emergence from the charnel-house. Charlemont's sojourn in the churchyard thus culminates in his sublime conviction that his sufferings have been justified; that heaven has made him 'satisfaction' for his 'wrongs' by reserving him for the 'worthy work' which has just now crowned the actions of his life (IV.iii.179–85). This unspeakable exaltation of conscience and spirit continue to sustain him throughout the trial-scene, where his impregnable courage in the face of death prompts D'Amville to request his body after execution, in order to find out by his 'anatomy' the efficient cause of a 'contented mind' (V.ii.167). 'My wit', says D'Amville,

> Has reached beyond the scope of Nature; yet
> For all my learning I am still to seek
> From whence the peace of conscience should proceed.
> (V.ii.156–9)

But the peace of conscience is not to be achieved either by 'art' or by 'Nature'; nor is it within the comprehension of a merely naturalistic 'Philosophy' (V.ii.161, 166); rather, as Charlemont affirms, it 'rises in itself', being a spiritual state of purely supernatural origins. In all these assumptions, the atheist displays the insufficiency of his reason, for the moral serenity and guiltless courage of his victims are the imputative effects of Divine grace; and it is specifically to heaven, therefore, that Charlemont in the end attributes all his blessings, including those 'gracious motives' which *made* him 'still forbear/To be mind own revenger' (V.ii.275–7).[32]

Just as the congruent pattern of events in the graveyard confirms Charlemont in the mysteries of a luminous faith, so a parallel series of events, by their very *un*naturalness, contribute to the overthrow of D'Amville's proud reason, and enforce him to a final recognition that there is a power above nature. The providence that safeguards the innocent and emancipates them to the beatific consolations of a liberated conscience, in like manner and by similar extraordinary processes, so binds the unregenerate conscience of D'Amville that he succumbs, like Macbeth, to its stricken imaginings. Paradoxically, his conscience becomes increasingly susceptible, as it veers towards unreason, to the evidence of that order of supernatural truth by definition incommensurable with a view of life rooted exclusively *in rerum natura*. Ghostly apparitions, real or imagined, combine to remind him inescapably of the 'loathsome horror' of his sin; and Charlemont's macabre disguise precipitates him to that state of distraction where such sights as the staring death's-head (IV.iii.211), the vision of Montferrer's ghost in 'A fair white cloud' (IV.iii.235), and its later manifestations in a dream (V.i.27–31), prove inexorably vexatious to his conscience, and awaken it, hitherto benumbed or seared, to the sinful enormity of his crimes. He is reduced, like Faustus, to that abject state of morbid terror said to afflict unrepentant sinners, and particularly atheists, once they became subject to intimations of their own mortality. Like Faustus, he suffers apocalyptic visions of annihilation, crying out in an agony of guilt to be overwhelmed by mountains, or consumed in the elements, so that his body, 'circumvolved' within a cloud, might be scattered by thunder to 'nothing in the air' (IV.iii.249–52).[33] Like Faustus, his soul is shaken by paroxysms of despair as it confronts the truth it has hitherto desired to avoid: accusing himself of cowardice, D'Amville admits that

> the countenance of
> A bloodless worm might ha' the courage now
> To turn my blood to water. The trembling motion
> of an aspen leaf would make me, like
> the shadow of that leaf, lie shaking under it.
> (IV.iii.236–40)

Tourneur's portrayal of D'Amville's spiritual desperation, and the leaf-like tremblings of his conscience, seems influenced by Calvin's doctrine that even among those who 'deny the being of a God', a sense of deity is nevertheless engraved upon their consciences; of atheists the *Institutes* affirm:

> The most audacious despiser of God is most easily disturbed, trembling at the sound of a falling leaf. How so, unless in vindication of the divine majesty which smites their consciences the more strongly the more they endeavour to flee from it. They all, indeed, look out for hiding-places, where they may conceal themselves from the presence of the Lord, and again efface it from their mind; but after all their efforts they remain caught within the net.
> . . . [In such cases] the gnawings of conscience is not unlike the slumber of the intoxicated or the insane, who have no quiet rest in sleep, but are continually haunted with dire horrific dreams.[34]

But having put, for the moment, his brain in 'order', making it the 'happy instrument' both of Charlemont's rearrest and the sealing up of his own 'assurance', D'Amville endeavours to evade all further excoriations of conscience by closeting himself with the gold coins for which he murdered his brother, 'ravishing' his 'sense' with their angels' voices (V.i.9). Moreover, he takes ironic refuge in what Tourneur evidently sees as an habitual and characteristic blasphemy inherent in the atheist's creed: the sacrilegious denial of astrological influence. Like Shakespeare's naturalist Edmund, who denies not only an 'enforced obedience' to the planets, but also their 'divine thrusting on' (*King Lear*, I.ii.130–1), D'Amville despises the 'ignorant astronomer' whose 'wandering speculation' would make the stars the arbiters of 'men's fortunes' (V.i.10–12). Instead, his reductivist faith equates the stars with gold, and reason with God:

> These are the stars, the ministers of fate,
> And man's high wisdom and superior power
> To which their forces are subordinate.
> (V.i.24–6)

Reassured in his convictions by this profane conceit, D'Amville falls asleep; but the complacency of his beliefs and the counterfeit security they represent are almost immediately countermined by his nightmare vision of the ghost of Montferrers, who refutes his atheistical presumption by reminding him that 'with all thy wisdom th'art a fool', and by predicting the imminent destruction of all his projects. We recall, with Calvin, that for the audacious despiser of God there can be no quiet rest in sleep, and prepare to behold the atheist finally caught up in the 'net' of providence, his conscience smitten by the divine wrath the more he endeavours to evade it.

Now the precise relationship between providential power and astrological fate was a subject of considerable controversy during the Renaissance, and the uses to which these concepts are put in *The Atheist's Tragedy* has occasioned a degree of critical dissension, if not outright confusion.[35] Tourneur appears to align himself with a leading proponent of judicial astrology, Sir Christopher Heydon, who, in *A Defence of Judiciall Astrologie*, affirms that 'the providence of God in the ordinarie government of the world, doeth as well shine in disposing the meanes, as in ordaining the ende', and holds that such ends can be effected *inter alia* through stellar influence.[36] And indeed, throughout the play, D'Amville's blasphemous denigration of all such influence is answered by ominous and unnatural portents in the heavens, which culminate, as we have seen, in the nightmare appearance of Montferrers. Thus on the occasion of the murder, D'Amville and Borachio gloat upon the macabre elegance of their plot, carried unobserved through the very eye of observation, by the unwitting but 'instrumental help' of servants made drunk for the purpose; and its successful execution through the agency of others, suggests to D'Amville's scornful pride a heinous comparison, which credits himself with

> That power of rule philosophers ascribe
> To him they call the supreme of the stars,
> Making their influences governors
> Of sublunary creatures, when their selves
> Are senseless of their operations . . .
>
> (II.iv.136–40)

In thus denying the ability of the stars to exert a governing influence upon the sublunary world, D'Amville is, of course, denying the existence of a power beyond them whose rule they merely reflect and mediate. However, this assertion is ironically interrupted in mid-sentence by thunder and lightning, clearly intended as a spectacular augury of heaven's power over nature, which D'Amville attempts to rationalize scientifically as a 'mere effect of Nature' (II.iv.142). The thunder and lightning motif recurs in Act IV, where Castabella, propositioned by D'Amville's 'argument' of 'love' (IV.iii.83), petitions heaven to express its wrath in thunderbolts and enflame the skies with lightning, rather than thus endure the burden of man's wickedness. And in due course, its power is asserted, and wickedness warded off, if not precisely in the manner desiderated by Castabella's entreaty, then at least no less auspiciously by the happy intervention of Charlemont, providentially preserved for this 'blessed purpose' by the protecting hand of God. A few lines later, D'Amville re-enters distractedly; stricken now with guilty horror, the sight of the stars, so far hidden in apparent complicity with his black and deep desires, convinces him that their present luminescence challenges 'payment' of him (IV.iii.230). Similarly the sky, hitherto darkened and obscured until the 'close deed/Was done' (IV.iii.223–4), now meets him in the face with her 'light corrupted eyes' (IV.iii.229): the empyreal witnesses of that divine power which is has been his temerity to deny.

Now in all these instances, Tourneur seems at least partly concerned to show the astrological scepticism of the atheist emphatically contravened by the manifest evidence of God's power as revealed in his creation; for the awesome impressiveness of the firmament, with its infinite multitude of stars, was held to be one proof of the existence of its creator. This is in fact the conventional Calvinist dogma, unexceptionable either to polemicists against astrology or against atheism. So the anonymous W. P. in his *Foure Great Lyers*, maintains that the firmament is 'an Alphabet written in great letters, in which is described the majestie of God', and that the 'wonderfull varietie of Starres' is so convincingly the work of his hands as 'maketh sinners and wicked menne inexcusable before the judgement seate of God'.[37] John Dove's *A Confutation of Atheisme* declares in similar vein that

> No man is such a rusticke, so brutish and voyde of common sense and reason, but as often as he looketh up to heaven, if he deny this, his own eyes shall witnes against him, for although this be not sufficient to bring him to the perfecte understanding of that God by whose providence he seeth the world is governed, yet what his eye hath seene, his tongue may tell.[38]

The difficulty here is that Tourneur goes beyond this to a cosmological theory in which the stars are not merely the latent and inert corruscations of God's glory, but specifically the active agents of his providence, and their subordinate influence upon the fortunes and destiny of the atheist is manifestly proportionate to his denials of their significance. The playwright's association with Sir Christopher Heydon (to whom he dedicated *The Transformed Metamorphosis*[39]) has apparently led him to adopt in these instances a somewhat intrusive and anomalous metaphysic of astrological determinism, logically at odds with his more typical concern to show God's direct intervention in the affairs of men, and strictly inconsistent with the mainstream Calvinist orthodoxy which elsewhere informs the play. Somewhat ironically, therefore, D'Amville's scorn for the 'planet-struck' ignorance of the astronomer is actually closer in spirit to those theologians of the period who accused astrologists of a contempt for God's providence, and whose characteristic objection to the sort of astrological fate developed in *The Atheist's Tragedy* was that, even where it postulated God as first cause, it assumed his will to be irreversibly expressed in the order of the stars, thus confining to second causes what was by definition supernatural and unknowable.[40] It is true that it was the judicial phase of the art which most antagonized its opponents. But to dogmatic reformists, even the moderate claims of a Heydon, that the divine government might shine as well in disposing the means as in ordaining the ends, infringed the Calvinist doctrine of special providence, according to which no phenomenal causes must be sought for except the secret will of God. Thus John Chamber, whose *Treatise Against Judicial Astrologie* was the immediate inspiration for Heydon's *Defence*, reasons that astrology must necessarily be opposed to divinity in that 'The hearts and wayes of all men are in the hands of God, who doth dispose and turne them, as seemeth best to him.'[41] Calvin himself in *A little booke concernynge offences* uncompromisingly proscribes not just astrology, but all notions of secondary causation and conditional necessity which threaten to usurp God's immediate regulation of the universe: 'For we neither dreame of intricate knottes of causes with the Stoikes, nor submit the governance of the worlde to the Starres, nor imagine a necessitie of things in the very nature of things it selfe.'[42]

But in fact, what seems a philosophic inconsistency in *The Atheist's Tragedy* is perhaps more apparent than real. D'Amville's scepticism, though counterposed somewhat inaccurately to a thematic systasis of religion and astrology, is in fact bred partly of an established stage convention in which any systematic repudiation of stellar influence (of the sort to which, for example, Edmund, Fletcher's Alquazier, and Chapman's Byron are prone) is to be equated, if not in every case with outright villainy, then with certain dangerous and autarchic tendencies of mind and will, which immediately triggered the still medieval prejudices and suspicions of a Renaissance audience. Indeed, as Don Cameron Allen suggests, the assumptions of astrology were so widely accepted at all levels of society, that in spite of the theological ordinances against it, a disbelief in its major hypotheses could be regarded paradoxically as a sinister aberration,[43] eminently consonant, therefore, with the unregenerate and irreligious scepticism of a D'Amville. And it is primarily at this level, where theology merges with popular superstition and a polymorphous dramatic tradition, that the genesis of Tourneur's beliefs must be sought; indeed, a popular Calvinism seems not to have been entirely incompatible with at least a modified form of *astrologia naturalis*. The Huguenot poet, Du Bartas, for example, manages to combine a belief in the unilaterality of the divine will, with an equally firm conviction that its dispositions may be predicted in the 'fatal influence' of the planets:

> I hold, that God (*as The first cause*) hath given
> Light, Course and Force to all the Lampes of Heav'n:
> That still he guides them, and his Providence
> Disposeth free, their *Fatall* influence:
> And that therefore, (the rather) we below
> Should studie all, their Course and Force to know.[44]

Even Calvin, as we have seen, does not totally repudiate the interposition of what he calls inferior causes, and in *An Admonicion against astrology judiciall* actually goes so far as to concede the principle that 'god can use the naturall meanes to chasten men withall'.[45] For in fact to argue that the divine decrees were exclusively effected without the intercourse of natural causes was to labour the freedom of God's will at the expense of all logic, human or divine, inviting the obvious charge, levelled in this instance by Sir Christopher Heydon, that 'God governeth inordinately, and so most absurdly, disturbing the order of causes. . . . For that cannot be truely said to be naturall, which is effected immediately by the powerfull and outstretched arme of God . . .'[46] But, allowing for a certain rhetorical exaggeration, this is very close to what the doctrine of special providence actually implied: that God indeed arranges his government so as to declare by the clearest manifestations that even where his justice is effected by natural means, it is necessarily above nature's corrupted law, and proclaims itself most strikingly in a specifically *un*natural irrelatedness to the order of causes. Ultimately, the question resolves itself into one of attribution, and a more exact definition of what is 'natural' than is usual in contemporary treatises, or for that matter in Tourneur's thought: there is, after all, no literal *deus ex machina* in *The Atheist's Tragedy*, and the wickedness of its protagonist is punished by 'natural' means, but so unnaturally disposed as to suggest, as far as lies within the limits of conventional realism, the active intervention of the 'powerfull and outstretched arme of God'. On this minimal definition of what is natural, all the extraordinary punishments which bring out the destruction of D'Amville have individually a material cause; but Calvinists would argue that God is the first, efficient and active cause from which such punishments proceeds, sin (rather than the stars, or any generalised instinct of nature) being the true impulsive cause, which provokes God into sending them.

So it is that in the opening scene of Act V, the overweening presumption which leads D'Amville to credit his 'real wisdom' with the creation of a state that will 'eternize' his 'posterity', and ironically to ridicule the foolish worshipper of a 'fantastic providence', is countered promptly by the providential annihilation of his posterity and the 'wisdom' by which it was to be sustained. His closet-bound meditations are interrupted by servants who enter with the body of Sebastian, 'Slain by the Lord Belforest' (V.i.49); while simulteneously the dying groans of the sickly Rousard emanate from a chamber 'within'. In each instance, the wages of sin have been wrought through a material cause; but the dramatic effect of the untimely deaths is naturalistically indefensible,[47] intended to suggest the unmistakable intervention of that efficient cause from which all such retribution derives. This effect is confirmed in Rousard's case when we recall how, on the 'very day' of his marriage to Castabella, an inexplicable 'weakness' surprised his health:

> As if my sickness were a punishment
> That did arrest me for some injury
> I then committed.
>
> (III.iv.65–7)

And indeed the idea that sickness can have, in such cases, a moral rather than a strictly natural cause – so explicit, moreover, as to be capable of bringing even atheists to acknowledge God – is endorsed by Martin Fotherby's *Atheomastix*, which states that 'even Physitians themselves doe finde in many sickenesses, that they be divine punishments'.[48] At this prospect of death, D'Amville's conscience succumbs once again to brain-sick and fatal visions, and for a moment its incandescent imaginings confuse the face of the messenger with that 'prodigious apparition' which had haunted his dream. Calling for a doctor, he offers him gold to inspire 'new life' into the bodies of his sons; but he learns too late that neither gold nor the 'radical ability of Nature' (V.i.85) can restore the heat of life to those in which it is palpably extinguished. Confronted thus by the incomprehensible dissolution, apparently by nature, of the very monument he had raised in her honour, and deprived further of his meretricious faith in wealth, D'Amville appeals amazedly to the doctor, who confirms his dawning suspicion that there must indeed be a 'power above Nature', by rehearsing the classic argument against atheism, a proof drawn *a posteriori* of the existence of God:

> A power above Nature?
> Doubt you that, my lord? Consider but
> Whence man received his body and his form:
> Not from corruption like some worms and flies,
> But only from the generation of
> A man, for Nature never did bring forth
> A man without a man; nor could the first
> Man, being but the passive subject, not
> The active mover, be the maker of

Himself; so of necessity there must
Be a superior power to Nature.
(V.i.104–14)

Increasingly distracted and troubled in his conscience, D'Amville curses treacherous nature for having 'abused his trust', and determines to arraign her as a forger of false assurances in the 'superior court' of 'yond Star Chamber' (V.i.118–20); and the pun here evidently implies his oblique recognition that the stars have, after all, a power to influence man's destiny, and that his own ultimate fate will be decided in the high court of divine justice. In the eschatology of the play's final scene, D'Amville opposes for the last time the providence of his reason to the providence of God, and his downfall enacts the widespread Renaissance belief not only that few atheists escaped unpunished, but that the manner of such punishments, in the words of Fotherby, 'inforceth divers of those *Atheists* to confesse [God] who before had denied him'.[49]

Thus, at the tragic climax, D'Amville interrupts the trial of Snuffe, Cataplasma and the minor workers of iniquity, entering 'distractedly, with the hearses of his two sons borne after him', appealing to the judges for 'Judgement, judgement' (V.ii.68). His own guilt-stricken terror of death causes him to marvel at the cheerful courage of Charlemont and Casta-bella, who, falsely accused for murder and adultery, mount the scaffold with the joyous alacrity of spirit which comes of a clear conscience. Whereas Charlemont calls for a glass of water, the apprehension of his victims' imminent end so harrows D'Amville's soul, freezing up 'the rivers of his veins', that, in contrast to his nephew, he calls for wine to bolster his courage; but again, his conscience becomes a prey to that stricken and phantasmagoric state in which 'nothing is but what is not', and the wine appears to change into blood, the 'filthy witness' of his own past crimes.[50] Having wrought himself up, by its consumption, to a 'bastard valour', and goaded by his conscience to an unreasoning and frenzied desperation, he dismisses the executioner, determining himself to become the 'noble' instrument of his nephew's death. As he raises up the axe, and Charlemont prepares himself for an 'unexampled dignity of death', D'Amville acciden-tally strikes out his own brains, a dramatic coup intended by Tourneur to demonstrate that in the theatre of God's justice, the atheist has secured both the judgment for which he came, and the due measure of his deserts, accomplished, moreover, by the extraordinary intervention of the deity.

For the Judge, as for all who behold it, the strangeness of this counter-stroke exhibits the same power of eternal providence which has made of Charlemont's griefs the instruments of his new-found blessings: an unimpeachable conclusion, given the Calvinistic certainties upon which the play is founded, and one that would be echoed fulsomely by Fotherby, for whom such signal displays of Divine retribution were a cause as much for the godly to 'rejoyce' as for the ungodly to tremble. Indeed, if we assume what on the evidence seems likely, that Tourneur's play is in its ideological structure a dramatic redaction of academic treatises on atheism, then the pervasive and laboured moralism by which it is contrived, and the curiously epiphanic tone of its ending, may have been suggested by just such a passage as follows from *Atheomastix*, which in its summary exposition of Tourneur's plot could as well serve as a homiletic prologue for *The Honest Man's Revenge*, as a cautionary epitaph upon *The Atheist's Tragedy*. 'For if we looke with judgement', says Fotherby,

> into the lives and deaths, of those prophane persons, that have beene Gods most direct and professed Enemies, and, most gloried and triumphed in their impieties and blasphemies, as though there were no God at all to regard them; wee may easily observe, that none of them hath escaped the revenging hand of God, but that all of them have constantly falne into great calamity, and evermore ended their ungodly lives, with unnaturall, untimely, and unfortunate deathes. Which constancy, in those mens so certaine infelicity (more than in other mens, that are in other kindes wicked) doth openly proclaime, that this their punishment commeth not out of the dust; neither is it sent unto them by blind chance and fortune (for, *there* is no such constancie) but that it onely proceedeth from that divine providence, which both heareth, and seeth, and knoweth all things: Yea, and taketh speciall notice of those that are *Atheists*, as of his most daring and audacious enemies: culling them out by the head, from among all other men, to be the selected spectacles of his wrath and indignation. That they who disclaimed him in their lives, yet might proclaime him in their deaths: declaring unto all men, that the God, whom they denied, had now, by their punishment, prooved himselfe a God indeed.[51]

Culled out 'by the head' in this manner, to be the selected spectacle of the divine wrath, it need hardly be added that D'Amville is damned for his sins, not only because he dies in the commission of murder, but as a reprobate atheist, the sentence of damnation has already been passed upon him.[52] Indeed, Fotherby alludes to one of the darker implications of the doctrine of predestination, when he infers that God ordains the spectacular crimes of atheists and their equally spectacular punishments, according to his secret will: 'As though he had made them to no other purpose, but to glorifie himselfe, by taking just vengeance upon their ungodliness.'[53] But by the more palpable evidence of his revealed will, D'Amville's profane faith in reason and his blasphemous exaltation of nature are anathema; and in his dying moments, the atheist proclaims their demonstrable insufficiency, driven by his conscience to render himself inexcusable before 'yond' power' that struck him down:

There was the strength of natural understanding
But Nature is a fool. There is a power
Above her that hath overthrown the pride
Of all my projects and posterity.

(V.ii.257–60)

8

The Duchess of Malfi

The nightmare oppressiveness of the Websterian cosmos – in which a womanish and fearful mankind gropes blindly towards a necessary fate it can neither see nor avoid – is, in its gloomy pessimism and pronounced *tedium vitae*, a yet more powerfully imagined testament than is *The Atheist's Tragedy* to the sceptical and nominalist temper of the age.[1] Embodying a shadowy world of claustral and miasmic evil, Webster's two principal tragedies are lit only by the flickering and insubstantial pageants of worldly pomp, and the brief pale fire of diamonds cut, like sinners, with their own dust. Here men stumble to their deaths in bloodstained obscurity, like dead walls and vaulted graves, yielding no echo. Webster's vision is, in truth, inexorably Augustinian in its harsh awareness of the pitiful inadequacy of man's reason, and the irredeemable depravity of that 'deep pit of darkness' which is for him the natural order of things (*The Duchess of Malfi*, V.v.100). Sharing in large measure Tourneur's bleak determinism, Webster has far less of his contemporary's facile faith in cosmic justice. An operant justice of sorts there undoubtedly is, inscrutable as in Tourneur's tragedies, and which, in a like arbitrary manner, divides the darkness as it pleases. But it is a justice that manifests itself even to the virtuous as a scourge, and by whose cryptic workings the unregenerate mass, wretched things of blood, must perforce stand condemned. As Ralph Berry has pointed out, the overwhelming weight of suggestion is that humanity is 'irretrievably prone to corruption and error'.[2] Cursed with the gift of consciousness, deluded and baffled by the imperfect light of reason, Webster's worldings rush to do what they can least prevent, suffered neither to do good when they have a mind to it, nor acquitted by conscience for the evil they seem powerless to resist.

In both these tragedies, but particularly in *The Duchess of Malfi*, Webster exhibits a hideously deformed universe, a fallen world demonstrative of human frailty and wickedness that is not only appallingly alien to the moral rationality of Shakespeare's vision, but profoundly inimical to the scholastic axiologies which sustained it. Here there is no sense, as Frost points out, of a universe fundamentally antagonistic to evil, purging itself of corruption in a series of convulsive catharthes,[3] nor indeed, of a tragic nemesis auspicated logically in an anterior matrix of causes.

Although, in *The Devil's Law Case*, we find articulated an apparently orthodox *sententia* of Richard Hooker ('Obedience of creatures to the Law of nature/Is the stay of the whole world', IV.ii.241–2), its truth is in general entirely irrelevant to that metaphysically separated universe which the two major tragedies essentially describe. For not only is the obedience of creatures an ideal for the most part rendered philosophically void in the self-evidently unstayed world in which they struggle to thrive, but the nescience in which they end suggests in the majority an invincible ignorance of that Law by which, according to a more optimistic ideology, the chaos might potentially have been stayed. On the contrary, the knowledge of nature and the world is for Webster incurably tainted and debased, of some transient and politic advantage, perhaps, in a drossy and ambitious age, but opposed absolutely to the Law Divine, of whose arcane mysteries a chosen few, chastened in suffering and made majestic in adversity, may be permitted some saving intimation. *'While we look up to heaven'*, observes Flamineo, *'we confound/Knowledge with knowledge'*;[4] but, as Herndl rightly suggests, the conflict of the two laws may be better observed in Bosola,[5] whose dilemma of conscience consists in being forced to recognize the good – indeed, to be the cause of goodness in others – whilst enslaving himself fatalistically to the prosecution of all the ill man can invent. Contemptuous of the corrupted world, yet inescapably dependent upon its o'er-laden and forbidden fruits, Bosola's defective intelligence remains imprisoned within the profane knowledge of what will best serve the world. Conscience is thus sedated by cynicism which denies both the viability of honesty in these 'dog-days' and the very possibility of virtue in an age where, so he rationalizes, 'the only reward/Of doing well, is the doing of it' (I.i.39,33–4). An actor in 'the main of all', Bosola's scepticism and world-hatred are writ large in a play of which he is at once the cynosure and focus of its themes. But if the Duchess is a luminous exception to its pejorative estimate of mankind, it remains true that virtue, forever a hidden or purely nominal concept for the wicked, is even for her a state well-nigh unattainable, born as it is out of hideous suffering, and crowned at last only in death.

If Webster's work thus evinces a consistency of moral tone, its philosophical aetiology is by no means so readily distinguishable. As studies by Dent and Whitman have shown, the very diversity of the playwright's immediate borrowings and the apparent irrelatedness of his sources make it extremely difficult to determine precisely how the plays are to be understood.[6] How far do such borrowings represent the accidents, as opposed to the substance, of Webster's philosophy? Are they superficial adornments merely, upon a profounder core of belief, or the functional, if somewhat miscegenated, elements of its true inspiration? The overwhelming weight of Webster's immediate indebtedness is threefold. His pervasive emphasis upon the vanity of life and of all earthly pretensions is clearly derivative of the medieval tradition *de contemptu mundi*, or at any rate, of its chief Renaissance exemplar, Sir William Alexander.[7] At the same time, his profound distrust of either the rationality of the universe, or the perfectibility of human reason is even more obviously attributable, often through direct quotation, to the Protestant nominalism of Sidney, or the Catholic scepticism of Montaigne.[8] As Whitman has shown, a large number of borrowings in *The Duchess* reflect the playwright's preoccupation with a theme rehearsed repeatedly in the *Arcadia*, namely, the imponderability of virtue in an uncertain and predestined world. Book V of Sidney's work, for example, supplies Bosola's disillusioned conviction, having inadvertently slain Antonio, that 'We are merely the stars' tennis-balls, struck and banded/Which way please them' (V.iv.53–4);[9] while Gynecia's apostrophe in Book II of the *Arcadia* – 'O Vertue, where doest thou hide they selfe? . . . or is it true that thou wert never but a vain name, and no essential thing?'[10] – is of course reiterated by Ferdinand in Act III of the play, and reverberates throughout as an important dramatic theme. Similarly, Montaigne's Pyrrhonist contempt for the 'inconstant vanitie and vaine inconstance'[11] of human reason, and the undependable nature of its judgments re-emerges in *The Duchess* as a recurrent refrain. Thus Bosola's sceptical aspersion, 'the opinion of wisdom is a foul tetter' (II.i.80), inaugurates a speech concerning the folly of wisdom which is itself reconstituted from a series of disparate phrases in *The Apologie of Raymond Sebonde*.[12]

But if it be conceded that Webster read widely in the works of Alexander, Sidney and Montaigne because individually they epitomized the moral perplexities of the age, it is by no means legitimate to describe him, by inference, as *merely* a sceptic, because he shared with Montaigne a conviction that the absolute truths of the universe are unknowable, any more than it would be to describe him as *merely* a fideist, because he espoused Pope Innocent III's opposed conviction that such truths are all that are worthy of being known. Even if it were possible to describe either of these apparently disparate strains in Webster's art, or for that matter, in the culture which sustained it, as a coherent, systematic philosophy in itself, it seems critically naive to make the assumption of just such a psychic dislocation in the literary analysis of his work – as if the external traditions which inform it, and the themes it embodies, could exist in an artificial and mutually opposed isolation, the sceptic in the artist forever warring with the fideist.

Historically, of course, the antithesis was more apparent than real. Montaigne was not so rigorously a Pyrrhonist, nor indeed, so indifferently a Christian, as to disallow finally a fideist appeal to that truth which

'God alone, and faith, have told us'.[13] Nor was *De Contemptu Mundi* so pietistically otherworldly a document that it did not have much to say, like Montaigne, concerning the *hubris* of reason, and the ephemerality and sinful hypocrisy of all worldly endeavour.[14] Robert Hoopes, in fact, argues persuasively that during the Renaissance fideism and scepticism were to become so complexly interfused that it is doubtful whether any historical distinction between them is practicable, and that impulses originally either fideistic or sceptical, as he says, 'often blend in the minds of sixteenth-century thinkers to produce the same result'.[15] What prompted this coalescence above all was the impact of reformist doctrines which incorporated, and hence prospered, the Pyrrhonist attitude that man's reason is fallible, and justified it with the premise, derived *de contemptu mundi*, that all mankind – and indeed nature itself – is subject to the postlapsarian dominion of sin.[16] The fact was that Pyrrhonism and traditional world-hatred were nowhere more relentlessly exploited than in Books I and II of Calvin's *Institutes*; and both attitudes were made peculiarly congenial to the voluntarist temper of the Jacobean age by the diaspora of numerous Puritan tracts and sermons in which they were the dominant motif. It is undoubtedly for this reason that European scepticism is often accommodated in a context orthodoxly fideistic in England; so that, for example, in the following (Calvinistic) lines from Thomas Adams's *The Soul's Sicknesse* (a divine with whose works Webster is known to have been acquainted)[17] we find a more or less typical seventeenth-century denunciation of both reason and the world, curiously reminiscent of *The Duchess* in its general hypochondriasis of tone:

> The *Sicknesse* of this *World* is *Epidemicall*, and hath with the invisible poyson of a generall pestilence infected it to the heart. For *Vice* in manners, as *Heresie* in doctrine, distilleth insensible contagion into the fountaine of Life; and *dum unum interficit, centum altos inficit*, in killing one, banes many. Whether . . . from the Devils malice, or mans securenesse, Iniquity is growne from a mist to a *Mysterie*, Ignorance to arrogance, nescience to negligence, simple imprudence to politicke impudence, and I know not how, too much light hath made men blinde . . . Sicknesse in mens *Soules* are bred like diseases in naturall, or corruptions in civill bodies; with so insensible a progresse, that they are not discerned, till they be almost desperate.[18]

Here the Arcadian labyrinth is grown from a mist to a mystery, the modest nescience of the *Apologie* exacerbated to a culpable negligence; the innocent pastoralism of the one, and the temperate reasonableness of the other, perceptibly darkened by the fideistic fact of original sin, which for Adams as much as for Webster, discharges an 'insensible contagion' into the 'fountaine of life'. Nor is such eclecticism confined only to works of theology, although the example from Adams could be replicated exhaustively from similar sources. Even in ostensibly secular writing, such as Raleigh's *The Sceptic*, or Greville's *Treatie of Humane Learning*, the lapse into theism is, as Baker has suggested, the almost inevitable resort of the Renaissance sceptic.[19] The Pyrrhonism of Montaigne is, of course, in no way synonymous with the Pyrrhonism of the Reformer, for whom it presupposes an entirely different dialectic. The *Institutes*, after all, declare not so much a concern for reason's inadequacy as for its wickedness; and the fideistic logic so ruthlessly developed therein, derives its energy, unlike the *Apologie*, from what Hoopes described as a 'primary notion . . . of the metaphysical status of good and evil', grounded in the inexorable doctrines of original sin.[20] But if none of this is to be found in Sidney or Montaigne, Webster's moral universe is indubitably one where sin is answered by sorrow; and grief causatively explained in terms of heavenly retribution for sin.

As Bosola's funeral dirge implies, men are by nature, inherently corrupt:

> *Sin their conception, their birth weeping:*
> *Their life, a general mist of error,*
> *Their death, a hideous storm of terror.*
>   (IV.ii.184–6)

Moreover, they inhabit what is emphatically a decayed and fallen world; a world which takes its tone from a multiplication of images evoking disease, rankness, and the slow poison of corruption infecting unseen the external shows of virtue. It is, above all, a dark and necessitated world in which virtue is hidden, honesty impossible to find; wherein conscience seem powerless to deter, sufficient only to accuse; and man seems doomed to sin for ends he is least fated to find. In short, it is not, perhaps, unreasonable to infer from this evidence that behind Webster's overt indebtedness to Alexander, Sidney, and Montaigne, lies what Baker calls the 'skeptical obscurantism' of Calvin,[21] and the bleak antinomian pieties of the faith to which a seventeenth-century scepticism inevitably paid tribute. Indeed, Webster himself could not better evoke the Websterian universe than does Calvin: for him, as for Webster, the light of reason is immersed in darkness, the soul's acuteness, mere blindness; and concerning the corruption of man's estate, the *Institutes* declare:

> Let it stand therefore, as an indubitable truth, which no engines can shake, that the mind of man is so entirely alienated from the righteousness of God that he cannot conceive, desire, or design anything but what is wicked, distorted, foul, impure, and iniquitous; that his heart is so thoroughly envenomed by sin, that it can breathe out nothing but corruption and rottenness; that if some men occasionally make a show

of goodness, their mind is ever interwoven with hypocrisy and deceit, their soul inwardly bound with the fetters of wickedness.[22]

If a Calvinist ethos does indeed contribute a philosophic substance to Webster's work, this fact alone goes far towards explaining that curious ambivalence in *The Duchess of Malfi*, concerning the attribution of moral responsibility, a refractivity of vision which permits all human judgments to return double-edged to plague the inventor, implicating each character in a universal and disabling context of guilt of which he is only partially aware. Bosola is of course the prime example of this pervasive moral obliquity, railing at the very things he most wants, yet loathing the evil he must do to obtain them (I.i.25); purging in the Duchess the glories of blood and state, yet, given the means, as 'Bloody, or envious, as any man' (I.i.27); saving his victim's soul in the act of murder, yet powerless to save his own. Antonio, too, is ostensibly a 'complete man' (I.ii.352), and comments perceptively on the corrosive solution of black melancholy and frustrated ambition which inwardly rots the souls of both the Cardinal and Bosola (I.ii.79–89; I.i.73–81). Yet his own covert advancement as consort of the Duchess is none the less characterized by her as in some sense a payment for virtue (I.ii.356), and is, moreover, subtly compromised in his own estimation by the devil ambition (I.ii.329), just as Bosola's instatement to 'place and riches' is less ambiguously compromised by those 'devils/Which hell calls angels' (I.ii.211,184–5). The Aragonian brethren – both, like Bosola, devils that can preach – spin a web of corruption and poisonous calumny which is first and foremost a projection of their own evil.[23] Yet the Duchess is so far entangled in its insidious coils as to answer Ferdinand's charge of luxury with an ironical appeal to those birds in nature which 'carol their sweet pleasures to the spring' (III.v.20) and implicates herself still further in his charge of hypocrisy by her own confession of a necessary doubleness, a fearful equivocation, in the face of those 'violent passions' which force her to 'leave the path/Of simple virtue' (I.ii.361,362–3). These inferences, in the case of the Duchess, are naturally mere shadows on an otherwise alabaster purity, the inherent weaknesses, perhaps, of 'flesh, and blood' (I.ii.369). But the fact is that, to adapt a phrase of Bradbrook, everyone in this perverted and degenerate world is inescapably tainted with original, if not personal, sin.[24] Here, as in *The White Devil*, there are 'degrees of evils'; but even the lives of the good are of a mingled yarn, their souls infected with that inherited residuum of guilt, which Calvin describes as a 'spring of evil . . . perpetually sending forth desires that allure and stimulate . . . to sin'.[25] All action in *The Duchess* is therefore evil or fated because it proceeds from an original corruption of the will; as in *The Atheist's Tragedy*, a helpless and driven passivity is all that can pass current for virtue.

There is more than a suggestion of all this in the long exordial speech in which Antonio's recent sojourn at the court of France enables him implicitly to describe the French king's palace, significantly termed 'His Master's master-piece', as a microcosm of creation itself, and its reduction to a 'fix'd order' as the 'work of Heaven' (I.i.6,10). He continues the analogy in theological metaphors reminiscent of Adams and of Calvin, which evoke inescapably that atavistic sickness of the world, which 'in killing one, banes many'. 'A Prince's court', says Antonio,

> Is like a common fountain, whence should flow
> Pure silver-drops in general. But if't chance
> Some curs'd example poison't near the head,
> *Death and diseases through the whole land spread.*
> And what is't makes this blessed government,
> But a most provident Council, who dare freely
> Inform him, the corruption of the times?
> Though some o'th' court hold it presumption
> To instruct Princes what they ought to do,
> It is a noble duty to inform them
> What they ought to foresee.

> (I.i.12–22)

But the moral referents of this homily, if clear in a timeless and universal sense, are less clear in the immediate context, where their meaning is ineffectuated by that insidious and reticulated guilt in which all are enmeshed. The court of Amalfi is indubitably poisoned 'near the head'; but the 'curs'd example[s]' most obviously the source of its general corruption – the Duchess's Machiavellian brethren – become less uniquely culpable when it is considered that she, after all, is its prince. Clearly it must be, as Antonio goes on to say, a 'noble duty' to inform such princes of 'the corruption of the times'; but whether such a duty impinges upon Bosola, the 'only court-gall' (I.i.23), or upon Antonio himself, the 'great master' of the Duchess's household (I.ii.8) is less easily decided. Both evade the moral imperatives of the French court; none seem able to resist the anamorphous evil of Amalfi. Here indeed is a mist grown mysterious, in a civil body insensible to the poison that consumes it, and where morality itself is ranged over the dark and occluded spectrum which extends from 'nescience to negligence, simple imprudence to politicke impudence', terminating in a blindness that makes men desperate.

But if in this necessitated universe, moral responsibility remains indeterminate, it is none the less sufficient; if the God that rules it remains inaccessible, his will shrouded in darkness, no man can thereby plead ignorance for sin. For it is a universe conditioned by Calvinist paradoxes: a universe of human motive ultimately neutralized, of voluntary intentions summarily negated in the *vis inertiae* of a providential and counteracting will. Ferdinand, presented with incontrovertible evidence of the Duchess's

marriage, laments the 'imperfect light of human reason' by which he
foresaw what he could least prevent (II.ii.78–80). His victims resign themselves to sorrow, attributing their sufferings to heaven's interference
(III.v.60,77–8); and Antonio, half in love with easeful death, approaches
the Cardinal's house mindless of his safety, under the strong conviction
that 'necessity compels' him to do so: to the cautious Delio he says

> Make scrutiny throughout the passages
> Of your own life; you'll find it impossible
> To fly your fate.
>
> (V.iii.33–5)

Bosola, too, attempts to atone for murder by the prosecution of a 'most
just revenge' (V.ii.338); but his final struggle to escape the 'sensible hell'
(IV.ii.337) of his own remorse is aborted in the accidental death of
Antonio, which effectively renders any such escape impossible. Man is
here possessed with free will and conscience sufficient to render him
culpable; but it is a freedom compatible only with depravation, and a
conscience subject to the secret inspiration of heaven. There is no suggestion, therefore, as in Hooker or Shakespeare, that 'evil as evil cannot be
desired',[26] or that, like Hamlet, men are merely deceived by the shows of
virtue. On the contrary, the consummately wicked – Ferdinand and the
Cardinal – dwell, by what is to all intents their own choice, in the very
'suburbs of hell' (V.ii.332), lapped in carnal security until the terminal
convulsions of a hitherto benumbed conscience deliver them up to the
madness or despair, depriving them, like D'Amville, of all pretext or
excuse. Bosola too, refutes the doctrine of ignorance; fatally divided
between goodness and the world, compelled to destroy the one in the
damnable service of the other, he is plagued by a tormenting sense of sin
deeper than that of either Ferdinand or the Cardinal; and though blinded
to the light of virtue by 'The devil, that rules i'th' air' (II.i.97), is none
the less able to approve in conscience what in reason he professes to deny.
His case is aptly described by Calvin, who flatly denies the possibility of
all attempts, by such deliberate sinners, to evade the judgments of good
and evil in the conscience. Although such judgments are far from sound
and entire, he says, by them

> the sinner . . . is ever and anon dragged forward, and not permitted to
> wink so effectually as not to be compelled at times, whether he will or
> not, to open his eyes, it is [therefore] false to say that he sins only
> through ignorance . . . : for the turpitude of the crime sometimes
> presses so on the conscience, that the sinner does not impose upon
> himself by a false semblance of good, but rushes into sin knowingly and
> willingly. Hence the expression, – I see the better course and approve
> it: I follow the worse (Medea of Ovid.).[27]

Bosola, too, sees the better course, and approves it, yet invariably follows the worse. Like the diabolic brethren whose familiar he becomes, he dwells over-long in the suburbs of hell; and when eventually a terrible self-reproach awakens him from his 'sweet and golden dream' (IV.ii.318), the cup of his new-found penitence is dashed from his lips, reprobated just as surely as his concomitant good intentions, and he is delivered up to that 'direful misprision' (V.iv.79) which is at once both the occasion and the seal of a consuming and nihilistic despair.

By comparison with their persecutors, Antonio and the Duchess are presented entirely sympathetically, the exemplars of innocence in a world grown old in evil. But theirs is an innocence none the less subtly denatured, necessarily diverted from the 'path/Of simple virtue' (I.i.362–3) by the encroachments of vice, and intrinsically flawed also by the latent suggestions of something disordered and excessive in the idea of action itself. There has, of course, been exhaustive critical discussion concerning the precise nature of the Duchess's guilt, much of it invoking external evidence such as the source-book charges in Painter of immodesty and incontinence,[28] or the theoretical objections to the remarriage of widows said to be operative in the contemporary culture.[29] Webster's own attitude appears to be one of 'controlled and sympathetic irony'.[30] The Duchess's brothers certainly refer to the 'spotted' livers of those that will 'wed twice' (I.ii.218), and see in her marriage a betrayal of blood and honour. But their allegations are offset partly by the spirit in which they are made, partly by the self-sustaining ideality of the contract itself, which to the mutual pair seems triumphantly exempt from the 'discord' and 'tempest' of the world in which it must be consummated (I.ii.384,387). And yet even within the 'circumference' of their love, its hermetic sublimity of value is shadowed by intimations of the evil it is supposed to exclude: on the Duchess's side, by hints of a self-indulgent rashness which seems in its urgency to confess the promptings of 'flesh and blood' (I.ii.369); on Antonio's by the presentiments of an incipient ambition which mars his own motives (I.ii.329). From an objective point of view also, the union is chorically condemned for its recklessness by Cariola; and its worth is obliquely undermined still further by the later and parallel wooing of Bosola by Julia, where the courtship of ambition by lust is less ambiguously played out.

In fact both Antonio and the Duchess enter a 'wilderness', only dimly aware that the moral complexities of action and motive will leave 'nor path, nor friendly clew' to guide them (I.ii.278,279); both glimpse the dangers, but choose to ignore them. Antonio's declaration that 'You have made me stark blind' (I.ii.328), is but an echo of the Duchess's 'let old wives report/I wink'd, and chose a husband' (I.ii.267–8), and merely confirms that their blindness here is to some extent a determination not to see, their ignorance a deliberate evasion of conscience. The words of

Calvin apply as much to them as to the incorrigibly wicked: no one is 'permitted to wink so effectually as not to be compelled at times, whether he will or not, to open his eyes'. But their awakening, when it comes, is not to the hopeless incomprehension of remorse, but to the wisdom that 'begins at the end' (I.ii.247); not to despair, but to a patient fortitude in which they can recognize a justice in suffering, as well as their own need for correction. For Antonio, affliction is the means by which lives 'out of frame' are brought by the hand of Heaven 'in better order' (III.v.62–3); an order which in the Duchess brings her finally to acknowledge

> That I perceive death, now I am well awake,
> Best gift is, they can give, or I can take.
> (IV.ii.220–1)

As Clifford Leech has pointed out, there is no easy dichotomy in the play between good and evil,[31] the corrupt and the regenerate. Antonio is to the Duchess 'a complete man' (I.ii.352); she to him 'stains the time past: lights the time to come' (I.ii.131). Compared to the obdurate villainy of their Machiavellian persecutors, their faults partake more of 'nescience' than 'negligence','simple imprudence' than 'politicke impudence'. The actions of the lovers are ostensibly as natural as they are pure; but in so far as action itself is disordered, and what is natural is thereby rendered impure, they both belong inescapably to their brothers' crepuscular world, unavoidably prone to its corruptions and errors. For even in the good, says Calvin, the appetites are 'vicious', the faculties 'vitiated', so that

> *all* human desires are evil, and we charge them with sin not in as far as they are natural, but because they are inordinate, and inordinate because nothing pure and upright can proceed from a corrupt and polluted nature. [Augustine] says (ad Bonif.) that *the law of sin remain*[s] *in the saints, the guilt only is taken* away.[32]

Inasmuch, therefore, as the law of sin implies bondage, characters here differ only in the degree to which they are so bound; and the morality of all action has a significance merely in the degree to which an inherent guilt is taken away.

But if the *hamartia* of Antonio is ambition and that of the Duchess a permission of the will,[33] this does not mean that Webster condones what the world makes inevitable. Indeed the world and the flesh are consistently linked with the devil. Sensuality is repeatedly seen as sinful, synonymous with the act of shame (II.v.41); honour, riches, place – these too are the 'bribes of shame' (I.ii.211), vain chimeras and insubstantial shadows, in striving for which men insensibly endanger their souls, lulling their consciences in the false cradles of security. The Aragonian brethren, incarnations both of the world's condition at its worst, symbols of its inveterate and characteristic evils, are consistently imaged as diabolic; and, like the

Devil, each candies his own sins o'er with a veneer of righteous hypocrisy (I.ii.196–7). The Cardinal – ambitious, avaricious, a politic contriver of deep plots in which he 'would not be seen' (I.ii.146) – is able, according to Bosola, 'to possess the greatest devil, and make him worse' (I.i.46–7). Ferdinand – likewise avaricious, and an unscrupulous patron of 'crows, pies, and caterpillars' (I.i.51) – corrupts Bosola with 'devils/Which hell calls angels', and creates him his familiar, 'a very quaint invisible devil in flesh' (I.ii.184–5,181). Both are twins in quality, passionately enslaved to the sins they so virulently condemn in the Duchess and Antonio (I.ii.94). The Cardinal affects indignation that his sister is 'Grown a notorious strumpet' (II.v.4), and informs the Pope of her 'looseness' (III.iv.30), while masking his own lust in a secret affair with Julia. The intensity of Ferdinand's reaction, moreover, makes of him a thing 'so deform'd, so beastly' (II.v.58) as to argue an interest in his sister's chastity still more darkly compromised, the morbid prurience of a nature 'perverse and turbulent' (I.ii.91).

Similarly, their declared concern for the integrity of the Duchess's honour – genuine in so far as it is *their* honour that is betrayed, *their* blood infected – conceals an undeclared concern for her wealth. The Cardinal, enraged at the tainting of the 'royal blood of Aragon and Castile' (II.v.22), implies, unconsciously at least, more pragmatic motives for this revenge, in his tale of the old woman 'murther'd/By her nephews, for her riches' (V.ii.91–2); while Ferdinand, infuriated no less by the Duchess's betrayal of blood as by the evidence of its rankness, confesses over her dead body his hope

> Had she continu'd widow, to have gain'd
> An infinite mass of treasure by her death:
> (IV.ii.278–9)

Theirs is a dropsied honour, a spurious concern for the name, rather than the substance of honour, which in Ferdinand's case becomes so obsessively an aspect of his wounded pride that he is wholly blinded to the objective reality of goodness. 'Virtue, where art thou hid?' he interpolates in Act III; but he persistently misjudges it by its appearance in his estimate both of Antonio ('A slave, that . . . / . . . nev'r in's life look'd like a gentle-man', III.iii.71–2) and the Duchess herself (in whom whiteness shows 'like leprosy', III.iii.62).

His creature Bosola, on the other hand, though himself ambitious for 'place and riches' (I.i.211), is not so blinded by his desires that he cannot sincerely commend the Duchess for preferring 'A man merely for worth: without these shadows/Of wealth, and painted honours' (III.ii.278–9). He exploits such goodness to his own advantage not because, like Ferdinand, he cannot see it for what it is, but because of his cynical conviction that, in a world where virtue is its own reward (I.i.32–3), it must perforce remain ever 'barren' and 'beggarly' (III.v.121). For Bosola, greatness itself grows 'crooked' (I.i.50); honour is but a 'mercenary herald' (III.ii.259); and to hang upon the one in the miserable expectation of the other entails the moral separation of greatness from goodness, honour from virtue, and the obviation of all scruple with the rationalization that 'every quality i'th world/Prefers but gain, or commendation' (III.ii.326–7). Advanced thus by greatness to honourable office in the Duchess's household, Bosola accepts the provisorship in the full knowledge that his corruption 'Grew out of horse-dung' (I.ii.208), just as he later betrays both the confidence of his mistress and the identity of her lover, in the certainty that the deception must imperil his soul. 'Now for this act, I am certain to be rais'd' (III.ii.328), he observes complacently; but the act is executed at the expense of a conscience which can recognize the evil thereof, even as it is insensibly hardened by it:

> A politician is the devil's quilted anvil,
> He fashions all sins on him, and the blows
> Are never heard; he may work in a lady's chamber,
> As here for proof. What rests, but I reveal
> All to my lord? Oh, this base quality
> Of intelligencer!
>
> (III.ii.321–6)

'Securitie is the very suburbs of Hell', adjures Thomas Adams, in a passage from 'The Gallant's Burden' which clearly suggested more to Webster than an apt quotation:

> *Miserius nihil est misero, se non miserante*, there is nothing more wretched, then a wretched man, that reckes not his own miserie: an insensible Heart is the Devils Anvile, he fashioneth all sinnes on it, and the blowes are not felt.[34]

Bosola sees what is good, but follows the worse; knowing what is due to heaven, he remains a creature of the world, bound by the law of sin in his soul, and increasingly inured to the judgments of his own conscience.

The claims of virtue and honour, heaven and the world are finally arbitrated, according to the Duchess's parable of the salmon and the dogfish, at the bar of God's judgment;[35] and the moral of the tale may be extended to Bosola's ambition for 'gain and commendation', as to those 'great men' who *oft are valued high, when th'are most wretch'd* (III.v.140). That the only true value resides in goodness, rather than rank, and that 'Man is most happy, when's own actions/Be arguments and examples of his virtue' (III.v.119–20) is substantiated once again by Thomas Adams:

> Greatnesse is the fairest object to the eye of the world, Goodnesse to

the eye of Heaven: There is glorious splendour in pompous Honour to draw the eyes of admiration after it: it little affects the sight of God, if Vertue gives it not a *Lustre* . . .

There are infinite wayes that conduct to seeming Honour, excluding Vertue; the end of them all is shame: since of a naturall man it is true, that (*Quanto ornatior, tanto nequior*) The more adorned, the more wicked: our Bonnets vaile, our Knees bow to many, whom the sight of Heaven and Vertue, scornes: This imparity of men living, is made even by death, who sweepes all (Beggar and Prince) with his impartiall Beesome, into one Bagge: and when Judgement comes, they are made odde and unequall again.[36]

Bosola, of course, likewise comes to the belated realization that 'There are a many ways that conduct to seeming/Honour, and some of them very dirty ones' (V.ii.300–1); but he does so only after remorse for the murder of the Duchess plunges him into a desperation 'Below the degree of fear' (IV.ii.358), in which his conscience is finally suffered to apply to his own conduct the mortifying truths by which, ironically, he saved the Duchess from despair.

As Ralph Berry has pointed out, Bosola is morally unintegrated, 'a grey zone of warring good and evil',[37] genuinely outraged by the world as he finds it, but in some obscure sense enslaved to its insidious evil. This fatal division of consciousness is reflected, of course, primarily in his attitude to the Duchess: so far is his own cynicism discountenanced by her fortitude in adversity, that he is brought paradoxically to pity whom he intends to destroy, and comfort whom he intends to torment.[38] He embodies in a curious sense a double role: the familiar of the Aragonian brethren, suborned to their infernal purposes, he is simultaneously the means by which those purposes are defeated, their power to hurt mysteriously subsumed in a larger economy in which good is brought finally out of evil, justice out of injustice. The instrument both of God and the Devil, Bosola is, like Richard III and (to a lesser extent) Hamlet, a minister and scourge; for in acting as he does against the will of heaven, he becomes the medium by which its will is accomplished. In one sense, at least, he seems aware, as does the Duchess, of the paradox he represents. His strangely hieratic role in expurgating the soul of his victim is foreshadowed in a gnomic allusion to his own corruption – 'Sometimes the devil doth preach' (I.ii.212) – and unmistakably implied in the ambiguity with which the Duchess challenges him on learning of her impending durance: 'What devil art thou, that counterfeits Heaven's thunder?' (III.v.97). In an equal and opposite sense he is unaware; the minister of a providential design he cannot in the nature of things comprehend, he remains infatuated with the vanities of the world and obtuse to the precepts of his own conscience. Blinded in this manner by the secret counsels of heaven, and yet punished for his blindness, he dies in a mist of ignorance, his most significant utterance ('We are merely the stars' tennis-balls', V.iv.53) a hopeless attempt to scan the syntax of a will ultimately unknowable, in whose arbitrary and unavoidable mysteries his fate seems sealed.

But the contradictions in Bosola's role point only to a deeper engima at the heart of Christian suffering itself, the neo-stoic paradox by which the regenerate 'account it praise to suffer tyranny' (III.v.74), and see in affliction the signs rather of God's favour, than of his hatred. Banished from Ancona, divided by their brothers' vengeance, Antonio and the Duchess not only recognize the 'heavy hand' of heaven in their sufferings, but see in them also the means to make 'patience a noble fortitude' (III.v.75,70). Both acknowledge the world's evil as a discipline to be endured, bitter and painful in itself, but which teaches a necessary wisdom. '*Man*', says Antonio, '*like to cassia, is prov'd best being bruis'd*' (III.v.72), and the Duchess refers similarly to her need of correction: 'nought made me e'er go right,/But Heaven's scourge-stick' (III.v.77–8). In the ethos of determinism, as Dominic Baker-Smith has pointed out, morals lose something of the significance they possessed for Shakespeare.[39] Indeed it seems obvious that for Webster, value is founded not so much on the inherent goodness of the Duchess as on her suffering; not so much in the acknowledgement of sin as in the achievement of a majesty in adversity. For if the play is not quite, as it has been described, a 'work of theodicy',[40] it at any rate seeks an uneasy consolation in the knowledge that if suffering is inevitable in a world of ordained evil, it is none the less the means by which some, at least, are delivered from the world's condemnation. 'God dooms us to destruction', says Calvin, 'if he does not, by correction, call us back when we have fallen off from him';[41] and although it is true that in the play all are doomed, all destroyed, what divides the darkness is that the good, as opposed to the desperately wicked, are schooled by suffering to patience, and trained to an obedience which redeems them. It is above all in their attitude to suffering – the uses to which the experience is put – which distinguishes in Webster's tragedy, what John Downame calls 'the children of God' from 'the children of wrath'; in *The Christian Warfare*, he says of afflictions

> though in their owne nature they be evill, yet through the wisdome and gracious providence of our God, they turne to the good of his children; and though to the wicked they are plagues and punishments, yet to the godly they are but trials and fatherlie chastisements . . . For as they are trials, they serve to shew unto all the world, and especially to our selves, our faith, hope patience, obedience, constancie . . . And as they are chastisements they serve for sharpe eye-salves to cleere our dimme sight, so as we may see our sinnes, and truelie repent of them. . . . They are that wormewood, wherby the Lord weaneth us from the

love of the world, whose pleasing delights we would ever suck without wearines if our mouthes were not distasted with some afflictions.[42]

To the wicked in the play, such 'plagues and punishments' are inflicted in the characteristic form of a desperate and guilt-stricken conscience. In Bosola, the agonies of remorse occasioned in him by the death of the Duchess, plunge him into a 'sensible hell' from which he never escapes (IV.ii.337); while in Ferdinand and the Cardinal, remorse conducts inexorably to madness and despair, a re-creation in themselves of that hell to which they would have consigned their sister. The sufferings of the Duchess, on the other hand, become a 'dismal preparation' for a wholly different voyage, administered ironically by Bosola. As a result, she is weaned from the love of a world from which he cannot be weaned; is reduced to an obedience which she can wish on her brothers, 'to do them good' (IV.ii.167); and is restored to a clarity of vision which can perceive death, not as the storm of terror to which her brothers succumb, but as a welcome release.

A scenario such as this, in which the instrumentality of the wicked is employed not only to the destruction of evil, but to the justification of virtue, inevitably recalls *The Atheist's Tragedy*, whose dramatic structure is defined by a similar Augustinian paradox: there, too, innocence is vindicated in suffering, and goodness is accomplished by the evil wills of those dedicated to its destruction.[43] But it also suggests the extent to which both plays share a common fund of inspiration in the Book of Job, the archetype of all attempts to reconcile human suffering with divine justice. *The Duchess of Malfi*, in particular, constantly invokes its themes and imagery.[44] To the author of Job, as to Webster, God is an inscrutable, exalted and transcendant force, whose ultimate responsibility for the evil which Satan inflicts upon the world is never in doubt; like the Duchess, Job attributes his sufferings not to his enemies, but to God, who merely uses the counter-agency of the forces of evil to bring his servant to patience and integrity of conscience.[45] But if God is the instigator of Job's trial, he endures it at the hands of those whose motives in inflicting it are wholly discrete: Satan's purpose (like Ferdinand's) is to drive his victim to madness by despair; the Sabeans' interest (like Bosola's) is in worldy gain; but in so far as they succeed at all in their intentions, they do so only to the extent that they are permitted, the diversity of their efforts contributing in the end to the vindication of good. The parallels are manifold: the Duchess, like Job, cries out in bitter complaint, becoming wayward and impatient at the moment of her 'greatest torture' (IV.i.70);[46] like Job, she passionately apprehends 'Those pleasures she's kept from' (IV.1.15);[47] like Job, she curses the stars,[48] and pleads in her despair for death as a surcease from pain:

There is not between heaven and earth one wish
I stay for after this . . .

(IV.i.61–2)

'Looke upon *Job*', says John Downame, in *The Christian Warfare*,

who is renowned for patience, and you shall finde that while the hand
of God was upon him, hee bewraieth the corruption of the flesh and
sheweth notable impatiencie, cursing the day of his nativitie, and wish-
ing that he had never been borne, or else that hee had presentlie after
his birth swallowed up in the jawes of death, Job.3. So chap 6.8.9. he
thus crieth out like a man utterly desperat: *O that I might have my
desire, and that God would graunt me the thing I long for.9. That is,
that God would destroy me: that he would let his hand goe and cut me
off. . . .* Where *Job* seemeth to deale with God as a condemned malefactor with a just and severe judge, who seeing the anger of the Judge
incensed against him . . . onlie desireth a mitigation of the tortures,
and that hee may quicklie be dispatched and ridde out of his paine:
nam misericordiae genus est cito occidere, it is a kinde of mercie to be
speedie in execution.[49]

'Who must dispatch me?', cries the Duchess, robbed like Job, of her
wealth and, to all intents, of her children also:

Go, howl them this: and say I long to bleed.
It is some mercy when men kill with speed.

(IV.i.108–9)

The correspondences between Webster's play and the Old Testament
poem (or at any rate, contemporary commentaries upon it) ought not, of
course, to be pushed too far; they are enough to suggest an important
philosophic congruence between the two works, particularly in their
approach to the problem of evil, rather than a straightforward analogy.
Bosola's role, it need hardly be said, has a unique complexity which in
some respects subsumes the parts played by the Sabeans and the Comfor-
ters in the Biblical story, but is finally unconformable to either as a mere
antetype. The Duchess, too, has a warm-hearted passional beauty in
suffering, unforeshadowed by anything in the Book of Job, and indeed,
these are the very qualities that inspire Bosola to outgrow his role as a
mere instrument of evil. Impressed by her nobility of bearing in prison,
moved also by her loveliness, which shows 'More perfect in her tears,
than in her smiles' (IV.i.8), he increasingly dissociates himself from the
damnable purposes of Ferdinand, offering her 'comfort' and 'pity'
(IV.i.18,88).

The effect of Ferdinand's demoniac impulse 'To bring her to despair'
(IV.i.115) is thus constantly ameliorated by his agent: 'Come, you must

live' urges Bosola (IV.i.69), and rebukes her impulse to revive the 'dead example' of a Roman wife with the words, 'O fie! despair? remember/You are a Christian' (IV.i.74–5). 'Plagu'd in art' by the ghastly effigies of death she takes to be the corpses of her family, the Duchess is tormented still further by the wild consort of madmen placed by her brother about her lodging. But Bosola will go no further in cruelty; appalled by the satanic compulsions of Ferdinand, he urges that the means of penance, 'beads and prayerbooks' (IV.i.119), should be furnished her, and refuses henceforward to see her in the shape 'forfeited' by his 'intelligence' (IV.i.132). But that the stirrings of penitence have already commenced in the Duchess's soul is implicitly suggested by her reprehension of Ferdinand's venomous taunts concerning the legitimacy of her children:[50]

> Do you visit me for this?
> You violate a sacrament o'th' Church
> Shall make you howl in hell for't.
> (IV.i.38–40)

The grotesque tableaux of death and madness by which she is surrounded have thus an effect contrary to what was intended; for they not only bring her to that calm acceptance of her own death in which she can contemplate the life to come, but also to the wisdom, nascent and embryonic at first, which enables her ultimately to transcend the inchoate madness of the world. 'I am not mad yet, to my cause of sorrow' (IV.ii.25), she laments to Cariola; but the malediction she invokes upon herself is paradoxically one of the curses for disobedience in the Book of Deuteronomy,[51] and its very repetition jolts her to a new sense of compliance:

> Th' heaven o'er my head seems made of molten brass,
> The earth of flaming sulphur, yet I am not mad.
> I am acquainted with sad misery,
> As the tann'd galley-slave is with his oar.
> Necessity makes me suffer constantly.
> And custom makes it easy.
> (IV.ii.26–31)

(Cf. Deut.28:23, 'And thy heaven that is over they head shall be brass, and the earth that is under thee shall be iron.') That the significance of these lines is not lost upon the Duchess is suggested by her refusal to be overwhelmed by her own anguish; to see in her 'sad misery' a 'necessity' which 'custom' makes easy. Suffering is thus once more accepted as correction, waywardness transmuted to patience; and the Duchess curses no more, implicitly recalled to the dangers of impenitence and desperation which Perkins, in an exegesis of these lines, makes clear is their real purpose:

The miserie over [the sinner's] head, is the wrath of God, which he testifies in all manner of judgements from heaven, in daunger of which every impenitent sinner is every houre . . . The miserie under his feete, is *hell fire*: for every man till he repent, is in as great danger of damnation, as the traytour apprehended of hanging, drawing, and quartering.[52]

Thus when the madmen are loosed upon her, their incoherent allusions to judgment and hell, the devil and the day of doom, have no longer the power to appal; and the Duchess can declare herself 'chain'd to endure' the tyranny they represent (IV.ii.61), delivered now of any further temptation to despair.

But the Duchess's ordeal is not yet over, nor her 'dismal preparation' complete; for she must be separated from that love of the world and its vanities of which Bosola perceives her still to be sick – the more dangerously, since her 'sickness is insensible' (IV.ii.119). Invulnerable now to despair, she must be alerted also to the dangers of its insidious opposite, carnal security, which, we recall with Adams, breeds a fatal oblivion in the soul with 'so insensible a progresse' that its condition remains undiscerned until 'almost desperate'. 'The Lord sendeth afflictions to mortifie in us the old man, the flesh and unregenerate part',[53] says John Downame in *The Christian Warfare*; and Bosola's appearance in the guise of an 'old man' is symbolic of that unregenerate Adam which in the Duchess he will bring 'By degrees to mortification' (IV.ii.174). Bosola's homily is all wormwood therefore, designed to render nugatory the illusory delights of the world: the flesh is frail, 'a little cruded milk, fantastical puff-paste' (IV.ii.124–5); our bodies perishable, 'weaker than those paper prisons boys use to keep flies in' (IV.ii.125–6). Rank, greatness, the additions of honour are vanities of the world's estimation, contemptible in the sight of heaven and virtue; and when the Duchess affirms, 'I am Duchess of Malfi still' (IV.ii.139), this is not a final assertion of tragic sufficiency, but a residual and now superfluous attachment to worldly eminence which must still be chastened in her. 'That makes thy sleeps so broken', affirms Bosola,

> *Glories, like glow-worms, afar off shine bright,*
> *But look'd to near, have neither heat nor light.*
> (IV.ii.140–2)

Repentance, so Calvin informs us, consists of two parts, the 'mortification of the flesh' and the 'quickening of the spirit'. Mortification implies.

the entire destruction of the flesh, which is full of perverseness and malice. It is a most difficult and arduous achievement to renounce ourselves, and lay aside our natural disposition. For the flesh must not be thought to be destroyed unless everything that we have of our own is abolished.[54]

And so it is with the Duchess: forced to part with everything she has owned or loved, reduced to the point even of renouncing her own identity, her mortification is at last accomplished; and she can welcome her brothers' 'present' of coffin, cords and a bell, as the harbingers of a 'last benefit' and a 'last sorrow' (IV.ii.168):

> Let me see it.
> I have so much obedience, in my blood,
> I wish it in their veins, to do them good.
> (IV.ii.165–7)

Bosola can thus commence the second stage of her purification, and announces himself as a 'common bellman' in order both to reconfirm in the Duchess the sense of her own mortality, and induce in her that 'quickening of the spirit' in which she can look forward with measured confidence to the promise of her own salvation. His funeral dirge has thus a double import: intoned to the dismal clangour of the passing-bell, its mordant harmonies meditate yet again upon the vanity and worthlessness of this life, but in doing so emphasize by contrast the peace and serenity of the next.[55] Bosola therefore calls upon the Duchess to 'don her shroud', invoking Job's insight that the world's condition is but pain and warfare, and the insisting *de contemptu mundi* upon its wretched sinfulness:

> *Of what is't fools make such vain keeping?*
> *Sin their conception, their birth, weeping:*
> *Their life, a general mist of error,*
> *Their death, a hideous storm of terror.*
> (IV.ii.183–5)

But death, whatever its terrors for those unquiet in conscience, is the means for the regenerate by which 'a perfect peace is sign'd' (IV.ii.182); and the Duchess, tempered by suffering to a new integrity of spirit, surpasses even Bosola's expectations by the equanimity with which she can face the grisly instruments of her own quietus. 'Doth not death fright you?' he marvels, and her answer reveals that the source of her courage is the certain knowledge of her own redemption:

> Who would be afraid on't?
> Knowing to meet such excellent company
> In th'other world.
> (IV.ii.207–9)

Unlike Cariola, who struggles pitifully with her executioners, the Duchess is awakened by the 'sharpe eye-salves of affliction' to the unshrinking acceptance of death as the best gift 'they can give, or I can take' (IV.ii.221). She submits to it on her knees, moreover, in an attitude of Christian humility which seems to recognize not just that (in Adam's phrase) the 'imparity of men living is made even by death', but that those worldly antinomies of goodness and greatness, virtue and honour, can be perfectly reconciled only in heaven:

> Pull, and pull strongly, for your able strength
> Must pull down heaven upon me:
> Yet stay, heaven gates are not so highly arch'd
> As princes' palaces: they that enter there
> Must go upon their knees.
>
> (IV.ii.226–30)

Weaned thus from the glories of earthly state, delivered ultimately from the corruptions of the world and the flesh, the Duchess dies innocent, and the sight of her stainless purity in death forces Ferdinand to see at last her true quality:

> Cover her face. Mine eyes dazzle: she di'd young.
> (IV.ii.259)

In the unhallowed rituals that precede her death, Bosola has been her guide and conscience, the arch-priest of her purification and sacrifice. But a recurrent irony invests these scenes, since the truths he so bloodily approves in the case of his victim are never once brought to bear upon the morality of his own acts. His conscience deadened in the security from which he has so recently reclaimed the Duchess, his passions blinded by the invidious glories of the world, Bosola continues throughout in the damnable service of Ferdinand; and it is not until his diabolic paymaster denies him the reward due to his service, that he finally comes to realize the mortal extent to which his soul has been infected by the 'sweet and golden dream' of place and riches (IV.ii.318). Only at this point, when he can recognize the inevitability of divine retribution ('blood flies upwards', IV.ii.258), and his own 'dejection' at last removes the anodyne for guilt[56] – only then does remorse take hold in the fragmented psyche of Bosola, and he yearns for a 'peace of conscience' which, were the deed to do again, he would not change either for the 'wealth' he has been denied, or the 'painted honour' he can now reject (IV.ii.334,335,330). For a brief instant, the Duchess revives, and repentance seems a momentary possibility; but then the cords of life break, and the heaven that seemed so auspiciously to open is closed finally against him. The realization of his own sinfulness has come too late, and Bosola is overwhelmed by irremediable agonies of conscience, giving himself up to the hideous overthrows of a black and deep despair:

> O sacred innocence, that sweetly sleeps
> On turtles' feathers: whilst a guilty conscience
> Is a black register, wherein is writ

> All our good deeds and bad; a perspective
> That shows us hell . . .
>
> (IV.ii.349–53)

The notion of conscience as a register is, of course, a commonplace of contemporary treatises upon the subject: Burton mentions it,[57] as does the puritan divine Richard Bernard, where, in his *Christian, See to thy Conscience*, he describes '*the fourth act and office of Conscience*' as '*Gods Register, or Notarie*, to keepe in record all things which man doth here in the body, whether it bee good or evill, against the Judgement Day, where account must be made of all things'.[58] But for Bosola, the account is already heavily weighted: the growing preponderance of his own desperation makes him see *all* his deeds, good and bad alike, in the gloomy perspective of hell. As perdition catches his soul, he becomes ever more chillingly convinced, in retrospect, that he has never been free to change his fate. Overborne by despair, and the intimations of a destiny inscrutably beyond his control, he succumbs to the conviction that his 'penitent fountains' were 'frozen up', and that he could not 'be suffer'd' to do the good he intended (IV.ii.359,360,353) – the passive voice in each case communicating an almost Faustian sense of powerlessness, and opening up those vistas of determinism in which his new-found penitence will so tragically miscarry. Sorrow is indeed '*the eldest child of sin*' (V.v.54); but the moral necessity which occasions the downfall of the wicked demonstrates also that in the Duchess's death, as Gunby has put it, 'evil did not vanquish good, but was itself defeated'.[59] Both Bosola and the 'wretched eminent things' he so unwillingly served end in a 'kind of nothing' (V.v.78), leaving

> no more fame behind 'em, than should one
> Fall in a frost, and leave his print in snow,
> As soon as the sun shines, it ever melts
> Both form and matter. . . .
>
> (V.v.113–16)

Fittingly, they exemplify the fate of the unregenerate in the Book of Job, whose 'remembrance shall perish from the earth':

> Drought and heat consume the snow waters: so doth the grave those which have sinned. The womb shall forget him; the worm shall feed sweetly on him; he shall be no more remembered, and wickedness shall be broken as a tree.
>
> (Job 18:17; 25:19,20)[60]

But if, as in Job, goodness is vindicated by the agency of evil, and innocence by suffering brought to a continuing integrity, this raises yet again the fundamental issue of moral responsibility. And if Bosola has been unwittingly coadjutant in this design – the minister and scourge of a providence which not only exploits the instrumentality of the wicked, but preconditions their necessary choices – then the thinking behind the play, like that of the Book of Job, seems to call in question both the ordination of evil in the world, and the justice by which it is punished. Webster seems to provide an answer to such questions, but he does so via the Augustinian logic which insists that in a universe of predestined evil, the same act can betray the inveterate guilt of man, even as it manifests the ineffable justice of God. If Bosola in his wickedness merely executes the providential judgments to which he subsequently falls forfeit, it is equally clear that for Webster this neither mitigates his responsibility for his own misdeeds, nor criminates the justice by which they are eventually condemned. 'For', says Calvin,

> we must hold, that while by means of the wicked God performs what he had secretly decreed, they are not excusable as if they were obeying his precept, which of set purpose they violate according to their lust.[61]

Man is a 'voluntary slave,'[62] therefore; and Bosola in his unfree freedom is both the minister of God's secret decrees, and a scourge who violates the divine precepts according to his own lust. Calvin reasserts the thesis of man's necessitated guilt in another passage which has a bearing on the play, not least in its invocation of a common paradigm in the Book of Job. By analogy with the biblical story, Calvin considers how the same act can be attributable both to God and to the wicked, 'without excusing Satan by the interference of God, or making God the author of evil'; this can be done, he says,

> if we look first to the end, and then to the mode of acting. The Lord designs to exercise the patience of his servant by adversity; Satan's plan is to drive him to despair; while the Chaldeans are bent on making unlawful gain by plunder. Such diversity of purpose makes a wide distinction in the act. In the mode there is not less difference. The Lord permits Satan to afflict his servant; and the Chaldeans, who had been chosen as the ministers to execute the deed, he hands over to the impulses of Satan, who, pricking on the already depraved Chaldeans with his poisoned darts, instigates them to commit the crime.
> . . . We thus see that there is no inconsistency in attributing the same act to God, to Satan, and to man, while from the difference in the end and mode of action, the spotless righteousness of God shines forth at the same time that the iniquity of Satan and of man is manifested in all its deformity.[63]

As we have seen, Bosola too is corrupted by worldly gain, and pricked on by the impulses of the satanic brethren to bring the Duchess to despair. But, as Calvin's analysis makes clear, in the context of determination, responsibility settles on the 'end and mode' of action, rather than its outcome, and justice is defined by the Augustinian equation: 'That men sin is attributable to themselves: that in sinning they produce this or that result, is owing to the mighty power of God.'[64] There is thus no concurrence between the purposes of Bosola, Ferdinand and the Cardinal, and the divine purposes to which their diabolic motives are so inscrutably correlated; and if it be enquired how God can will that to be done which by his will is also forbidden, Calvin declares this to be a 'hidden mystery',[65] taking refuge, like Webster, in the fideistic obfuscation which asserts that 'when we look up to heaven/We confound knowledge with knowledge'. And as the remainder of the play demonstrates the ineluctable condemnation of the wicked, driven by the secret counsels of providence to do what they ought not to do, we can only echo the words of St Augustine, who asks rhetorically: 'Who can refrain from trembling at those judgements when God does according to his pleasure even in the hearts of the wicked, at the same time rendering to them according to their deeds?'[66]

Bosla, therefore, sunk in despair 'Below the degree of fear' (IV.ii.358) attempts in vain to recompense for his past crimes by seeking out Antonio in order to join him in a 'most just revenge' (V.ii.338). Not only is his conscience haunted by visions of the Duchess (V.ii.340–1), but its terrors are exacerbated by a new awareness of his own spiritual danger, for which the Cardinal's complacency stands as a terrible precedent:

> I must look to my footing;
> In such slippery ice-pavements men had need
> To be frost-nail'd well; they may break their necks else.
> The president's here afore me: how this man
> Bears up in blood! seems fearless! Why, 'tis well:
> Security some men call the suburbs of hell,
> Only a dead wall between.
>
> (V.ii.327–33)

But Bosola's cognizance of his soul's precariousness is insufficent to prevent its damnation. The remainder of his sins will no longer, it is true, proceed from a preconceived malice, but even where the intention is good, so Calvin informs us, 'Our reason is exposed to so many forms of delusion, is liable to so many errors, stumbles on so many obstacles, is entangled by so many snares, that it is ever wandering from the right direction.'[67] But in the divided consciousness of Bosola, his motives are still fatally mixed, and his intention to protect Antonio is flawed by the deluded conviction that a private revenge can also be 'most just'. The example of the Cardinal notwithstanding, Bosola continues to bear up in blood; and the 'sword of justice' (V.ii.340) he attempts to wield in Antonio's behalf becomes the instrument of a terrible miscarriage, a double-edged and ambiguous symbol of all earthly attempts to arbitrate justice. For Bosola, the accidental death of the one man 'I would have sav'd 'bove mine own life!' (V.iv.52) is unutterably meaningless, evidence only of human futility in the face of an aribitrary and uncomprehending fate:

> We are merely the stars' tennis-balls, struck and banded
> Which way please them . . .
>
> (V.iv.53–4)

But in the gulf which separates divine and human estimations of justice, the same act, we may recall with Calvin, can possess a metaphysical ambiguity, declaring simultaneously the guilt of man and the ineffable rightness of God. Though to Bosola, his attempt to execute justice ends in that 'mist' (V.v.93) in which all merely human intentions are finally abrogated, his revenge is made 'perfect', not only in the killing of Ferdinand and the Cardinal (V.v.62), but, by an occult paradox, also in the fortuitous stabbing of Antonio, for whom he unwittingly ends a 'long suit' and gives a 'benefit in death' (V.iv.46,48). For just as life is merely a 'preparative to rest' (V.iv.67) in the vexed and sin-laden world of Webster's play, so suffering is the preparative to death, whether it be the penultimate terrors of the damned, or the divine chastizements of the redeemed. There is no sense here, as in *The Atheist's Tragedy*, that the meek shall inherit the earth; the earth's blessings, on the contrary, are the wages of Satan, and, for the virtuous at least, it is only in death that a perfect peace is signed. The play's stoic philosophy of pain echoes St Paul's dictum that 'we are chastened of the Lord, that we should not be condemned with the world' (I.Cor. 11:32); and in the dying utterance of Antonio, there is an implicit recognition, born of his ordeal, of the extent to which he too had been infected by the world, by ambition and its dream of greatness:

> In all our quest of greatness,
> Like wanton boys, whose pastime is their care,
> We follow after bubbles, blown in th'air.
>
> (V.iv.63–5)

'For what in truth', asks John Downame, in *The Second Part of the Christian Warfare*.

> is this false fame and glorie of the worlde, but a smoake or vapour, which is tossed to and fro with the breath of every ones mouth? . . . What do [wordly men] but like wanton and foolish boyes run after a sopie bubble, raysed with the breath of their companions mouthes, because it seemeth beautiful through varietie of colours, although it commonly vanish in the pursuing, or at least breake as soone as it is but touched?[68]

In the final act Ferdinand and the Cardinal, pre-eminently creatures of the world, are given up in death to the devil they served in life. Ferdinand's remorse over the corpse of his sister recapitulates the opaque motives for which he had her murdered; motives in which avarice, betrayed honour, and sexual jealousy are all incoherently intertwined.[69] Horrified by the 'deed of darkness' he has commissioned, stricken too late by the conscientious fear of 'him which binds the devils' (IV.ii.329,309) Ferdinand is possessed by the devil indeed, and is precipitated into that frenzy which is both a 'fatal judgement' (V.ii.83) upon his crimes, and a hideous projection of his own bestiality.[70] He whose life had been wholly given over to worldly gain and the claims of a meretricious honour, who had trodden the slippery ice-pavements of carnal security, is now engulfed in a madness which makes penitence impossible, rapt in a sleep of the mind the very symbol of his spiritual lethargy. On the eve of his death, the midnight watchers at his door tell of the storm in which his chamber 'shook like an osier', a manifestation to Malateste, of that 'pure kindess' of the devil, by which he 'rock[s] his own child' (V.iv.19–21). Of the predicament of such worldlings, John Downame writes:

> For alas, what will their passed pleasures, honours and riches, now profit them . . . if they die of a spiritual lethargie, and be rocked asleepe of the divell in the cradle of security, and so carried quietly into hell; so as they have no leasure to think of these things, or time to entertaine these fearfull meditations; yet how much more hellish horror have they when they are awakened out of their deep sleep, with those intollerable tortures?[71]

On the very verge of death, Ferdinand seems momentarily, as Bosola says, 'to come to himself' (V.v.68), but is sufficiently conscious of sin only to acknowledge the providential justice of his end:

> *Whether we fall by ambition, blood, or lust,*
> *Like diamonds we are cut with our own dust.*
> (V.v.71–2)

The Cardinal is also brought, by Bosola's sword-thrust, to a similar recognition that he suffers now 'for what hath former bin' (V.v.53); but whereas in his brother, conscience has been frozen in an attitude of presumption, paralysed in the narcosis of a diabolically induced madness, in the Cardinal, presumption leads by a more orthodox pathogenesis into the consuming horrors of despair. He meditates obsessively, after the poisoning of Julia, on the varieties of infernal torment, his soul harrowed by the tedium of a guilty conscience, and haunted by a grim prolepsis of the *poena damni*, in the shape of 'a thing, arm'd with a rake', which seems to strike at him (V.v.6). Like Faustus, he is unable to pray, and goes to his death in the abject terror of all those in whom the apprehension of their own sin outweighs the expectation of divine mercy. A politic churchman, the cruel murderer of his sister and of the lustful Julia, he dies as he had lived, cut off even in the blossoms of his sin; and his cowardice in death is the final demonstration that the worldly greatness for which he had sinned, was, in the words of Bosola, 'only outward' (V.v.41). Of 'Presumption running into despaire', Thomas Adams has this to say:

> Sinne, and judgement for sinne, make the most cruell men cowardly. Tyrants whose frownes have been death; oppressours . . . now tremble themselves: and would change firmenesse with an Aspine leafe. They that care not for the acte of sinne, shall care for the punishment . . . They that have made others weepe shall desperately howle themselves.[72]

But, as the Cardinal observes in his dying moments, Bosola, too, has received the death-wound that is for him also, a fatal judgment: 'Thou has thy payment too' (V.v.73). His fate has moved ever more swiftly following the direful misprision in which the innocent Antonio is stabbed, and by it he is swept up into the carnage of the last scene, the avenging instrument of a moral design in which '*black deeds*', his own as well as others', '*must be cur'd with death*' (V.iv.40). His erstwhile conversion from the world to 'justice', from sin to penitence, thus subverted in the apparently causeless logic of Antonio's death, he abjures all codes, all obligations, both 'Christian breath' and the world's 'desert' (V.iv.39), in a desperate nihilism from which emerges, nevertheless, an austere sense of value, a self-sufficient integrity in being 'mine own example' (V.iv.81). He dies overcome by an uncomprehending weariness of soul, blind to the significance of his own life, and blind also to the significance of that greater cause by which goodness has been brought out of evil, and in whose operant and unsearchable judgments he has been 'naught but [the] sword' (V.v.40).

> Oh this gloomy world,
> In what a shadow, or deep pit of darkness
> Doth, womanish, and fearful, mankind live?
> (V.v.99–101)

But in spite of this, there has been some development, a shadowy *anagnorisis* that has grown out of the welter of blood, pain, and death, and which – though comprehending no more than the autarchic integrity in which he ends – communicates to the soul of Bosola an exiguous and partial satisfaction. For the man who had in the beginning denied conscience, and justified wickedness by the cynical rationalization that the only 'reward of doing well, is the doing of it', now finds a saving consolation in the knowledge *suum cuique*, that 'doing well' must remain his only reward, and that if in the end he dies neglected by both the worlds, his death was not entirely in vain. Indeed, the pathos of Bosola's death makes it difficult to avoid the conclusion that in *The Duchess of Malfi* we witness more than the Duchess's tragedy: that Bosola, in the words of Herndl, functions as 'bewildered Jacobean Everyman' confounded ultimately by the knowledge which confounds knowledge.[73] The world is indeed a 'deep pit', a very crucible of suffering: and the earthly predicament of man is a tragic storm of darkness and terror, in which the wages of sin and virtue alike are paid in the common currency of death. But if the earth is made of flaming sulphur, the sky above seems no more pitying in its implacable judgments; and whether his ultimate destination be heaven or hell, man has first to be acquainted with the 'sad misery' which is the very essence, the absolute condition of being human. Webster, like Calvin, can see a moral quality in the determined act, can assert the reality of sin even in an order in which it is preordained; but the stark assumptions of this moral vision are tinged with pathos, tempered by an implicit compassion which sees value itself as tenuous, responsibility uncertain, in the tragic enigma by which a man can be 'an actor in the main of all' (V.v.84), yet impelled to be so against the deepest instincts of nature and conscience.

9

The Unnatural Combat and *The Renegado*

Massinger's reputation as a somewhat stolid moralist has undergone little serious revaluation since Swinburne's contention that his 'highest and most distinctive claims to honour' were rather 'moral and intellectual . . . than imaginative and creative'.[1] Indeed, this is the sort of faint praise which is damningly recapitulated in the verdict of his chief biographer and critic, T. A. Dunn, who avers that in Massinger, whatever else his merits, the 'artistic conscience always succumbs to the conscience of the moralist'.[2] It is true that his morality, like that of the Jacobean dramatists in general, is frequently condemned as corrupt or decadent. But unlike theirs, as T. S. Eliot, the best-known exponent of this generalization, makes clear, this decadence has less to do with any profound metaphysical dislocation in the universe of his plays, than with a kind of emotional exhaustion, a perceptible inanition of those energies which it is the function of morality to order and restrain.[3] Massinger's genius, in fact, has little in common with the cankered muse of a Tourneur or a Webster, whose bleak determinism portrays man's estate as either irremediably vicious or utterly helpless. On the contrary, his plays declare at every turn an invincible optimism concerning man's natural prospects, and exhibit a moral design in which evil, far from necessary or incomprehensible, merely graces the triumph of a strident and declaratory virtue. All too often, indeed, Massinger evinces a fatal willingness to sacrifice consistency of character to an overall moral tendentiousness, truth to a kind of sentimental and idealized piety, so that implacable villainy is forced to denounce itself, and patient fortitude caused infallibly to prevail over evil, in accordance with some governing abstraction, inflexibly applied. By a curious paradox, it is Massinger's all too patent concern to use the drama for moral ends, that makes his drama insipid and his morality morbid. This paradox arises principally in his refusal to admit the existence of recalcitrant reality and – what follows – a strange bloodlessness on the part of his unimpassioned characters that permits them to undergo completely unconvenanted changes of motive, renouncing their own natures in accordance with the facile requirements of a happy ending, and the polite demands of a moral system which is thus made to seem little more than a branch of etiquette.[4]

Of more immediate concern for present purposes is the nature of that system, its intellectual determinants and philsophical derivation. Massinger's plays are constructed on the fundamental premise of man's freedom of will, upon his rational capacity both to subdue his passions and to know and choose the good within the framework of a morality essentially in harmony with reason and nature. His characters, as T. A. Dunn has observed, are 'reasoners more or less at odds with passions'.[5] But their ethical psychology is predicated on the assumption that, far from being enslaved to those passions, as are the tormented worldlings of Tourneur and Webster, men in general possess an unimpaired power of natural reason, in relation to which faith, where super-added, exists as a necessary and appropriate complement. The universe of Massinger's plays exhibits, therefore, a moral design which, in its evident conservatism, looks backward to the medieval synthesis of nature and grace. But at the same time it declares such an obvious debt to the Renaissance neo-Stoic revival[6] as to be at the same time symptomatic of that larger growth of deism and religious rationalism that was itself a seventeenth-century reaction to Calvinism. There are, indeed, occasional hints, in his plays, of that bifurcated world that we find so graphically portrayed in the tragedies of Massinger's contemporaries: testimony, perhaps, of the extent to which, whatever the orientation of Massinger's personal convictions, the primary concepts of nature, law, and conscience had been irreversibly conditioned by postreformist theological usages and habits of thought. Thus, by Sir Giles Overreach, the 'atheist' of *A New Way to Pay Old Debts*, we find articulated that voluntarist doctrine of the two laws by which Bosola's worldly ambitions had been so arbitrarily confounded; like Webster's anti-hero, Sir Giles too 'would be worldly wise, for the other wisdome/That does prescribe us a well-govern'd life . . ./I value not an Atome (*ANW*, II.i.23–4,26). In *The Renegado*, also, there is an observable tendency to make religion, rather than reason, the proper exercise of man's faculties, and to postulate God, rather than nature and nature's Law, as the legitimate object of conscience. One could point, furthermore, to those suggestions of anti-rationalism in Vitelli's perception of God as the utterly transcendent manipulator of providence, whom he refers to in the authentic accents of Calvinist self-abasement as 'That most inscrutable, and infinite essence', 'at whose nod/The fabricke of the World shakes' (IV.iii. 116,113–14). It might even be hypothesized that the curious convertibility of Massinger's characters, their susceptibility to sudden and surprising conversions and reversions which is so typical a convention of the Beaumont and Fletcher school in general, is due in some obscure sense to the seventeenth-century decay of that natural-law belief in the study of character in what Herndl calls its 'aspect of causal moral relation to event'.[7] As clues to the substantive qualities of Massinger's thought, these pointers and allusions are, of course, merely circumstantial. But they do none the less provide linguistic and imaginative testimony of the widespread absorption of voluntarist beliefs into the general contemporary culture, eclectic and syncretist as that culture was, and which manifested itself vestigially in the psychic and intellectual profile of one who was, by all accounts, very far from being a Calvinist.

In essence, and for the most part, therefore, it may be said that Massinger's plays evince an implicit belief in the fundamental rationality of man and God, together with the apprehensibility by reason of the dictates of the Law of Nature. If that Law no longer imposes a causal relationship between action and its consequences, as it does in Shakespeare, then it none the less provides the basis for an intrinsically natural morality. And if, in some cases (as in *The Rengado*, for instance) the appeal to reason is allowed only a conditional, as opposed to an absolute, validity, reason nevertheless exists in a hierarchical, rather than dialectical relationship with that grace by which Vitelli is enabled to master 'The rebell appetite of flesh and blood . . .' (*The Renegado*, IV.iii.27). There are, indeed, fleeting evocations of a more radical orthodoxy in Massinger's work; but the atmosphere is, on the whole, entirely inhospitable to the anti-rationalist thesis so remorselessly developed in *The Atheist's Tragedy* and *The Duchess of Malfi*. His metaphysics are embedded in that epistemological continuum which stretches from Plato and Aristotle, via the Thomistic rehabilitation of the axiom of knowledge, through to its Renaissance extension in the works of Hooker and the neo-Stoic revivalists such as Lipsius and Du Vair.

On the other hand, the viability of reason and nature in Massinger's plays certainly raises the contrary possibility: that of the playwright's hypothetical conversion to Catholicism, first conjectured by Gifford, and left open by subsequent commentators for lack of conclusive evidence either way. The arguments from external evidence – that his putative conversion at Oxford alienated Pembroke,[8] that the high cost of his burial in Southwark was because it involved Roman rites[9] – consists almost wholly in unverifiable conjecture, and, having been adequately demolished by Dunn[10] and Lawless,[11] need not concern us here. On the question of internal evidence, the majority of critics – Boyle,[12] Keoppel,[13] Chelli,[14] Cruikshank,[15] together with the plays' latest editors, Edwards and Gibson[16] – all declare themselves more or less uncommitted; indeed, only Sir Leslie Stephen[17] and T. A. Dunn[18] address themselves at all seriously to its consideration, and their 'proofs' of Massinger's at any rate formal adherence to the Church of Rome are neither incontrovertible, nor, in some cases, very persuasive. Some of the more obvious machinery of stage Catholicism – for example, the impulse of several female characters

(Beaumelle, Sophia, Camiola) to take the veil, the incidence of auricular confession in *The Emperor of the East*, and the prominence given to Friar Paulo in *The Maid of Honour* and even to the Jesuit Francisco in *The Renegado* – can be explained in terms of a quite conventional desire on Massinger's part to give authentic colouring to plots derived largely from French, Spanish and Italian sources. The 'grotesque' indications of Massinger's Catholicism that Sir Leslie Stephen affects to find in Vitelli's quandary as to the validity of lay baptism, and the regenerative effect of the sacrament upon the Muslim convert Donusa, are quite simply ill-founded. Cartwright's famous controversy with Whitgift, over two decades before *The Renegado* is assumed to have been written, had in part concerned the issue of private baptism;[19] and Hooker[20] also makes it clear that for Anglicans lay baptism, *ante mortem*, was an absolute necessity – a view conditioned largely by their belief in just such a dynamic expectation of grace through the sacraments, as Donusa is shown to experience.[21] More convincing, perhaps, is Dunn's study of *A City Madam*, where the London setting consorts strangely with the evident Catholicism of the brothers Frugal, a fact less easily offset by purely conventional considerations of local colour.[22] But if some of the plays argue a familiarity with doctrines such as expiatory penance,[23] for example, or the efficacy of works[24] that would indeed come strangely from someone who had not a distinct tolerance towards Rome, there is in truth very little that could not ultimately be accommodated within the broad doctrinal compass of the Anglican *via media*, especially in its pre-Civil War Arminian tendencies. Somewhere within that compass, for example, almost certainly originates the dramatic formulation of the decree of reprobation which occurs in *The Roman Actor*, duly modified in the light of Anglican doctrines upholding the principle of Divine 'permission' versus 'will': in the heavenly retribution which will befall the Emperor Domitian, we are assured, in words reminiscent of Hooker,[25] that

> [The immortall powers] in their secret judgements, doe determine
> To leave him to his wickednesse, which sinckes him,
> When he is most secure . . .

> (III.i.64–6)

There is, without doubt, a certain tolerant eclecticism in Massinger's thought which is unusual, though by no means unique, in an age not noted for an enlightened liberalism in matters of faith, and particularly sensitive to the expression of such matters on the public stage. Makkink has called him an 'apostle of tolerance';[26] the kind of tolerance, indeed, for which one of his own characters stands as a surprisingly apt spokesman. Asked what is his religion, Gazet, in the opening scene of *The Renegado*, insists:

> I would not be confin'd
> In my beliefe: when all your Sects, and sectaries
> Are growne of one opinion, if I like it
> I will professe my selfe, in the meane time
> Live I in *England, Spaine, France, Rome, Geneva*
> I am of that Countryes faith.
>
> (I.i.32–7)

One might recognize in this a plea for the sort of *sensus communis* which Donne calls for in the *Pseudo-Martyr;* Rome and Geneva, sects and divisions, he implies, are all in quest of the same goal, and make 'but one Church, journeying to one Jerusalem, and directed by one guide, Jesus Christ'.[27] In short, there is very little that is explicit in what Coleridge described as Massinger's 'half-in-half hankering for Popery',[28] much less that possesses the hard-edged status of evidence. We may acknowledge in him a latitudinarianism somewhat ahead of his time, but if we go further than the indisputable facts of his baptism and burial within the Anglican fold, we must hypothecate a 'conversion' upon terms of reference patently imprecise, a conversion, moreover, which left a residuum of Augustinian Protestantism in the rationalist waters of his new-found faith, to be further muddied by his evident interest in the Jacobean neo-Stoic revival. In practice, the problem of critical interpretation is perhaps best resolved by approaching his work as in some sense related to the central stream of Christian humanism, of which Shakespeare and Hooker are the best-known English exemplars, and to which the Christian neo-Stoic treatises of Justus Lipsius[29] and Guillaume Du Vair[30] were early seventeenth-century tributaries.

Certainly the aetiology of conscience within the corpus of Massinger's plays illustrates just this kind of broad receptivity to the contemporary cross-currents of English thought. To a degree shared by no other dramatist of the age, the philosophical antitheses of scholasticism and its Calvinist reaction are here embodied in the literary inventions of one man, the historical process this account seeks to explore thus uniquely arrested in the intellections of a single mind. Hence the idea of conscience as developed in several plays demonstrates at any rate an acquaintance with the sort of concepts and terminology already familiar from predominantly Puritan casuistical treatises. In *The Unnatural Combat* and *The Roman Actor*, for example, Malefort Snr and Caesar respectively refer to their own moral insensibility in the by now common-place terms of a 'sear'd up' conscience (*UC*, V.ii.280; *RA*, V.i.142) – that almost pathological condition of remorseless villainy to which Macbeth and Webster's Cardinal are brought. In the last-named play, Caesar furthermore displays all the orthodox signs of what we have come to recognize as carnal security: full of a reckless confidence which arms him against the manifold auguries of his own destruction, he falls victim to a 'sudaine but a secure drousinesse' in which he is visited by the apparitions that drive him to distraction (V.i.155). Caesar, 'that would be stilde a God', is cast down, like Faustus and Damville, for an overweening presumption and, like them, waxes desperate as the hour of death approaches, experiencing all the hideous terrors of those in whom a hitherto inconfined ambition is made subject to the remorseless circumcriptions of time and mortality. Advised to appease the gods, he laments:

> 'Twill be fruitlesse,
> I am past hope of remission. Yet could I
> Decline this dreadfull houre of five, these terrors
> That drive me to despaire would soon flye from me . . .
> (V.i.285–8)

This account of Caesar's desperation is paralleled by the full-length study of despair in *The Renegado*, where Grimaldi, the 'hell-breed Villaine' (I.i.131) of the play's title, undergoes all the spiritual agonies and self-destructive impulses of the irremediably wounded in conscience, until he is rescued in Act IV and taught to repent through the benign ministrations of Francisco. Theological despair was not, of course, a Protestant phenomenon. But it is difficult to believe that the detailed portrayal of Grimaldi's decline, gravid with 'blacke guilt, and misery' (III.ii.62) does not owe at least something to that tradition, both religious and dramatic, which originated in the story of Francesco Spiera, whose notorious recusancy and psychic paralysis in the face of death so traumatized the consciousness of Protestant Europe, that it could still be invoked in one of the neo-Stoic treatises of Joseph Hall over half a century later, a treatise, moreover, which Massinger might well be presumed to have read.[31]

But it is precisely this interest of Massinger's in Stoic philosophy that prevents any straightforward ascription of his ideas concerning conscience and moral choice to the mainstream of English casuistical literature.[32] Seneca, for example, is directly invoked as a moral philosopher in *The Maid of Honour* (IV.iii.25), in *The Roman Actor* (III.ii.72) and in *The Emperor of the East* (V.i.113), while the Stoic ideals of virtue, constancy and temperance appropriate to the 'wise man' are consistently and everywhere upheld. It is clearly beyond the scope or competence of this study to determine definitively whether or not this influence came to Massinger directly (through the widely available editions of Epictetus, Seneca, Cicero and Marcus Aurelius) or indirectly (through the Renaissance attempts, by Lipsius, Du Vair, de Mornay, and Hall, to fuse Stoic thought with Christian theology). In all probability there was a compound debt involved: the strongly pietistic overtones in much of Massinger's work suggest that he was one of those Christian humanists who, as Baker says, welcomed neo-Stoicism 'as a discipline with both classical authority and Christian colouring'.[33] For the reconciliation of divine law with human reason which we find in his plays, and which was so characteristic an assumption of the neo-Stoic expositors, was itself an evolutionary development of that natural religion which the Renaissance had inherited from Aquinas. Some vestiges of literary Senecanism, that theatrical genre for which the motifs of blood and revenge, macabre apparitions, and a wooden indifference to calamity and death were the veritable stock-in-trade, are assuredly to be found in Massinger. But it seems likely that it was to the positive moral content of Stoicism rather than to the *Tenne Tragedies* that he was drawn, and that its generalized philosophical codex, naturally more congenial to his rationalist temper, had a deeper influence upon his work than on that of his less conservative contemporaries. Indeed, whatever the wider sociological reasons for the seventeenth-century revival of Stoicism,[34] Massinger's recourse to it as a dramatist is likely to have been that of a conservative and deeply moral mind which saw in Stoicism a more expedient outlet for religious formulas whose overt expression on the contemporary stage would have been unacceptable either to law or custom. In the theatre of Massinger, therefore, Stoic values thus become a kind of extended periphrasis of Christian doctrines, the direct presentation of which would have been proscribed; as George Stanhope was later to put it, 'by a light change of Philosophy into Religion, and Plurality of Divine Beings into the only True God . . . any considering Christian may here find a scheme of what Himself ought to be.'[35] It is to the 'considering Christian' above all that Massinger's dramatic homilies are addressed; and if the moral 'schemes' through which he sets out to edify his audience are in some instances predominantly Stoic, in others predominantly Christian in tone, he none the less stands as a dramatist in the same field of ideas as those other non-dramatic polemicists in whom the metaphysical synthesis was more systematically developed.

Hence the general principles of Stoic thought – its conception of a hierarchically ordered universe of cause and effect, its equation of virtue with reason and nature, and its emphasis upon the values of moral responsibility and duty to others – are all implicit, albeit in varying emphasis, in Massinger's plays. For the dramatist, as for the Stoics, virtue is the supreme good of mankind, rooted in that perfection of right reason which consists in following nature. 'Virtue', says Seneca, 'is the only good; at any rate there is no good without virtue; and virtue itself is situated in our nobler part, that is, in the rational part.' Asked what is the greatest good man can possess, he is adamant: 'It is to conduct oneself according to what nature wills.'[36] Cicero, too, insists that the great office of man is to live in harmony with nature, the pursuit of which leads to the acquisition of the four cardinal virtues:

If we follow Nature as our guide, we shall never go astray, but we shall be pursuing that which is in its nature clear-sighted and penetrating (Wisdom), that which is adapted to promote and strengthen society (Justice), and that which is strong and courageous (Fortitude). But the very essence of propriety is found in . . . (Temperence).[37]

Massinger's ethical psychology, which identifies virtue with the sover-iegnty of reason over passions in the soul of man is, of course, a Renaiss-ance commonplace as old as Plato's *Republic* and Aristotle's *Ethics;* but the dramatist's sources seem to have been, in the immediate case, as much Roman as Greek. For the Stoics, too, the wise man aspires to moral goodness by the rational exercise of justice, fortitude, and temperance, which in turn makes him aloof both to outward calamity and the inward rebellion of his passions. As Cicero explains, in terms which almost exactly define the comparatively simple organization of Massinger's characters:

the essential activity of the spirit is two-fold: one force is appetite . . . which impels a man this way and that; the other is reason, which teaches and explains what should be done and what should be left undone. The result is that reason commands, appetite obeys.[38]

The faculty of moral choice for Massinger is therefore almost wholly intellective; and whatever the evidence for his cognizance of the (largely Calvinistic) conventions of English casuistry, we must recognize at the same time that in some of his plays the key philosophical denominators are essentially pagan. Not only is the identification of virtue, nature, and reason for all practical purposes complete, but this moral axis is often allowed an absolute validity, unconditioned by any notion of man's fall.

Hence in these plays, Massinger's characters act within an objective and consistently realizable ideology of good and evil.[39] There is no sense either of reason's inadequacy or virtue's obliquity, nor even, as in Shakespeare, that the apprehension of the good lies in the application of reason to particular moral instances. Malefort Snr, tormented by the pangs of inces-tuous love, succumbs at last to his 'victorious passions' (*Unnatural Combat*, IV.i.120) but recognizes, even as he chooses the worst, that he has 'reason to discerne the better way' (IV.i.151). Elsewhere, the 'true victory' of reason is couched in authentically Stoic accents: in *The Fatal Dowry*, Romont describes its triumph as a conquering of 'our intestine foes,/Our passions breed within us . . .' (V.ii.103–4); in *The Bondman*, Cleora echoes Cicero in affirming that 'noble temperance (the Queene of vertues)' can bridle 'rebellious passions' (IV.iii.124–5); and in *A Very Woman* there is a similar exaltation of 'passive fortitude' as 'the best vertue' in him 'Who fights/With passions, and overcomes 'em' (IV.ii.153–5). A purely natural morality, presided over by an anonymous

'Power' or 'Powers', is clearly posited in *The Unnatural Combat;* throughout the play, the notion of order is modulated in terms of a constant
semantic interplay between the imperatives of 'nature' and 'unnatural'
considered as categories of moral value; and the Stoic conceptions of the
jus gentium, which the Renaissance retrospectively equated with Natural
Law,[40] is positively identified with 'moral honesty' in *Believe As You List*
(I.ii.33). In all of these instances, conscience as the arbiter of moral choice
is effectively synonymous with reason. The laws of well-doing are the
dictates, not of revelation, but of right reason,[41] and the subjective satisfactions that derive from the attainment of virtue are not so much the
transcendental serenities of a fulfilled conscience, as the earth-bound consolations of a purely Stoic philosophy. Thus, in *The Roman Actor*, the
condemned senators Rusticus and Sura 'take a leaf of *Seneca*' (III.ii.72)
to render themselves insensible to a horrible death; both meet their ends
unflinchingly in that virtuous fortitude which is the explicit debt they owe
to 'grave Philosophie' and the 'Stoicks frozen principles' (III.ii.99,75).

But the paramountcy of reason and nature, in the above instances more
or less absolute, is qualified in other plays of Massinger by what Stanhope
called that 'light change of Philosophy into Religion'; here, though the
Stoic substratum remains, it is interfused and permeated by that Christian-
ized ethos that is so characteristic of the neo-Stoic treatises of Lipsius and
Du Vair. Not only is the 'Plurality of Divine Beings' transmuted by
Massinger into 'the only True God', but the ramparts of reason and nature
are at once partially undermined by the doctrines of original sin and
subordinated, albeit in a contiguous, rather than wholly dialectical
relationship, to the supervenient necessities of grace and faith. What
Baker has remarked of the neo-Stoic impulse in a more general sense, is
equally true of a certain phase of Massinger's work. By a subtle metamorphosis, the cardinal Stoic virtues are modulated into familiar Christian
morals, so that fortitude becomes resignation, resolution and constancy
become a pious trust in the providence of God.[42] So in *The Maid of
Honour*, what Camiola calls 'Th' Adamant chaines of nature and religion'
(III.iii.145) coexist as harmonizable ethical imperatives; but that religion
is specifically Christian, and not only sanctions the pursuit of virtue (in the
form of the heavenly plaudits of 'bless'd Saints' and Seraphique Angells',
V.i.88–9), but in one case actually displaces the Stoic ethic by disallowing
to Adorni the 'Roman resolution of selfe – murther' (IV.iii.117).[43] In
The Renegado, Francisco schools the conscience of Vitelli to a Christian
resignation whose best exemplars are saints rather than philosophers:

> I exacte not from you
> A fortitude insensible of calamitie,
> To which the Saints themselves have bowde and showne

> They are made of flesh, and bloud; all that I challenge
> Is manly patience.
>
> (I.i.76–80)

And in *The Virgin Martyr*, the persecuted Theophilus is possessed of the rapturous assurance in the face of death which is the mark of a Christian conscience, and his extraordinary capacity to ensure 'beyond/The sufferance of man' (V.ii.)* is attributable, not to an indifference bred of *ataraxia*, but to his other-worldly vision of Dorothea and her fellow-martyrs, who extend to him the heavenly crown which is the specifically Christian solution to the problem of evil. But it is in *The Renegado* chiefly, that the unqualified ascendency of *recta ratio* is subordinated to religion and tempered by its post-lapsarian orthodoxies. In Act III, Vitelli attempts to extenuate his surrender to the seductive embraces of Donusa, and condemns his weakness as an example of that inherited 'humane frailety' which pursues him 'In scorne of reason, and what's more, religion' (III.v.12,15). Later on, having successfully resisted a second temptation, he cedes the moral victory, not to unaided reason, but to the fortifying effects of grace:

> I grant to have master'd
> The rebell appetite of flesh and blood
> Was far above my strength; and still owe for it
> To that great power that lent it.
>
> (IV.iii.26–9)

In short, we may apply to the somewhat tergervizating impulses of Massinger's moral philosophy, the apology urged in defence of Justus Lipsius by his English translator, John Stradling:

> *That he writeth so highly in commendation of RIGHT REASON, although som times with the words of the Ancients: yet he accopteth no reason pure or right except it be directed by God and illuminated by faith.*[44]

Indeed, Stradling's parentheses serve to point up the most significant distinctions to be made between the two plays under immediate discussion. *The Unnatural Combat* and *The Renegado:* in the earlier play 'Right Reason' and 'the words of the Ancients' provide for the most part its prevailing ethos, while in the latter, this largely secular morality is overlaid by the supra-rational mysteries of 'God' and 'faith'.

Thus while *The Unnatural Combat* contains ethical motifs whose source is essentially Christian – the proscription of revenge and incest, for example – these are subjoined to an overwhelmingly Stoic conception of natural justice. Its very title suggests the clue to the interpretation of its otherwise rather curious morality: a morality that begins and ends in the Ciceronian

* Gifford edition.

command, *sequere naturam*. That structural disunity which T. S. Eliot and Chelli[45] have pointed out – the first part of the play concerning the hatred of Malefort for his son, the second his passion for his daughter – becomes less serious a fault if the two actions are seen as aspects of a single theme. The parent-child relationship is, after all, the common denominator in both parts, and its violation in either instance is subjected to the sanctions of a natural morality: the nemesis that overtakes the father's unnatural love for his daughter is clearly related to the nemesis that prevents the son's attempt, by means of an unnatural combat, to execute justice upon his own father. The causal means of this nemesis is not, as has been remarked, the Christian God, but is variously apostrophized as 'Thou searcher of men's hearts' (I.i.342), or as an 'Immortal' Power or Powers (II.i.189; I.i.382), whose providence entails upon man a necessary fate. There is an almost organic synthesis between the gods and nature in the play: both are merged in the numinous dynamic of a single will, so that there is no practical distinction between that 'Power above' which enforces its edicts in the name of what is natural, and the purely natural instruments of its just revenge. The logic by which Malefort Snr is brought to justice is thus primarily Stoic, rather than scholastic. It is entrained, not by a series of causes in human affairs (he is destroyed for, rather than by, his sins), but by a bolt of lightning, his offences against nature in this manner quite literally punished by nature. The natural law here is above all a law of kind, uniting ruler and subject, father and child, the state and the citizen; but its morality is sternly indivisible, and its first priority is the preservation of that universal order which transcends the individual. The pirate son's challenge to his father ostensibly champions the cause of murdered innocence; but his cause is seen as unnatural, not simply because it involves preying upon the country of his birth and the equally impious purpose 'to kill him, from whom/He receiv'd life' (II.ii.19–20), but because it represents, in Seneca's words, a larger failure to 'conduct oneself according to what nature wills'. It is interesting to note that Malefort Jnr shares with Hamlet a common cause – the murder of a parent. But in the case of the latter, his attempt at revenge is unilaterally vetoed, and himself slain, in order to preserve the integrity of those fixed and unvarying principles upon which the ethical homogeneity of the Stoic universe rests. Thus Seneca, speaking of the essential oneness of virtue, writes: 'The advantage of the state and that of the individual are yoked together . . . to human virtues only one rule applies. For right reason is single and of but one kind.'[46] And Marcus Aurelius expresses this moral uniformity in terms of a monolithic cosmos:

Constantly regard the universe as one living being, having one substance and one soul; and observe how all things have reference to one perception, the perception of this one living being; and how all things are the cooperating causes of all things which exist; observe too the continuous spinning of the thread and the contexture of the web.[47]

In the beginning of the play, therefore, Malefort Jnr's career as a pirate is repeatedly described as unnatural, not only by the father who stands accused of complicity in his son's crimes against the state, but by all concerned. As a pirate he is denounced by the Governor as a 'bloudy/And fatall enemie' (I.i.214–15) in seeking the ruin of his country, and his challenge to his father is variously anathemized as 'impious' (II.ii.18), 'Strange and prodigious' (I.i.361), and 'against all ties of nature' (I.i.380). *Prima facie* the issue, resting as it does upon the son's implacable hostility towards an apparently blameless father, appears unnatural; but even the son himself, who is in possession of those facts at first hidden from the audience (i.e. the father's murder of the son's mother) recognizes his course as a revenge forbidden by nature. Thus he entreats his pirate captains to be charitable in their censure of him for 'undertaking that/ Which must be, when effected, still repented' (II.i.54–5). The perturbation of his soul is not due to a 'servile fear of death' but rather to the fact that both discourse and reason tell him that he 'can nor live, nor end a wretched life' but 'both ways' be rendered impious (II.i.58–61). To Malefort Snr, on the other hand, the challenge to single combat comes as a quite literal answer to prayer, for it dissolves the immediate charges upon which he had been falsely accused: aiding and abetting his son's raids on the harbour of Marseilles. Arraigned before the Council of War, fettered in the ruins of his former military glories, the Admiral appeals to heaven to proclaim his innocence:

> Thou searcher of mens hearts,
> And sure defender of the innocent,
> (My other crying sinnes, a while not lookd on)
> If I in this am guiltie strike me dead,
> Or by some unexpected meanes confirme,
> I am accusd unjustly.
>
> (I.i.342–7)

The 'unexpected meanes' seem to be confirmed in the opportune arrival of the sea-captain, who interrupts the proceedings to invite Malefort to a trial of arms with his son, over what patently concerns an issue of private revenge, rather than the issues of public justice over which the Admiral stands accused. According to his messenger, Malefort Jnr desires that

> It may be understood no publike hate,
> Hath brought him to Marsellis, nor seekes he
> The ruine of his countrie, but aimes only
> To wreake a private wrong . . .
>
> (I.i.350–3)

In the event, the bloody arbitrament is determined in the father's favour. In the death of Malefort Jnr, the gods appear to sanction a natural morality which dictates that the combat upon which the pirate son engaged was unnatural not simply because it involved his own father, but because it implies the setting of himself up as judge in a purely private cause. The ethical interdict concerning revenge, effectively dramatized by Tourneur, is repeatedly endorsed elsewhere in Massinger's work: in *The Renegado*, for instance, Francisco advises Vitelli, 'Leave your revenge to heaven' (I.i.146); and in *The City Madam* those who entertain it are condemned as 'strangers/To morall honestie, and never yet/Acquainted with religion' (I.iii.94–6). Though motivated by an entirely just anger over his mother's murder (albeit to the world undiscovered), Malefort Jnr attempts to obtain a personal satisfaction for her injuries in a course of action over which, on his own admission, 'Pietie will weepe, and filiall dutie mourne' (II.i.141). Certainly in the England of Massinger's time, any such referral of controversy to the arbitrary conclusions of trial by combat would have been anathema to civil and ecclesiastical authority alike: Perkins, in considering the question 'whether a man may reskue himselfe or other by combate', condemns the practice as morally indistinguishable from private revenge:

> First, it is the expresse commandement of God, *Thou shalt not kill*. In which, all private men are forbidden to kill or slay, but in the case of just and necessary defense. Secondly, we may not hazard our lives, without some speciall warrant from God: if we doe, it is a flat tempting of God: and this is done in every combate . . .
>
> There is no warrant in Gods word, for a private man to accept a chalenge. Nay, it is rather flat against the word. For God saies, *Revenge is mine*. The private man saies the contrarie. The wrong is mine, and I will be avenged of him that hath done it.[48]

By an irony which costs him his life, Malefort Jnr refuses to make public the grounds of his complaint; out of a wrong-headed concern for his father's honour, he declares that he will 'Speake' his 'griefes' indirectly, in a 'perplext forme and method', which only the Admiral can interpret by the 'guiltie knowledge' in his bosom (II.ii.116–19). The consequence of this misplaced delicacy is that the son himself becomes guilty of that hazard of his life which is a 'flat tempting' of the play's presiding deity, and is destroyed for it. At the same time, his death effectively vindicates Malefort Snr of the public and immediate charges for which he stood trial, while the private issues ('My other crying sinnes, awhile not lookd on') await a public and spectacular redress at the end of the play. The general verdict on the son's defeat and death is articulated in Theocrine's exclamation, 'Heaven is just!' (II.ii.29); and if this is a provisional verdict on the perceived facts of the case, it is none the less underwritten by the appearance, in the final scene, of the ghosts of Malefort's victims, who urge him to a similar interpretation of his son's destruction:

> Yet, thou being my sonne,
> Were't not a competent judge mark'd out by heaven
> For her revenger, which thy falling by
> My weaker hand confirm's. Tis granted by thee.
>
> (V.ii.294–7)

Massinger's narrative technique is governed largely by his desire to create suspense, so that the logic of incident and event proceeds according to something very like that 'perplext forme and method' by which young Malefort alludes to what he dare not speak. Hence the springs of action and motive – the son's mysterious hatred for an apparently honourable father, Montreville's hypocritical friendship and subsequent villainy – are hinted at, but never fully revealed until Act V. Only then does it become clear that Malefort's overthrow was forged upon the 'anvile of [his] impious wrongs' (V.ii.284), both towards Montreville, whose mistress he stole, and towards the long-dead mother of his son, whom he murdered in order thus to indulge his lust. Once the tragic climax is reached, the play's moral design becomes in retrospect intelligible; for it is then that we realize that the combat of the play's title is not an isolated incident, but one in a series of unnatural acts that have characterized the gradual disintegration of a moral persona – of which Malefort's incestuous love for his own daughter is the ultimate and most heinous expression. In the past, the Admiral's poisoning of his first wife out of an adulterous passion for his friend's mistress constituted a sundering of the moral bonds of nature, just as the remorseless killing of his own son is, in the manner of it, equally unnatural. As the quotation from Perkins makes clear, the ethical embargo on single combats of this kind applied equally to those who accept as well as those who issue such challenges; but Malefort's invidious abuse of his son's corpse indicates that he fought not in self-defence, but in order to silence for ever the sharer of his guilty secret, and to escape the 'power of Fate' again to make him wretched:

> Were a new life hid in each mangled limbe,
> I would search, and finde it. And howere to some
> I may seeme cruell, thus to tyrranize
> Upon this senslesse flesh, I glorie in it.
> That I have power to be unnaturall,
> Is my securitie.
>
> (II.ii.204–9)

But in spite of the general esteem in which he is everywhere held, there are early suggestions of his 'power to be unnaturall', evidence of those seeds of corruption which are brought, during the action of the play, to so perverse a fruition. The oblique comments of the Usher in the opening scene hint at Malefort's obscure affinity with Montreville: from the beginning they have been twins in quality, 'joynt purchasers,/In fire, and waterworks, and trukt together' (I.i.54–5). In Act III, Beaufort Snr explains his earlier hesitation to exercise judgment in the prospective marriage of his son to Theocrine, in an observation upon her father's character which looks behind the superscriptions of honour to the inner reality of long-engrafted vice:

> I have knowne him
> From his first youth, but never yet observ'd
> In all the passages of his life, and fortunes,
> Vertues so mix'd with vices. Valiant the world speakes him
> But with that bloody; liberall in his gifts too,
> But to maintaine his prodigall expence,
> A fierce extortioner; an impotent lover
> Of women for a flash, but his fires quench'd,
> Hating as deadly . . .
>
>   (III.ii.31–9)

In such a man, sudden, violent and sensual, the growth of an incestuous passion for his daughter – a daughter, moreover, who so clearly evokes in him the remembrance of those 'sweet pleasures, and allowd delights' (II.iii.94) he once tasted from the mother – is a logically coherent development. Even if, as Eliot suggests, there is no inevitable chain of causation between the two actions of the play, there is none the less, therefore, a consistency between Malefort's earlier crimes and his final attempt on his daughter, which is conceived primarily in terms of the inherent degeneracy of his character, and its progressive violations of what is natural. The unifying principle of Massinger's drama is rooted essentially in the integrity of its underlying moral order; all Malefort's crimes offend against that order, and the punishment meted out to the son in the first half of the play is just as surely meted out to the father in the second. Since sin here by definition consists in a separation from nature, both characters come to represent a cognate threat to its indivisible morality. The good, we may recall with Seneca, is in every instance subject to the same laws; just as 'right reason is single and of but one kind', so to human virtue 'only one rule applies'.

It is the rule of virtue and of right reason, already infringed in the killing of his wife and son, that Malefort's unnatural lust for his daughter entirely subverts. His moral struggle is couched primarily in terms of the classico-Christian correlatives of soul, and ends in that spiritual disequilibrium in which reason is undermined by a will perverted and disordered by the passions, which, in the words of Theocrine's page, are man's 'worst masters' (III.ii.119). Malefort's conscience, in the light of which he fully realizes the objective nature of what he intends, is here effectively synonymous with his reason: for Massinger, as for the neo-Stoics in general, the coefficients of moral discrimination are essentially rational in character. Lipsius, for example, speaks not only of the concomitance of reason and the conscience, but also of their final inestinguishability:

> Reason hath her offspring from heaven, yea from God: and *Seneca* gave it a singular commendation, saying (a) *That there was hidden in man parte of the divine spirit.* This reason is an excellent power or faculty of understanding and judgement . . .
>
> Here hence come those stings of Conscience in wicked men: Here hence those inward gnawings and scourges: here hence also commeth it that the wicked even against their wils approove vertuous living and commend it. For this good part in man may somtimes be pressed down, but never oppressed: and these fiery sparks may be covered, but not wholly extinguished.[49]

Just before Malefort's destruction, the ghosts of his first wife and his son will come to lance what he declares to be his 'sear'd up' conscience (V.ii.280), but it is none the less a conscience that, however 'pressed down' in the onrush of his guilty desires, never ceases to testify to the foul reality of his misdeeds, actual or potential.

Hence the full significance of that cumulative series of dark hints – Malefort's excessive interest in his daughter's personal adornment, his almost lubricious praise of her womanly attractions – is finally discovered in his aside at the banquet given in his honour, in which he confesses his own growing unease with the direction of his impulses:

> And yet I nourish strange thoughts, which I would
> Most willingly destroy.
>
> (III.iii.3–4)

Yet the assertion only adumbrates our perception of the disordered tendencies of those thoughts, and the increasing degeneracy of the will by which they ought to be destroyed. When Beaufort Jnr proposes a general toast to 'the worthiest of Women' (III.iii.6), Malefort is swept up into fervid praise of his daughter, above anything due to 'forraigne Queenes/Nor yet our owne' (III.iii.9–10), and ending in a defiant threat to pronounce a villain anyone who dares to doubt its validity. Like Macbeth, he becomes the prey to irrational motives: 'chimeras' and those false creations which proceed from the heat-oppressed brain impress themselves upon his 'phantasie', so that he gives vent to the amazing suspicion that his daughter is being stolen away from him, in danger to be lost forever:

> Phantasies? They are truths.

> Where is my *Theocrine?* You have plotted
> To rob me of my Daughter:
>
> (III.iii.142–3)

Informed that his daugher is safe, and exchanging the very courtship with young Beaumont for which he had brought her, he demands to be taken to see for himself the love-scene being enacted: 'ere she delivers up her virgin fort' to her betrothed, he insists

> I would observe what is the art he uses
> In planting his artillery against it;
> She is my only care, nor must she yield
> But upon noble termes.
>
> (III.iii.153–6)

And as he intrudes unobserved upon the modest exchanges of the two lovers, Malefort succumbs further, in a series of asides, to the uncontrollable jealousy which seemed implicit in his role as voyeur: 'O how my bloud boyles!' (III.iv.36); 'I am ruin'd if/I come not fairely off' (III.iv.45–6). Asked for his consent to the match, he appeals in desperation for some 'strange invention' to aid him, and excuses his evident reluctance to agree to it by the transparent subterfuge that his daughter is not yet worthy of the marriage for which he had so earnestly sued, and that 'so great/A good as then flow'd to her, should have beene/With more deliberation entertain'd' (III.iv.65–7). The subversion of rational control is now complete. Despite the amazement of his hearers, he determines to use his 'will' to defer the marriage, yielding 'no further reason' in the disposition of what is his own, and exits with Theocrine, complaining of the inward fires of lust which threaten to consume him.

At the beginning of Act IV Malefort enters *solus*, and in a long soliloquy confesses his appalled recognition that the flames fanned by his wild desires are not those of an honourable love lighted at Cupid's altars, but an 'infernal brand' thrown into his 'guiltie bosome' by the 'snake-hair'd Sisters' (IV.i.5–8). The guilt of his past crimes still sticks upon him, and he feels himself 'Accurs'd in having issue' (IV.i.8); his conscience, heavy with the blood of his son, shrinks at the unnatural thoughts he entertains in regard to his daughter. He berates himself for having 'by the false shadowes of a fathers kindnesse' (IV.i.24) long deceived himself; 'wilfully' he forgot the name of his daughter, and cherished obscene hopes in his slumbers, whose ravishing temptations ('My eyes being open', IV.i.39) were never condemned in his waking hours. Yet still he determines to reassert a rational control over his will, and master his rebellious passions:

> Yet spight of these temptations I have reason
> That pleads against 'em, and commands me to
> Extinguish these abhominable fires,

> And I will doe it. I will send her backe
> To him that loves her lawfully.
>
> (IV.i.41–5)

But his will is atrophied, long since habituated to evil by that 'power to be unnatural' that had facilitated his earlier sins; and the intention is almost immediately subverted by passion as soon as he looks upon Theocrine:

> But all my boasted power of reason leaves me,
> And passion againe usurpes her Empire . . .
>
> (IV.i.47–8)

In a moving interview with his daughter, torn between the conflicting impulses of his being, he tells her incoherently, in a 'perplexd, and misterious method' (IV.i.80) that her perfections are to him 'foule blemishes,/ And mulcts in nature' (IV.i.83–4), for in her beauty he drank the poison he now feels dispersed in his blood. Her dutiful care to please his will merely compounds her unlawful attraction to him, defeating all his rational attempts to oppose it:

> my rankes of reason
> Disbanded, my victorious passions fell
> To bloody execution, and compeld me
> With willing hands to tie on my owne chaines . . .
>
> (IV.i.119–22)

By a curious inversion of value, therefore, itself obliquely suggestive of his moral confusion, his daughter's 'plurisie of goodness' is become, in its capacity to make him guilty, her chiefest 'ill', her 'vertues vices' merely (IV.i.131–2); and in desperation he banishes her from his sight, lamenting his own sense of powerlessness:

> O that I
> Have reason to discerne the better way
> And yet pursue the worse
>
> (IV.i.150–2)

The poignancy of Malefort's dilemma, suspended as he is between the perceived imperatives of knowledge and a fatal impotence of mind, between an unassenting conscience and an almost involuntary thraldom of the will, contains inevitable echoes of Bosola's tragic predicament, and, indeed, of those Calvinist formularies of moral choice[50] by which Webster's anti-hero was bound. But here, there is no question that Malefort cannot choose the good rationally perceived: the chains that seem to bind him to what he fully recognizes as evil, are tied on with 'willing hands' (IV.i.122), his capacity to sin undertaken 'with a kinde of flattering joy' (IV.i.123). In Webster's necessitated universe, on the other hand, the possibility of choice is negated; man's only freedom consists in doing evil, and his conscience is sufficient merely to provide no pretext or excuse for wickedness. Malefort, it is true, is an authentically Stoic believer in a personal destiny: the slaying of his son was in part a surety against the power of fate, and he remains convinced that his present impasse is determined by his 'crosse fates' (IV.i.159). Yet a belief in fate, for Stoic and neo-Stoic alike, was perfectly compatible with the free moral act. The Roman concept of *fatum* inhered in an eternal ordinance of God, executed in an immutable order of secondary causes; liberty of the will and moral responsibility were preserved, in that man's only duty lay in aligning his will with that of the gods, his sole responsibility to endure virtuously whatever destiny laid upon him. Seneca insists that man's moral agency is effectively dependent upon fate:

> I am constrained to nothing, I suffer nothing against my will, nor am I God's slave, but his willing follower, and so much the more because I know that everything is ordained and proceeds according to a law that endures for ever. The fates guide us . . . ; every cause depends upon some earlier cause: one long chain of destiny decides all things, public or private.[51]

Lipsius, too, agrees with Seneca as to the equipoise of fate and free will, only modifying the iron 'bandes of destiny' with an orthodox Christian insistence upon contingency, of which human choice is an important instance:

> Is there FATE? Yea. But it is the firste and principall cause, which is so farre from taking away the middle and secondary causes, that (ordinarilie and for the most part) it worketh not but by them: and thy will is among the number of those secondary causes thinke not that God forceth it, or wholly taketh it away.[52]

Yet, if Malefort's attempt to criminate fate rather than his own will is rendered illegitimate by the presiding axiologies of his universe (just as it will be emphatically disannulled at the moment of his death), so, too, is his specious appeal to nature as the arbiter and exemplar of bestial licence. Conjured by the hypocritical Montreville into confessing his guilty passion, and persuaded that absence from Theocrine may yield a 'kinde of intermission' to the 'fury of the fit' (IV.i.236–8), he commends her to the dubious protection of his treacherous friend. But her absence, on the contrary, provokes anew his passion, and he curses himself for being 'tender-consciencd' (Since 'twas my fate, and not to be declin'd' V.ii.14,13) and invokes the precedent of 'Universall nature' which every day allows incest to creatures of all kinds.

> The gallant horse
> Covers the Mare to which he was the sire,

> The bird with fertile seed gives new encrease
> To her that hatchd him. Why should envious man then
> Brand that close act which adds proximity
> To whats most neere him, with the abhorred title
> Of incest?
>
> (V.ii.29–34)

But Malefort's rationalizations are here a perversion of reason and a blasphemy upon nature: for the measure of man's station in the universe *vis-à-vis* the beasts, is overwhelmingly a function of his nature and his reason. The injunction *sequere naturam* is to do in nature what it behoves a rational creature to do. So, in the *Meditations*, Marcus Aurelius insists that 'the true joy of a man is to do that which properly belongs unto a man';[53] and in the *Discourses*, Epictetus avouches that what properly belongs to man is wholly separate from what belongs to the animals:

> for them it is sufficient to eat and drink and rest and procreate, and whatever else of the things within their own province the animals sever-ally do; while for us, to whom [God] has made the additional gift of the faculty of understanding, these things are no longer sufficient, but unless we act appropriately and methodically, and in conformity each with his own nature and constitution, we shall no longer achieve our own ends . . . Wherefore, it is shameful for man to begin and end just where the irrational animals do; he should rather begin where they do, but end where nature has ended in dealing with us.[54]

Nature is, of course, invoked elsewhere in Jacobean drama to sanction acts which are inimical to grace and faith, either by rationalistic atheists such as D'Amville and Levidulcia, or by victims, such as Bosola and the Duchess, crushed relentlessly between the metaphysical antinomies of a voluntarist universe. But whereas in these instances the natural order is perceived as corrupt, here nature is seen as the very measure of morality, the rule of reason and the proper object of conscience. Malefort attempts to rationalize an act which, in the words of Epictetus, begins and ends 'just where the irrational animals do'; and, as the evil Montreville is shortly to point out, his intent:

> made natures selfe run backward,
> And done, had caus'd an earth-quake.
> (V.ii.251–2)

Later, his daughter raped and murdered while under 'the treacherous guard/Of Goatish Montreville' (V.ii.210–11), an inexorable correspon-dence between action and nemesis, between the violation of nature and the earthquakes of its inevitable retribution, is exhibited in the fates of both Malefort and the unrelenting victim of his own past crime. Montreville's castle is surprised by the forces of the Governor, and its owner, obdurate to the last, is led away, Iago-like, to torture and death. In an agony of grief and remorse, Malefort enters in the 'storme and darknesse of the night' (V.ii.255), and, like Lear on the heath, taxes the elements that are not only the cosmic expression of his unnatural and bemadding sorrow, but the means also whereby the gods find out their enemies:

> Doe, doe, rage on, rend open *Aeolus*
> Thy brazen prison, and let loose at once
> Thy stormy issue; blustring *Boreas*,
> Aided with all the gales, the Pilot numbers
> Upon his compasse, cannot raise a tempest
> Through the vast region of the ayre, like that
> I feele within me . . .
>
> (V.ii.258–64)

But unlike the largely innocent Lear, Malefort has still within him undivulged crimes; nor are the convulsive dislocations in nature that are their direct consequence primarily tutelary in character, but are here ultimately destructive of those pent-up guilts that now begin to lacerate his soul:

> I am possess'd
> With whirle-winds, and each guilty thought to me is
> A dreadfull Hurricano; though this centre
> Labour to bring forth earthquake, and hell open
> Her wide-stretch'd jawes, and let out all her furies,
> They cannot adde an atome to the mountaine
> Of feares and terrors that each minute threaten
> To fall on my accursed head.
>
> (V.ii.264–71)

The revelational echoes of that precipitate mountain of 'feares and terrors', which in previous chapters threatened the heads of such notable sinners as Faustus and D'Amville, here completes the dramatic irony inherent in Malefort's earlier response to his son's challenge in Act I. There, the rhetoric of honour had insisted that to dare to live were as easy as to repent 'when mountaines of my sins orewhelme me' (I.i.372); to fight for 'a second life' as easy as to plead for mercy 'At my last gaspe' (I.i.373). Now, at the final crisis of that second life, at the limit of a lease borrowed circumstantially of nature and eternity, Malefort finds that the divine prospects of mercy and repentance are as far away as ever, subject now to that fatal trepidation of the conscience which is the symptom of its own decline into despair. The ghosts of his past victims appear to his deranged fancy, identifiably Senecan in their blood-boltered and ghoulish aspect: young Malefort, 'naked from the wast' and 'full of wounds', leads in the shade of his mother, 'her face leprous'. By signs and gestures, the apparitions communicate their embassy: they come to 'launce' his 'sear'd up conscience' (V.ii.280), and to instruct him that 'those thunderbolts'

> That hurl'd me headlong from the height of glory
> Wealth, honours, wordly happinesse, were forg'd
> Upon the anvile of my impious wrongs . . .
>   (V.ii.281–4)

Impelled by horror, and the objectified images of his own guilt, he confesses that his lust caused him to poison his wife, and was in turn the cause (to the world now discovered) of his son's repudiation of his 'filial duty' (V.ii.289). Yet, as we have already seen, the son's revenge, unnatural in itself, was by nature countermanded in his death, allowing to the father that hiatus in which his own crimes against nature, wrought up to an overweening pitch and presumption, should come to a full and public reckoning. The disappearance of the ghosts reduces him to the desperate conviction that his guilt is beyond expiation, his crimes finally beyond the scope of penance. He accuses his fate, and 'those starres' cross to him in his birth, whose malign influences forbid him now to die 'With peace of conscience like to innocent men', but rather to curse his 'cause of being' (V.ii.300–6). Yet the reason for his present downfall and imminent destruction, though in a manner pre-ordained in that perpetual chain of causes by which the Stoic universe is governed, lay not so much in his destiny, as within the orbit of his own will; for as Du Vair explains, 'this Destinie that hath fore-ordained all things, hath decreed that our Will shall bee free; so that if there bee any necessitie in our will, it is this, that it is necessarily free'.[55] Ultimately, Malefort is killed by a flash of lightning, struck down by that avenging thunder that his son had seemed to predict for him (II.i.190). Yet though, like D'Amville, he dies a self-convicted atheist and murderer, the manner of his death does not, like that of D'Amville, constitute an intermission in nature, but a foreclosing of its proper instruments; not a Calvinistic intrusion of providential retribution, but a purely rationalistic nemesis arising out of a great cosmic impulse to order. That power above which Beaufort Snr, pointing the tragic moral, cites as the punisher of 'murther, and unlawfull love' (V.ii.343), is not significantly different from the Stoic conception of providence, which Seneca describes as a 'power over all things' and in which all causes, including the most unexpected accidents of nature, have their individual reasons. In a passage which perhaps provides a sufficient and final comment upon the destruction of sinners such as Malefort against the moral interflux of universal nature, the philosopher writes:

> this great frame of the world could not be sustained without som governor and superintendent . . . even those things which seeme most

incertain and confused, I speak of cloud and raines, of the claps of thunder and lightning, of fires and flames that enforce their passage thorow the tops of the highest mountaines, . . . and other accidents, which that part of nature which is most stormie and tempestuous . . . how sudden and unexpected soever they be, are never raised without reason.[56]

In *The Renegado*, on the other hand, while the Stoic motifs of constancy in resolution and fortitude in suffering contribute much to the dramatic ethos, the coordinates of reason and nature are permitted only a provisional legitimacy. Indeed, the play as a whole dramatizes not so much a sin against nature, but a violation of a purely religious morality, in which the sufficiency of reason is no longer an absolute premise. In the Jesuit Francisco's opening advice to his impetuous disciple Vitelli, but lately arrived in Tunis in search of his abducted sister, stoical fortitude is augmented with Christian patience, reason with revelation, nature with grace. The priest's homily makes it clear that the wisdom that triumphs over fortune and the passions is specifically religious in character, and that suffering may be endured because its purpose is ultimately moral:

> I exacte not from you
> A fortitude insensible of calamitie,
> To which the Saints themselves have bowde and showne
> They are made of flesh, and bloud; all that I challenge
> Is manly patience. Will you that were train'd up
> In a Religious Schoole, where divine maximes
> Scorning comparison, with morall precepts,
> Were daily taught you, beare your constancies triall
> Not like *Vitelli*, but a Village nurse
> With curses in your mouth: Teares in your eyes?
> How poorly it showes in you!
>
> (I.i.76–86)

The completion of virtue by religion, or 'morall precepts' by 'divine maximes' that Francisco's speech so precisely articulates, is wholly consonant with that characteristic neo-Stoic subordination of *recta ratio* to the higher mysteries of faith. So in *Vertues Commonwealth* or *The High-Way to Honour*, the neo-Stoic apologist Henry Crosse prefaces his treatise with the orthodox deference that any such account of pagan philosophy was required to make in the direction of revealed truth. In an exhortation which in many respects parallels that of Francisco, he writes:

> We must not rest then upon the morall vertue, and make that the chiefe good, which are but steppes to clyme up thereunto, as the wise Heathen taught . . . here is a maine difference, let no man repose himselfe, upon such a sandie and shallow foundation, if he will stand sure: but build

on Christ the Rocke, the bright starre of the immortall majestie, on him to cast Anchor. . .[57]

As Dunn has pointed out, the central issue debated by the play concerns that of 'religious versus amatory obligation'.[58] Vitelli throughout the first three acts wavers between the 'divine maximes' of his spiritual mentor Francisco, and the seductive allurements of the Muslim princess Donusa, to whose charms he temporarily falls forfeit. This subjective moral struggle in the soul of the protagonist is objectified also in the wider contrast between Christian orthodoxy and Islam: the Christians either redeem themselves from temptation, or resist it altogether by subduing their passions to rational control; a control which is in direct contrast to the cruelty and sensuality of the Turks, whose 'Religion' allegedly 'Allowes all pleasure' (I.ii.49–50). There is thus a somewhat Puritan identification of virtue with sexual chastity in *The Renegado*, the practical attainment of which lies with the spiritual competence of the Christians only. Vitelli, it is true, succumbs to the embraces of Donusa, and in doing so believes momentarily that 'Vertue's but a word' (II.iv.136); but he is thereafter armed in its exercise by religion, and the trial of his constancy is undertaken with the help of 'holy thoughts, and resolutions' (III.v.38). In the non-Christians, however, virtue by itself is patently inadequate: Donusa is unable to resist the force of her desires, and capitulates to them within a framework of value wherein the available antinomies of choice are purely secular – that is, between 'Virgin pride' and honour on the one hand, and 'ill fame' and the *'Siren* notes' of 'lust' on the other (II.i.24–34).

As in *The Unnatural Combat*, Massinger dramatizes in *The Renegado* two separate actions, but this time more successfully integrated, both at the levels of plot and theme. Vitelli's love affair with Donusa and subsequent imprisonment by the Turkish Vice-Roy Asambeg, is counterpointed by what is, in spite of the title, effectively a sub-plot involving his sister's abduction by the piratical renegade Grimaldi. The two actions are technically united in the key role of Grimaldi, who is both the initiator of the catastrophe, and, via his reconversion to the cause of Christianity, the means of its triumphant resolution. Thematically considered, Vitelli's amatory lapse, followed by a triumph over his flesh and blood worthy of the 'Saints themselves', is paralleled in the secondary plot by Grimaldi's religious renegadism and redemptive agonies of despair. In protagonist and antagonist alike, the motives of sensual 'pleasure' (I.ii.50) give way to the more lasting satisfactions of a regenerate conscience; both suffer a period of incarceration during which they are either strengthened in, or recalled to, Christian principle, partly through exposure to affliction, and partly through the ministrations of that 'most religious man' (IV.i.6), Father Francisco.

The respective predicaments of Vitelli and Grimaldi illustrate two of the divine purposes of suffering as defined and set forth by Justus Lipsius: in the case of Vitelli, his afflictions appear to belong in that category sent to the good as trials of 'Constancy';[59] of Grimaldi, that sent to the bad as chastizements, for their 'amendment'.[60] In both play and treatise alike, that insensible fortitude of the Stoics is harnessed to a Christian sense of purpose: things may be borne in patience because they come from an ultimately beneficient Deity. The cause of adversity in the good, so Lipsius asserts,

> is Gods love towards us, and not hatred. For this our exercising further-eth us more waies than one: it confirmeth or strengtheneth us; it trieth or prooveth us; it maketh us mirrours of patience unto others.
>
> It doth strengthen us, for that same is (as it were) our school-house, wherein God traineth up his servants in Constancy and vertue.[61]

So it is that vitelli, having confessed to Francisco his former surrender to the weaknesses of the flesh, determines to expiate his fall from grace by a renewed attempt to bear his 'constancie's trial', in the pursuit of which he returns once more to the Viceroy's palace to brave not only the continued temptations represented by Donusa, but the imminent risk of capture and execution by her guardian Asambeg. Scornful of Francisco's injunction 'not to goe, but send' (III.ii.15), he rejects the latter course with a fully Stoic resolution, as a 'pettie triall/Not worth one so long taught, and exercisde/Under so grave a master' (III.ii.15–17). But this self-imposed exercise of his virtue is very nearly disabled from the outset: brought again into the company of Donusa, Vitelli finds the force of her allurements threatening once more to overthrow his reason. Asked whom it is that he fears, he replies in terms of original corruption:

> That humane frailety I tooke from my mother,
> That, as my youth increas'd, grew stronger on me
> That still pursues me, and though once recover'd
> In scorne of reason, and what's more, religion,
> Againe seekes to betray me.
>
> (III.v.12–16)

The dialectical relationship between reason and instinct, conscience and the baser passions, which so clearly conditions the moral struggle of Malefort, is here encapsulated within the more orthodox metaphysical co-ordinates of 'religion' and inherited 'humane frailty'. The case of Vitelli's conscience implies to this extent a reordering by Massinger, in this play at least, of the determinants of moral choice, so that reason is reinforced by religion, just as 'flesh and blood' is infected with a natural corruption. An awareness of this neo-Stoic revaluation assists in the correct interpret-ation of Donusa's reply, which, once again, invokes the equivocal sanctions of universal nature: to turn rebel to her embraces, she insists, would be to

> turne rebell to
> The lawes of nature, the great Queene, and Mother
> Of all productions, and denie alleageance,
> Where you stand bound to pay it.
>
> (III.v.17–20)

But the philosophy which makes virtue coextensive with nature is, as we have seen, essentially pagan in origin; and its invocation in this case is seen as evil not because, as with Malefort, it is beyond doubt a specious rationalization, but because it is wholly unconditioned by specifically Christian formulas concerning the post-lapsarian corruption of the natural world. The love that to Donusa is authorized by the 'great Queene, and Mother/Of all productions' therefore, becomes to the increasingly precisian conscience of Vitelli, a 'poyson' received into his 'entrayles' (III.v.46); and her present argument from natural morality appears to him no more than the defence raised by lust to 'maintaine a precipice/To the Abisse of looseness!' (III.v.67–8).

Having in this manner mastered the internal rebellion of his passions, the captured Vitelli faces the trial of purely external afflictions with an invincibly Stoic fortitude, built nevertheless upon the rock of his religion. Thrown into prison by the Viceroy Asambeg for having compromised the virtue of the Sultan's niece, Vitelli endures torture with a patience so impressive that it wins the admiration of his jailers: Mustapha confesses that since he studied and knew what man was, he

> was never witnesse
> Of such invincible fortitude as this Christian
> Showes in his sufferings; all the torments that
> We could present him with to fright his constancy
> Comfirm'd, not shooke it; and those heavy chaines
> That eate into his flesh, appear'd to him
> Like bracelets made of some lov'd mistrisse hayres
> We kisse in the remembrance of her favours.
>
> (IV.ii.45–52)

Thus in his 'manly patience' and 'commanding' virtue, Vitelli attains the very apotheosis of the Stoical 'wise man'; but it is a wisdom illuminated by faith and a clear conscience, of which Joseph Hall in his *Characters of Vertues and Vices* has this to say:

> His passions are so many good servants, which stand in a diligent attendance ready to be commanded by reason, by religion . . .
> Hee is Gods best witnesse, and when he stands before the barre

for truth . . . hee with erect and setled countenance heares his unjust sentence, and rejoyces in it. The Jailers that attend him are to him his pages of honour; his dungeon the lower part of the vault of heaven; his racke or wheele the staires of his ascent to glorie; he challengeth his executioners, and incounters the fiercest paines with strength of resolution; and while he suffers, the beholders pitie him.[62]

So exemplary a witness for Christian truth does Vitelli determine to become, that when Francisco visits him in prison to applaud his disciple's fulfilment of the precepts of virtue and religion, he declares fulsomely that his achievements so far are 'but beginnings, not/The ends of my high aimes' (IV.iii.25–6), and that his final objective is nothing short of a martyr's crown. Francisco praises his constant bearing, assuring him that the 'Sun' of his 'cleere life' will lend to 'good men light' (IV.iii.39–40); indeed, such a 'mirrour of patience' does he become, that Donusa, attempting his conversion in order to save her own life, is herself converted to Christianity by his evident fearlessness in the face of death. Thus Vitelli's conduct is seen as a triumphant vindication of the purposes of providence in afflicting the virtuous: for, as Lipsius assures us, such trials as Vitelli endures to the extremity of life itself, have an exemplary effect on those who behold them:

> they serve in steed of mirrours or presidents. For that the constancie and patience of good men in miseries, is as a cleare light to this obscure world. They provoke others thereunto by their example, and tread the path wherin they should walk . . . *Regulus* was unworthily put to death by torments; but his worthy example of keeping promise liveth yet. *Papinianus* was murthered by a tyrant: but the same butcherly axe that cut off his head, emboldneth us to suffer death for justice sake.[63]

In the sub-plot too, the renegade Grimaldi's crisis of conscience adumbrates the play's leit-motif of redemption through suffering: his agonies of remorse illustrate, in the words of Lipsius, 'An other ende why God sendeth afflictions, [that] is for our Chastisement'.[64] To this purpose, continues Lipsius,

> [God taketh] from us our goodes, which we abused to luxuriousnesse. Our liberty, which wee abused licentiouslie. And so with this gentle correction of calamities, he dooth . . . purge and washe awaie our wickednesse.[65]

Grimaldi, in whom licence and sensuality are personified, and for whom moral scruples are the 'ragges of chastitie, and conscience' merely (I.iii.49), finds himself imprisoned by the Viceroy his master, on charges of treachery to the Ottoman power; and in passing sentence, Asambeg confiscates both his goods and his liberty in terms ironically suggestive both of the pirate's future reformation, and Lipsius's testimony to the correcting power of all such 'calamities':

> Ceize upon him;
> I am not so neere reconcild to him
> To bid him die: that were a benefit
> The dog's unworthy of. To our use confiscate
> All that he stands possesde of: Let him tast
> The miserie of want, and his vaine riots
> Like to so many walking Ghosts affright him
> Where ere he sets his desperate foote.
>
> (II.v.80–7)

When we next meet Grimaldi, his demeanour is miraculously changed: self-confessedly 'tame and quiet' in comparison to his former self, his dejection and remorse would seem to have grown out of his imprisonment and disgrace. Now, the 'miserie of want', and the guilty remembrance of his 'vaine riots' induce in him that moral torpor and sense of irremediable loss which are the classic symptoms of a despairing conscience:

> Why should I study a defence, or comfort?
> In whom blacke guilt, and misery if ballanc'd,
> I know not which would turne the scale. Looke upward
> I dare not, for should it but be beleev'd,
> That I (dide deepe in hells most horrid colours,)
> Should dare to hope for mercy, it would leave
> No checke or feeling, in men innocent
> To catch at sinnes the divell nere taught mankind yet.
> No, I must downeward, downeward: though repentance
> Could borrow all the glorious wings of grace,
> My mountainous waight of sins, would cracke their pinions,
> And sincke them to hell with me.
>
> (III.ii.61–72)

His pangs of conscience, typical in that they anticipate the very fires of hell, convince him that he is a devil already (III.ii.77). Invoking the Platonic/Aristotelian theory of the four elements, by which each may afford liberty to the soul after death, Grimaldi elects to make the sea his grave, for there he 'ploude up/Mischiefe as deepe as Hell' (III.ii.91–2); and he is only restrained from these self-destructive impulses by the inter-vention of Francisco, who applies to the wounded conscience of the pirate such cures as heaven and his own office have lent him.

The definitive cure is deferred to a climacteric scene at the beginning of Act IV. As is clear from the dialogue between the Master and the 'Boteswaine', Grimaldi's despair has been to some extent alleviated, but exacerbates as soon as mention is made of 'The Church, or the high Altar' (IV.i.12). According to the Master, his remembrance is tormented by a sacrilege he once committed at St Mark's in Venice, when in a fit of 'wanton irreligious madnesse' (IV.i.29), he seized from the priest the 'sanctifide meanes' and 'Dash'd it upon the pavement' (IV.i.32–3). Grimaldi's general despair is thus compounded by his somewhat idiosyncratic persuasion that, in the words of the Master

> he cannot receave pardon
> For this fowle fact, but from his hand against whom
> It was committed.
>
> (IV.i.40–2)

At this point, Grimaldi himself enters, studying a book on the subject of penitential satisfaction, his still suicidal melancholy implied in his preparedness to execute a bloody justice on himself to purchase a pardon from all those he has caused to suffer. His deliberations are, in turn, cut short by the entry of Francisco, attired, in accordance with the stage directions, 'in a Cope like a Bishop'. Confronted, like Malefort, with the very image of his 'fiend-like' deed, Grimaldi falls anew to remorse; but Francisco is none the less able to grant him the personal pardon his condition seems to require. His absolution is therefore, by implication at least, a sacramental one; and afterwards, Grimaldi feels the regenerating effects of grace and determines to confirm his repentance by 'good deeds' (IV.i.96):

> What celestiall balme
> I feele now pour'd into my wounded conscience!
> What penance is there Ile not undergoe
> Though nere so sharpe and rugged, with more pleasure
> Then flesh and blood ere tasted . . .
>
> (IV.i.88–92)

In this manner, Grimaldi is brought to the neo-Stoic recognition that his sufferings are but the 'gentle correction of calamities' and that, in his own words, the stripes of true sorrow 'Arm'd with an iron whip' are nothing more than the 'gentle touches of a hand,/That comes to cure . . .' (IV.i.93–6). Adversity has proved for him one of those divine chastizements, which, in the words of Lipsius,

> is the best and gentlest that may be for our amendment. It helpeth and healeth us two manner of waies. Eyther as a whippe when we have offended: Or as a bridle to hold us backe from offending. As a whip, because it is our fathers hande that dooth often scourge us when wee doo amisse: but it is a butcherly fist that striketh seldome, and then

payeth home for all at once. As fire or water are used to purge filth: So is this Purgatorie of persecutions to our sinnes.[66]

The precipitate and, indeed, improbable conversions of both Grimaldi and Donusa – the one a hardened criminal, the other a niece of the Grand Turk himself – have been criticized as typical of that naive facility by which Massinger transforms the whole bias of plot and character in order to adumbrate an exemplary moral.[67] According to this view, his drama sacrifices much of its logical consistency to theatrical expediency, and if we are to believe in it at all, we must do so at the expense of applying realistic criteria to conventions which are so manifestly at the service of a primarily homiletic purpose. Putting the point at its most extreme, Maurice Chelli has said of the characters in *The Renegado*,

> ils ne sont que comme des indices à la position desquels nous reconais-
> sons la marche des événements. Donusa embrasse le christianisme
> comme naguère elle cassa les assiettes de Vitelli! Il est inutile de s'at-
> tarder à discuter une psychologie qui fut le moindre souci de l'auteur.[68]

While it would be impossible to deny the pietistic animus to which Massinger's reversions and transformations are traceable, their apparent incredibility is perhaps mitigated by a proper understanding of the concept of suffering in the play, and in particular an awareness of the central importance of this theme in neo-Stoic philosophy. Once the dramatic significance of this theme is grasped, the motivation of characters, as well as what Chelli calls 'la marche des événements' can be seen to be governed, if not by a natural logic of cause and effect, then at any rate by a logic which, for Massinger, is located in the moral responsiveness of human beings to pain and adversity. This process is neither as impressively nor as thoroughly worked out as it is in Shakespearean tragedy, for example; but it is true, none the less, that Massinger's sinners are redeemed, no less than is King Lear, by the experience, actual or vicarious, of what Lipsius designates as a 'Purgatorie of persecutions'. Constancy in resolution is the neo-Stoic theme of *The Renegado*, together with the associated idea, voiced by Francisco, that 'such as suffer, overcome' (V.ii.96). But constancy in virtue, and the fortitude to withstand suffering, prove impossible without the endorsement of faith; and it is this almost Websterian inability to go right but for heaven's scourge-stick, that, above all, prompts the spiritual metamorphoses in the personages of Massinger's drama.

Grimaldi is therefore recruited to the cause of the Christians, and eventually becomes the instrument of their safe delivery from Tunis, principally out of a sense of obligation to Francisco for his own deliverance from the torments of his conscience:

> doe I owe
> A peace within heere, Kingdoms could not purchase,

> To my religious creditor, to leave him
> Open to danger . . .
>
> (V.ii.11–14)

And Vitelli is able to convert Donusa, not so much through the patent triviality of his arguments (IV.iii.128) as by the fortitude he displays in the face of his approaching death, which in turn instructs her in the supposed insufficiency of her own faith. What apparently finally impresses her is the last of his arguments, which directly addresses her own 'fear to die' (IV.iii.135):

> Can there be strength in that
> Religion, that suffers us to tremble
> At that which every day, nay hower wee haste to?
>
> (IV.iii.135–7)

to which her reply is at best comprehensible as a psychological response to the immediacy of her own end: 'This is unanswerable, and there's something tells mee/I erre in my opinion' (IV.iii.138–9). Vitelli, however, interprets this as a 'Heavenly prompter', a motion of divine grace, which alone can shore up the constancy of Donusa's new-found resolution. He urges her to marry him and to die in the faith, a transcendental consummation above and beyond the debased impulses of 'flesh and blood'. Reassured that Vitelli, through the sacrament of baptism, will procure the means by which her conversion may be endorsed, Donusa spits at Mahomet, a gesture which, not unnaturally, seals her death-warrant.

The climax of the play is simultaneously the climax of their spiritual aspirations. Vitelli and Donusa enter the place of execution to the sounds of 'A dreadful musicke', displaying a rapt exaltation of conscience reminiscent of Charlemont and Castabella, and armed with an almost Calvinistic assurance in the prospects of their own salvation. Vitelli acclaims his bride's fearlessness in the face of those euphoric pains, which, in ending life, are no more than the prologue to 'immortall pleasures' (V.iii.72). He declares, moreover, that he will neither insult her 'minds fortitude' by enquiring how she can brook her coming ordeal, nor tell her of the ineffable joys of the 'Haven' in which that ordeal will be terminated. There, in that ultimate destination, their souls will become heirs to those unspeakable satisfactions of which Du Vair speaks, satisfactions that attend upon the testimony of a clear conscience, and the triumph of constancy over adversity:

> Now besides the pleasure we receive in our soule . . . and that constancy worketh in a manner, and wrastleth with adversitie, there remaines after-wards unto us a greater taste of it, when wee are delivered, and are come into a safe harbour. For there is nothing more pleasant in the world, nor that gives a greater contentment to our soules, then the

testimony our conscience beareth unto virtue . . . . We are filled then with an unspeakable pleasure, and the splendour of a true and sound glory seemeth to shine about us, and give us some preeminence amongst men.[69]

But the progress of Vitelli and his bride to martyrdom, though allowed to proceed, for maximum homiletic effect, to the moment when glory seems most to shine about them, is summarily arrested by the dramatic intervention of Paulina, hitherto 'mewde up' (II.v.140) in the Viceroy's seraglio. High drama is thus converted to anti-climax, and comedy wrested out of the very jaws of tragedy by a series of rapid and skilful peripeteias, in which Paulina is able to discover to Donusa not only her true identity, but also the ruse, devised by an ever-resourceful Francisco, by which they are all to escape from Tunis. Hence the moral triumph of the Christians, symbolized in Donusa's conversion and Vitelli's constancy, is practically underwritten in their safe deliverance from the Turks, an outcome which Vitelli puts down to a 'pious miracle' (V.ii.16), and Francisco attributes to the inscrutable purposes of providence (V.ii.86). Yet at the same time, the moral victory of Christianity over Islam is somewhat tarnished by the adroit misappropriation, on the part of the sainted defectors, of the Viceroy's 'choysest jewels'; and to this peculiarly discordant morality may be added the plangent disharmonies of what Dunn calls the play's 'dying fall'.[70] In the closing lines, Vitelli intones the predictable moral, while the grief-stricken Asambeg blames the loss of his captives on his own credulity; but the trite complacencies of triumphant virtue are ironically deflated in the baffled cry of the man it has defeated, who is left 'without one mans compassion' to hide his head among the 'desarts', or some cave filled with shame (V.viii.36–7).

In conclusion, it may be said that Massinger's treatment of the idea of conscience clearly represents a conservative deviation in the general dramatic and philosophic tendencies which this book attempts to trace. But this fact alone does not seriously endanger the hypothesis upon which that attempt is based; on the contrary, and to adapt a Polonian maxim, it is a task of scholarship by just such indirections to find directions out. As we have seen, Massinger displays unmistakable traces of Calvinist anti-rationalism even as he reacts against it, and is in that sense as much a product of the voluntarist ethos of his age as are Tourneur, Webster or Ford. The corpus of his work displays a mind highly sensitive to the cultural cross-currents of the early seventeenth century; indeed, it is possibly this sensitivity to thought rather than to emotion, to moral abstraction rather than to empirical observation, which accounts not only for a certain philosophical eclecticism, but also for that dissociation of sensibility which Eliot claimed to have detected in Massinger's plays.[71] At all events, his cultural susceptibility gives ample testimony in literary form of that continued dynamic interplay between the opposing impulses of humanistic rationalism and the Calvinist reaction by which it was all but destroyed; in this sense, he may be seen as a symbol of that theological uncertainty whose available recourse was to the secular authority of neo-Stoic thought. He is clearly a believer in man's ability to go right, and to follow his conscience if he so determines: man is, for him, *rationis capax*, capable, at least, of rational action. But, like the neo-Stoics to whom he was indebted, he is far less certain as to what extent the dictates of reason are invalidated in a fallen world, or indeed, whether in such a world, nature or revelation provides the appropriate correlatives for conscience.

10

'Tis Pity She's a Whore

In so far as he draws upon the same neo-Stoic tradition as Massinger we may detect in the somewhat remittent impulses of Ford's non-dramatic works a similar epistemological uncertainty. In *The Golden Mean* and *A Line of Life*, virtue is construed once again according to the familiar classical formulae as a victory over the insurrections of passion and the vicissitudes of fortune.[1] But even in these avowedly neo-Stoic treatises, the uncertainty of that victory is far more deeply etched than in the blandly optimistic axioms of his contemporary. If Ford allows a partial sufficiency to man's reason, he is careful to insist simultaneously upon its invincible susceptibility to error in what the latter pamphlet deprecates as the 'Labyrinth and Maze of this naturall . . . Race of frailtie'.[2] It is, indeed, primarily in the concessions made by the two pamphlets to the doctrines of total depravity wherein consists their most obvious affinity with the antinomian world of *'Tis Pity She's a Whore*; for, although the drama brings into somewhat equivocal play such common philosophical denominators as 'fate' and 'resolution', there is, in this instance at any rate, no real ideological commerce between Ford's stoical beliefs and his distinctly Calvinist theology.[3] The moral perspectives of *'Tis Pity*, in fact, are those in which the claims of philosophical naturalism are unconditionally abrogated in the obscurantist ethos of orthodox fideism; a hierarchy of values which clearly owes far more to that other product of Ford's rigorous piety, *Christes Bloodie Sweat*, where the metaphysical abasement of 'prone mortalyty accurst' is a theme powerfully suggestive of the drama it precedes.[4]

Just as this poem exists within the dark penumbra of Calvinistic dogmatism, so *'Tis Pity* exists at the outer edge of that bleak territory of the imagination already colonized by Tourneur and Webster; an eclipsed and ever more decadent universe, animated now only by the febrile energies of a vast and cosmic despair. Both poem and play affirm the dangers of rational speculation and the spurious exaltation of vitiated natural impulse as guides to morality; both, too, invoke the necessary theological sanctions; but if there is a mercy to be found in such judgments, it remains an occluded and half-glimpsed prospect, overshadowed in a divine economy which graces the graceless in the arbitrary coils of an inscrutable will. *'Tis Pity*, in truth, is a reversion to that bifurcated world of the two laws described in earlier chapters, a reopening of that dialectical chasm between the realms of faith and reason so nearly bridged in the drama of Massinger. Here, as Richardetto comes to recognize 'All human worldly courses are uneven' (IV.ii.20), while what justice there is has 'fled to Heaven' (III.ix.62), where it resides ineffably beyond reason's capacity to descry or nature's to obey. 'Nature is in Heaven's positions blind' is the Friar's fideistic premise (II.v.34); and it is a premise ominously borne out in the corrupt world of the play, where, in the words of *Christes Bloodie Sweat*, 'Intrusted jurisdiction' is habitually 'over-sway'd/By partiall favour', scholarship misapplied to 'paynt the grosenes of unlawfull love', and 'Inchanting sinne . . . Rockes [men] in Lethargies' of lust to their ultimate confusion and damnation.[5] Here none are perfect; all, in varying degrees, are 'Slaves to disorder, servants to delight';[6] and since, in Calvin's phrase, 'Guilt is from nature',[7] it follows that even the spokesman for the moral order, the Friar, admits to its unintelligibility, and is irreparably tainted, both by the inadequacy of his counsel, and the very obligation to act in a world which makes action itself guilty. Like Webster's Amalfi in this, Ford's Parma evinces a similar dependence upon necessity and fate, or, what amounts to the same thing, an inexorable providence, before which man must acknowledge himself 'A wretch, a worm, a nothing' (I.i.76). At the same time, the humanist in Ford, as before in Webster, protests just so far as to secure compassion for the pitiable plight of mankind, caught up in the cosmic paradox by which to do what nature impels is to succumb inescapably to the whips of conscience and the rod of divine vengeance. Giovanni, indeed, is yet another Jacobean Everyman, and the ambiguities of the audience's response to him are exactly proportionate to the moral perplexities of his predicament – a predicament wrought up to the pitch of tragedy in so far as it compels pity and terror as emotions mutually counterpoised. Hence, inasmuch as he is an heroical lover, helplessly infatuated by a misplaced love for his sister, we concede to his experience something of that pity and even admiration seemingly authorized by the inwrought richness of the verse and its appeal to the values of *amour courtois*.[8] In so far as that love is objectively corrupt, and sets in train the crimes of blasphemy, atheism, and murder, we accede to its just condemnation by the statutes of conscience and of civil use. Terror resides in the inexorable steps by which Giovanni, impaled as he is upon the laws of Burtonian necessity[9] and a reprobate conscience, and struggling in vain to rationalize his perversity in terms of nature and Platonic casuistry, nevertheless proceeds ineluctably to the 'mischief' an angry heaven has remarked him for

(IV.v.10). He is in very truth one of Calvin's voluntary slaves, wilfully electing himself to a destiny that is also a predestined doom.

Giovanni's incestuous love is not, as with earlier Jacobean sinners, the 'libertine corollary'[10] of his atheism, so much as a passion which must be made consistent with that rational morality of which he is so distinguished a scholar. At the same time, it is a morality conceived exclusively by 'nature's light', against whose latent dangers he has 'Long ago' been cautioned by the Friar, containing as it does the seeds of 'ignorance in knowledge' (II.v.31,27). Giovanni's opening arguments are doubtless, therefore, intended to appear specious, unlikely 'school-points' (I.i.2), inferring the necessary collocation, insistently propounded in Fotherby's *Atheomastix* and related works,[11] of 'devilish atheism' with mere foolishness (I.i.8). (Indeed, it is doubtful, especially in view of Giovanni's subsequent vacillations, whether atheism was possible as a formal philosophical creed; since according to such seventeenth-century confutations, full conviction would always be betrayed by the workings of conscience, from which an understanding of the deity could never entirely be rooted out.)[12] 'The Fool hath said in his heart, There is no God', says the Psalmist;[13] and the Friar's response, albeit resting upon obscuration and manifestly deficient as an answer to the youth's 'fond' questions, is primarily intended to underscore this very foolishness. The propositions of philosophy, erected upon man's enfeebled wit, lead to a natural speculation which is in heaven's positions mere blindness; a Calvinistic assertion that negates not only the centuries-old fusion of philosophy and revelation, but flatly disannuls the humanistic assumptions of Hooker and Shakespeare.[14] The purely secular knowledge, which in *Faustus* has been seen as a synthetic element in the plot of 'scholarism grac'd', is here inflexibly reprobated as presumption, while the law of nature in which it is grounded becomes an unholy licence to commit sin, in direct contravention of him who is 'above the sun' (I.i.II). Moreover, whereas Faustus's desire for knowledge unlimited is seen as partially legitimate, Giovanni's intellectual presumption, like D'Amville's, is dedicated to reconciling the promptings of blood with the vitiated impulses of reason in order to justify the inglorious pursuit of what he himself recognizes to be lust (I.ii.154).

In sum, Giovanni's is the atheistic conscience of the natural man; since what he proposes is, by his own account, 'in religion sin' (I.ii.145), he abjures religion, seeking rather to regard his actions exclusively in the moral aspect of 'nature's light' which alone can instance 'some defence' (II.v.31-2). The implication of the Friar's argument is that all of Giovanni's reckless defences, comprising as they do the spurious syllogisms concerning consanguinity (I.i.28-34), neo-Platonism (II.v.14-26) and fate, employ but a single term in the metaphysical equation that might validate them. In so far as they evoke only the 'philosophers/Of elder times'

(II.v.31–2), and excise the coefficients of grace and faith, his arguments remain smothered in darkness.

Hence Giovanni's Aristotelian proposition, advanced in the first act, that nearness in blood persuades a 'nearer nearness in affection' (I.ii.236), ignores the Thomistic gloss that the very ardency of such a love is what makes incest a 'determinate species of lust'.[15] In similar fashion, the ladder of love argument, by which 'Virtue itself is reason but refined,/And love the quintessence of that' (II.v.20–1) turns out to be a ladder that terminates this side of idolatry, denying Ficino's caveat that all earthly desires must end in the perception of divinity.[16] That perception is extinguished ultimately, of course, in Giovanni's moral capitulation to the immanence of fate, the apparent inefficacy of his repentance setting the seal upon his atheism, and vindicating in him that metonymic logic by which nature becomes his law, and 'fate' his 'god' (I.i.84).[17] 'Lost. I am lost. My fates have doomed my death', he cries in the incipient onrush of theological despair (I.ii.139); his 'prayers' unanswered, and his 'tears' to all intents in vain, Giovanni's Faustian response to the metaphysical void is to banish altogether the claims of a heaven that will give no token of itself, as 'dreams' and 'old men's tales' (I.ii.151). But the vanity of all such attempts to redefine the governing axiologies of his universe, typical of the atheist, is attested to by Robert Burton: speaking in *The Anatomy* of those who in their 'innate blindness' hold religion a 'fiction, opposite to Reason and Philosophy', he says,

> In spiritual things God must demonstrate all to sense, leave a pawn with them, or else seek some other creditor. They will acknowledge nature and fortune, yet not God: though in effect they grant both: for . . . as . . . *Calvin* writes, *Nature* is God's order . . . *Fortune* his unrevealed will.[18]

Enslaved to a passion incurable by prayer, made hopeless in the certainty of his own ruin, Giovanni attempts to exonerate his actions in what he increasingly comes to see as a cosmic determinism by exalting nature and fate above a grace inexplicably withheld and a providence baffling in its arbitrary sway.

This gives to his love for Annabella all the exhilaration and poignancy of desperation, its bright incandescence made fragile by the very brittleness of the vows that sustain it. Like that of the Duchess and Antonio before them, the love of Giovanni and Annabella is given poetic affirmation, and acquires in its ideal mutuality an hermetic self-signification. External judgments convert in the prismatic conflux of their love to a spectrum of moral evaluation in which knowledge becomes ignorance, sin a species of virtue. But unlike the Duchess, who repents, Giovanni's attempt to do so leads directly to the Satanic conviction of his own reprobation, releasing him in turn to that deciduous euphoria which is the mark of the benumbed and secure conscience. His case is rather that of D'Amville: in both, their discovery of the nearest way to hell is ordained by the irredeemable sin of atheism; and from the outset, Giovanni's will remains fixed in the transvaluating logic of a corrupt love and an equally corrupted conscience, devoid of grace. The conscience of the natural man, says Thomas Morton in *A Treatise of the threefolde state of man*, albeit imbued with 'some reliques of knowledge', remains but a 'false witnes, and doth judge of right and wrong, of life and death so as a blind man judgeth colours, saying that blacke is white, and white is blacke, that evill is good, and good evil'.[19] So it is with Giovanni. His moral sense, never quite extirpated in its down-pressing dread of 'the rod/Of vengeance' (I.i.83–4), remains yoked to the exactions of an 'unrevealed will' in its aspect of a personal fate, and thereafter commits itself to that perverted series of justifications by which the religion of love replaces the love of religion, Annabella's repentance is seen as faithless treachery (V.v.4–10), and the terrible revenge that follows becomes a glorious triumph (V.vi.10). It is true that, like Faustus's Good Angel,[20] the Friar maintains to Giovanni that 'The throne of mercy is above your trespass' (II.v.64); but the promise is disannulled, not only by his pupil's atheism, but in the numerous prophecies implying that heaven has marked him down beyond the 'compass' of prayer (cf.I.i.67; II.v.9–10; II.v.38–9; V.iii.70). The lover's experience wins for them an abbreviated happiness, fluctuating between ambrosial contents and an intoxicated hubris; but Giovanni's decline, beginning with his lie to Annabella concerning the approval of 'holy church' (I.ii.237) through to his growing jealousy and final obduration, is that of a man existing in the chill and stricken desolation of an incommutable doom.

What lends a seeming value to the experience of the lovers is partly its romantic *afflatus*, drawing upon that courtly tradition stretching from Capellanus to the Caroline love-cult, partly the rank corruption of a world which seems well lost for it. The rottenness of the social context has doubtless a dramatic function in putting, as Kaufmann says, the 'unthinkable within the access of thought';[21] but a generalized contempt for a fallen world uniformly immersed in what John Downame calls 'the vanitie of honours, riches, and pleasures',[22] is just as surely a characteristic trait of the Calvinist imagination. All here are so immersed. Grimaldi's is a painted honour, the sham impress of his princely connections and noble birth, whose obligations he betrays in the bungled revenge which results in Bergetto's death. Similarly, Soranzo's 'still rising honours' (III.ii.4) conceal a proclivity to sensual pleasure, and permit of perjury and murder as the means to obtain it. The material baits of wealth and position go far, in Florio's case, to explain his evident preference for Soranzo as suitor to his daughter, in spite of what Parma 'long hath rumoured' (IV.i.43) concerning his sordid affair with Hippolita; while Donado and Richardetto, more openly venal, variously conspire to milk the 'Golden calf',

Bergetto, of his riches, by marrying him off to their own advantage (I.ii.120). Soranzo's creature Vasques, a villainous contriver of all harms, and reminiscent of Bosola in his moral irrelatedness, seeks to uphold his master's counterfeit honour by assassination and torture, righting his wrongs by a cold-blooded vengeance masquerading as justice. Justice here has indeed fled to heaven; while in its earthly minister, the Cardinal, entrusted jurisdiction is manifestly overswayed in the interests of mercenary self-enrichment, or the partial favour extended to 'blood' and nobility.

The overall effect is to re-create that familiar Jacobean world of closeted lust and secret intrigue: the corrupted affection of Giovanni and Annabella, incestuous in itself, is insidiously affined with the murderous adultery of Soranzo and Hippolita, and the behind-door work by which the latter seduces Vasques to her baneful designs; all of which, the typical impostumes of the times, fester and run to head in the multiple attempts at vengeance. 'O horrible!', declares the disingenuous Vasques, having elicited from Putana the identity of her mistress's lover: 'To what height of liberty in damnation hath the devil trained our age' (IV.iii.233–4); and his verdict is suggestive of that same enmeshing web of guilt as Ford himself intimates in *Christes Bloodie Sweat*, where such infirmity is the shared inheritance of mankind, and entails

> faults so great,
> As scant is one amongst a thousand good
> And yet that one of thousands, if the letter
> Of life were surely scand, might bee much better.[23]

Just such an exception is Friar Bonaventura: 'one of thousands' in his benevolent earnestness and genuine desire for the spiritual welfare of Giovanni and Annabella, his good qualities are marred by the 'moral obliquity'[24] which is his debt to nature. His practical attempts to save 'a pair of souls' (II.v.69) from the world's condemnation are tainted by a necessary compromise with that world, falling far short of the moral order whose claims he professes to mediate. His advice to Annabella,

> First, for your honour's safety, that you marry
> The Lord Soranzo; next, to save your soul,
> Leave off this life, and henceforth live to him
> (III.vi.36–8)

is well-intentioned in so far as it contrives to secure Annabella's redemption through her marriage, and builds, moreover, upon the *de facto* consideration that the order for the union with Soranzo has already been taken by her father. But this is expedience merely, affecting neither the honour nor the morality it is designed to confirm; for, as Irving Ribner has pointed out, 'To earn the grace of heaven she must cheat Soranzo'; while to save her own honour she must impugn that of her future husband.[25] 'Real honour', says the philosopher Tecnicus in *The Broken Heart*, 'Is the reward of virtue, and acquir'd by/Justice' (III.i.261–3); and the Friar's politic contrivances, albeit defined by the proprieties of place and occasion, remain by this criterion neither properly virtuous nor truly honourable. His wisdom is tainted in its very pragmatism, and founders at length in a world whose corruptions it unavoidably compounds.

So Annabella acquiesces in the Friar's suggestion that she marry Soranzo, but her later conduct reveals that she does so in order to satisfy the purely nominal conditions of the Friar's exhortations to virtue and honour. In a subsequent interview with her outraged husband, she admits that she chose him 'but for honour' (IV.iii.23), and there is clear evidence that the Friar's rehearsal of the religious sanctions appropriate to 'secret incests' (III.vi.26) does not for long deter her from a resumption of her affair with Giovanni (cf. V.iii.1–12).[26] Her repentance thus remains equivocal, her marriage a *pro forma* concession to those external circumstances which had conditioned her confessor's counsel. As a consequence, the grace that had appeared to work 'New motions' in her heart is temporarily overborne by the 'baits of sin', which, as the Friar recognizes, 'Are hard to leave' (III.vi.32,39–40). Her obduracy is doubtless a reflection of the Calvinistic emphasis upon the difficulty of true repentance, and the Friar's insight, which in turn quotes from *Christes Bloodie Sweat*, is elaborated therein according to the voluntaristic formulae. For he that addicts himself to sin, says Ford,

> tis almost impossible to change,
> From bad to good though God in mercy woe
> Mortality, to tast of mercies treasure,
> Yet O, tis hard to leave the baites of pleasure.[27]

Passion tempts her 'above [her] strength to folly' (IV.iii.134) and her will remains for a time bound to the impulses of flesh and frailty. Nevertheless, in time she is brought, by a now-familiar process, through affliction to a more profound sense of remorse: imprisoned in her chamber, 'Barred of all company', she has had time 'To blush at what hath passed', and can vow unshakably 'a leaving of that life' she has long 'died in' (V.i.49,51,36–7). Although, unlike her brother, she has never attempted to justify her passion according to philosophy or nature,[28] her conscience, like his, had remained inimical to grace, prone to the blasphemous inversions which accord a divinity to her lover, and responsibility to fate (cf. IV.iii.36–42; IV.iii.15). Now, an almost Faustian sense of the abridgments of time and fortune produce in her conscience an indictment of her 'weary life' with 'depositions charactered in guilt' (V.i.2,10); and not only is she restored to those perspectives in which she can see her love as 'lust', but she is brought to credit heaven, rather than fate, with the timely arrival of the Friar, by 'providence ordained' to be minister and embassy in her 'behoof' (V.i.28, 38–9). In contrast to Giovanni, she learns the limited scope of those neo-Platonic syllogisms which for him had endorsed their love; that in the state of corrupted nature, beauty, far from being synonymous with virtue, 'Is cursed if it be not clothed with grace' (V.i.13). She dies, appropriately, in an odour of sanctity, her recantation (and, by implication, her salvation) made complete in her final motives of mercy and forgiveness.

To Giovanni, however, is permitted no such recantation. He becomes, on the contrary, a prey to the irrationality that invariably attends upon the hardened in conscience, compounded, moreover, by the psychological decline determined by his humorous disposition, which proceeds according to a Burtonian prognosis, through *'Hope and Fear, Jealousy, Fury'* to *'Desperation'*.[29] His atheism, originating in 'unlikely arguments' and mere 'school-points', becomes ever more hubristic, challenging the slavish fear of Hell, and anathemizing 'religion-masked sorceries' (V.iii.20,29). At the same time, his love, born in the forbidden contemplation of 'Beauty's sweet wonder' (II.i.3), coarsens perceptibly in the metamorphosis to mere Epicureanism, so that by Act V, the romantic affirmation implied in the 'glory/Of two united hearts' coexists uneasily with the Faustian vaunt that 'A life of pleasure is Elysium' (V.iii.11–12,16). To atheism and incest is added adultery; and the temper of his mind, hitherto 'unexperienced' (V.iii.3), becomes by habitual indulgence both more audacious and more avowedly salacious, ever more vulnerable in its moral eclipse to those sanctions, which, as Hippolita had earlier discovered, wait upon 'lust and pride' (IV.i.101). Giovanni is, in very truth, marked out for heaven's vengeance. His conscience is, as the Friar affirms, 'seared' (V.iii.30), proof against the 'warning' implied in Soranzo's discovery of their love, and wrought up, in the fury of desperation, to strike 'deep in slaughter' in the plot of his own ruin (V.iii.62). The Friar, understandably, leaves him to 'despair' (V.iii.70); but, unlike Faustus, D'Amville and Malefort, he experiences none of its terminal convulsions. Instead, Giovanni appears to be inured to interior torment, one of those whose atheism makes them secure and prone to revenge, and who, in the words of St Paul, fall headlong to their destruction, 'heaping wrath to themselves against the day of wrath' (Rom. 2:5). Slain by their own blindness, such atheists, according to Burton, reason thus in a reprobate sense:

> For the rest of Heaven and Hell, let children and superstitious fools believe it: for their parts they are so far from trembling at the dreadful day of judgement, that they wish with *Nero, me vivo fiat*, let it come in their times: so secure, so desperate, so immoderate in lust and pleasure, so prone to revenge, that . . . it shall not be so wickedly attempted, but as desperately performed, whate'er they take in hand.[30]

Hence despair or the tortures of a thousand hells are alike indifferent

to him, while 'the curse/Of old prescription' by which he stands condemned only whets him to the courage which, 'desperately performed',
will enrol him in the prospects of a 'glorious death' (V.iii.74–5,76). If he
now holds 'fate/Clasped in [his] fist' (V.v.11–12), it is only because, as H.
J. Oliver infers, he has made that death as inevitable as it is welcome;[31]
he thus collaborates triumphantly in his impending doom, and willingly
enables its 'bad fearful end' (V.iii.65). He goes to his destruction in a
kind of lethargy: asleep in his blindness, hugging the confusion that per-
petuates in his conscience those fatal reversals of value, he can see Annabella's repentance only as a species of betrayal, her access to faith a
faithless revolt; while her death becomes the grotesque fulfilment of a
bloody revenge, whose 'glory' will darken the 'bright sun', make 'midday
night' (V.v.79–80).

Since Giovanni is an outcaste to the 'laws of conscience and of civil use'
(V.v.70), and has long since yielded to the idolatry of making Annabella's
love his heaven and 'her divine' (II.v.36), virtue and honour for him
consist uniquely in their fidelity to each other and to their mutual vows,
endowed with an almost sacramental significance in the religion of his
love. Thus, reasoning as he does in a reprobate sense, Annabella's
secession from the strict terms of her vow renders her forfeit to its dread
compulsion: 'Love me, or kill me, brother' (I.ii.252). But, like the heart
upon the dagger which is its grisly correlative, Annabella's death assumes
a protean significance in the morbid paralogic of Giovanni's mind; a
mind which, as Morris has said, struggles confusedly to reconcile its own
experience with the orthodox meanings of honour, fame and revenge.[32]
For him, her murder, honourable in being justified by her 'treachery', is
also 'glorious' in that it saves her fame from the triumph of 'infamy and
hate' (V.v.104) and 'brave' in that it avenges the 'reaching plots' of the
man who would destroy them both (V.v.100). All these motives, the error-
struck perversions of a deadened conscience impervious to the counter-
claims of 'any value balanced' (V.vi.27), coalesce in the ultimate gross
distortion which appears to vindicate them: 'honour doth love command'
(V.v.86). But in *A Line of Life*, Ford speaks of 'the truest honour *A
deserved fame*, which is one . . . of the best and highest rewards of
vertue';[33] and in subordinating his love to the claims of a purely self-
referent honour, Giovanni neither escapes the opprobrium of a world
which damns him ('Inhuman scorn of men':V.vi.70), nor preserves his
sister's 'fame' from the detraction of its final verdict (''tis pity she's a
whore':V.vi.160).

But the world which condemns Giovanni does not thereby escape condemnation; indeed, in the moral perspectives of 'prone mortalyty accurst';
his degradation in the bondage of illicit passion can be seen as an ever
more complete immersion in its corrupted values. In the antinomian gloom
of the play's ending, Giovanni, guilded in the reeking blood of his victims,

becomes no more than a symbol for those other worldly attempts to institute private justice – Grimaldi's, Hippolita's, Soranzo's – in which the motives of revenge are in like manner gilded in the claims of a spurious honour. Only Richardetto, at best an equivocal spokesman for the divine order, desists from his attempt on the life of Soranzo, in the numinous presentiment of 'One/Above' who 'begins to work' (IV.ii.8–9). At the same time, other, and perhaps more reliable, references to the working out of providential justice (for example, those of the Friar, of Florio at III.ix.67–8, of Annabella at V.i., and Donado at V.vi.109), seem calculated to confirm the inevitability of its (albeit arcane) intervention in the chaos of human affairs, and to underscore the general truth of Florio's *sententia*:

> Great men may do their wills, we must obey;
> But Heaven will judge them for't another day.
> (III.ix.67–8)

There is, indeed, little doubt that we are intended to see the play's spectacular conclusion in the aspect of just such a judgment; to behold, if we will, how the multiple acts of vengeance, whose cumulative logic determines the final carnage, are coordinated to the higher purposes of 'One/Above' and transmuted according to those purposes in the *vis inertiae* of Augustinian determinism: 'That men sin, is attributable to themselves: that in sinning they produce this or that result, is owing to the mighty power of God'.[34]

Thus, for Soranzo and Hippolita, revenge proves but a bloody instruction, in the latter's case commending quite literally the ingredients of the poisoned chalice to her own lips; while Vasques, who engineers the death of Giovanni, becomes, like Bosola, the unholy instrument of a righteous design, a vessel of wrath in his eventual condemnation. As for Giovanni, who till the end honours his revenge as a species of fate (V.vi.37), himself its triumphant arbiter, now finds in the fullness of that fate a doom which necessity perfects.[35] His blasphemous claim to control the 'twists of life', the impious assertion that 'revenge is mine' (V.vi.72,75), are merely the ashen fruits of an atheism fanned in the morbid hysteria of his final moments to an hubristic arrogation of the divine prerogatives. But his faith in nature, already compromised in the dispatch of Annabella to fill a throne in heaven (V.v.65), cannot sustain him long; the comminations of the Friar and the ruin long since augured forth in his own seared conscience, foreclose upon him in the encircling sword-thrusts of the banditti, themselves the ministers of a strange and miraculous justice (V.vi.109). It is true that Giovanni's cry of 'Mercy? Why, I have found it in this justice' (V.vi.103), and his unredeemed determination to die in the grace of Annabella, alike reconstruct the orthodox moral hierarchies,[36] and suggest a continued imprisonment in the moral chiasmus by which he lives and dies. But as D'Amville had discovered, and as seventeenth-century polemicists aver, atheism proves a flawed creed, incapable, in the end, of extinguishing the 'reliques' of conscience; and accordingly, Giovanni is made to acknowledge its 'laws', if not their 'rigour', and to extenuate his unbelief in the uncertain agnosticism of his final couplet:

> Where'er I go, let me enjoy this grace,
> Freely to view my Annabella's face.
> (V.vi.107–8)

In thus kissing the rod he had all along sought to escape, Giovanni bows, though far less abjectly than had Faustus, D'Amville, or Malefort, to the sanctions imposed by an implacable providence. In a manner reminiscent of Marlowe's protagonist, he is a representative figure, caught between an older order of harshly orthodox belief, and a newer world of emergent individualism and an emancipated faith in nature;[37] and Ford can see tragedy in the moral uncertainty of mankind thus symbolized, torn by the divergent claims upon his soul. In both, a species of intellectual rebellion is crushed by traditional morality; in both, the crime and its punishment are philosophically considered; but, like a later specialist in this theme, Dostoevski, Ford dramatizes the issues at their most sensational and extreme, driving to the point of shocking antinomy and barely resolvable paradox the insistent claims of man's nature in relation to the irresistible moral law by which they are abrogated. Hence we are made to see Giovanni and Annabella as 'Gloriously fair', even in their 'infamy';[38] to see 'pity' in the fate of sinners, 'so young, so rich in nature's store', reduced by the very statutes of nature to incest and murder. This leads, as the diversity of criticism itself suggests, to wide inconsistencies in our final response, which refuses to accede to the imposed harmonies of the play's ending; and no wonder, since to do so would be to acquiesce in the spectacle of a humanity forfeited to its own deepest instincts, of conscience, deadened in the sleep of errant reason, condemned by the ineffable laws of its own being.

Conclusion

It is an irony perhaps inseparable from this kind of literary scholarship that the sort of ideological conductions and transactions it attempts to describe, and for which previous pages are offered in evidence, should be, in the last analysis, unsusceptible to proof. In the flux and interflux of medieval and post-Reformation thought concerning the conscience and the moral status of man, theoretical precision is a concept sufficiently recondite and abstruse, even in the work of those theologians, philosophers, and encyclopaedists whose professional business it was to analyse and organize such ideas in the cause of a putative enlightenment. In the work of those whose less precise business it was to exploit such complexities at second hand and for a variety of literary and theatrical purposes – for whom, indeed, the process of analysis and organization were weighted according to altogether less conscious and systematic criteria – a forensic clarity of exposition must perforce remain a notional or relative concept.

Such a caveat notwithstanding, I believe that the evidence adduced in this study consolidates, at any rate circumstantially, the hypotheses by which it was prefaced: that sixteenth- and seventeenth-century drama not only reflects and illuminates at a popular and subliminal level ideas about conscience rendered academically specific in medieval and contemporary instruments of moral theology, but documents also the historical evolution of those ideas, attendant upon profound dichotomies in the shifting substrata of belief, from the predominantly scholastic configuration evinced in the early interludes and in Shakespeare, to the overwhelmingly reformist dialectic by which it was evidently displaced in the drama of the earlier seventeenth century. The universe of Shakespeare's plays, fundamentally medieval in character, has inherently a legal basis; its moral axes are intelligibly rational, and it is permeated by a conception, scholastic in origin, of the Natural Law, to which all creation is bound, and to whose cyclic and teleological operations the conscience of man functions as an internal and spiritual witness. The intellective and rational nature of the conscience as formulated in the great medieval treatises, enables its operations to be described in terms of a syllogism, according to which basic deontic premises intuitively apprehended in the *synderesis* are actualized in the *conscientia*, and applied therein to particular cases and instances. Moreover, the act of moral discrimination takes place in an unconditioned moral ethos, which centres responsibility firmly in man: Shakespeare's tragic heroes are like Hooker's voluntary agents and act according to a free will counselled by conscience, which is, in turn, dispositionally oriented towards the ultimate good. Evil, therefore, cannot be desired as such, but only in so far as its very ambiguity gives to it the specious coloration of good, making plausible the pretexts of audacity and imprudence alike, and lending to the desperate all the treacherous courage of despair. Thus Richard rationalizes his depravity in terms that show it to be a choice freely undertaken, while Hamlet's conscientious scruples concerning the course to which the Ghost and the animus of his own disordered passions solicit him are subjected to a recurrent process of ratiocination whose moral coordinates are, if not immediately clear, at least philosophically unconfined. In *Macbeth*, the theological axes of prescience versus determinism, free-will versus fore-ordination are held in a less auspicious counterpoise, rendering perceptibly more oblique those slippery ice-pavements by which a man may consign himself, by destruction, to an involuntary doom. But here again, the Shakespearean protagonist is seen to will into hideous being the embryonic evil within his soul, which mortifies his conscience even as it eclipses, by a fatal and incremental logic, his original freedom to act. In short, the appeal to knowledge and reason, evidently endorsed within the context of this study by the two pre-Reformation moralities, *The World and the Child* and *Impatient Poverty*, is allowed an almost unconditional validity within the moral framework of Shakespeare's plays. Moreover, while that validity is to a degree qualified in *Doctor Faustus* – the old medieval hierarchies made suspect in the dialectics of humanist revolt – Marlowe, too, sufficiently upholds the scholastic orthodoxies by which it is crushed as to construe the act of conscience and its metaphysical correlatives as exercised not as a function of divine fiat, but within the ambit of divine permission. For Marlowe, as for Shakespeare, the evil that men do is neither caused nor requited in the active and undetermined decrees of a providence to which all causes in nature are arbitrarily subjoined, but exists rather as a derogation from the good, a defiance of man's true nature, a cosmic malignancy which is expurgated ultimately in a coherent nexus of proximate and reactive impulses in the Natural Law, to whose violated precepts the guilt-stricken conscience attests.

The nominalist equation of divine will and human nescience, on the other hand, though more pervasively an element in the moral ethos of Jacobean tragedy, is, as we have seen, perceptibly at work in some of the later moralities herein surveyed, where both the Law of Nature and the judgments of the conscience are seen as desecrated and corrupt, the one disannulled in the superintendent mysteries of a special providence, the other mortally disabled by an irreparable tendency to error, only selectively assuaged in a metaphysical economy whose effective agencies – grace and faith – are bestowed *de potentia absoluta*. Counterpointed to that dramatic development in the interlude tradition, by which Conscience was assimilated to the soul of the protagonist or emancipated to a fuller theatrical presence, is discoverable an equally marked doctrinal change in which early suggestions of its inveterate corruption and complicity in evil (as in the interpolated scenes of *Impatient Poverty*, for example) are complemented by an increasingly fideistic appeal to the Scriptures, and to the coadjutant properties of prevenient grace. The natural order, a universal systasis of faith and reason which has a literary ancestry at least as venerable as Chaucer,[1] is seen in the post-Reformation moralities of Woodes and Wilson as perverted and vitiated, merely anticipating its more decisive disintegration in the antinomian tragedies of Tourneur, Webster, and Ford.

It is this metaphysical disintegration which above all characterizes the occluded and inexpiably sin-laden world of Jacobean drama. Here man's earthly state has become synonymous with a deep pit of darkness, the light of reason clouded in ignorance, the soul's acuteness in regard to moral categories coextensive with a blindness that makes men desperate. Whether in those tragedies of knowledge – Tourneur's and Ford's – in which the hubris of a puny rationalism is reprobated in the mysteries of a providence it would pretermit, or in the necessitated universe of Webster, where all human volitions are bound by a law of sin in the soul, there exists a profound dissonance between nature and an inaccessible morality, between conscience and the grace that might redeem it, between an invidious knowledge of the world and the incommensurable edicts of an inscrutable heaven. Here man's responsibility is minimal, though sufficient, action, both evil and pre-ordained; while the conscience in its residual capacity is merely a yoke, driving and convicting the soul in the compulsions of its necessary guilt to denounce itself before the bar of eternal judgment. In such a universe, condemnation is the very keynote of existence, suffering the anacrusis of that storm of terror which ends in death; and to seek to innoculate the conscience in the transient consolations of the world, or to transcend its exiguities by the blasphemous exaltation of mere reason, is to court, like D'Amville, Bosola and Giovanni, that demoniac pathogenesis by which carnal security and presumption alike conduce ineluctably to despair.

It is true that there is a half-glimpsed mercy discoverable in the arbitrary sanctions by which the stature of man is confined, a tenuous placability in the rigour by which virtue is shriven and wickedness broken as a tree.

Though affliction and death are the common inheritance of man, there are none the less degrees of evil, segregated in the moral obliquity by which all are tainted, winnowed and refined according to the gospel paradox that such as suffer, overcome. Thus it is that Charlemont, Webster's Duchess, and Ford's Annabella, though abandoned in that general mist of error to which all humanity is forfeit, are brought at length by heaven's scourge-stick to mortification, and redeemed in a purgatory of persecutions to the unearthly satisfactions of a sound conscience. In Massinger's characters, this paradox, though more optimistic, is merely made more explicit; for in so far as their philosophical composition draws intermittently upon both the neo-Stoicism of Calvin and the fideism of the neo-Stoic revivalists, Vitelli and Grimaldi are converted to goodness by adversity, and weaned from a love of the world either by those trials which are the proofs of constancy, or those chastizements which are the amendments of evil.

In spite of these great religious and philosophical contrasts, there exist as well recurring leitmotifs in the hagiography of conscience, reiterated themes in the vast interlocking pattern of man's redemption and heaven's high ordinance whose transitional variations and modulations these plays indirectly trace. The dual classification of the warning and the accusing conscience, for example, is reflected at intervals throughout the dramas here surveyed. The former is frequently seen metaphorically as a register or witness of sin, premonitory of the Last Judgment, as, for instance, in *The Three Ladies, Richard III*, and *Macbeth*; or again as a precursor of spiritual death, as in *Appius and Virginia, Faustus*, and *'Tis Pity*. The latter, on the other hand, is more often conceived of either as a whip of correction, or less positively, as a rod of divine vengeance, in either case lurid with the kind of visions and appalling sights that excoriate the guilt-stricken souls of Macbeth, Faustus and D'Amville. The case of *Hamlet* is of course unique as a study of the doubting or erroneous conscience and the scholastic taxonomy of *synderesis* and *conscientia* by which it is implicitly sustained. But those morally discrepant and unrelated impulses in Hamlet's psyche, inherent in the ambiguities of his providential role, are re-echoed in the consciences of Bosola and Vasques, whose less equivocal adhesion to evil is coopted to the sifting of virtue, and coordinated to the unrevealed purposes of a universal good. The correlatives of conscience, expressed in terms of the Aristotelian motives of 'measure' and 'discrecyon' in the three earlier moralities, and mediated in terms of a classical-scholastic synthesis of nature and reason in the Shakespearean canon, are replaced by the Calvinistic formularies of moral choice symbolized most powerfully in the Good Angel's advice to Faustus to 'Read, read the Scriptures' (*Doctor Faustus*, I.i.72), and, of course, recapitulated as a Protestant theme in the moral dilemmas of Poverty, Philologus and Charlemont. Coincident with all these theological developments in the drama is the increasing evidence of its growing secularization, seen most pronouncedly in the morality tradition and its subsequent exploitation by Marlowe and Shakespeare. In the course of this transition, the crude theological determinants of the early plays are transmuted in the ever-deepening wells of cerebration to the point where the psychomachia becomes, if not altogether internalized, then more intimately related to characterization, and subordinated to a profounder noesis of ideation, will, and the conscience. *Faustus* is, as in other respects, an evolutionary hinge in this development; for the spirit visitants which attend upon the exercise of the Doctor's will, have, in their capacity to influence it, a symbolic and psychological significance which is, if anything, dramatically augmented by their objective corporeality.

But to judge from the dramatists here surveyed, it is the chilling dynamics of reprobation which appear most to have engrossed the collective imagination of the age, the eternal judgements by which, in the words of Milton, 'the hard [are] hardened, the blind [are] blinded more' (*Paradise Lost*, iii.200). The bleak imperatives of the *conscientia desperata*, which are implied archetypally in the Spiera syndrome, are documented succinctly by Perkins: the notorious malefactor, he suggests, commences in obstinacy and perversity, and habituates himself thereafter to the occasions of sin, so that 'the light of nature is extinguished: and then commeth the *reprobate minde*, which judgeth evil good, and good evill: after this follows the *seared conscience*, in which there is no feeling or remorse'.[2] These are the leaden declensions of the evil conscience, the inexorable stations of its own descent into despair; and such themes resonate inauspiciously throughout a majority of the plays under discussion, and never more ominously that in those where the predestinarian enigma is an implied or dominant motif. From Philologus to Macbeth, from Faustus to Giovanni – all preface their careers in sin, whether construed in the active or passive mode, with a perverse obstinacy which renders them contumaciously resistant to the motions of grace. All, too, are inured in conscience to the light of nature, where ontologically a consideration, cancelling its precepts by which Downame calls 'customable sinning and habituall wickednesse'.[3] In similar fashion, all remain fixed in the transvaluating logic of the 'reprobate minde', impelled by an unholy irony of inversion into seeking a spurious redemption of the devil. And finally, all are brought to experience the 'seared conscience', that state of moral annihilation in which 'nothing is but what is not', and in whose terminal convulsions they are wrought up to a pitch of destructive desperation, or reduced, by an equally destructive cycle, to callousness, negativity, and the torpid resignation of despair.

Notes

Introduction

1 See David Little, *Religion, Order and Law: A Study in Pre-Revolutionary England* (Oxford: Basil Blackwell, 1970), pp. 31–115; John F. H. New, *Anglican and Puritan: The Basis of Their Opposition, 1558–1640* (London: A. & C. Black, 1964), pp. 5–25; Daniel Horton Davies, *Worship and Theology in England*, 5 vols. (London: Oxford University Press, 1965–70), I (1970), pp. 17–59. The complex philosophical and theological currents of thought which extend from the Middle Ages to the Reformation and beyond have, of course, been charted by numerous scholars upon whose efforts this study is, in a general sense, necessarily dependent. See, for example, Herschel Baker, *The Wars of Truth: Studies in the Decay of Christian Humanism in the Earlier Seventeenth Century* (Cambridge, Mass: Staples Press; 1952); Robert Hoopes, *Right Reason in the English Renaissance* (Cambridge, Mass: Harvard University Press, 1962); Basil Willey, *The English Moralists* (London: Chatto & Windus, 1964); Etienne Gilson, *History of Christian Philosophy in the Middle Ages* (London: Sheed & Ward, 1955); F. Copplestone, *A History of Philosophy*, 7 vols. (London: Burns, Oates & Washbourne 1953, reprinted 1963), II and III; Paul Oskar Kristeller, *Renaissance Thought: The Classic, Scholastic, and Humanist Strains* (New York: Harper, 1961); *The Protestant Reformation*, ed. Hans J. Hillerbrand (London and Melbourne: Macmillan, 1968); George C. Herndl, *The High Design: English Renaissance Tragedy and the Natural Law* (Lexington, Kentucky: University of Kentucky Press, 1970).

2 *The Summa Theologica of St Thomas Aquinas*, trans. the Fathers of the English Dominican Province, second and revised edition, 22 vols. (London: Burns, Oates & Washburne, 1921?–32). Part II.i. Questions 90–4.

3 It is clear, says Luther, 'that, as the soul needs only the Word of God for its life and righteousness, so it is justified by faith alone, and not any works; for if it could be justified by anything else, it would not need the Word, and consequently, it would not need faith.' 'The Freedom of a Christian', trans. W. A. Lambert, rev. Harold J. Grimm, in *Luther's Works*, general eds. Jaroslav Pelikan (vols. 1–30) and Helmut T. Lehmann (vols. 31–55), 55 vols. (St Louis and Philadelphia: Concordia, 1956–67), XXXI: *Career of the Reformer* I, ed. Harold J. Grimm (Philadelphia, 1957), p. 346.

4 John Calvin, *Inistitutes of the Christian Religion*, trans. Henry Beveridge, 2

270

vols. (London: James Clark, 1953), III.ii.1–43; II.i.1–11. All references to the *Institutes* hereafter will be to this edition, and expressed thus in book and chapter headings.

5 See Little, *Religion, Order and Law*, pp. 38–51.

6 *Institutes*, III.xix.15, III.xix.1–5.

7 See New, *Anglican and Puritan*, pp. 6–8.

8 Louis B. Wright, *Middle-class Culture in Elizabethan England* (New York: Cornell University Press 1958), pp. 228–96.

9 A number of the treatises explored in following chapters have been surveyed by J. W. Hogan in 'The Rod and the Candle: Conscience in the English Morality Plays, Shakespeare's *Macbeth*, and Tourneur's *The Atheist's Tragedy*' (unpublished Ph.D. dissertation, City University of New York, 1974), pp. 48–97.

10 *The High Design*, p. 111.

11 See Willey, *The English Moralists*, pp. 100–47; Herndl, *The High Design*, pp. 138–52.

12 John Calvin, *A Commentary upon Genesis*, VI:5, trans. John King, 2 vols. (in 1) (London: The Banner of Truth Trust, 1965), p. 247.

13 All dates referred to in the Introduction are taken from A. Harbage, *Annals of English Drama*, rev. S. Schoenbaum (London: Methuen, 1964). Editions of plays used are listed in the first section of the Bibliography.

14 These terms of reference have had, in some cases, to be somewhat rigorously applied in order to avoid peering yet more darkly through a glass already sufficiently obscure. There are, of course, opportunities for further research in a number of plays either not included in this study, or mentioned only in passing. Some of the more obvious candidates for inclusion, Shakespeare's *Measure for Measure, The Tempest* and *Henry VIII*, for example, have been omitted on the grounds that the idea of conscience, though present, is not a presiding or dominant theme. Others, such as Greene's *The Scottish History of James the Fourth*, or Heywood's *A Woman Killed with Kindness*, are excluded where such a theme is merely implied rather than overtly stated, and the dramatic action invites critical discourse in terms rather of remorse or penitence than of conscience as a linguistically specific concept. Neither is Beaumont and Fletcher's *A King and No King* represented here: the case of Arbaces' conscience is undercut, his moral dilemma made spurious by a contrived solution which not only sunders the moral connection between cause and consequence, but subverts from the very outset the seriousness of the play's philosophical pretensions.

Chapter 1

1 W. C. Curry, *Shakespeare's Philosophical Patterns* (Baton Rouge, Louisiana: Louisiana State University Press, 1959), pp. 107–9.

2 See Baker, *The Wars of Truth*: pp. 135–7; Hoopes, *Right Reason in the English Renaissance*, pp. 73–88; Gilson, *History of Christian Philosophy in the Middle Ages*, pp. 454–71; Curry, *Shakespeare's Philosophical Patterns*, pp. 105–9; Herndl, *The High Design*, pp. 88–109.

3 St Jerome, *Commentary upon Ezekiel*, 1.7 (Latin text in Migne, *Patrologia Latina*, vol. 25, col. 22). Timothy C. Potts (trans.), *Conscience in Medieval Philosophy* (Cambridge: Cambridge University Press, 1980), pp. 79–80. This, and subsequent passages quoted from the minor scholastic treatises over the following section of the chapter, are taken from Potts's invaluable compen-

dium of translations from medieval texts upon the subject, and are cited, where applicable, with reference to the appropriate page numbers in Potts.

4 Peter Lombard, *Books of Judgements*, 2.39 (Latin text in *Magistri Petri Lombardi Sententiae in IV libros distinctae*, tom.I, pars II. Grottaferrata (Rome), *Collegium S. Bonaventurae Ad Claras Aquas* (Quarrachi), 1971, pp. 553–6) (Potts, p. 93).

5 *Batman uppon Bartholome, his Booke De Proprietatibus Rerum* (London, 1582), sig.D2. Cited by Ruth Leila Anderson, *Elizabethan Psychology and Shakespeare's Plays*, University of Iowa Humanistic Studies, 3, IV (Iowa, 1927), p. 9.

6 Phineas Fletcher, *The Purple Island, or The Isle of Man* (London, 1633), sig.K1ᵛ. Cited by Anderson, *Elizabethan Psychology*, p. 20.

7 Timothy Bright, *Treatise of Melancholie* (London, 1586), sig.E5.

8 Robert Burton, *The Anatomy of Melancholy*, ed. A. R. Shilleto, 3 vols. (London: Bell 1896), I, pp. 189–90.

9 *Commentary upon Ezekiel*, 1, 7 (Potts, pp. 79–80).

10 Potts, *Conscience in Medieval Philosophy*, pp. 10–11.

11 *Debated Questions on Truth*, 16, 1 (Latin text in *S. Thomae Aquinatis, Opera Omnia*, vol. 22. *Quaestiones disputatae de veritatae*, Rome: *ad Sancta Sabinae*, 1972, pp. 501–28) (Potts, p. 122).

12 ibid., 16.1, Discussion (Potts, pp. 123–5).

13 ibid., 17.1 (Potts, pp. 130–2). A similar distinction is made in the *Summa Theologica*, Part I. Q.79, Arts. 11–13.

14 *Debated Questions on Truth*, 16.2, Replies 1 and 2 (Potts, p. 128).

15 ibid., 16.3, Discussion (Potts, pp. 128–9).

16 *Summa Theologica*, Part II.i. Q.77, Art.1.

17 *Debated Questions on Truth*, 17.4 (Potts, p. 135).

18 ibid., 17.3–4 (Potts, pp. 134–6).

19 *Summa Theologica*, Part II.i. Q.91, Art. 2.

20 ibid., Part I.i. Q.79, Art. 12.

21 ibid., Part II.i. Q.93, Art.6.

22 'The Laws of Ecclesiastical Polity', I.ii.2, in *The Works of That Learned and Judicious Divine Mr. Richard Hooker*, arranged by John Keble, seventh edition, 3 vols. (Oxford: Clarendon Press, 1888). Hereafter cited as 'The Laws of Ecclesiastical Polity', and referred to throughout in this edition by book and chapter headings.

23 ibid., I.iii.2.

24 ibid., I.iii.2.

25 ibid., I.iii.1; I.v.1–2.

26 ibid., I.viii.7.

27 ibid., I.viii.7.

28 M. M. Reese, *The Cease of Majesty* (London: Edward Arnold, 1961), p. 16. The correlations between Elizabethan drama and Renaissance theories of cosmic order have been explored in a general sense by a number of commentators. See, for example, Theodore Spencer, *Shakespeare and the Nature of Man* (New York: Cambridge University Press, 1943); E. M. W. Tillyard, *The Elizabethan World Picture* (London: Chatto & Windus, 1943), and *The English Renaissance: Fact or Fiction?* (London: Hogarth Press, 1952); Willard Farnham, *The Medieval Heritage of Elizabethan Tragedy* (Berkeley, Calif: University of California Press, 1936); A. O. Lovejoy, *The Great Chain of Being* (Cambridge, Mass: Harvard University Press, 1936); Hardin Craig, *The Enchanted Glass* (New York: Oxford University Press, 1936); Douglas

Bush, *The Renaissance and English Humanism* (Toronto: University of Toronto Press, 1939); John F. Danby, *Shakespeare's Doctrine of Nature: A Study of 'King Lear'* (London: Faber & Faber, 1949); Curry, *Shakespeare's Philosophical Patterns*.

29 A. Harbage, *Shakespeare and the Rival Traditions* (New York, Macmillan: 1952), p. 135.

30 'The Sermon of Obedience', in *Certain Sermons or Homilies Appointed to be Read in Churches in the Time of Queen Elizabeth of Famous Memory*, pub. under the direction of the Tract Committee (London, 1864) pp. 109–10.

31 Thomas Wright, *The Passions of the Minde in Generall* (London, 1630), sigs. B2^{v}–B4^{v}; D7–D7^{v}. Cited by Anderson, *Elizabethan Pschology*, p. 80.

32 Pierre de La Primaudaye, *The French Academie. Fully Discoursed and finished in foure Bookes* (London, 1618), sig.Ss1. Cited by Anderson, *Elizabeth Psychology*, p. 82.

33 Anderson, *Elizabethan Psychology*, p. 89.

34 Potts, *Conscience in Medieval Philosophy*, pp. 26–8.

35 Plato, 'The Timaeus', in *The Dialogue of Plato*, trans. B. Jowett, 4 vols. (Oxford: Clarendon Press 1871) II, 580. Cited by Anderson *Elizabethan Psychology*, p. 143.

36 Francis Bacon, *The Advancement of Learning*, ed. G. W. Kitchin (J. M. Dent, London: 1973), p. 107.

37 Bishop Nemesius, *The Nature of Man*, Englished by Geo. Wither (London, 1636), sigs.Bb10–Bb10^{v}. Cited by Anderson, *Elizabethan Psychology*, pp. 144–5.

38 Robert Speaight, *Nature in Shakespearean Tragedy* (London: Hollis & Carter, 1955), p. 47.

39 My own account of *Macbeth* is influenced by Curry's exposition of the play in terms of school philosophy. See *Shakespeare's Philosophical Patterns*, pp. 53–137.

40 'A Discourse of Conscience', in *William Perkins 1558–1602, English Puritanist: His Pioneer Works on Casuistry*, ed. Thomas F. Merrill (Nieuwkoop: Nieuwkoop B. De Graaf, 1966), pp. 67–8. All references to Perkins's casuistical works will be cited hereafter from this edition.

41 ibid., pp. 68, 40.

42 *The Anatomy of Melancholy*, III, 449–50.

43 'A Discourse of Conscience', p. 72.

44 Thomas Playfere, *Hearts delight (The power of praier. The sickmans couch*) (London, 1611), sig.18.

45 'The Laws of Ecclesiastical Polity', I.ix.1.

46 Clifford Leech, *Shakespeare's Tragedies and Other Studies in Seventeenth Century Drama* (London: Chatto & Windus, 1950), pp. 40–1.

47 For full discussions of the thirteenth- and fourteenth-century decline of scholasticism, and the disputes over universals, see Gilson, *History of Christian Philosophy in the Middle Ages*, pp. 489–500; Coplestone, *A History of Philosophy*, III, 49–61; Baker, *The Wars of Truth*, pp. 135–46; Hoopes, *Right Reasons in the English Renaissance*, pp. 88–93; Herndl, *The High Design*, pp. 103–9; Gordon Leff, 'Nominalism – Realism', in *A Dictionary of Christian Theology*, ed. Alan Richardson (London: SCM Press, 1969), pp. 232–3.

48 Quoted by Leff, 'Nominalism – Realism', in *A Dictionary of Christian Theology*, p. 232.

49 Thomas M. McDonough, *The Law and the Gospel in Luther* (Oxford: Oxford University Press, 1963), pp. 33–41.
50 *The Table-Talk of Martin Luther*, CXVIII, trans. and ed. W. Hazlitt (London: G. Belland Sons, 1911), p. 52.
51 *The Law and the Gospel in Luther*, p. 40.
52 *Institutes*, I.xvii.2.
53 ibid., I.xvii.2.
54 ibid., II.i.8–9.
55 ibid., II.i.5.
56 ibid., II.i.7.
57 ibid., II.iii.2,5.
58 Herndl, *The High Design*, pp. 160–5. I wish to acknowledge a generalized indebtedness in the following argument to Herndl's excellent analysis of the decline of natural-law beliefs in Jacobean tragedy.
59 Massinger is an eclectic in matters of moral philosophy, combining an apparent belief in a stoic universe of law with a markedly fideistic view of man's place within it. For a full discussion, see Chapter 9.
60 'The Freedom of a Christian' in *Luther's Works*, XXXI, 361.
61 Sir Philip Sidney, *The Countess of Pembroke's Arcadia*, ed. Maurice Evans (Harmondsworth: Penguin, 1977), p. 817. The metaphors of fatalism have a strange consonancy, and are doubtless intended (especially in the case of Bosola) to suggest that despairing tendency of man's carnal nature, which in Calvin's words 'inclines us to speak as if God were amusing himself by tossing men up and down like balls'. *Institutes* I.xvii.1.
62 Fulke Greville, 'A Treatie of Humane Learning' in *The Works in Verse and Prose Complete . . .* , ed. A. B. Grosart, 4 vols. (Edinburgh 1870, reprinted New York: Arris Press, Inc., 1960), II, 11.
63 John Marston, 'Satyre IIII', in *The Scourge of Villainie* (London, 1599) facsimile edition, ed. G. B. Harrison (Edinburgh: Edinburgh University Press, 1966), p. 45.
64 The quotation is from A. H. Bullen's collected edition, *The Works of John Marston*, 3 vols. (London: John C. Nimmo, 1937), I.
65 I. F., *Christes Bloodie Sweat, or the Sonne of God in his Agonie* (London, 1613), sig.C4ᵛ.
66 McDonough, *The Law and the Gospel in Luther*, p. 31.
67 *Institutes*, II.ii.22.
68 ibid., II.ii.13.
69 ibid., II.i.9; II.ii.12,13.
70 McDonough, *The Law and the Gospel in Luther*, p. 32.
71 *Institutes*, II.ii.12.
72 ibid., III.xxiii.4.
73 ibid., II.ii.22.
74 ibid., II.ii.24.
75 ibid., II.xix.15.
76 ibid., III.xix.2–4.
77 ibid., III.xix.4–5.
78 ibid., II.iii.7.
79 ibid., II.iii.6.
80 ibid., II.ii.7.
81 'The Laws of Ecclesiastical Polity', I.iii.2.
82 *Institutes*, I.xvi.1–3.
83 *The High Design*, p. 132.

84 *Worship and Theology in England*, I, 407.
85 Camille Wells Slights, *The Casuistical Tradition in Shakespeare, Donne, Herbert, and Milton* (Princeton, New Jersey: Princeton University Press, 1981). The major premise of this stimulating study is that what she calls the 'casuistical paradigm' evolved in the works of Perkins, Ames, Sanderson, Taylor, and Baxter, expresses itself in other literary genres, and that the characteristic methods of the Protestant casuists in resolving practical cases of conscience can illuminate the decision-making process in the imaginative literature of their contemporaries.

Any study of English casuistry which shares common ground with this book must declare, at any rate, a partial indebtedness; but apart from obvious differences of scope and chronology, the central impulse of my own exploration is to show the extent to which the Protestant theology of conscience not only derives from the medieval sources outside the purview of Prof. Slights's investigation, but was riven and factionalized in the process of transmission. It is partly true, as she says, that 'Casuistry . . . shows no clear Anglican/Puritan split' (p. 28), but only if absolute clarity can be any more than a relative concept in such a discussion; and her somewhat limited sample of the five or six major works of casuistry leads her to over-emphasize its common conceptual framework, overlooking fundamental doctrinal propensities and differences in her desire to forge a standardized instrument of literary analysis. Applied to rationalists such as Donne, Herbert and Milton, this lack of specificity may not be all that apparent; but in making distinctions between man's moral capacity in Shakespeare, and his manifest incapacity in the dramatic universe of a Webster or a Ford, we must surely take account of profound metaphysical transformations, whose significance Miss Slights, within the context of her book, clearly has less cause to labour.
86 For full discussions of the major seventeenth-century casuists who wrote about cases of conscience, see H. H. Henson, *Studies in English Religion in the Seventeenth Century* (London: John Murray, 1903), pp. 171–210; H. R. McAdoo, *The Structure of Caroline Moral Theology* (London: Longman, Green), 1949), pp. 64–97; Thomas Wood, *English Casuistical Divinity During the Seventeenth Century: With Special Reference to Jeremy Taylor* (London: SPCK, 1952); Elliot Rose, *Cases of Conscience: Alternatives to Recusants and Puritans under Elizabeth I and James I* (Cambridge: Cambridge University Press, 1975); Kevin Kelly, *Conscience: Dictator or Guide? A Study in Seventeenth Century English Protestant Moral Theology* (London: Geoffrey Chapman, 1967).
87 'A Discourse of Conscience', p. 5.
88 ibid., p. 5.
89 Robert Bolton, *A Discourse About the State of True Happinesse* (London, 1611), sig.P3^v (Greek characters transliterated).
90 Richard Carpenter, *The Conscionable Christian, or the Indevour of Saint Paul* (London, 1623), sigs.G3^v–G4.
91 'A Discourse of Conscience', p. 6.
92 ibid., p. 10.
93 Jeremiah Dyke, *Good Conscience: Or a Treatise shewing the Nature, Meanes, Marks, Benefit and Necessity Thereof* (London, 1624), sigs.B6^v–B7.
94 Immanuel Bourne, *The Anatomie of Conscience* (London, 1623), sig.B4.
95 Thomas Morton, *A Treatise of the threefolde state of man* (London, 1596), sigs.R7^v–R8.

96 John Downame, *A Guide to Godlyness, Or a Treatise of a Christian Life* (London, 1622), sig.G4ᵛ.
97 ibid., sigs.G4ᵛ–G5.
98 'A Discourse of Conscience', pp. 10, 42.
99 *A Guide to Godlynesse*, sig.H1.
100 *The Conscionable Christian*, sig.K1ᵛ.
101 'A Discourse of Conscience', pp. 41–2.
102 William Ames, *Conscience with the Power and Cases Thereof* ([n.p.], 1639), sig.C2.
103 ibid., sig.C1ᵛ.
104 John Woolton, *Of the Conscience* ([London], 1576), sig.M4.
105 *The Conscionable Christian*, sig.H1.
106 *Good Conscience*, sig.B8.
107 Richard Bernard, *Christian See to thy Conscience, Or, A Treatise of the nature, the kinds and manifold differences of Conscience* . . . (London, 1631) sigs.D11–F1ᵛ.
108 William Jones, *A Commentary Upon the Epistles of Saint Paul to Philemon, and to the Hebrewes* (London, 1635), sigs.Aaa3–Aaa3ᵛ.
109 *The Anatomie of Conscience*, sigs.C4.
110 ibid., sig.D1.
111 *Good Conscience*, sigs.D1ᵛ–D2.
112 Ibid., sigs. D4–D4ᵛ.
113 Robert Harris, *Six Sermons of Conscience*, second edition (London, 1630), sig.C3.
114 *Conscience with the Power and Cases Thereof*, sig.G3ᵛ.
115 ibid., sig.F2.
116 Christopher Lever, *The Holy Pilgrime, leading the way to Heaven* (London, 1618), sig.I1ᵛ.
117 *Six Sermons of Conscience*, sigs.C2–C2ᵛ.
118 *A Treatise of the threefolde state of man*, sigs.S5ᵛ–S6.
119 ibid., sigs.S6ᵛ–S7.

Chapter 2

1 All the dates of printing or publication of the plays dealt with in this chapter are, as in the Introduction, taken from A. Harbage, *Annals of English Drama*, rev. S. Schoerbaum (London: Methuen, 1964). Sources of individual speculation as to dates of composition are as cited in the text, and in notes.
2 *Summa Theologica*, Part II.i.Q.90, Art. 1; Q.91, Art. 3, Reply Obj. 2.
3 *The Ethics of Aristotle*, trans. J. A. K. Thompson, (London: Allen & Unwin, 1953), p. 91.
4 *Summa Theologica*, Part II.i.Q.90; Q.109, Art. 4.
5 David M. Bevington, *From 'Mankind' to Marlowe: Growth of Structure in the Popular Drama of Tudor England* (Cambridge, Mass: Harvard University Press, 1962), p. 119.
6 McKerrow assigns its composition to the period 1550–8, but suggests that its 'general roughness of style' would indicate an even earlier date. See *A newe interlude of Impacyente Povertye*, from the quarto of 1560, ed. R. B. McKerrow, (W. Bang (ed.) Materialien zur Kunde des älteren englischen Dramas, Bd.33) (Louvain: A. Uystpruyst, 1911), p. x. Harbage gives as its date limits, 1547–58 (*Annals of English Drama*, p. 30).
7 ibid., p. x.

8   *From 'Mankind' to Marlowe*, p. 20.
9   Peter J. Houle, *The English Morality and Related Drama: A Bibliographical Survey* (Hamden, Conn.: Archon Books, 1972), p. 53.
10 *A newe interlude*, p. x.
11 'The Pagan Servitude of the Church', reproduced in *Martin Luther; Selections from his Writings*, ed. John Dillenburger (New York: Anchor Books, 1961), pp. 322–3.
12 See *Summa Theologica*; Part II.ii.Q.62, Art. 1; Q.78, Art. 1.
13 Martin Luther, *Table-Talk*, ed. and trans. Theodore G. Tappert, in *Luther's Works*, LIV, 398.
14 Charles Hardwick, *A History of the Articles of Religion* (London: George Bell & Sons, 1881), appendix III, p. 295.
15 *The Later Writings of Bishop Hooper*, ed. Charles Nevinson, Parker Society (Cambridge: Cambridge University Press 1852), p. 44.
16 Johan Bale, *Comedy Concernynge Thre Lawes*, ed. M. M. Arnold Schroeer, (Halle: Max Niemeyer, 1882), 11.1181–4.
17 See Bevington, *From 'Mankind' to Marlowe*, p. 32. Date-limits in Harbage are from 1559–67 (*Annals of English Drama*, p. 38).
18 C. F. Tucker Brooke, *The Tudor Drama*, (Cambridge Mass: Houghton Mifflin, 1911), p. 206.
19 Peter Happe, 'Tragic Themes in Three Tudor Moralities', *SEL*, 5 (1965), 207–27, (p. 220).
20 See F. P. Wilson, *The English Drama, 1485–1585*, ed. G. K. Hunter (Oxford: Clarendon Press, 1969), p. 48, and also Judith Anne Wall, 'An Edition of R. B.'s *Appius and Virginia*' (unpublished MA thesis, University of Birmingham, 1972), p. lxviii.
21 'Tragic Themes in Three Tudor Moralities', p. 222.
22 ibid., pp. 220–7; 'An Edition of R. B.'s *Appius and Virginia*, pp. lxx-lxxxiii.
23 'Tragic Themes in Three Tudor Moralities', pp. 224–5.
24 *Summa Theologica*, Part II.i.Q.93, Art. 6.
25 'An Edition of R. B.'s *Appius and Virginia*', p. lxxxv.
26 See Bevington, *From 'Mankind' to Marlowe*, pp. 56–8; Brooke, *The Tudor Drama*, p. 120; Robert Potter, *The English Morality Play* (London and Boston: Routledge & Kegan Paul, 1975), p. 121.
27 *From 'Mankind' to Marlowe*, p. 58.
28 The play is reproduced as it was originally issued in Nathaniel Woodes, *The Conflict of Conscience*, facsimile edition, Marlowe Society (Oxford: Oxford University Press, 1952). The second issue is identical with the first, apart from the cancel leaves containing the title, prologue and last scene, which are reprinted separately in the Marlow Society edition.
29 Celesta Wine, 'Nathaniel Wood's *Conflict of Conscience*', *PMLA*, 50 (1935), 661–78 (pp. 667–72). There are full accounts of Spiera's biography in this article (pp. 663–5) and also in that of Lily B. Campbell, 'Doctor Faustus: A Case of Conscience', *PMLA*, 67 (1952), 219–39 (pp. 225–30).
30 *From 'Mankind' to Marlowe*, p. 250.
31 *Institutes*, III.iii.15.
32 *A notable and marveilous Epistle of the famous Doctour, Matthew Gribalde, Professor of Lawe, in the Universitie of Padua: concernyng the terrible judgemente of GOD, upon hym that for feare of men, denieth Christ and the knowne veritie: with a Preface of Doctor Calvine* (London, [1570]), sig.A.3.
33 *From 'Mankind' to Marlowe*, p. 249.

34 'Commentary upon Ezekiel', 2:2. Quoted by T. F. Torrance, *Calvin's Doctrine of Man* (London: Lutterworth Press, 1949), pp. 132–3.
35 *The English Morality Play*, p. 122.
36 *The English Morality and Related Drama*, p. 136.
37 *The Tudor Drama*, p. 141.
38 *Of the Conscience*, sig.A1ᵛ.
39 H. S. D. Mithal, 'An Edition of R(obert) W(ilson)'s *The Three Ladies of London* and *The Three Lords and Three Ladies of London*' (unpublished Ph.D. thesis, University of Birmingham, 1959), p. xxii.
40 *Institutes*, II.i.7.
41 p. lxxxvi.

Chapter 3

1 Nicholas Brooke, *Shakespeare's Early Tragedies* (London: Methuen, 1968), p. 52.
2 For other treatments of the theme of conscience in *Richard III*, see Robert Heilman, 'Satiety and Conscience: Aspects of *Richard III*', *Antioch Review*, 24 (1964), 57–73, reprinted in *Essays in Shakespearean Criticism*, ed. J. Calderwood and H. E. Toliver (Englewood Cliffs, New Jersey: Prentice Hall, 1970), pp. 137–51; Richard P. Wheeler, 'History, Character and Conscience in *Richard III*', *Comparative Drama*, 5 (1971–2), 301–21; William B. Toole, 'The Motif of Psychic Division in *Richard III*', *Shakespeare Survey*, 27 (1974), 21–32; Slights, *The Casuistical Tradition in Shakespeare, Donne, Herbert, and Milton*, pp. 68–79.
3 R. G. Moulton, *Shakespeare as a Dramatic Artist* (Oxford: Clarendon Press, 1901), pp. 107–30.
4 A. P. Rossiter, *Angel with Horns and Other Shakespearean Lectures*, (London: Longmans, 1961), p. 6.
5 Raphael Holinshed, *The Third Volume of Chronicles* (London, 1586), sig.3L4ᵛ.
6 Rossiter, *Angel with Horns*, p. 7.
7 M. M. Reese, *The Cease of Majesty* (London: Edward Arnold, 1961), p. 222.
8 Sen Gupta, *Shakespeare's Historical Plays* (Oxford: Oxford University Press, 1964), p. 97.
9 Reese, *The Cease of Majesty*, p. 223.
10 Lily B. Campbell, *Shakespeare's 'Histories': Mirrors of Elizabethan Policy* (San Marino, Calif.: Huntingdon Library, 1947), pp. 307–8.
11 Aquinas, *Summa Theologica*, Part II. i.Q.91, Art. 2.
12 Aquinas, *The Summa Contra Gentiles*, trans. the English Dominican Fathers, 4 vols. in 5 (London: Burns, Oates & Washbourne, 1923–9), Book II.i. Chapters 72–6.
13 ibid., Chapter 77.
14 *Summa Theologica*, Part I.i.Q.22, Art. 1, Reply Obj. 2; Part I.i. Q.22, Art. 3; Part II.i.Q.93, Art. 3; Part II.i.Q.94, Art. 1, Reply, Obj. 2.
15 *Certain Sermons or Homilies Appointed to be Read in Churches*, p. 110.
16 Wolfgang Clemen, *A Commentary on Shakespeare's 'Richard III'* (London: Methuen, 1968), p. 72.
17 Henry Smith, 'The betraying of Christ', in *The Sermons of Master Henrie Smith* (London, 1592), sig.Ggg3ᵛ.
18 'A Discourse of Conscience', p. 68.
19 ibid., p. 66.

20 'The betraying of Christ', in *The Sermons*, sig.Ggg3ᵛ.
21 Wilbur Sanders, *The Dramatist and the Received Idea* (Cambridge: Cambridge University Press, 1968), p. 79.
22 ibid., p. 104.
23 See Alan Hobson, *Full Circle: Shakespeare and Moral Development* (London: Chatto & Windus, 1972), p. 117. Hobson writes on the psychological revelations afforded by Richard's portrayal in *3 Henry VI*, and my argument has availed itself of a number of his insights.
24 ibid., p. 118.
25 The following discussion of Richard's moral disintegration is indebted at several points to Sanders, *The Dramatist and the Received Idea*, pp. 104–9.
26 Clemen, *A Commentary on Shakespeare's 'Richard III'*, p. 219.
27 'A Discourse', p. 8.

Chapter 4

1 A number of studies demonstrate the indebtedness of Shakespeare and his contemporaries to the Morality tradition. See, for example, J. Dover Wilson, *The Fortunes of Falstaff* (Cambridge: Cambridge University Press, 1943), pp. 15–35; Bernard Spivack, *Shakespeare and the Allegory of Evil* (New York: Columbia University Press, and London: Oxford University Press, 1958), p. 79 *et passim*; Bevington, *From 'Mankynde' to Marlowe*; Alan C. Dessen, *Jonson's Moral Comedy* (Evanston, Illinois: Northwestern University Press, 1971), pp. 8–36; Potter; *The English Morality Play*; Edmund Creeth, *Mankynde in Shakespeare* (Athens, Georgia: University of Georgia Press, 1976); Catherine Belsey, 'The Case of Hamlet's Conscience', *SP*, 76 (1979) 127–48. Also John Vyvyan, in *The Shakespearean Ethic* (London: Chatto & Windus, 1959), pp. 33–61, interprets Hamlet's as an allegorical struggle between the powers of heaven and hell within his soul, while for Irving Ribner in *Patterns of Shakespearean Tragedy* (London: Methuen, 1960), Hamlet's life journey is essentially symbolic, 'the emotional equivalent of a Christian view of human life' (p. 65).
   The interpretation offered here is based on the Arden edition of *Hamlet*, ed. Harold Jenkins (London: Methuen, 1982). It thus presupposes as integral to the text material (including the passage here cited) which the New Oxford editors consign to an appendix in accordance with their theory that Shakespeare revised his own text, and that these authorial revisions are preserved in the Folio version. However, nobody has seriously contended that the ampler Q2 text is not Shakespearean, or that the cuts were made for interpretative rather than theatrical reasons; what we appear to have are two authorial inscriptions of the text representing different stages in its evolution from study to theatre. As it is, a discussion of Hamlet's conscience is furthered in passages which are present only in Q2 and I have therefore opted to use a modern edition which preserves the traditional text in its entirety. For full discussions of the textual problems in *Hamlet*, see G. R. Hibbard (ed.), *Hamlet*, The Oxford Shakespeare (Oxford and New York: Oxford University Press, 1987); Gary Taylor, Stanley Wells, *et al.*, 'Hamlet' in *William Shakespeare: A Textual Companion* (Oxford and New York: Oxford University Press, 1987); David Bevington, 'Determining the Indeterminate: The Oxford Shakespeare', *Shakespeare Quarterly*, 38 (Winter, 1987), 501–19; Paul Werstine, 'The Textual Mystery of Hamlet', *Shakespeare Quarterly* 39 (Spring, 1988), 1–26.

2 *Macbeth*, I.iii.130.
3 John Lawlor, *Tragic Sense in Shakespeare* (London: Chatto & Windus, 1960), p. 73.
4 Ribner, *Patterns of Shakespearean Tragedy*, p. 79.
5 'The Case of Hamlet's Conscience', p. 137.
6 T. McAlindon, *Shakespeare; and Decorum* (London: Macmillan, 1973), p. 61.
7 Eleanor Prosser, *Hamlet and Revenge*, second edition (Stanford, Calif: Stanford University Press, 1971), p. 203.
8 ibid., p. 210.
9 J. Dover Wilson, *What Happens in Hamlet*, third edition (Cambridge; Cambridge University Press, 1970), p. 224.
10 G. R. Elliott, *Scourge and Minister* (New York: Duke University Press, 1965), p. 30.
11 See Dover Wilson, *What Happens in Hamlet*, pp. 60–6; B. L. Joseph, *Conscience and the King* (London: Chatto & Windus, 1953), pp. 32–6; Prosser, *Hamlet and Revenge*, pp. 97–117. Other studies of Elizabethan spirit lore relating to *Hamlet* are Roy W. Battenhouse, 'The *Ghost* in Hamlet; a Catholic "Linchpin"?', *SP*, 48 (1951), 161–92; I. J. Semper, 'The Ghost in *Hamlet*: Pagan or Christian?', *The Month*, 9 (1953), 222–34; John Erskine Hankins, *The Character of Hamlet and Other Essays* (Chapel Hill, North Carolina: University of North Carolina Press, 1941); Sister Miriam Joseph, 'Discerning the Ghost in *Hamlet*', *PMLA*, 76 (1961), 493–502; Robert H. West, *Shakespeare and the Outer Mystery* (Lexington, Kentucky: University of Kentucky Press, 1968), pp. 56–68.
12 Deuteronomy 32:35; Hebrews 10:30; Romans 12:19.
13 See Dover Wilson, *What Happens in Hamlet*, pp. 84–5; West, *Shakespeare and the Outer Mystery*, p. 63; Ribner, *Patterns of Shakespearean Tragedy*, p. 72.
14 Vyvyan, *The Shakespearean Ethic*, p. 29.
15 This, indeed, is the main thesis of Eleanor Prosser's *Hamlet and Revenge*.
16 Joseph Hall, *The Works*, 12 vols. (Oxford: D. A. Talboys, 1837–9), I, 348. (*The Works* were first published as a collected edition in 1625.)
17 ibid., p. 319.
18 *Richard III*, I.iv.204–5.
19 *King Lear*, III.vi.78–9.
20 Geoffrey Bush, *Shakespeare and the Natural Condition* (Cambridge, Mass.: Harvard University Press, 1956), p. 83.
21 Richard Hooker, 'The Laws', I.vii.7.
22 'The Case of Hamlet's Conscience', pp. 141–2.
23 Bush, *Shakespeare and the Natural Condition*, p. 83.
24 'The Laws', I.x.1.
25 ibid., I.vii.6.
26 ibid., I.vii.7.
27 William Perkins, 'A Discourse of Conscience', pp. 41–2; 'The Whole Treatise of Cases of Conscience', p. 100.
28 John Woolton, *Of the Conscience*, sigs.M1ᵛ–M3ᵛ.
29 Immanuel Bourne, *The Anatomie of Conscience*, sigs.C3ᵛ–C4ᵛ.
30 William Ames, *Conscience with the Power and Cases Thereof*, sigs.C1–D2.
31 See also Richard Carpenter, *The Conscionable Christian, or the Indevour of Saint Paul*, sigs.I3–K2; Robert Harris, *Six Sermons of Conscience*, sig. D2;

William Jones *A Commentary upon the Epistles of Saint Paul to Philemon, and to the Hebrewes*, sig.Aaa 3.
32 'A Discourse', p. 41.
33 *Of the Conscience*, sig.M3ᵛ.
34 Timothy Bright, *A Treatise of Melancholie*, sig.E5.
35 Robert Burton, *The Anatomy of Melancholy*, I, 189–90.
36 'A Discourse', p. 5.
37 Robert Bolton, *A Discourse about the State of True Happiness*, sig.P3ᵛ (Greek characters transliterated).
38 Philip the Chancellor, *Summa de Bono*, 3, Reply AI. (Latin text in O. Lottin, *Psychologie et morale aux XIIᵉ et XIIIᵉ siècles* (Gembloux: J. Duculot, 1948), vol. 2, pp. 140–2, 145–8, 150–2, 153–6) (Potts, p. 104).
39 ibid., 2, Reply (Potts, p. 102).
40 Aquinas, *Debated Questions on Truth*, 16, Discussion (Potts, pp. 123–5).
41 ibid., 17.1 (Potts, p. 130).
42 ibid., 16.2, Reply 1 (Potts, p. 128).
43 ibid., 16.2, Discussion (Potts, p. 128).
44 ibid., 16.3, Discussion (Potts, p. 129).
45 ibid., 16.3, Discussion (Potts, p. 129).
46 *Summa Theologica*, Part II.i. Q.77, Art. 1.
47 *Debated Questions on Truth*, 16.3, Discussion (Potts, p. 128).
48 *Summa Theologica*, Part II.i. Q.77, Art. 1.
49 'The Case of Hamlet's Conscience', p. 142.
50 Cf. the Second Murderer in *Richard III* elects to ignore the warnings of conscience preparatory to dispatching Clarence: 'I'll not meddle with it; it makes a man a coward' (I.iv.128); an incident which anticipates Richard's misgivings on the eve of Bosworth: 'O coward conscience, how dost thou afflict me!' (V.iii.180). A similar equation of conscience with cowardice occurs in *Appius and Virginia*, pp. 510–675.
51 See Vyvyan, *The Shakespearean Ethic*, p. 59.
52 *What Happens in Hamlet*, pp. 245–6.
53 A. C. Bradley makes this point in *Shakespearean Tragedy*, second edition (London: Macmillan, 1932), pp. 134–5.
54 Derek A. Traversi, *An Approach to Shakespeare*, third edition (London: Hollis & Carter, 1969), II, 61.
55 See *Conscience and the King*, p. 80.
56 See, for example, Perkins, 'A Whole Theatise', where, in speaking of the erroneous conscience, he says, 'For the error of the judgement cannot take a way the nature of that which is simply evill. Sinne is sinne, and so remaineth, notwithstanding any contrarie perswasion of the conscience' (p.100). In this, he is supported by Bishop Hall: 'Ignorance cannot acquit, if it can abate, our sin' (*The Works*, I, 329).

Chapter 5

1 See Sanders, *The Dramatist and the Received Idea*, p. 267.
2 John Wilders, *The Lost Garden* (London: Macmillan, 1978), p. 63.
3 Sanders, *The Dramatist and the Received Idea*, p. 279.
4 ibid., p. 282.
5 For other studies which discuss the theme of conscience in Macbeth, see Willard Farnham, *Shakespeare's Tragic Frontier: The World of His Final Tragedies* (Berkeley and Los Angeles, Calif: University of California Press,

1950), pp. 107–10; Henry N. Paul, *The Royal Play of 'Macbeth'* (New York: Macmillan, 1950), pp. 134–5; William Rosen, *Shakespeare and the Craft of Tragedy* (Cambridge, Mass.: Harvard University Press, 1960), pp. 87–8; Paul A. Jorgensen, *Our Naked Frailties: Sensational Art and Meaning in 'Macbeth'* (Berkeley and Los Angeles, Calif.: University of California Press, 1971), pp. 181–4; A. L. and M. K. Kistner, 'Macbeth: A Treatise of Conscience'. *Thoth*, 13 (1973), 27–43; W. H. Toppen, *Conscience in Shakespeare's 'Macbeth'* (Groningen: J. B. Wolters, 1962); Slights, *The Casuistical Tradition in Shakespeare, Donne, Herbert, and Milton*, pp. 106–32.

6 Toppen, *Conscience in Shakespeare's 'Macbeth'*, p. 219.
7 'A Discourse of Conscience', p. 68.
8 Toppen, *Conscience in Shakespeare's 'Macbeth'*, pp. 240–1.
9 See G. Wilson Knight, *The Wheel of Fire*, paperback edition (London: Methuen, 1961), p. 156.
10 Henry Smith, *Sermons* (London, 1593). Quoted by Peter Milward in *Shakespeare's Religious Background* (London: Sidgwick & Jackson, 1973), p. 133.
11 Curry, *Shakespeare's Philosophical Patterns*, p. 134.
12 This, indeed, in the Augustinian thesis we find propounded by St Thomas in the *Summa Theologica*. Speaking of the providence of God, he says:

Since, then, all particular causes are included under the universal cause, it could not be that any effect should take place outside the range of that universal cause . . . Since God, then, provides universally for all being, it belongs to His Providence to permit certain defects in particular effects, that the perfect good of the universe may not be hindered. If all evil were prevented, much good would be absent from the universe . . . Thus Augustine says: *Almighty God would in no wise permit evil to exist in His works, unless He were so almighty and so good as to produce good even from evil.*
(Part I.i.Q.22, Art.2, Reply Obj. 1 and 2)

A better known version of the same theodicy occurs in *Paradise Lost*, where by a similar prevarication, Satan's free will is preserved, and his designs permitted, only to

Heap on himself damnation, while he sought
Evil to others, and enrag'd might see
How all his malice serv'd but to bring forth
Infinite goodness, grace, and mercy . . .
(*PL*, i.215–18)

Chapter 6

1 Roy W. Battenhouse, *Marlow's Tamburlaine: A Study in Renaissance Moral Philosophy* (Nashville, Tennessee: Vanderbilt University Press, 1941). This is the inference he draws of all Marlowe's protagonists, that their 'tragic fall is both a consequence and a punishment of sin', p. 17. The phrase quoted is that of M. M. Mahood, *Poetry and Humanism* (London: Jonathan Cape, 1950), p. 54.
2 Una M. Ellis-Fermor, *Christopher Marlowe* (London: Methuen, 1927), pp. 62–3.
3 This, essentially, is the position taken by Leo Kirschbaum, 'Marlowe's *Faustus*: A Reconsideration', *RES*, 19 (1943), 225–41; and G. I. Duthie, 'Some Observations on Marlowe's *Doctor Faustus*', *Archiv*, 203 (1966), 81–96.

4   Clifford Davidson, 'Doctor Faustus of Wittenburg', *SP*, 59 (1962), 514–23.
5   Sanders, *The Dramatist and the Received Idea*, pp. 243–51; Pauline Honder-
    ich, 'John Calvin and Doctor Faustus', *MLR*, 68 (1973), 1–13.
6   See J. P. Brockbank, *Marlowe: Dr Faustus* (London: Edward Arnold, 1962),
    pp. 13–18; Douglas Cole, *Suffering and Evil in the Plays of Christopher
    Marlowe* (Princeton, New Jersey: Princeton University Press, 1962), pp.
    194–210; Arieh Sachs, 'The Religious Despair of Doctor Faustus', *JEGP*,
    63 (1964), 625–47.
7   Robert Speaight, 'Marlowe: The Forerunner', *REL*, 7 (1966), 25–41, p. 36.
    For similar evaluations, see Duthie, 'Some Observations on Marlowe's
    Doctor Faustus', pp. 84–5; Kirschbaum, 'Marlowe's *Faustus*: A Reconsider-
    ation', p. 229; T. M. McAlindon, 'Classical Mythology and Christian Tra-
    dition in Marlowe's *Doctor Faustus*', *PMLA*, 81 (1966), 214–23; and James
    L. Smith, 'Marlowe's *Dr Faustus*', *Scrutiny*, 8 (1939–40), 36–55.
8   Sanders, *The Dramatist and the Received Idea*, p. 209.
9   *The First Anniversarie: An Anatomy of the World*, 1.205.
10 La Primaudaye, *The French Academie*, sig.Hhhh^v.
11 Leif Grane, *Peter Abelard: Philosophy and Christianity in the Middle Ages*,
    ed. Derek Baker, trans. F. and C. Crowley (London: Allen & Unwin, 1970),
    p. 118.
12 Helen Gardner, 'The Tragedy of Damnation', *Essays and Studies*, 1 (1948),
    46–66, reprinted in *Elizabethan Drama: Modern Essays in Criticism*, ed. R.
    J. Kaufmann (New York: Oxford University Press, 1961), 320–41, p. 323.
13 William Perkins, 'Of the nature and practise of repentance', in *Two Treatises*,
    second edition (Cambridge, 1597), sig.A5^v.
14 ibid., sig.A5^v.
15 ibid., sig.A5^v.
16 Perkins, 'A Discourse of Conscience', p. 102.
17 Sachs, 'The Religious Despair of Doctor Faustus', p. 644.
18 Sanders, *The Dramatist and the Received Idea*, p. 228.
19 Most notably, of course, by Lily B. Campbell in 'Doctor Faustus: A Case
    of Conscience', but see also Bevington, *From 'Mankind' to Marlowe*, pp.
    245–62; Brockbank, *Marlowe: Dr Faustus*, pp. 16–18; and Sachs, 'The
    Religious Despair of Doctor Faustus'.
20 Nathaniel Woodes, *The Conflict of Conscience*, 1.2151.
21 *The Dramatist and the Received Idea*, p. 228.
22 *Article XVII*: 'Of Predestination and Election'.
23 *A Golden Chaine or The Description of Theologie* (London, 1592), sig.U^v.
24 'Fragments of an Answer to the Letter of Certain English Protestants', in
    The Works, Book V, Appendix 1, paragraphs 42, 34.
25 ibid., paragraph 42.
26 ibid., paragraph 42.
27 ibid., paragraph 34.
28 Robert Bolton, *Instructions for a Right Comforting Afflicted Consciences*
    (London, 1631), sig.F3^v.
29 Grane, *Peter Abelard: Philosophy and Christianity in the Middle Ages*, p. 23.
30 II.ii.19.
31 Sanders, *The Dramatist and the Received Idea*, p. 219.
32 ibid. I am indebted at several points in the following argument to Sanders's
    invaluable discussion of the nature of the supernatural in *Doctor Faustus*.
    See *The Dramatist and the Received Idea*, pp. 213–18.
33 See 'Marlowe's *Dr Faustus*', p. 38.

34 J. B. Steane makes a similar point in *Marlowe: A Critical Study* (Cambridge: Cambridge University Press, 1964), p. 160.

35 Sanders, *The Dramatist and the Received Idea*, p. 217.

36 There are a number of discussions relating *Doctor Faustus* to the Morality tradition, notably those of Bevington, *From 'Mankind' to Marlowe*, pp. 245–62; Campbell, 'Doctor Faustus: A Case of Conscience'; Brockbank, *Marlowe: Dr Faustus*, pp. 18–23; Cole, *Suffering and Evil in the Plays of Christopher Marlowe*, pp. 231–43; R. B. Heilman, 'The Tragedy of Knowledge: Marlowe's Treatment of Faustus', *QRL*, 2 (1945–6), 316–32.

37 *The Conflict of Conscience*, Prologue, 1.44, second issue.

38 That is, according to arguments marshalled by Campbell, 'Doctor Faustus: A Case of Conscience', pp. 230–9; Bevington, *From 'Mankind' to Marlowe*, p. 245; and Spivack, *Shakespeare and the Allegory of Evil*, p. 474.

39 This point is argued by Douglas Cole, who, from an analysis of the characteristic dramatic activity of personified vices and virtues in various Morality plays, concludes that since the Angels never interact between themselves or with any other character, they are in this respect atypical of the dramatic convention. See *Suffering and Evil in the Plays of Christopher Marlowe*, pp. 235–6.

40 Richard Kilby, *The Burthen of a loaden conscience or the miserie of sinne* (Cambridge, 1608), sigs.A4, A4ᵛ.

41 Cole, *Suffering and Evil in the Plays of Christopher Marlowe*, pp. 209, 210.

42 ibid., p. 206. See also Brockbank, *Marlowe: Dr Faustus*, p. 38.

43 Sig.I5.

44 Cf. Brockbank, *Marlowe: Dr Faustus*, p. 40.

45 Cf. Cole, *Suffering and Evil in the Plays of Christopher Marlowe*, p. 209.

46 The similarities to *Macbeth* at this point have been remarked by J. B. Steane. See *Marlowe: A Critical Study*, pp. 136–7.

47 See Mahood, *Poetry and Humanism*, p. 68. Also Kirschbaum, 'Marlowe's Faustus: A Reconsideration', p. 235, and Harry Levin, *The Overreacher: A Study of Christopher Marlowe* (London: Faber & Faber, 1952), p. 142.

48 *The Burthen of a loaden conscience*, sig.A4.

49 Mahood, *Poetry and Humanism*, p. 71.

50 See John D. Jump (ed.), *Doctor Faustus*, The Revels Plays (London: Methuen, 1962), p. liv.

51 Richard Greenham, *Two Treatises of the comforting of an afflicted conscience* (London, 1598), sig.F2ᵛ.

52 Woolton, *Of the Conscience*, sig.02.

53 'Marlowe's *Dr Faustus*', p. 42.

54 Cf. Mahood, *Poetry and Humanism*, p. 72.

55 Robert Linaker, *A Comfortable Treatise for the reliefe of such as are afflicted in conscience*, second edition (London, 1601), sig.B4ᵛ (first edition published in 1590).

56 *Instructions for a Right Comforting Afflicted Consciences*, sigs.G7, G7ᵛ.

57 Numerous critics have pointed out the increasing degeneracy and triviality of the satisfactions for which Faustus sold his soul. Some of the more prominent are Mahood, *Poetry and Humanism*, p. 73; Levin, *The Overreacher*, p. 143 and W. W. Greg in 'The Damnation of Faustus', *MLR*, 41 (1946), 97–107. In subscribing to this argument, I accept, as do most recent commentators, Marlowe's authorial responsibility, at any rate, for the text as we have it.

58 Sigs.C2, C2ᵛ.

59 Cf. McAlindon, 'Classical Mythology and Christian Tradition in Marlowe's *Doctor Faustus*', p. 215.
60 Brockbank, *Marlowe: Dr Faustus*, p. 54.
61 See Luke 22:31.
62 Cole, *Suffering and Evil in the Plays of Christopher Marlowe*, p. 220.
63 *Instructions for a Right Comforting Afflicted Consciences*, sig.C3.
64 See Brockbank, *Marlowe: Dr Faustus*, pp. 56–7, and Arthur M. Mizener, 'The Tragedy of Marlowe's *Dr Faustus*', *College English*, 5 (1943), 70–5.
65 Levin, *The Overreacher*, p. 156.
66 Respectively 10:8; 23:30; 6:16.
67 *Instructions for a Right Comforting Afflicted Consciences*, sig.G5ᵛ.
68 See Roma Gill (ed.), *Doctor Faustus*, The New Mermaids (London: Benn, 1965), p. xxvi.
69 *A Golden Chaine, or The Description of Theologie*, sigs.C6, C6ᵛ.
70 R. Niebuhr, *The Nature and Destiny of Man*, 2 vols. (London: Nisbet, 1941–3, New York: Charles Scribner's Sons, 1945), I, 317.
71 See Frederick S. Boas, *Christopher Marlowe: A Biographical and Critical Study* (Oxford: Clarendon Press, 1940); Paul H. Kocher, *Christopher Marlowe: A Study of His Thought, Learning and Character* (Chapel Hill, North Carolina: Russell & Russell, Inc., 1946, reprinted New York, 1962); A. L. Rowse, *Christopher Marlowe: A Biography* (London: Macmillan, 1964); Levin, *The Overreacher*.

Chapter 7

1 Robert Ornstein, *The Moral Vision of Jacobean Tragedy* (Wisconsin: University of Wisconsin Press, 1960) p. 123.
2 For a more sustained comparison of *The Atheist's Tragedy* and *Doctor Faustus*, see Ornstein, *The Moral Vision*, pp. 122–4, and Irving Ribner (ed.), *The Atheist's Tragedy*, the Revels Plays (London: Methuen, 1964), lxiii.
3 *Institutes*, I.v.4.
4 *Institutes*, I.xvi.3.
5 For discussions of *The Atheist's Tragedy* in the context of the revenge tradition see Fredson Bowers, *Elizabethan Revenge Tragedy*, 1587–1642 (Princeton, New Jersey: Princeton University Press, 1940), pp. 139–43; and Brian Morris and Roma Gill (eds.), *The Atheist's Tragedy*, New Mermaids Edition (London: Benn, 1976), pp. xviii–xxiv; also T. M. Tomlinson, 'The Morality of Revenge: Tourneur's Critics', *Essays in Criticism*, 10 (1960), 134–47.
6 *Institutes*, I.v.7–8. For a Calvinist interpretation of the play see Michael H. Higgins, 'The Influence of Calvinistic Thought in Tourneur's *Atheist's Tragedy*', *RES*, 19 (1943), 255–62.
7 M. C. Bradbrook, *Themes and Conventions of Elizabethan Tragedy* (Cambridge: Cambridge University Press, 1935), p. 184.
8 Herndl, *The High Design*, p. 163. I have at several points found Herndl's discussion of natural law beliefs in Jacobean tragedy invaluable.
9 *Institutes*, II.ii.22.
10 Cf. Ribner (ed.), *The Atheist's Tragedy*, xxxvii.
11 Ornstein, '*The Atheist's Tragedy* and Renaissance Naturalism', *SP*, 51 (1954), 194–207; see also *The Moral Vision*, p. 120.
12 See '*The Atheist's Tragedy* and Renaissance Naturalism'; *The Moral Vision*. For more general discussions of Renaissance atheism see E. A. Strathmann, 'Elizabethan Meanings of Atheism', in *Sir Walter Raleigh: A Study in Eliza-*

bethan Skepticism (New York: Columbia University Press, 1951); G. T. Buckley, *Atheism in the English Renaissance* (Chicago: Chicago University Press, 1932); P. H. Kocher, *Science and Religion in Elizabethan England* (San Marino, Calif.: Huntingdon Library 1953).

13 Peter B. Murray, *A Study of Cyril Tourneur* (Philadelphia: University of Pennsylvania Press, 1964), pp. 60–1.

14 *Institutes*, II.ii.12.

15 Cf. Murray, *A Study of Cyril Tourneur*, p. 87.

16 I am indebted, as are all who have written on this subject, to the avenues of research suggested by Strathmann's major study: *Sir Walter Raleigh: A Study in Elizabethan Skepticism*.

17 *Institutes*, I.iii.2.

18 William Vaughan, *The Golden-grove* (London, 1600), sig.C2.

19 Martin Fotherby, *Atheomastix: Clearing four Truthes, Against Atheists and Infidels* (London, 1622), sig.M5⁴.

20 John Dove, *A Confutation of Atheisme* (London, 1605), sig.A4.

21 Cf. Murray, *A Study of Cyril Tourneur*, p. 62.

22 This transformation has been noticed by Una Ellis-Fermor in *The Jacobean Drama: An Interpretation* (London: Methuen, 1936), p. 166, and by Murray, *A Study of Cyril Tourneur*, p. 100. I am indebted also in the following paragraphs to Murray's perceptive comments on the relationship between honour and reason in Charlemont, ibid., pp. 99–104.

23 Thomas Morton, *A Treatise of the threefolde state of man*, sigs.S6ᵛ, S7.

24 Cf. Brian Morris and Roma Gill (eds.), *The Atheist's Tragedy*, p. xiv.

25 Cf. Herndl, *The High Design*, p. 223.

26 *Institutes*, II.i.7.

27 *A Treatise of the threefolde State of man*, sig.S5.

28 ibid., sig.S5.

29 *Institutes*, I.xvii.11.

30 *Institutes*, I.xvii.11.

31 *Institutes*, I.xvii.9.

32 My italics.

33 See Hosea 10:8; Luke 23:30; Revelation 6:16. For a more general discussion of Tourneur's borrowings see Ornstein, *The Moral Vision*, pp. 120–6.

34 *Institutes*, I.iii.2.

35 See J. M. S. Tompkins, 'Tourneur and the Stars', *RES*, 22 (1946), 315–19; Ribner (ed.), *The Atheist's Tragedy*, pp. xliii-xlvi; Bradbrook, *Themes and Conventions of Elizabethan Tragedy*, pp. 176–8. Murray disagrees with the determinist interpretations of the above-mentioned critics when he states that the stars 'do not function as they should, if they were truly in control of the actions of men' (*A Study of Cyril Tourneur*, p. 95). For more general studies see Kocher, *Science and Religion in Elizabethan England*, pp. 201–24 and Don Cameron Allen, *The Star-Crossed Renaissance* (Durham, North Carolina: Duke University Press, 1941).

36 Sir Christopher Heydon, *A Defence of Judiciall Astrologie* (Cambridge, 1603), sig.q4ᵛ.

37 W. P., *Foure Great Lyers, Striving who shall win the silver Whetstone* (London, 1585), sig.B7. W. P. is identified as William Perkins by H. Dick in 'The Authorship of Foure Great Lyers (1585)', *The Library*, IV, 19 (1938–9), 311–14.

38 Sig.C4.

39 According to the hypothesis advanced by Kenneth Cameron in 'Tourneur's *Transformed Metamorphosis*', *RES*, (1940) 18–24, p. 20.
40 Cf. Kocher, *Science and Religion in Elizabethan England*, p. 215.
41 John Chamber, *A Treatise Against Judiciall Astrologie* (London, 1601), sig. D1.
42 Jean Calvin, *A little booke concernynge offences*, trans. A. Goldinge (1567), sig.F7ᵛ.
43 *The Star-Crossed Renaissance*, pp. 184–5.
44 *Guillaume de Saluste du Bartas: his devine weekes and workes*, trans. J. Sylvester (London, 1605), sig.L2ᵛ.
45 Jean Calvin, *An admonicion against astrology judiciall*, trans. G. G(ylby) (London, 1561), sig.C3.
46 *A Defence of Judiciall Astrologie*, sig.q4ᵛ.
47 Bradbrook, *Themes and Conventions of Elizabethan Tragedy*, p. 178.
48 Sig.T6ᵛ.
49 ibid., sig.N2.
50 *Macbeth*, I.iii.141, II.ii.48.
51 *Atheomastix*, sigs.N2, N2ᵛ.
52 See John Dove, sig.A4, quoted above.
53 *Atheomastix*, sig.N2ᵛ.

Chapter 8

1 Ornstein, *The Moral Vision of Jacobean Tragedy*, p. 134.
2 Ralph Berry, *The Art of John Webster* (Oxford: Clarendon Press, 1972), p. 107.
3 David L. Frost, *The School of Shakespeare* (Cambridge: Cambridge University Press, 1968), p. 129.
4 *The White Devil*, V.vi.256–7.
5 Herndl, *The High Design*, p. 196.
6 R. W. Dent, *John Webster's Borrowing* (Berkeley and Los Angeles, Calif.: University of California Press, 1960); Robert F. Whitman, *Beyond Melancholy: John Webster and the Tragedy of Darkness*, Salzburg Studies in English Literature, ed. James Hogg (Salzburg: University of Salzburg, 1973). All who write on Webster must incur numerous obligations to Dent's compendious study, and I wish to record in advance a general indebtedness to the suggestions it makes regarding Webster's sources and influences.
7 Dent, *John Webster's Borrowing*, p. 16 *et passim*; Whitman, *Beyond Melancholy*, p. 164.
8 Dent, *John Webster's Borrowing*, p. 16 *et passim*; Whitman, *Beyond Melancholy*, pp. 165–91.
9 Whitman, *Beyond Melancholy*, p. 169.
10 Sir Philip Sidney, *The Countesse of Pembrokes Arcadia* (1590), ed. Albert Feuillerat (Cambridge: Cambridge University Press, 1922), p. 146. Quoted by Whitman, *Beyond Melancholy*, p. 168.
11 From *The Essayes*, trans. John Florio, ed. J. I. M. Stewart (New York, 1933), p. 525. Quoted by Whitman, *Beyond Melancholy*, p. 173.
12 Whitman, *Beyond Melancholy*, pp. 174–5; Dent, *John Webster's Borrowing*, p. 194.
13 *The Essays of Montaigne*, trans. E. J. Trechmann with an introduction by J. H. Robertson, 2 vols. (London: Humphrey Milford, 1927), I, 556.
14 'Truely Man is made of Earth, conceyved in Sinne, and borne to paine . . .

Through his wickedness he shal become foode to the fire, meat for wormes, and a lumpe of putrefaction loathsome to beholde . . . Man is made of dust, of claye, of ashes: hee is conceyved in the wanton desire of fleshly lust, in the heate of carnall appetite, in the foule delight of Leacherie, and which is worse, in the spotte of Sin' (Pope Innocent III, *The Mirror of Man's Lyfe*, Englished by H. Kirton (London, 1586), sigs.B1ᵛ–B2).

15 Hoopes, *Right, Reason in the English Renaissance*, p. 97.
16 ibid., p. 121.
17 See Dent, *John Webster's Borrowing*, pp. 36–7 *et passim*.
18 Thomas Adams, 'The Soules Sicknesse', in *The Workes of Tho: Adams* (London, 1630), sig.004ᵛ. First published under the title *Diseases of the soule: a discourse* (London, 1616).
19 Baker, *The Wars of Truth*, p. 152.
20 *Right Reason in the English Renaissance*, p. 116.
21 *The Wars of Truth*, p. 153.
22 *Institutes*, II.v.19.
23 Elizabeth M. Brennan (ed.), *The Duchess of Malfi*, The New Mermaids (London: Benn, 1964), p. xii.
24 She concludes that the Duchess's 'was original sin, not personal sin.' See Bradbrook, *Themes and Conventions of Elizabethan Tragedy*, p. 209.
25 *Institutes*, III.iii.10.
26 Hooker, 'The Laws of Ecclesiastical Polity', I.vii.6.
27 *Institutes*, II.ii.22,23.
28 See in particular Bradbrook, *Themes and Conventions*, pp. 197–202, and Peter B. Murray, *A Study of John Webster* (The Hague and Paris: Mouton, 1969), p. 126.
29 See Clifford Leech, *John Webster: A Critical Study* (London: Hogarth Press, 1951), p. 69; Bradbrook, *Themes and Conventions*, p. 199; F. W. Wadsworth, 'Webster's *Duchess of Malfi* in the Light of Some Contemporary Ideas on Marriage and Remarriage', *Philological Quarterly*, 35 (1956), 394–407.
30 T. B. Tomlinson, *A Study of Elizabethan and Jacobean Tragedy* (Cambridge: Cambridge University Press, and Melbourne: Melbourne University Press, 1964), p. 231.
31 *John Webster: A Critical Study*, p. 77.
32 *Institutes*, III.iii.12.
33 Cf. Berry, *The Art of John Webster*, p. 126.
34 *The Workes*, sig.A3. 'The Gallant's Burden' was first published in 1612. The borrowing is cited in Dent, *John Webster's Borrowing*, p. 216.
35 Cf. Brennan (ed.), *The Duchess of Malfi*, p. xxi. 'The use of capitals in the first quarto suggests a parabolic interpretation of this apparently simple fable: the Fisher is God: the gathering in of the fishes is a harvest at which not wheat and tares, but good and bad fish are to be judged; the Market is the Judgement . . .'.
36 'The Gallant's Burden', in *The Workes*, sig.A1ᵛ. Cf. Dent, *John Webster's Borrowing*, p. 254.
37 *The Art of John Webster*, p. 107.
38 D. C. Gunby, '*The Duchess of Malfi*: A Theological Approach', in *John Webster*, ed. Brian Morris, Mermaid Critical Commentaries (London: Benn, 1970), pp. 181–204 (p. 190).
39 Dominic Baker-Smith, 'Religion and John Webster', in *John Webster* ed. Brian Morris, Mermaid Critical Commentaries (London: Benn, 1970), pp. 207–28 (p. 227).

40 Gunby, '*The Duchess of Malfi:* A Theological Approach', p. 181.
41 *Institutes*, III.viii.6.
42 John Downame, *The Christian Warfare* (London, 1608), sigs.L7ᵛ, L8.
43 'For the things which God rightly wills, he accomplishes by the evil wills of bad men' (*August. Enchirid. ad Laurent.* cap. 101), quoted by Calvin in *Institutes*, I.xviii.3.
44 The parallels between *The Duchess of Malfi* and the Book of Job have been noted by V. F. Hopper and G. B. Lahey (eds.), *The Duchess of Malfi* (New York: Barron's Educational Series, 1960), pp. 52, 54–5, and more especially by P. B. Murray, to whose account in *A Study of John Webster*, pp. 130–4, I am indebted at several points in the following discussion.
45 Cf. Job 31:6: 'Let me be weighed in an even balance, that God may know mine integrity.' Cf. Murray, *A Study of John Webster*, p. 130.
46 Cf. Job Chs 6–12.
47 Job Chs 29–30.
48 Job 3:9. Cf. Murray, *A Study of John Webster*, p. 131.
49 Sig.M5.
50 Bradbrook says of the Duchess here that 'she is at present experiencing the sacrament of penance'. See *Themes and Conventions of Elizabethan Tragedy*, p. 206.
51 Noticed by M. C. Bradbrook in 'Fate and Chance in *The Duchess of Malfi*' from 'Two Notes Upon Webster' in *MLR*, 42 (1947), 281–91, p. 281.
52 William Perkins, *The Works of that Famous and Worthy Minister of Christ*, 3 vols. (London, 1612–13, and Cambridge, 1613), I, Rr1ᵛ.
53 Sig.M1.
54 *Institutes*, III.iii.8.
55 Cf. Gunby, '*The Duchess of Malfi*: A Theological Approach', pp. 195–6.
56 ibid., p. 198.
57 Robert Burton, *The Anatomy of Melancholy*, III, 458.
58 Bernard, *Christian See to they Conscience*, sigs.E6, E6ᵛ.
59 Gunby, '*The Duchess of Malfi*: A Theological Approach', p. 197.
60 Cited in Murray, *A Study of John Webster*, p. 134.
61 *Institutes*, I.xviii.4.
62 ibid., II.ii.7.
63 ibid., II.iv.2.
64 ibid., II.iv.4.
65 ibid., I.xviii.3.
66 *De Grat. et Lib. Arbit. ad Valent*, c. 20. Cited in *Institutes*, I.xviii.4.
67 *Institutes*, II.ii.25.
68 John Downame, *The Second Part of the Christian Warfare*, (London, 1611), sigs.V4–V4ᵛ. Borrowing cited in Dent, *John Webster's Borrowing*, p. 259.
69 On these and related questions see, McD. Emslie, 'Motives in Malfi', *Essays in Criticism*, 9 (1959), 391–405; and W. G. Dwyer, *A Study of Webster's Use of Renaissance Natural and Moral Philosophy*, Salzburg Studies in English Literature, ed. James Hogg (Salzburg: University of Salzburg, 1973).
70 Bradbrook, 'Fate and Chance in *The Duchess of Malfi*', p. 284.
71 *The Second Part of the Christian Warfare*, sig.VV2ᵛ. Borrowing noted by Dent, *John Webster's Borrowing*, p. 258.
72 'Presumption running into Despaire', in *The Workes*, sig.Ttt5.
73 *The High Design*, p. 196.

Chapter 9

1 A. C. Swinburn, 'Philip Massinger', *Fortnightly Review*, 46 N.S. (July, 1889) 1–23, p. 23.

2 T. A. Dunn, *Philip Massinger: The Man and the Playwright* (Ghana and London: Thomas Nelson, 1957), p. 74.

3 T. S. Eliot, 'Philip Massinger', in *Elizabethan Dramatists* (London: Faber & Faber, 1963), pp. 143–4.

4 Sir Leslie Stephen, *Hours in a Library*, 3 vols. (London: Smith Elder & Co., 1892), II, 160–4.

5 *Philip Massinger: The Man and the Playwright*, p. 192.

6 Massinger's debt to Stoic philosophy is discussed by B. T. Spencer in his chapter on Philip Massinger in *Seventeenth Century Studies*, ed. R. Shafer (Princeton, New Jersey: Princeton University Press, 1933), 3–119 (pp. 7–78).

7 *The High Design*, p. 230.

8 *The Plays of Philip Massinger*, ed. W. Gifford, second edition, 4 vols. (W. Bulmer and Co., London, 1813), pp. xlii–xliv.

9 J. Phelan, 'The Life of Philip Massinger', *Anglia*, 3 (1880), 361–8. Quoted by Dunn, *Philip Massinger: The Man and the Playwright*, pp. 50–1, whose critical study of Massinger includes a useful survey of the 'evidence' for and against his alleged conversion. See also pp. 184–91.

10 *Philip Massinger: The Man and the Playwright*, p. 51.

11 Donald S. Lawless, *Philip Massinger and His Associates*, Ball State Monograph 10, Publications in English 6 (Muncie, Indiana: Ball State University, 1967), p. 10.

12 R. Boyle, 'Philip Massinger', *DNB*, XIII, 10–16, p. 10.

13 E. Koeppel, 'Philip Massinger', *CHEL*, VI, 141–65, p. 150.

14 Maurice Chelli, *Le Drame de Massinger* (Lyon: M Audin 1923), p. 337.

15 A. H. Cruikshank, *Philip Massinger* (Oxford: Blackwell, 1920), p. 3.

16 *The Plays and Poems of Philip Massinger*, ed. Philip Edwards and Colin Gibson, 5 vols. (Oxford: Clarendon Press, 1976), I xlv.

17 *Hours in a Library*, II, 153.

18 *Philip Massinger: The Man and the Playwright*, pp. 184–91. Dunn, whose consideration is by far the most thorough, admits that 'the question is still arguable' (p.191).

19 Whitgift, *The Works*, ed. John Ayre, Parker Society, 3 vols. (Cambridge: Cambridge University Press, 1851–3), I, 207–8; II, 525, 529, 537–9. Quoted in New, *Anglican and Puritan*, p. 66.

20 'The Laws of Ecclesiastical Polity', II.v.61. For a full discussion of the Anglican belief in baptism as a vehicle of grace, see New, *Anglican and Puritan*, pp. 60–76.

21 Cf. *The Renegado*, where the newly baptized Donusa exclaims

> I am an other woman; till this minute
> I never liv'd, nor durst thinke how to dye.
> How long have I beene blinde? Yet on the suddaine,
> By this blest meanes I feele the filmes of error
> Tane from my soules eyes.
>
> (V.iii.121–5)

22 See in particular Luke Frugal's speech at V.iii.14–36.

23 *The Maid of Honour*, V.ii.208–20.

24 *The Renegado*, IV.i.96.

25 The wicked, according to Hooker's statement of the classic Anglican position

on reprobation, are abandoned by God because they resist the grace offered indiscriminately to all: 'And for this cause, that will of God which sin occasioneth to decree the just condemnation of many, is by the same necessity enforced to leave many unto themselves, where the greatness of sin hath constrained him to set down the sentence of death.' 'Fragments of an Answer to the Letter of Certain English Protestants', in *The Works*, Book V, Appendix 1, paragraph 42.

26 Henri Jacob Makkink, *Philip Massinger and John Fletcher; A Comparison* (New York: Haskell House, 1966), p. 130.
27 Quoted in Baker, *The Wars of Truth*, p. 118.
28 *Coleridge on the Seventeenth Century*, ed. R. F. Brinkley (Durham, North Carolina: Duke University Press, 1955), p. 515.
29 Justus Lipsius's *De Constantia* (1584) was translated into English by John Stradling as *Two Books of Constancie* (London, 1595), to which edition all future references were made.
30 Guillaume du Vair's *De la Constance et Consolation és Calamitez Publiques* was translated in 1622 by Andrew Court as *A Buckler Against Adversitie* and reissued a year later as *The True Way to Vertue and Happinesse: Intreating Specially of CONSTANCIE in publicke Calamities, and private Afflictions,* (London, 1623). Other neo-Stoic writers were Philippe de Mornay whose *Excellent Discours de la Vie et de la Mort* was translated in 1592 by the Countess of Pembroke, and the 'English Seneca', Joseph Hall, in his *Heaven upon Earth* (London, 1606) and *Characters of Vertues and Vices* (London, 1608). The original philosophical works of Epictetus, Cicero, Marcus Aurelius and Seneca were all widely available, both in Greek or Latin, and the vernacular. For a useful discussion of the Renaissance neo-Stoic revival, see Hoopes, *Right Reason in the English Renaissance*, pp. 33–45 and 132–45; Baker, *The Wars of Truth*, pp. 110–16; Gilles Monsarrat, 'Les Themes Stoiciens Dans La Litterature de La Renaissance Anglaise' (unpublished thesis, University of Paris, 1974).
31 Joseph Hall, *Heaven upon Earth*, sig.E12:

> None but those who have hearde the desperat complaints of some guilty *Spyra*, or whose soules have beene a little scorched with these flames, can enough conceive of the horror of this estate [of despair]; it beeing the policie of our common enemie to conceale it so long, that wee may see and feele it at once: least wee should feare it, before it be too late to bee avoyded.

32 B. T. Spencer's essay in *Seventeenth-Century Studies* explores Massinger's debt to Roman Stoicism and to Seneca in particular, and the following discussion owes much to his study.
33 *The Wars of Truth*, p. 111.
34 Some of these are explored by Hoopes, *Right Reason in the English Renaissance*, p. 135.
35 *Epictetus his Morals*, trans. George Stanhope, second edition (London, 1700), sigs.A7ᵛ–A8. Quoted in Baker, *The Wars of Truth*, p. 114.
36 Seneca, *Ad Lucilium Epistulae Morales*, LXXI. 32, trans. Richard N. Gunmere, 3 vols. (Cambridge, Mass: Harvard University Press, 1920), II.
37 Cicero, *De Officiis*, I.xxviii.100, trans. Walter Miller (Cambridge, Mass: Heinemann and Harvard University Press, 1913).
38 *De Officiis*, I.xxviii.101.
39 Cf. Dunn, *Philip Massinger: The Man and the Playwright*, p. 122.

40 See 'Natural Law', *Encyclopaedia Britannica*, fifteenth edition (1981), XII, 863–5.
41 The phrase is, of course, borrowed from Hooker. Compare 'The Laws of Ecclesiastical Polity', I.vii.4.
42 *The Wars of Truth*, p. 114.
43 Cf. Spencer, 'Philip Massinger', p. 74.
44 *Two Bookes of Constancie*, sig.A3.
45 *Elizabethan Dramatists*, p. 142; *Le Drame de Massinger*, p. 133.
46 *Ad Lucilium Epistulae Morales*, LXVI, 10.
47 Whitney Oates (ed.), 'The Meditations of Marcus Aurelius Antoninus' in *The Stoic and Epicurean Philosophers* (1940), p. 514. Quoted in Hoopes, *Right Reason in the English Renaissance*, p. 42.
48 Perkins, 'The Whole Treatise of Cases of Conscience', in *William Perkins: English Puritanist*, p. 179.
49 *Two Bookes of Constancie*, sigs.C1^v, C2.
50 See *Institutes*, II.ii.23.
51 L. Annaeus Seneca, *Minor Dialogues*, trans. Aubrey Stewart (London, 1889), p.16.
52 *Two Bookes of Constance*, sig.H2.
53 *The Golden Book of Marcus Aurelius*, trans. Meric Casaubon (London: J. M. Dent and New York, 1906), p. 94.
54 Epictetus, *The Discourses as Reported by Arrian*, I.vi.12–21, trans. W. A. Oldfather, 2 vols. (London: Heinemann, and Cambridge, Mass: Harvard University Press, 1925).
55 *The Ture Way to Vertue and Happiness*, sig.K4^v.
56 *The Workes of Lucius Annaeus Seneca, Both Morall and Naturall*, trans. Thomas Lodge (London, 1614), sig.Tt4^v. I have cited the contemporary translation here as its phrasing and vocabulary are rather more illuminating than that of any modern translation.
57 Henry Cross, *Vertues Common-Wealth or The High-Way to Honour* (London, 1603), sig.B2.
58 *Philip Massinger: The Man and the Playwright*, p. 177.
59 *Two Bookes of Constancie*, sig.L3^v.
60 ibid., sig.L4^v.
61 ibid., sig.L3^v.
62 Sigs.B.5, D4^v, D5.
63 *Two Bookes of Constancie*, sig.L4.
64 ibid., sig.L4^v.
65 ibid., sig.L4^v.
66 ibid., sig.L4^v.
67 Cf. Dunn, *Philip Massinger: The Man and the Playwright*, p. 70; Cruikshank, *Philip Massinger*, pp. 73–6; Stephen, *Hours in a Library, II*, pp. 162–6.
68 *Le Drame de Massinger*, p. 133
69 *The True Way to Vertue and Happinesse*, sig.N5^v.
70 *Philip Massinger: The Man and the Playwright*, p. 72.
71 *Elizabethan Dramatists*, pp. 138–40.

Chapter 10

1 For the purposes of my argument, I accept, as do all recent commentators, Ford's authorship of the two prose pamphlets, *The Golden Mean* (1613) and *A Line of Life* (1620) and, in addition, the religious poem *Christes Bloodie*

Sweat (1613). See M. Joan Sargeaunt, 'Writings Ascribed to John Ford by Joseph Hunter in *Chorus Vatum*', *RES*, 10 (1934), 165–76; R. Davril, *Le Drame de John Ford* (Paris: Marcel Didier, 1954), pp. 83–4; H. J. Oliver, *The Problem of John Ford* (Melbourne: Melbourne University Press, 1955), pp. 12–21; C. Leech, *John Ford and the Drama of his Time* (London: Chatto & Windus, 1957), p. 22; G. F. Sensabaugh, *The Tragic Muse of John Ford* (Stanford: Stanford University Press, and London, 1944), p. 174.

2 John Ford, *A Line of Life: Pointing at the Immortalitie of a Vertuous Name* (London, 1620), sig.B5.

3 See Monsarrat, 'Les Themes Stoiciens Dans La Littérature de La Renaissance Anglaise', p. 602. He writes categorically that 'Le stoicisme est absent de deux tragédies: *Love's Sacrifice* et *'Tis Pity She's a Whore*'.

4 I. F., *Christes Bloodie Sweat*, sig.C1^v.

5 Sigs.C2^v, C3, H4^v.

6 ibid., sig.F2.

7 *Institutes*, II.i.7.

8 See Sensabaugh, *The Tragic Muse of John Ford*, pp. 95–172. This writer's well-known thesis is that Ford was decisively influenced by Queen Henrietta Maria's cult of Platonic love, which 'featured in her new English court ideals of beauty and love reminiscent of the sonnets of Petrarch, of sixteenth-century Italian pastorals, of Spanish romances, of French Renaissance poetry and prose, and even of tales of medieval chivalry' (p. 106).

9 Several scholars have traced the influence of Burton's popular science upon Ford's characterization of Giovanni. See Stuart Sherman, 'John Ford's Debt to His Predecessors and Contemporaries, and His Contribution to the Decadence of the Drama' (unpublished dissertation, Harvard University, 1906), pp. 175ff., 405; Mary E. Cochnower, 'John Ford', in *Seventeenth Century Studies*, ed. Robert Schafer (Princeton, New Jersey: Princeton University Press, 1933), pp. 123–275 (pp. 123–201); S. Blaine Ewing, *Burtonian Melancholy in the Plays of John Ford* (Princeton, New Jersey: Princeton University Press, 1940), pp. 71–6; Sensabaugh, *The Tragic Muse of John Ford*, pp. 24–93; Mark Stavig, *John Ford and the Traditional Moral Order* (Madison, Milwaukee: University of Wisconsin Press, and London, 1968), p. 109. Sensabaugh argues that Giovanni suffers from Burtonian 'Love Melancholy', Cochnower and Ewing that he is a victim of 'Religious Melancholy in defect'. The two states do not seem to me to be mutually exclusive: his main symptoms – sighs, tears, incurable sadness, over-bookishness, decline into eventual desperation – are capable of both diagnoses, and my references to Burton are not intended in any case to indicate any presupposition, nor to re-open an old debate.

10 Ornstein, *The Moral Vision*, p. 204.

11 See Fotherby, *Atheomastix*: 'all impious *Atheists*, and deniers of God . . . are, in very deede, no better than meere fooles.' Sig.M5^v.

12 See Vaughan, *The Golden-grove*, sig.C2; Dove, *A Confusation of Atheisme*, sig.D1^v.

13 Psalms 14:1; 53:1.

14 Herndl, *The High Design*, p. 261.

15 *Summa Theologica*, Part II. ii. Q. 154, Art. 9.

16 *Marsilio Ficino's Commentary on Plato's Symposium*, the text and a translation with an introduction by Sears Reynolds Jayne, University of Missouri Studies, XIX, 1 (Columbia, Missouri, 1944). As Jayne makes succinctly clear in his introduction, 'Ficino insists that we realize that, in this life, body and

soul are inseparable, intimate partners in the same activity; that our ladder
of love must begin with love of the body, that the desires of the body are
not wicked in themselves . . . but are wicked only as man loses the sense of
proportion which enables him to see that earthly desires are only the beginning of the path up which we trudge to the perception of divinity' (p. 26).

17 Cf.

> All this I'll do, to free me from the rod
> of vengeance; else I'll swear my fate's my god.
>
> (I.i.83–4)

This initiates a series of references by Giovanni to the notion of being
governed by fate, rather than providence (cf. I.ii.139; I.ii.224–5; III.ii.20;
V.v.11–12; V.vi.11,72). This substitution is one of the more significant symptoms of his atheism. In one of his classic disquisitions upon the nature of
divine providence, Calvin in the *Institutes* excludes not only fortune and fate
from the governance of the universe, but the contingency which depends
upon human free will: 'no cause must be sought for but the will of of God'.
I.xvi.8.

18 *The Anatomy of Melancholy*, III, 440–1.
19 Thomas Morton, *A Treatise of the threefolde state of man*, sig.R7ᵛ.
20 Cyrus Hoy, ' "Ignorance in Knowledge"; Marlowe's Faustus and Ford's
    Giovanni', *MP*, 57 (1960), 145–54 (p. 148).
21 R. J. Kaufmann, 'Ford's Tragic Perspective', *Texas Studies in Literature and
    Language*, 1 (1960), 522–37, reprinted in *Elizabethan Drama: Modern Essays
    in Criticism*, ed. Kaufmann, pp. 356–72 (p. 366).
22 John Downame, *The Second Part of the Christian Warfare*, sig.V3ᵛ.
23 Sig.C1ᵛ.
24 Ellis-Fermor, *The Jacobean Drama*, p. 244.
25 Irving Ribner, *Jacobean Tragedy: The Quest for Moral Order* (London:
    1962), p. 168.
26 The point is made by Stavig, *John Ford and the Traditional Moral Order*,
    pp. 111–12: and by Derek Roper (ed.), *'Tis Pity She's a Whore*, The Revels
    Plays, (London: Methuen, 1975), pp. lii-iii.
27 Sig.D2.
28 See Cochnower, 'John Ford', pp. 203–4.
29 *The Anatomy of Melancholy*, III, 18.
30 ibid., III, 436.
31 Oliver, *The Problem of John Ford*, p. 95.
32 Brian Morris (ed.), *'Tis Pity She's a Whore*, New Mermaids, (London: Benn,
    1968), p. xv.
33 *A Line of Life*, sig.B10.
34 St Augustine is quoted by Calvin in the *Institutes*, II.iv.4.
35 Perkin Warbeck's words 'the fulness of our fate – Whose minister, necessity,
    will perfect – ' are yet another indication, if any further were needed, of
    Ford's deterministic viewpoint. *Perkin Warbeck*, III.ii.100–1. Cited from the
    Revels Plays edition, ed. Peter Ure (London: Methuen, 1968).
36 Cf. Ellis-Fermor, *The Jacobean Drama*, p. 235.
37 The historical 'accidents' of this struggle are different, of course; the ortho-
    dox beliefs in this case, are those mediated predominantly by Calvin; the
    'emergent individualism and emancipated faith in nature' is that impact of
    the 'new philosophy' which, in the later seventeenth century, was to make
    such wide distinctions between religion and science. For a full discussion of

the relation of some of these ideas to Ford, see Sensabaugh, *The Tragic Muse*.
38 Cf. the prefatory poem 'To My Friend the Author' by Thomas Ellice, l.10.

Conclusion

1 See, for example, Theseus's long philosophical speech in *The Knight's Tale* in defence of divine providence, a compound of Boethian Stoicism and medieval scholasticism, in which 'the faire cheyne of love' that orders the mutable and corruptive world, has its fount and origin in the divine source of all motion 'The Firste Moevere of the cause above'. *The Knight's Tale*, II.2987–8, in *The Complete Works of Geoffrey Chaucer*, ed. F. N. Robinson, second edition (London: Oxford University Press, 1957), p. 46.
2 'A Discourse of Conscience', p. 68.
3 *A Guide to Godlynesse*, sig.G5.

Bibliography

The first section comprises the editions used of those plays whose extended analysis forms the basis of individual chapters. The second section contains all other books and articles found useful or relevant in the preparation of this book.

I: PLAY TEXTS

B. R., *Apius and Virginia* (London, 1575), facsimile edition prepared by R. B. McKerrow, Malone Society (London: Chiswick Press, 1911)

Ford, John, *'Tis Pity She's a Whore*, ed. Brian Morris, The New Mermaids (London: Benn, 1968; reprinted 1978)

    A Newe Interlude of Impacyente Povertye, from the quarto of 1560, ed. R. B. McKerrow (W. Bang (ed.), *Materialen zur Kunde des älteren englischen Dramas*, 33) (Louvain: A. Uystpruyst, 1911)

Marlowe, Christopher, *Doctor Faustus*, ed. Roma Gill, The New Mermaids (London: Benn, 1965)

Massinger, Philip, *The Plays and Poems*, ed. Philip Edwards and Colin Gibson, 5 vols. (Oxford: Clarendon Press, 1976)

Shakespeare, William, *Hamlet*, ed. Harold Jenkins, The Arden Shakespeare (London: Methuen, 1982)

    King Richard III, ed. Anthony Hammond, The Arden Shakespeare (London: Methuen, 1981)

    Macbeth, ed. Kenneth Muir, ninth edition, The Arden Shakespeare (London: Methuen, 1962; reprinted 1966)

Tourneur, Cyril, *The Atheist's Tragedy*, ed. Brian Morris and Roma Gill, The New Mermaids (London: Benn, 1976)

Webster, John, *The Duchess of Malfi*, ed. Elizabeth M. Brennan, The New Mermaids (London: Benn, 1964)

W[ilson], R[obert], *A Right Excellent and Famous Comoedy called the Three Ladies of London* (London, 1584)

    The Pleasant and Stately Morall, of the Three Lordes and three Ladies of London (London, 1590)

Woodes, Nathaniel, *The Conflict of Conscience*, ed. Herbert Davis and F. P.

Wilson, facsimile edition, Malone Society (Oxford: Oxford University Press, 1952)

    The World and the Child: otherwise Mundus et Infans (1522), prepared under the Supervision and Editorship of John S. Farmer, Tudor Facsimile Texts (London: printed privately, 1909)

II: OTHER MATERIAL

Adams, Thomas, *The Workes* (London, 1630)

Alexander, Nigel, 'Intelligence in *The Duchess of Malfi*', in *John Webster*, ed. Brian Morris, Mermaid Critical Commentaries (London: Benn, 1970).

Allen, Don Cameron, *The Star-Crossed Renaissance* (Durham, North Carolina: Duke University Press, 1941)

Ames, William, *Conscience with the Power and Cases Thereof* ([n.p.], 1639)

Anderson, Ruth Leila, *Elizabethan Psychology and Shakespeare's Plays*, University of Iowa Humanistic Studies, 3, IV (Iowa, 1927)

Arber, Edward (ed.), *Transcript of the Register of the Company of Stationers of London*, 1554–1640 A.D. (London: printed privately (5 vols.), 1875)

Aristotle, *The Ethics of Aristotle*, trans. J. A. K. Thompson (London: Allen & Unwin, 1953)

    The Works, trans. under the editorship of J. A. Smith and W. D. Ross, 12 vols. (London: Clarendon Press, 1910–52; reprinted 1963–8)

Augustine, St, Bishop of Hippo, *The City of God*, trans. John Healey, ed. R. V. G. Tasker with an introduction by Sir Ernest Barker, 2 vols. (London: J. M. Dent, 1945, reprinted 1962)

    Earlier Writings, trans. with an introduction by John H. S. Burleigh, Library of Christian Classics, VI (London: SCM Press, 1953)

Aurelius Antoninus, Marcus, *The Golden Book of Marcus Aurelius*, trans. Meric Casaubon (London and New York: J. M. Dent, 1906)

    'The Meditations', in *The Stoic and Epicurean Philosophers*, ed. Whitney J. Oates (New York: Modern Library, 1940)

Babb, Lawrence, *The Elizabethan Malady: A Study of Melancholia in English Literature from 1580 to 1642* (East Lancing: Michigan State College Press, 1951)

Bacon, Francis, *The Advancement of Learning*, ed. G. W. Kitchin (London: J. M. Dent, 1973)

Bainton, Roland, *The Reformation of the Sixteenth Century*, fourth edition (London: Hodder & Stoughton, 1963)

Baker, Herschel, *The Wars of Truth: Studies in the Decay of Christian Humanism in the Earlier Seventeenth Century* (Cambridge, Mass: Staples Press, 1952)

Baker-Smith, Dominic, 'Religion and John Webster', in *John Webster*, ed. Brian Morris, Mermaid Critical Commentaries (London: Benn 1970)

Baldini, Gabriele, *John Webster e il linguagio della tragedia* (Rome: Edizioni deu'Ateneo 1953)

Bale, Johan, *Comedy Concernynge Thre Lawes*, ed. M. M. Arnold Schroeer (Halle: Max Niemeyer, 1882)

Barber, C. L., 'The form of Faustus' fortunes good or bad', *TDR*, 8 (Summer, 1964), 92–119.

Batman, Stephen, *Batman uppon Bartholome, his Booke De Proprietatibus Rerum* (London, 1582)

Battenhouse, Roy W., 'The Ghost in *Hamlet*; a Catholic "Linchpin"?', *SP*, 48 (1951), 161–92

    'Marlowe Reconsidered: Some Reflections on Levin's *Overreacher*', *JEGP*, 52 (1953), 531–42

   Marlowe's 'Tamburlaine': A Study in Renaissance Moral Philosophy (Nashville, Tennessee: Vanderbilt University Press, 1941, reprinted 1964)

Beaumont and Fletcher, *A King and No King*, ed. Robert K. Turner, Jr, Regents Renaissance Drama (London: Edward Arnold, 1964)

Belsey, Catherine, 'The Case of Hamlet's Conscience', *SP*, 76 (1979), 127–48

Bernard, Richard, *Christian See to thy Conscience, Or, A Treatise of the nature, the kinds and manifold differences of Conscience . . .* (London, 1631)

Berry, Ralph, *The Art of John Webster* (Oxford: Clarendon Press, 1972)

Bethell, S. L., *The Cultural Revolution of the Seventeenth Century* (London: Dennis Dobson, 1963)

Bevington, David M., 'Determining the Indeterminate: The Oxford Shakespeare', *SQ*, 38 (Winter, 1987)

   From 'Mankind' to Marlowe; Growth of Structure in the Popular Drama of Tudor England (Cambridge, Mass.: Harvard University Press, 1962)

The Bible: Authorized Version

Bluestone, Max, 'Libido Speculandi', in *Re-interpretations of Elizabethan Drama*, ed. with a foreword by Norman Rabkin (New York and London: Columbia University Press, 1969), pp. 33–83

Boas, Frederick, S., *Christopher Marlowe: A Biographical and Critical Study* (Oxford: Clarendon Press, 1940)

Bogard, Travis, *The Tragic Satire of John Webster* (Berkeley and Los Angeles: University of California Press, 1955)

Boklund, Gunnar, *'The Duchess of Malfi': Sources, Themes, Characters* (Cambridge, Mass.: Harvard University Press, 1962)

Bolton, Robert, *A Discourse About the State of True Happinesse* (London, 1611)
   Instructions for a Right Comforting Afflicted Consciences (London, 1631)

Bourne, Immanuel, *The Anatomie of Conscience* (London, 1623)

Bowers, Fredson, 'The Death of Hamlet', in *Studies in the English Renaissance Drama*, ed. Josephine W. Bennett, Oscar Cargill and Vernon Hall, Jr (London: Peter Owen and Vision Press, 1959)
   Elizabethan Revenge Tragedy, 1587–1642 (Princeton, New Jersey: Princeton University Press, 1940)

Boyer, C. V., *The Villain as Hero in Elizabethan Tragedy* (London: Russell & Russell, 1914)

Boyle, R., 'Philip Massinger', *DNB*, XIII, 10–16.

Bradbrook, Muriel C., 'Fate and Chance in *The Duchess of Malfi*', from 'Two Notes upon Webster', *MLR*, 42 (1947) 281–91
   'Marlowe's *Doctor Faustus* and the Eldritch Tradition', in *Essays on Shakespeare and Elizabethan Drama in Honor of Hardin Craig*, ed. Richard Hosley (Columbia, Missouri: University of Missouri Press, 1962), pp. 83–90
   Themes and Conventions of Elizabethan Tragedy (Cambridge: Cambridge University Press, 1935)

Bradley, A. C., *Shakespearean Tragedy* (London: Macmillan, 1932)

Brandes, Georg, *William Shakespeare: A Critical Study* (London: Heinemann, 1898)

Bredvold, L. I., 'The Naturalism of Donne in Relation to some Renaissance Traditions', *JEGP*, 22 (1923), 471–502

Brennan, Elizabeth, M., 'The Relationship between Brother and Sister in the Plays of John Webster', *MLR*, 58 (1963), 488–94

Bright, Timothy, *Treatise of Melancholie* (London, 1586)

Brissenden, Alan, 'Impediments to Love: A Theme in John Ford', *Renaissance Drama*, 7 (1964), 95–102

Brockbank, J. P., *Marlowe: Dr Faustus* (London: Edward Arnold, 1962)

Brooke, C. F. Tucker, *The Tudor Drama* (Cambridge, Mass.: Houghton Mifflin, 1911)

Brooke, Nicholas, 'The Moral Tragedy of Dr Faustus', *The Cambridge Journal*, 5 (1952), 662–87

    'Marlowe the Dramatist', in *Elizabethan Theatre*, ed. John Russell Brown and Bernard Harris, Stratford-upon-Avon Studies, 9 (London: Edward Arnold, 1966)

    Shakespeare's Early Tragedies (London: Methuen, 1968)

Brooke, Rupert, *John Webster and the Elizabethan Drama* (London: Sidgwick & Jackson, 1916, reprinted 1917)

Buckley, G. T., *Atheism in the English Renaissance* (Chicago: Chicago University Press, 1932)

Burton, Robert, *The Anatomy of Melancholy*, ed. A. R. Shilleto, 3 vols. (London: Bell, 1896)

Bush, Douglas, *The Renaissance and English Humanism* (Toronto: University of Toronto Press, 1939)

Bush, Geoffrey, *Shakespeare and the Natural Condition* (Cambridge Mass.: Harvard University Press, 1956)

Byfield, Nicholas, *Sermons upon the first chapter of the Epistle Generall of Peter* (London, 1617)

Calderwood, James L., '*The Duchess of Malfi*: Styles of Ceremony', *Essays in Criticism*, 12 (1962), 133–47

Calvin, Jean, *An admonicion against astrology judiciall*, trans. G. G.[ylby] (London, 1561)

    A little booke concernynge offences, trans. A. Goldinge ([n.p.], 1567)

Calvin, John, *A Commentary upon Genesis*, trans. and ed. John King, 2 vols. in 1 (London: The Banner of Truth Trust, 1965)

    Institutes of the Christian Religion, trans. Henry Beveridge, 2 vols. (London: James Clarke, 1953)

Cameron, Kenneth, 'Tourneur's *Transformed Metamorphosis*', *RES*, 16 (1940), 18–24

Campbell, Lily B. 'Doctor Faustus: a Case of Conscience', *PMLA*, 67 (1952), 219–39

    Shakespeare's 'Histories': Mirrors of Elizabethan Policy (San Marino, Calif.: Huntington Library, 1947)

    Shakespeare's Tragic Heroes: Slaves of Passion (Cambridge: Cambridge University Press, 1930)

    'Theories of Revenge in Elizabethan England', *MP*, 28 (1931), 281–96

Carpenter, Richard, *The Conscionable Christian, or the Indevour of Saint Paul* (London, 1623)

Cartwright, Thomas, *Cartwrightiana*, ed. Albert Peel and Leland Carlson (London: Allen & Unwin, 1951)

Cecil, David, *Poets and Story-Tellers* (London: Constable, 1949)

    Certain Sermons or Homilies Appointed to be Read in Churches in the Time of Queen Elizabeth of Famous Memory, published under the direction of the Tract Committee (London, 1864)

Chamber, John, *A Treatise Against Judicial Astrologie* (London, 1601)

Chaucer, Geoffrey, *The Complete Works*, ed. F. N. Robinson, second edition (London: Oxford University Press, 1974)

Chelli, Maurice, *Le Drame de Massinger* (Lyon: M. Audin, 1923)

Chew, Samuel, C., *The Pilgrimage of Life* (Yale: Yale University Press, 1962)

Cicero, *De Officiis*, trans. Walter Miller (London: Heinemann and Cambridge, Mass.: Harvard University Press, 1913)

Clemen, Wolfgang, *A Commentary on Shakespeare's 'Richard III'* (London: Methuen, 1968)

Cochnower, Mary Edith, 'John Ford', in *Seventeenth Century Studies*, ed. Robert Shafer (Princeton, New Jersey: Princeton University Press, 1933), pp. 123–275

Cole, Douglas, *Suffering and Evil in the Plays of Christopher Marlowe* (Princeton, New Jersey: Princeton University Press, 1962)

Coleridge, S. T., *Coleridge on the Seventeenth Century*, ed. R. F. Brinkley (Durham, North Carolina: Duke University Press, 1955)

Coplestone, Frederick, *A History of Philosophy*, 8 vols. (London: Burns, Oates & Washbourne, 1963)

Cowper, William, *The Anatomie of a Christian Man* (London, 1613)

Craig, Hardin, *The Enchanted Glass* (New York: OxfordUniversity Press, 1936)
    English Religious Drama of the Middle Ages (Oxford: Clarendon Press, 1955)
    An Interpretation of Shakespeare (New York: The Dryden Press, 1948)
    'Morality Plays and Elizabethan Drama', *SQ*, 1 (1950), 64–72

Craik, T. W., *The Tudor Interlude* (Leicester: Leicester University Press, 1958)

Creeth, Edmund, *Mankynde in Shakespeare* (Athens, Georgia: University of Georgia Press, 1976)

Crosse, Henry, *Vertues Common-wealth or The High-way to Honour* (London, 1603)

Cruikshank, A. H., *Philip Massinger* (Oxford: Blackwell, 1920)

Cruttwell, Patrick, 'The Morality of Hamlet – "Sweet Prince" or "Arrant Knave" ', in *Hamlet* ed. John Russell Brown and Bernard Harris, Stratford-upon-Avon Studies, 5 (London: Edward Arnold, 1963), pp. 110–28

Curry, W. C., *Shakespeare's Philosophical Patterns* (Baton Rouge, Louisiana State University Press, Louisiana, 1959)

Danby, John F., *Shakespeare's Doctrine of Nature: A Study of 'King Lear'* (London: Faber & Faber, 1949)

Davidson, Clifford, 'Doctor Faustus of Wittenburg', *PMLA*, 59 (1962) 514–23

Davies, C. W., 'The Structure of *The Duchess of Malfi*: An Approach', *English*, 12 (1958), 89–93

Davies, Daniel Horton, *Worship and Theology in England*, 5 vols. (London: Oxford University Press, 1966–70) I, (1970)

Davril, R., *Le Drame de John Ford* (Paris: Marcel Didier, 1954)

Dawley, Powell Mills, *John Whitgift and the Reformation* (London: A. & C. Black, 1955)

Dent, R. W., *John Webster's Borrowing* (Berkeley and Los Angeles, Calif.: University of California Press, 1960)

Dessen, Alan C., *Jonson's Moral Comedy* (Evanston, Illinois: Northwestern University Press, 1971)

Dick, H., 'The Authorship of *Foure Great Lyers* (1585)', *The Library*, IV, 19 (1938–9), 311–14

Dickens, A. G., *Reformation and Society in Sixteenth Century Europe* (London: Thames & Hudson, 1966)

Dodsworth, Martin, *Hamlet Closely Observed* (London and Dover, New Hampshire: Athlone Press, 1985)

Donne, John, *Essays in Divinity*, ed. E. M. Simpson, (Oxford: Clarendon Press, 1952)
    'The First Anniversarie: An Anatomy of the World', in *The Epithalamions*

Anniversaries and Epicedes of John Donne, ed. with introduction and commentary by W. Milgate (Oxford: Clarendon Press, 1978)

    Pseudo-Martyr (London, 1610)

Dove, John, *A Confutation of Atheisme* (London, 1605)

Downame, John, *The Christian Warfare* (London, 1608)

    A Guide to Godlynesse, Or a Treatise of a Christian Life (London, 1622)

    The Second Part of the Christian Warfare (London, 1611)

Du Bartas, Guillaume de Saluste, *Guillaume de Saluste du Bartas: his devine weekes and workes*, trans. J. Sylvester (London, 1605)

Dunn, T. A., *Philip Massinger: The Man and the Playwright* (Ghana and London: Thomas Nelson, 1957)

Duthie, G. I., 'Some Observations on Marlowe's *Doctor Faustus*', *Archiv*, 203 (1966), 81–96

Du Vair, Guillaume, *The True Way to Vertue and Happinesse: Intreating Specially of CONSTANCIE in publike Calamities, and private Afflictions* (London, 1623)

Dwyer, William, W. G., *A Study of Webster's Use of Renaissance Natural and Moral Philosophy*, Salzburg Studies in English Literature, ed. James Hogg (Salzburg: University of Salzburg, 1973)

Dyke, Jeremiah, *Good Conscience: Or a Treatise shewing the Nature, Meanes, Marks, Benefit and Necessity Thereof* (London, 1624)

Ekeblad, Inga-Stina, 'An Approach to Tourneur's Imagery', *MLR*, 64 (1959), 489–98

Eliot, T. S., *Elizabethan Dramatists* (London: Faber & Faber, 1963)

    Selected Essays, third edition (London: Faber & Faber, 1951)

Elliott, G. R., *Scourge and Minister* (New York: Duke University Press, 1965)

Ellis-Fermor, Una M., *Christopher Marlowe* (London: Methuen, 1927)

    The Jacobean Drama: An Interpretation (London: Methuen, 1936)

Elton, William, R., *'King Lear' and the Gods* (San Marino, Calif.: Huntington Library, 1966)

Emslie, McD., 'Motives on Malfi', *Essays in Criticism*, 9 (1959), 391–405

Epictetus, *The Discourses as Reported by Arrian*, trans. W. A. Oldfather, 2 vols. (London: Heinemann, and Cambridge, Mass.: Harvard University Press, 1925)

    Epictetus His Morals, trans. George Stanhope, second edition (London, 1700)

Ewing, S. Blaine, *Burtonian Melancholy in the Plays of John Ford* (Princeton, New Jersey: Princeton University Press, 1940)

F. I., *Christes Bloodie Sweat, or the Sonne of God in his Agonie* (London, 1613)

Farnham, Willard, *The Medieval Heritage of Elizabethan Tragedy* (Berkeley, Calif.: University of California Press, 1936)

    Shakespeare's Tragic Frontier: The World of his Final Tragedies (Berkeley and Los Angeles, Calif.: University of California Press, 1950)

Ficino, Marsilio, *Commentary on Plato's Symposium*, the text and a translation with an introduction by Sears Reynolds Jayne, University of Missouri Studies, XIX, 1 (Columbia, Missouri: University of Missouri Press, 1944)

Fisch, Harol, *Hamlet and the Word* (New York: Frederick Ungar, 1971)

Fletcher, Phineas, *The Purple Island, or the Isle of Man* (London, 1633)

Ford, John, *The Broken Heart*, ed. Brian Morris, The New Mermaids (London: Benn; 1965)

    The Golden Mean (London, 1613)

    A Line of Life: Pointing at the Immortalitie of a Vertuous Name (London, 1620)

    Perkin Warbeck, ed. Peter Ure, The Revels Plays (London: Methuen, 1968)

'Tis Pity She's a Whore, ed. N. W. Bawcutt, Regents Renaissance Drama Series (London: Edward Arnold, 1966)

'Tis Pity She's a Whore, ed. Derek Roper, The Revels Plays (London: Methuen, 1975)

Forker, Charles R., *The Skull Beneath the Skin* (Carbondale and Edwardsville, Illinois: Southern Illinois University Press, 1986)

Fotherby, Martin, *Atheomastix: Clearing four Truthes, Against Atheists and Infidels* (London, 1622)

Frost, David L., *The School of Shakespeare* (Cambridge: Cambridge University Press, 1968)

Frye, Roland M., 'Marlowe's *Doctor Faustus*: The Repudiation of Humanity', *South Atlantic Quarterly*, 55 (1956), 322–8

Gardner, Helen, *The Business of Criticism* (Oxford: Clarendon Press, 1959)

'The Tragedy of Damnation', *Essays and Studies*, 1 (1948), 46–66, reprinted in *Elizabethan Drama: Modern Essays in Criticism*, ed. R. J. Kaufmann (New York: Oxford University Press, 1961), 320–41

Gilson, Etienne, *History of Christian Philosophy in the Middle Ages* (London: Steed & Ward, 1955)

Goddard, Harold C., *The Meaning of Shakespeare* (Chicago: University of Chicago Press, 1951)

Goldman, Arnold, 'The Fruitful Plot of Scholarism Graced', *Notes and Queries*, 209, New Series, 11 (1964), 264

Grane, Leif, *Peter Abelard: Philosophy and Christianity in the Middle Ages*, ed. Derek Baker, trans. Frederick and Christine Crowley (London: Allen & Unwin, 1970)

Greene, Robert, *The Scottish History of James the Fourth* ed. J. A. Lavin, The New Mermaids (London: Benn, 1967)

Greenham, Richard, *Propositions containing answers to certaine demaunds in divers spirituall matters, specially concerning the conscience . . .* (Edinburgh, 1597)

Two Treatises of the comforting of an afflicted conscience (London, 1598)

Greg, W. W., 'The Damnation of Faustus', *MLR*, 41 (1946), 97–107

Greville, Fulke, *The Works of Verse and Prose Complete*, ed. with an introduction by A. B. Grosart, 4 vols. (Edinburgh, 1870, reprinted New York: Arms Press, Inc., 1960)

Gribaldi, Matthew, *A notable and marveilous Epistle of the famous Doctour, Matthewe Gribalde, Professor of Lawe, in the Universitie of Padua: concernying the terrible judgemente of GOD, upon hym that for feare of men, denieth Christ and the knowne veritie: with a Preface of Doctor Calvine* (London, [1570])

Gunby, D. C., 'The Duchess of Malfi: A Theological Approach', in *John Webster*, ed. Brian Morris, Mermaid Critical Commentaries (London: Benn, 1970)

Hall, Joseph, *Characters of Vertues and Vices* (London, 1608)

Heaven upon Earth (London, 1606)

The Works, 12 vols. (Oxford: D. A. Talboys, 1837–9)

Hankins, John Erskine, *The Character of Hamlet* (Chapel Hill, North Carolina: University of North Carolina Press, 1941)

Happé, Peter, 'Tragic Themes in Three Tudor Moralities', *SEL*, 5 (1965), 207–27

Harbage, A., *Annals of English Drama*, rev. S. Schoenbaum (London: Methuen, 1964) 3rd edn. rev. S. Stoler Wagonheim (London: Routledge, 1989)

Shakespeare and the Rival Traditions (New York: Macmillan, 1952)

Hardwick, Charles, *A History of the Articles of Religion* (London: Bell, 1881)

Harris, Robert, *Six Sermons of Conscience*, second edition (London, 1630)

Hart, A. Tindal, *The Man in the Pew: 1558–1660* (London: John Baker, 1966)

Heilman, Robert, B., 'Satiety and Conscience: Aspects of *Richard III*', *Antioch Review*, 24 (1964), 57–73, reprinted in *Essays in Shakespearean Criticism*, ed. J. Calderwood and H. E. Toliver (Englewood Cliffs, New Jersey: Prentice Hall, 1970), pp. 137–51

'The Tragedy of Knowledge: Marlowe's Treatment of Faustus', *QRL*, 2 (1945–6), 316–32

Heller, Erich, 'Faust's Damnation: The Morality of Knowledge', *Listener*, 67 (1962), 59–61

Henson, H. H., *Studies in English Religion in the Seventeenth Century* (London: John Murray, 1903)

Herndl, George C., *The High Design: English Renaissance Tragedy and the Natural Law* (Lexington, Kentucky: University of Kentucky Press, 1970)

Heydon, Sir Christopher, *A Defence of Judiciall Astrologie* (Cambridge, 1603)

Heywood, Thomas, *A Woman Killed with Kindness*, ed. R. W. Van Fossen, The Revels Plays (London: Methuen, 1961)

Higgins, Michael H., 'The Influence of Calvinistic Thought in Tourneur's *Atheist's Tragedy*', *RES*, 19 (1943) 255–62

Hillerbrand, Hans J. (ed.), *The Protestant Reformation* (London and Melbourne: Macmillan, 1968)

Hobson, Alan, *Full Circle: Shakespeare and Moral Development* (London: Chatto & Windus, 1972)

Hogan, J. W., 'The Rod and the Candle: Conscience in the English Morality Plays, Shakespeare's *Macbeth*, and Tourneur's *The Atheist's Tragedy*' (unpublished Ph.D. dissertation, City University of New York, 1974)

Holinshed, Raphael, *The Third Volume of Chronicles* (London, 1586)

Holloway, John, *The Story of the Night: Studies in Shakespeare's Major Tragedies* (London: Routledge & Kegan Paul, 1961)

Honderich, Pauline, 'John Calvin and Doctor Faustus', *MLR*, 68 (1973), 1–13

Hooker, Richard, *The Works of that Learned and Judicious Divine Mr. Richard Hooker*, arranged by John Keble, seventh edition, 3 vols. (Oxford: Clarendon Press, 1888)

Hooper, John, *The Later Writings of Bishop Hooper*, ed. Charles Nevinson, Parker Society (Cambridge, 1852)

Hoopes, Robert, *Right Reason in the English Renaissance* (Cambridge, Mass.: Harvard University Press, 1962)

Houle, Peter J., *The English Morality and Related Drama: A Bibliographical Survey* (Hamden, Conn.: Archon Books, 1972)

Howard, Douglas, *Philip Massinger: A Critical Reassessment* (Cambridge: Cambridge University Press, 1985)

Hoy, Cyrus, ' "Ignorance in Knowledge": Marlowe's Faustus and Ford's Giovanni', *MP*, 57 (1960), 145–54

Hughes, Daniel E., 'The "Worm of Conscience" in *Richard III* and *Macbeth*', *English Journal*, 55 (1966), 845–52

Hughes, John, *St Paul's Exercise, or a Sermon of Conscience* (London, 1622)

Huit, Ephraim, *The Anatomy of Conscience* (London, 1626)

Hunter, Robert, G., *Shakespeare and the Mystery of God's Judgements* (Athens, Georgia: University of Georgia Press, 1976)

Jackson, William A., 'Woodes's *Conflict of Conscience*', *LTLS* (7 September 1933), 592

James, D. G., *The Dream of Learning* (Oxford: Clarendon Press, 1951)

Jenkins, Harold, 'Cyril Tourneur', *RES*, 17 (1941), 21–36

Jerome, S., *Commentary Upon Ezekiel* (Latin text in Migne, *Patrologia Latina*, vol. 25, col. 22), ed. and trans. Timothy C. Potts, *Conscience in Medieval Philosophy* (Cambridge: Cambridge University Press, 1980), pp. 79–80

Jones, William, *A Commentary upon the Epistles of Saint Paul to Philemon, and to the Hebrewes* (London, 1635)

Jorgensen, Paul A., *Our Naked Frailities: Sensational Art and Meaning in 'Macbeth'* (Berkeley and Los Angeles, Calif.: University of California Press, 1971)

Joseph, Bertram L., *Conscience and the King* (London: Chatto & Windus, 1953)

Joseph, Sister Miriam, 'Discerning the Ghost in Hamlet', *PMLA*, 76 (1961), 493–502

Kaufmann, R. J., 'Ford's Tragic Perspective', *Texas Studies in Literature and Language*, 1 (1960), 522–37, reprinted in *Elizabethan Drama: Modern Essays in Criticism*, ed. R. J. Kaufmann (New York: Oxford University Press, 1961), pp. 356–72

Kelly, Henry Ansgar, *Divine Providence in the England of Shakespeare's Histories* (Cambridge, Mass.: Harvard University Press, 1970)

Kelly, Kevin, *Conscience: Dictator or Guide? A Study in Seventeenth Century English Protestant Moral Theology* (London: Geoffrey Chapman, 1967)

Kilby, Richard, *The Burthen of a loaden conscience or the miserie of sinne* (Cambridge, 1608)

Kirschbaum, Leo, 'Marlowe's *Faustus*: A Reconsideration', *RES*, 19 (1943), 225–41

Kistner, A. L. and M. K., '*Macbeth:* A Treatise of Conscience', *Thoth*, 13 (1973), 27–43

Kitto, H. D. F., *Form and Meaning in Drama* (London: Methuen, 1956)

Knight, G. Wilson, *The Golden Labyrinth: A Study of British Drama* (London: Phoenix House, 1962)

   The Wheel of Fire, paperback edition (London: Methuen, 1961)

Knights, L. C., 'The Strange Case of Christopher Marlowe', in *Further Explorations* (Stanford: Stanford University Press, and London: Chatto & Windus, 1965), pp. 75–98

Kocher, Paul H., *Christopher Marlowe: A Study of his Thought, Learning and Character* (Chapel Hill, North Carolina: Russell & Russell, 1946, reprinted New York, 1962)

   Science and Religion in Elizabethan England (San Marino, Calif.: Huntingdon Library, 1953)

Koeppel, E., 'Philip Massinger', *CHEL*, VI, 141–65

Kristeller, Paul Oskar, *Renaissance Thought: vol. 1 The Classic, Scholastic, and Humanist Strains* (New York: Harper, 1961)

Lamb, Charles, comp., *Specimens of English Dramatic Poets, who lived about the Time of Shakespeare* (London: J. M. Dent, 1911)

La Primaudaye, Pierre de, *The French Academie. Fully Discoursed and finished in foure Bookes* (London, 1618)

Lawless, Donald S., *Philip Massinger and His Associates*, Ball State Monograph 10, Publications in English, 6 (Muncie, Indiana, 1967)

Lawlor, John, *Tragic Sense in Shakespeare* (London: Chatto & Windus, 1960)

Leech, Clifford, *John Ford and the Drama of His Time* (London: Chatto & Windus, 1957)

   John Webster: A Critical Study (London: Hogarth Press, 1951)

   Marlowe: A Collection of Critical Essays (Englewood Cliffs, New Jersey: Prentice Hall, 1964)

Shakespeare's Tragedies and Other Studies in Seventeenth Century Drama (London: Chatto & Windus, 1950)

Leff, Gordon, 'Nominalism-Realism' in *A Dictionary of Christian Theology*, ed. Alan Richardson (London: SCM Press, 1969) pp. 232–3

Lever, Christopher, *The Holy Pilgrime, leading the way to Heaven* (London, 1618)

Levin, Harry, *The Overreacher: A Study of Christopher Marlowe* (London: Faber & Faber, 1954)

The Question of Hamlet (New York: Oxford University Press, 1978)

Lewis, C. S., '*Hamlet:* The Prince or the Poem?', *PBA*, 28 (1943 for 1942), 139–54

Linaker, Robert, *A Comfortable Treatise for the reliefe of such as are afflicted in conscience*, second edition (London, 1601)

Lipsius, Justus, *Two Bookes of Constancie*, Englished by John Stradling (London, 1595)

Little, David, *Religion, Order and Law: A Study in Pre-Revolutionary England* (Oxford: Blackwell, 1970)

Lovejoy, A. O., *The Great Chain of Being* (Cambridge, Mass.: Harvard University Press, 1936)

Luther, Martin, *Luther's Works*, general eds. Jaroslav Pelikan (vols. 1–30) and Helmut T. Lehmann (vols. 31–55), 55 vols. (St. Louis and Philadelphia: Concordia Publishing House, 1956–67)

Martin Luther: Selections from his Writings, ed. and with an introduction by John Dillenburger (New York: Anchor Books, 1961)

The Table-Talk of Martin Luther, trans. and ed. W. Hazlitt (London: Bell 1911)

McAdoo, H. R., *The Structure of Caroline Moral Theology* (London: Longman, Green, 1949)

McAlindon, T., 'Classical Mythology and Christian Tradition in Marlowe's *Doctor Faustus*', *PMLA*, 81 (1966), 214–23

Shakespeare and Decorum (London: Macmillan, 1973)

McCloskey, John C., 'The Theme of Despair in Marlowe's *Faustus*', *College English*, 4 (1942), 110–13

MacCracken, Henry N., 'A Source of *Mundus et Infans*', *PMLA*, 23 (1908), 486–96

McCullen, Joseph T., 'Dr Faustus and Renaissance Learning', *MLR*, 51 (1956), 6–16

McDonough, Thomas M., *The Law and the Gospel in Luther* (Oxford: Oxford University Press, 1963)

McGee, Arthur, *The Elizabethan Hamlet* (New Haven and London: Yale University Press, 1987)

McGrath, Patrick, *Papists and Puritans under Elizabeth 1* (London: Blandford Press, 1967)

Mack, Maynard, 'The World of Hamlet', *The Yale Review*, 41 (1952), 502–25

Mahood, M. M., *Poetry and Humanism* (London: Cape, 1950)

Makkink, Henri Jacob, *Philip Massinger and John Fletcher: A Comparison* (New York: Haskell House, 1966)

Marlowe, Christopher, *Doctor Faustus, 1604–1616*. Parallel texts ed. W. W. Greg (Oxford: Clarendon Press, 1950)

Doctor Faustus, ed. John D. Jump, The Revels Plays (London: Methuen, 1962)

The Plays, ed. Leo Kirschbaum (Cleveland and New York: Meridian Books, 1962)

Marston, John, *The Scourge of Villainie* (London, 1599), facsimile edition, ed. G. B. Harrison (Edinburgh: Edinburgh University Press, 1966)
  The Works, ed. A. H. Bullen, 3 vols. (London: John C. Nimmo (1877), 1931)
Massinger, Philip, *The Plays*, ed. William Gifford, second edition, 4 vols. (London: W. Bulmer, 1813)
  The Unnatural Combat, ed. Robert Stockdale Telfer, Princeton Studies in English, 7 (Princeton, New Jersey, 1932)
Maxwell, J. C., 'The Sin of Faustus', *The Wind and the Rain*, 4 (1947), 49–52
Mercer, Peter, *Hamlet and the Acting of Revenge* (Iowa: University of Iowa Press, 1987)
Milton, John, 'Paradise Lost', in *The Poetical Works of John Milton*, ed. Helen Darbishire, 2 vols. (Oxford: Clarendon Press, 1952, reprinted 1967), I
Milward, Peter, *Shakespeare's Religious Background* (London: Sidgwick & Jackson, 1973)
Mizener, Arthur M., 'The Tragedy of Marlowe's *Dr. Faustus*', *College English*, 5 (1943), 70–5
Montaigne, Michel de, *The Essayes*, trans. John Florio, ed. J. I. M. Stewart (New York: The Modern Library, 1933)
  The Essays, trans. E. J. Trechmann with an introduction by J. M. Robertson, 2 vols. (London: Humphrey Milford, 1927)
Mornay, Philippe de, *Excellent Discours de la Vie et de la Mort* (La Rochelle, 1581)
  A discourse of life and death . . . done in English by the countesse of Pembroke (London, 1592)
Morris, Ivor, *Shakespeare's God: The Role of Religion in the Tragedies* (London: Allen & Unwin, 1972)
Morton, Thomas, *A Treatise of the threefolde state of man* (London, 1596)
Mosse, George L., *The Holy Pretence: A Study in Christianity and Reason of State from William Perkins to John Winthrop* (Blackwell, Oxford: 1957)
Moulton, R. G., *Shakespeare as a Dramatic Artist* (Oxford: Clarendon Press, 1901)
Mulryne, J. R., '*The White Devil* and *The Duchess of Malfi*', in *Jacobean Theatre*, ed. John Russell Brown and Bernard Harris, Stratford-upon-Avon Studies, 1 (London: Edward Arnold, 1960), pp. 201–25
Murray, Peter B., *A Study of Cyril Tourneur* (Philadelphia: University of Pennsylvania Press, 1964)
  A Study of John Webster (The Hague and Paris: Mouton, 1969)
Nashe, Thomas, *The Works*, ed. Ronald B. McKerrow, reprinted with corrections and supplementary notes under the editorship of F. P. Wilson, 5 vols. (Oxford: Blackwell, 1958)
'Natural Law', *Enclopoedia Britannica*, fifteenth edition (1981), XII, 863–5
Nemesius, Bishop of Emesa, *The Nature of Man*, Englished by Geo. Wither (London, 1636)
Nevo, Ruth, *Tragic Form in Shakespeare* (Princeton, New Jersey: Princeton University Press, 1972)
The New Cambridge Modern History, I, *The Renaissance, 1493–1520*, ed. G. R. Potter (Cambridge: Cambridge University Press, 1957)
  II, *The Reformation, 1520–1559*, ed. G. R. Elton (Cambridge: University Press, 1958)
  III, *The Counter-Reformation and Price Revolution, 1559–1610*, ed. R. B. Wernham (Cambridge: Cambridge University Press, 1968)

New, John F. H., *Anglican and Puritan: The Basis of Their Opposition, 1558–1640* (London: A. & C. Black, 1964)

Niebuhr, R., *The Nature and Destiny of Man*, 2 vols. (London: Nisbet, 1941–3, New York: Charles Scribner's Sons, 1945)

Oliver, H. J., *The Problem of John Ford* (Melbourne: Melbourne University Press, 1955)

Oliver, Leslie, 'John Foxe and *The Conflict of Conscience*, *RES*, 25 (1949), 1–9

Ornstein, Robert, '*The Atheist's Tragedy* and Renaissance Naturalism', *SP*, 51 (1954), 194–207

    The Moral Vision of Jacobean Tragedy (Wisconsin: University of Wisconsin Press, 1960)

    'Marlowe and God: The Tragic Theology of *Dr. Faustus*', *PMLA*, 83 (1968), 1378–85

Owst, G. R., *Literature and Pulpit in Medieval England*, second edition (Oxford: Blackwell, 1961, reprinted 1966)

P. W., *Foure Great Lyers, Striving who shall win the Silver Whetstone* (London, 1585)

Palmer, D. J., 'Elizabethan Tragic Heroes', in *Elizabethan Drama*, ed. John Russell Brown and Bernard Harris, Stratford-upon-Avon Studies, 9 (London: Edward Arnold, 1966), pp. 11–28.

Paul, Henry N., *The Royal Play of 'Macbeth'* (New York: Macmillan, 1950)

Perkins, William, 'A Discourse of Conscience' and 'The Whole Treatise of Cases of Conscience', in *William Perkins 1558–1602, English Puritanist: His Pioneer Works on Casuistry*, ed. with an introduction by Thomas F. Merrill (Nieuwkoop: Nieuwkoop B. De Graaf, 1966)

    A Golden Chaine, or The Description of Theologie (London, 1592)

    Two Treatises, second edition (Cambridge, 1597)

    The Workes of that Famous and Worthy Minister of Christ in the University of Cambridge, 3 vols. (London, 1612–13, and Cambridge, 1613)

    The Works, ed. by Ian Breward (Appleford: Sutton Courtenay Press, 1970)

Peter Lombard, *Sententiae*, 2.39 (Latin text in *Magistri Petri Lombardi Sententiae in IV libros distinctae*, tom. I, pars II. Grottaferrata (Rome), *Collegium S. Bonaventurae Ad Claras Aquas* (Quarrachi), 1971, pp. 553–6), ed. and trans. Timothy C. Potts, *Conscience in Medieval Philosophy* (Cambridge: Cambridge University Press, 1980), pp. 90–3

Phelan, J., 'The Life of Philip Massinger', *Anglia*, 3 (1880), 361–8

Philip The Chancellor, *Summa de Bono* (Latin text in O. Lottin, Psychologie et morale aux XIIe et XIIIe siècles, vol. 2. Gembloux J. Duculot, 1948, pp. 140–2, 145–8, 150–2, 153–6), ed. and trans. Timothy C. Potts, *Conscience in Medieval Philosophy* (Cambridge: Cambridge University Press, 1980), pp. 94–109

Pineas, Rainer, 'The English Morality Play as a Weapon of Religious Controversy', *SEL*, 2 (1962), 157–80

Plato, *The Dialogues*, trans. with analyses and introductions by B. Jowett, 4 vols. (Oxford: Clarendon Press, 1871)

Playfere, Thomas, *Heart's delight (The power of praier. The sickmans couch)* (London, 1611)

Poirier, Michel, *Christopher Marlowe* (London: Chatto & Windus, 1951)

Pope Innocent III, *The Mirror of Man's Lyfe*, Englished by H. Kirton (London, 1586)

Potter, Robert, *The English Morality Play* (London: Routledge & Kegan Paul, 1975)

Potts, Timothy C. (trans.), *Conscience in Medieval Philosophy* (Cambridge: Cambridge University Press, 1980)

Price, Hereward T., 'The Function of Imagery in Webster', *PMLA* (1955), 717–39, reprinted in R. J. Kaufmann (ed.) *Elizabethan Drama: Modern Essays in Criticism* (New York: Oxford University Press, 1961)

Prior, Moody E., *The Language of Tragedy* (New York: Columbia University Press, 1947)

Prosser, Eleanor, *Hamlet and Revenge*, second edition (Stanford, Calif.: Stanford University Press, 1971)

The Protestant Dictionary, ed. Sydney G. Carter and G. E. Alison Weeks, second edition (London: The Harrison Trust, 1933)

Raleigh, Sir Walter, *Sir Walter Raleigh's Sceptick* (London, 1651)

Reese, M. M., *The Cease of Majesty* (London: Edward Arnold, 1961)

Ribner, Irving, *Jacobean Tragedy: The Quest for Moral Order* (London: Methuen 1962)

    'Marlowe's "Tragique Glasse" ', in *Essays on Shakespeare and Elizabethan Drama in Honor of Hardin Craig*, ed. Richard Hosley (Columbia, Missouri: University of Missouri Press, 1962), pp. 91–114

    Patterns in Shakespearean Tragedy (London: Methuen, 1960)

Rose, Elliot, *Cases of Conscience: Alternatives to Recusants and Puritans under Elizabeth I and James I* (Cambridge: Cambridge University Press, 1975)

Rosen, William, *Shakespeare and the Craft of Tragedy*, (Cambridge, Mass.: Harvard University Press, 1960)

Rossiter, A. P., *Angel with Horns and Other Shakespearean Lectures* (London: Longman, 1961)

Rowse, A. L., *Christopher Marlowe: A Biography* (London: Macmillan, 1964)

Sachs, Arieh, 'The Religious Despair of Doctor Faustus', *JEGP*, 63 (1964), 625–47

Sanders, Wilbur, *The Dramatist and the Received Idea* (Cambridge: Cambridge University Press, 1968)

Santos, Marlene Soares dos, 'Theatre for Tudor England; an Investigation of the Ideas of Englishness and Foreignness in English Drama c. 1485 – c. 1592, with Particular Reference to the Interludes' (unpublished Ph.D. thesis, University of Birmingham, 1980)

Sargeaunt, M. Joan, *John Ford* (Oxford: Blackwell, 1935)

    'Writings Ascribed to John Ford by Joseph Hunter in *Chorus Vatum*', *RES*, 10 (1934), 165–76

Schücking, Levin, *The Meaning of Hamlet* (London: Oxford University Press, 1937)

Semper, I. J., 'The Ghost in Hamlet: Pagan or Christian?', *The Month*, 9 (1953), 222–34

Seneca, Lucius Annaeus, *Ad Lucilium Epistulae Morales*, trans. Richard M. Gunmere, 3 vols. (London: Heinemann and Cambridge, Mass.: Harvard University Press, 1920)

    Minor Dialogues, trans. Aubrey Stewart (London: Bonn's Classical Library, 1889)

    The Workes of Lucius Annaeus Seneca. Both Morrall and Naturall, trans. Thomas Lodge (London, 1614)

Sen Gupta, S. C., *Shakespeare's Historical Plays* (Oxford: Oxford University Press, 1964)

Sensabaugh, G. F., *The Tragic Muse of John Ford* (Stanford, Calif: Stanford University Press, 1944)

Shakespeare, William, *Coriolanus*, ed. Philip Brockbank, The Arden Shakespeare (London: Methuen, 1976)
    Hamlet, ed. G. R. Hibbard, The Oxford Shakespeare (Oxford and New York: Oxford University Press, 1987)
    Julius Caesar, ed. T. S. Dorsch, sixth edition, The Arden Shakespeare (London: Methuen, 1955, reprinted 1966)
    The Second Part of King Henry IV, ed. A. R. Humphreys, The Arden Shakespeare, (London: Methuen, 1966)
    King Henry VI, ed. A. S. Cairncross, third edition, 3 pts, The Arden Shakespeare (London: Methuen, 1957–64)
    King Henry VIII, ed. R. A. Foakes, third edition, The Arden Shakespeare (London: Methuen, 1957; reprinted 1964)
    King Lear, ed. Kenneth Muir, ninth edition, The Arden Shakespeare (London: Methuen, 1952)
    King Richard II, ed. Peter Ure, fifth edition, The Arden Shakespeare (London: Methuen, 1961; reprinted 1964)
    Measure for Measure, ed. J. W. Lever, second edition, The Arden Shakespeare (London: Methuen, 1965; reprinted 1966)
    The Merchant of Venice, ed. John Russell Brown, seventh edition, The Arden Shakespeare (London: Methuen, 1955; reprinted 1966)
    The Tempest, ed. Frank Kermode, sixth edition, The Arden Shakespeare (London: Methuen, 1958; reprinted 1966)
    Troilus and Cressida, ed. Kenneth Palmer, The Arden Shakespeare (London: Methuen, 1982)
    Twelfth Night, ed. J. M. Lothian and T. W. Craik, The Arden Shakespeare (London: Methuen, 1975)
Sherman, Stuart, 'Ford's Debt to his Predecessors and Contemporaries, and his Contribution to the Decadence of the Drama' (unpublished dissertation, Harvard University, 1906)
Sidney, Sir Philip, *The Countesse of Pembroke's Arcadia*, ed. Maurice Evans (Harmondsworth: Penguin, 1977)
    The Countesse of Pembroke's Arcadia (1590), ed. Albert Feuillerat (Cambridge: Cambridge University Press, 1922)
Siegel, Paul, N., *Shakespeare in His Time and Ours* (Notre Dame, Indiana: University of Notre Dame Press, 1968)
    Shakespearean Tragedy and the Elizabethan Compromise (New York: New York University Press, 1957)
Sinfield, Alan, '*Macbeth:* History, Ideology, and Intellectuals', *Critical Quarterly*, 28, i-ii (1986), 63–77
Sisson, C. J., *Shakespeare's Tragic Justice* (London: Methuen, 1962)
Skulsky, Harold, 'Revenge, Honour and Conscience in *Hamlet*', *PMLA*, 85 (1970), 78–87
Slights, Camille Wells, *The Casuistical Tradition in Shakespeare, Donne, Herbert, and Milton*, (Princeton, New Jersey: Princeton University Press, 1981)
Smith, Henry, *The Sermons*, (London, 1592)
Smith, James, 'Marlowe's *Dr Faustus*', *Scrutiny*, 8 (1939), 36–55
Smith, Warren, D., 'The Nature of Evil in *Doctor Faustus*', *MLR*, 60 (1965), 171–5
Snyder, Susan, 'The Left Hand of God: Despair in Medieval and Renaissance Tradition', *Studies in the Renaissance*, 12 (1965), 18–59
Speaight, Robert, 'Marlowe: The Forerunner', *REL*, 7 (1966), 25–41
    Nature in Shakespearean Tragedy (London: Hollis & Carter, 1955)

Spencer, B. T., 'Philip Massinger', in *Seventeenth Century Studies*, ed. R. Shafer (Princeton, New Jersey: Princeton University Press, 1933)

Spencer, Theodore, *Shakespeare and the Nature of Man* (New York: Cambridge University Press, 1943)

Spivack, Bernard, *Shakespeare and the Allegory of Evil* (New York: Columbia University Press, and London: Oxford University Press, 1958)

Springer, Keith L., *The Learned Doctor William Perkins: Dutch Backgrounds of English and American Puritanism* (Urbana, Illinois: Univeristy of Illinois Press, 1972)

Stavig, Mark, *John Ford and The Traditional Moral Order* (Madison, Milwaukee and London: University of Wisconsin Press, 1968)

Steane, J. B., Marlowe: *A Critical Study* (Cambridge: Cambridge University Press, 1964)

Stephen, Sir Leslie, *Hours in a Library*, 3 vols. (London: Smith Elder & Co., 1892)

Stirling, William Alexander, 1st Earl of, *Poetical Works*, ed. by L. E. Kastner and H. B. Charlton, 2 vols. Publications of the University of Manchester, English Series, 10, 18 (Manchester, 1921–9)

Stoll, E. E., *John Webster: The Periods of his Work as Determined by his Relations to the Drama of his Day* (Boston, Mass.: Alfred Mudge 1905)

Strathmann, Ernest A., *Sir Walter Raleigh: A Study in Elizabethan Skepticism* (New York: Columbia University Press, 1951)

Swinburne, A. C., 'Philip Massinger', *Fortnightly Review*, 46 N.S. (July, 1889), 1–23

Symonds, H. Edward, *The Council of Trent and Anglican Formularies* (London: Oxford University Press, 1933)

Taylor, Gary, and Wells, Stanley, 'Hamlet' in *William Shakespeare: A Textual Companion* (Oxford and New York: Oxford University Press, 1987)

Thomas Aquinas, Saint, *Debated Questions on Truth*, 16–17 (Latin text in *S. Thomae Aquinatis, Opera Omnia*, vol. 22. *Quaestiones disputatae de veritatae*. Rome: *ad Sanctae Sabinae*, 1972, pp. 501–528), ed. and trans. Timothy C. Potts, *Conscience in Medieval Philosophy* (Cambridge: Cambridge University Press, 1980), pp. 122–9

> *The Summa Contra Gentiles*, translated by the English Dominican Fathers, 4 vols. in 5 (London: Burns, Oates & Washbourne, 1923–9)

> *The Summa Theologica* . . . , translated by the Fathers of the English Dominican Province, second and revised edition, 22 vols. (London: Burns, Oates & Washbourne, 1921?–32)

Tillyard, E. M. W., *The Elizabethan World Picture* (London: Chatto & Windus, 1943)

> *The English Renaissance: Fact or Fiction?* (London: Hogarth Press, 1952)

> *Shakespeare's Problem Plays* (London: Chatto & Windus, 1950)

Tomlinson, T. B., *A Study of Elizabethan and Jacobean Tragedy* (Cambridge: Cambridge University Press, and Melbourne: Melbourne University Press, 1964)

Tomlinson, T. M., 'The Morality of Revenge: Tourneur's Critics', *Essays in Criticism*, 10 (1960), 134–47

Tompkins, J. M. S., 'Tourneur and the Stars', *RES*, 22 (1946), 315–19

Toole, William B., 'The Motif of Psychic Division in Richard III', *Shakespeare Survey*, 27 (1974), 21–32

Toppen, W. H., *Conscience in Shakespeare's 'Macbeth'* (Groningen: J. B. Wolters, 1962)

Torrance, T. F., *Calvin's Doctrine of Man* (London: Lutterworth Press, 1949)

Tourneur, Cyril, *The Atheist's Tragedy*, ed. Irving Ribner, The Revels Plays (London: Methuen, 1964)
    The Transformed Metamorphosis (London, 1600)
Traversi, Derek, *An Approach to Shakespeare*, third edition, 2 vols (London: Hollis & Carter, 1969)
Tyler, Thomas, *The Philosophy of 'Hamlet'* (London: Williams & Norgate, 1874)
Vaughan, William, *The Golden-grove* (London, 1600)
Vernon, P. F., 'The Duchess of Malfi's Guilt', *Notes and Queries*, 10 (1963), 335–8
Versfield, Martin, 'Some Remarks on Marlowe's Faustus', *ESA*, 1 (1958) 134–43
Vyvyan, John, *The Shakespearean Ethic* (London: Chatto & Windus, 1959)
Wadsworth, F. W., 'Webster's *Duchess of Malfi* in the Light of Some Contemporary Ideas on Marriage and Remarriage', *PQ*, 35 (1956), 394–407
Walker, Roy, *The Time is Free: A Study of 'Macbeth'* (London: Andrew Dakers, 1949)
    The Time is Out of Joint: A Study of 'Hamlet' (London: Andrew Dakers, 1948)
Wall, Judith Anne, 'An Edition of R. B.'s *Appius and Virginia* (unpublished MA thesis, University of Birmingham, 1972)
Webster, John, *The Complete Works*, ed. F. L. Lucas, 4 vols. (London: Chatto & Windus, 1927)
    The Devil's Law-Case, ed. Elizabeth M. Brennan, The New Mermaids (London: Benn, 1975)
    The Duchess of Malfi, ed. John Russell Brown, The Revels Plays (London: Methuen, 1964)
    The Duchess of Malfi, ed. V. F. Hopper and G. B. Lahey (New York: Barron's Educational Series, 1960)
    The White Devil, ed. Elizabeth M. Brennan, The New Mermaids (London: Benn, 1966; reprinted 1978)
Werstine, Paul, 'The Textual Mystery of Hamlet', *SQ*, 39 (Spring, 1988)
West, Robert H., *Shakespeare and the Outer Mystery* (Lexington, Kentucky: University of Kentucky Press, 1968)
Westlund, Joseph, 'The Orthodox Christian Framework of Marlowe's *Faustus*', *SEL*, 3 (1963), 191–205
Wheeler, Richard P., 'History, Character and Conscience in Richard III', *Comparative Drama*, 5 (1971–2), 301–21
Whitgift, John, Abp of Canterbury, *The Works*, ed. John Ayre, Parker Society, 3 vols. (Cambridge: Cambridge University Press, 1851–3)
Whitman, Robert F., *Beyond Melancholy: John Webster and the Tragedy of Darkness*, Salzburg Studies in English Literature, ed. James Hogg (Salzburg: University of Salzburg, 1973)
Wilcox, Thomas, *A Profitable and Comfortable Letter for afflicted consciences* (London, 1582)
Wilders, John, *The Lost Garden* (London: Macmillan, 1978)
Willey, Basil, *The English Moralists* (London: Chatto & Windus, 1964)
Wilson, F. P., *The English Drama, 1485–1585*, ed. with a bibliography by G. K. Hunter (Oxford: Clarendon Press, 1969)
    Marlowe and the Early Shakespeare (Oxford: Clarendon Press, 1953)
Wilson, Harold S., *On the Design of Shakespearean Tragedy* (Toronto: University of Toronto Press, 1957)
Wilson, J. Dover, *The Fortunes of Falstaff* (Cambridge: Cambridge University Press, 1943)

What Happens in Hamlet, third edition (Cambridge: Cambridge University Press, 1970)

W[ilson], R[obert], *The Three Ladies of London and The Three Lords and Three Ladies of London*, ed. H. S. D. Mithal (unpublished Ph.D. thesis, University of Birmingham, 1959)

Wilson, Thomas, *A Christian Dictionary* (London, 1612)

Wine, Celesta, 'Nathaniel Woodes, author of the Morality Play *The Conflict of Conscience*', *RES*, 15 (1939), 458–63

'Nathaniel Wood's *Conflict of Conscience*', *PMLA*, 50 (1935), 661–78

Wood, Thomas, *English Casuistical Divinity During the Seventeenth Century: With Special Reference to Jeremy Taylor* (London: SPCK, 1952)

Woodson, William C., 'Elizabethan Villains and the Seared Conscience: The Application of a Theological Concept to Suggest the Credibility of Barabas, Aaron, Richard III and Iago' (unpublished Ph.D. dissertation, University of Pennsylvania, 1969)

Woolton, John, *A New Anatomie of the Whole Man* (London, 1576)

Of the Conscience ([London], 1576)

Wright, Louis B., *Middle-class Culture in Elizabethan England* (New York: Cornell University Press, 1958)

'William Perkins: Elizabethan Apostle of "Practical Divinity" ', *Huntingdon Library Quarterly*, 3 (1940), 171–96

Wright, Thomas, *The Passions of the Minde in Generall* (London: 1630)

Index